A
STEP-BY-STEP
INTRODUCTION TO
STATISTICS
FOR
BUSINESS

Sara Miller McCune founded SAGE Publishing in 1965 to support the dissemination of usable knowledge and educate a global community. SAGE publishes more than 1000 journals and over 800 new books each year, spanning a wide range of subject areas. Our growing selection of library products includes archives, data, case studies and video. SAGE remains majority owned by our founder and after her lifetime will become owned by a charitable trust that secures the company's continued independence.

Los Angeles | London | New Delhi | Singapore | Washington DC | Melbourne

A
STEP BY STEP
INTRODUCTION TO
STATISTICS
FOR
BUSINESS

Richard N. Landers

Los Angeles | London | New Delhi
Singapore | Washington DC | Melbourne

Los Angeles | London | New Delhi
Singapore | Washington DC | Melbourne

SAGE Publications Ltd
1 Oliver's Yard
55 City Road
London EC1Y 1SP

SAGE Publications Inc.
2455 Teller Road
Thousand Oaks, California 91320

SAGE Publications India Pvt Ltd
B 1/I 1 Mohan Cooperative Industrial Area
Mathura Road
New Delhi 110 044

SAGE Publications Asia-Pacific Pte Ltd
3 Church Street
#10-04 Samsung Hub
Singapore 049483

Editor: Kirsty Smy
Editorial assistant: Martha Cunneen
Assistant editor, digital: Chloe Statham
Production editor: Sarah Cooke
Copyeditor: Andy Baxter
Proofreader: Tom Hickman
Indexer: Martin Hargreaves
Marketing manager: Alison Borg
Cover design: Francis Kenney
Typeset by: C&M Digitals (P) Ltd, Chennai, India
Printed in the UK

Library of Congress Control Number: 2018954720

British Library Cataloguing in Publication data

A catalogue record for this book is available from the British Library

ISBN 978-1-4739-4810-5
ISBN 978-1-4739-4811-2 (pbk)

CONTENTS

To new beginnings, for Amy, Owen, Mia, Sophie, and in memory of Neko.

ACKNOWLEDGEMENTS

I would like to first thank those of you that adopted the first edition of this text. Without you, there would be no second edition, and I have incorporated your feedback and adapted this text to your needs as much as possible in this revision. But no textbook is ever truly 'complete', so if you have further suggestions or refinements, please don't hesitate to e-mail me (rlanders@tntlab.org) and I'll integrate them as best I can in the future.

In terms of the book content, I would like to thank and acknowledge Dr Amy Landers, who was an amazing sounding board for ideas and explanations on top of her writing many, many Test Yourself questions as a direct contribution to the text. Without her support, this book would not exist. Thank you for everything.

Finally, I would like to thank the many reviewers and editors who provided feedback at various stages of writing on both the first and second editions. I was and remain amazed at just how many people it takes to put together a textbook, and furthermore, that it all works so seamlessly. Your work made this text all it could be.

ABOUT THE AUTHOR

Richard N. Landers, Ph.D., is an Associate Professor of Psychology at the University of Minnesota and holds the John P. Campbell Distinguished Professorship of Industrial-Organizational Psychology. His research concerns the use of innovative technologies in assessment, employee selection, adult learning, and research methods. Recent topics have included big data, game-based learning, game-based assessment, gamification, unproctored Internet-based testing, mobile devices, virtual reality, and online social media. His work has been published in *Journal of Applied Psychology, Industrial and Organizational Psychology Perspectives, Computers in Human Behavior, Simulation & Gaming, Social Science Computer Review, and Psychological Methods*, among others, and his research and writing have been featured in *Forbes, Business Insider, Science News, Popular Science, Maclean's*, and the *Chronicle of Higher Education*, among others. In addition to authoring this textbook, he holds associate editorships at several journals and edited both *Social Media in Employee Selection*, and the *Cambridge Handbook of Technology and Employee Behavior*.

YOUR GUIDE TO THIS BOOK

What You Will Learn … and Data Skills You Will Master from This Chapter Highlight what you will understand and be able to do with data by the end of each chapter.

Case Study A real-world example of a business problem that needs to be solved with statistics.

Foundation Concepts Revises what you should already know from the previous chapter.

Finally, we plug these values into the z-test formula and solve for z (Figure 8.10).

$$z = \frac{\bar{x} - \mu}{\sigma_{\bar{x}}}$$
$$= \frac{57.669090 - 45}{2.309401}$$
$$= \frac{12.669090}{2.309401}$$
$$= 5.485877$$
$$= 5.49$$

GURE 8.10   Calculating the case study z-test

Annotated Formulas So you can see at a glance what the symbols mean.

Test Yourself To make sure you have understood what you have just read.

Data Skill Challenges To make sure you can put all your knowledge into practice and actually 'do' statistics.

NEW TERMS

case: conditions: constant: construct: continuous: control condition: correlational study: data: Data View: dataset: datum: dichotomous: discrete: experiment: hypothesis: interval: Likert-type item: Likert-type scale: nominal: operational definition: operationalization: ordinal: population: qualitative: quantitative: quasi-experiment: random assignment: ratio: representative: sample: scale of measurement: subject: theory: treatment condition: variable: Variable View:

Visit https://study.sagepub.com/landers2e **for free additional online resources related to this chapter.**

New Terms Revisits everything that was new to the chapter to help remind you what you have covered.

STATISTICS IN THE REAL WORLD

These web links can be accessed directly from the book's website.

Philip Evans, senior partner of Boston Consulting Group, describes how data are transforming the business world: www.ted.com/talks/philip_evans_how_data_will_transform_business.

How has the increasing availability of data fundamentally changed business? Can a business ignore data and still be successful?

National Numeracy, a UK charity, explains why fluency with numbers and statistics is critical to our futures as world citizens: www.nationalnumeracy.org.uk/why-numeracy-important.

What are the costs of ignoring numbers in the modern economy?

Statistics in the Real World Directs you to online articles and videos exploring real-world uses of statistics

FREQUENCIES IN EXCEL

Download the Excel dataset for the demonstration below as chapter2freq.xls. As you read this section, try to apply the terms you've learned in this chapter to the dataset and follow along with Excel on your own computer.

You can also get a video demonstration of the section below under Excel Videos: Chapter 2.

There are two worksheets in this dataset, which you can navigate between using the tabs at the bottom, as shown in Figure 2.24.

Excel Walkthroughs Step-by-step guides to computing and analysing statistics and datasets using the Excel program.

FREQUENCIES IN SPSS

Download the SPSS dataset for the demonstration below as chapter2freq.sav. As you read this section, try to apply the terms you've learned in this chapter to the dataset and follow along with SPSS on your own computer.

You can also get a video demonstration of the section below under SPSS Videos: Chapter 2.

Because SPSS is a program designed to conduct statistical analyses, creating frequency tables is quite easy. With the dataset open, click Analyze>Descriptive Statistics>Frequencies (see Figure 2.58).

SPSS Walkthroughs Step-by-step guides to computing and analysing statistics and datasets using the SPSS program.

ONLINE RESOURCES

GO ONLINE

Visit https://study.sagepub.com/landers2e for access to a wide range of online resources for students and lecturers.

FOR STUDENTS

- **Interactive flashcard glossary** – online flashcards will help you get to grips with the key terms introduced in the book. All the terms in the book's glossary can be found here.

- **Weblinks** – you can access the websites referred to in each chapter's 'Statistics in the Real World' feature directly from the website by clicking on the links provided.

- **Datasets** – Excel and SPSS datasets so you can practice the statistics skills you learn in this chapter.

- **Test and data skills answers** – take the tests and data skills challenges in this chapter and then check the answers online to see how you got on.

- **Tutorial Videos** – Excel and SPSS demonstrations from Richard N. Landers.

FOR LECTURERS

- **Instructor's manual** – tutor's notes, instructional objectives, and additional class and lab activities to help support your teaching.

- **PowerPoint slides** – with learning objectives, figures and tables, and key concepts from each chapter.

- **Lecturer Testbank** – a wide range of assessment questions, complete with model answers.

- **Test questions and answers** – additional 'Test Yourself' exercises from each chapter, to further challenge students.

PREFACE

Many years ago, I took my first undergraduate business statistics course at the University of Tennessee in the United States. At the time, the course seemed a bit haphazard. We did not follow the textbook closely, and the lecturer would often instruct us to skip chapters or portions of chapters because they were too confusing. He told us to ignore certain formulas, and he supplied us packets of photocopies as 'supplementary material' explaining concepts that were already in the text (although the photocopies were much clearer!). He also did not trust the questions in the text, advising us to ignore them entirely. So I asked the obvious question: 'Why did he make us buy a textbook that he doesn't want us to use?'

I attended graduate school at the University of Minnesota in industrial/organizational psychology, the application of psychology to human resources and organizational behaviour. There, I taught undergraduate statistics for the first time and quickly discovered the answer to my earlier question. There simply were no accessible textbooks. There were certainly many excellent handbooks and compendiums of all things statistical, but that's not what I wanted with an undergraduate statistics text. I wanted clear, succinct explanations with relatable examples. I wanted coverage of the core concepts of statistics that I had time to get to in a single semester, and no more. I wanted a visual emphasis, with figures and diagrams illustrating core concepts. I wanted simple, easy-to-understand language. That text simply did not exist.

I think the lack of texts in this style can be traced back to one major cause: statistics textbooks are typically written by academics trained to be statisticians. I suspect most academics would think that's a selling point, but it really isn't. Statistical reasoning is very abstract, and those that study statistics as their profession typically do so because statistics comes somewhat naturally to them. Statisticians write their textbooks for other statisticians-in-training. But, as anyone who has taught first-year undergraduate statistics knows, most students in such classes have very different career goals. For most of us, the process of learning statistics is anything but 'natural'.

By my second year teaching undergraduate statistics, I had grown frustrated with the text I had chosen. It was the best I could find, but it was still not quite enough. Most of the time, I needed to reframe the content to make it more accessible. And if I needed to do that, why have the text at all?

Thus began a span of experimental statistical teaching. I gave up on the book and using lecture slides, working entirely from a whiteboard with markers of several colours. Through this experience, I quickly learned that my statistical training – I was about six graduate statistics courses in at that point, some of which were from top psychometricians and statisticians in the world – was not very valuable in relating these concepts to undergraduates. I quickly realized that my personal experience conducting statistical analysis for research projects was much more relatable. By telling a story about my own experiences using statistics to solve problems that I personally found meaningful, I found that students were more inspired to learn the material than with the text I had been using previously. After a few students sent me end-of-semester e-mails saying, 'I thought statistics would be scary, but you made it fun!', I knew I had a winning formula.

This text, like many academic projects, was largely the result of serendipity. Several years after receiving my doctoral degree, I was serving on the executive committee of the organizational behaviour division of the US Academy of Management when a SAGE editor approached me. She had an innovative idea for a textbook – a concise one-semester introduction to statistics in business written for a general audience – and she wanted to find someone willing to write such a text. Given my previous experience, I jumped at the opportunity!

I wrote this text to take advantage of the lessons I learned while teaching statistics – that the best way to make statistics meaningful to students is simply to tell a story, emphasizing how statistics are used in the real world to solve real problems. Each chapter in this text thus tells the story of a young manager or entrepreneur faced with a realistic business problem (or problems!). Each chapter begins with the prologue to such a story presented as a case study alongside a dataset available on this book's companion website collected to solve that problem. Statistical concepts that are used to solve the problem are introduced throughout the chapter. This ties concepts directly to a real application that students are likely to face. Each chapter concludes with a new story that the student can explore to test themselves on the material. Everything is related in a conversational style, mimicking the many one-on-one conversations I had when students struggled with new concepts. For most, the use of statistics will be a valuable practical skill, and it is for this audience that I wrote this text.

I hope you find this text as enjoyable to learn or teach from as I found it to write. If you have any comments or suggestions, please don't hesitate to e-mail me.

Richard N. Landers

CHANGES IN THE SECOND EDITION

Here we are, several years after writing this book, and I'm back writing it again! We had several requests from readers and adopters which I have integrated into this new edition. I have preserved the order of chapters and almost all sections in order to save instructors from re-writing their syllabi too much, but additional content has been added throughout the text. Most significantly:

1 A Prologue has been added, providing a gentle review of essential mathematics.

2 A new section has been added to Chapter 4 to provide a bit more background on basic probability (a little renumbering there!).

3 New sections have been added to Chapter 13 to provide more guidance when choosing between statistical tests.

4 References to real-world resources have been added as a pedagogical feature at the end of every chapter (thank you to the instructor providing this suggestion!).

5 Links to online material have been made clearer.

6 Additional figures and worked examples have been added throughout the text, although more heavily in the second half.

7 Excel and SPSS sections of the text have been more clearly differentiated so that students can tell the difference between them a bit more easily.

8 A variety of small errors have been corrected, including the addition of missing glossary terms and fixing incorrect references to colours in a few figures.

If you have any further suggestions for what might make the text easier for you, your students, or your instructor, or if you spot any lingering errors, please e-mail me so that they can be corrected in the next edition!

Your still loyal author,
Richard N. Landers

INTRODUCTION

Welcome to the exciting world of business statistics! You might be suspicious of the words 'exciting' and 'statistics' in close proximity, but you shouldn't be! Statistics abound in almost all areas of our modern lives, from politics to product sales. They are used as a tool to explain complex ideas and relationships that we can't explain easily with words alone. This is the purpose of statistics: to make logical sense of a world filled with an overwhelming amount of information. As a result, statistical skills are among the most valuable skills you can gain to help manage a business successfully.

Statistics is a combination of two areas that students often find difficult to combine: abstract logical reasoning and mathematics. In my experience, there are two major ways that students approach statistics, driven by their impression of statistics when they begin the course. I encourage you to reflect on which describes your own beliefs before diving in.

1 'Statistics is just maths, and I'm good at maths, so I'll be good at statistics.' Before taking statistics, this student believes that statistics is essentially mathematics. Since he did well in mathematics, he believes he will do well in statistics. Students specializing in accounting are almost always in this group. Unfortunately, this student will soon be surprised. Statistics is in large part conceptual; many statistical concepts can't be expressed clearly with numbers alone (at least, not until you've had quite a large number of statistics classes for context). This type of student will find the conceptual component quite challenging and the mathematical component quite simple – nothing worse than multiplication, division and order of operations.

2 'I want to manage a business, not use a calculator.' Before taking statistics, this student doesn't see much value in statistics for business. She just wants to run her business or manage her team as makes logical sense. While statistics and numbers certainly play a role in a successful business, she believes that she can just hire someone else to take care of that part. This type of student is often uneasy about the idea of taking a statistics course; it seems very number-oriented and intimidating. Students specializing in human resources are almost always in this group. Fortunately, the study of statistics is not maths alone, and the maths used is relatively simple: multiplication and division are just about the worst you'll face. Much of statistics is abstract and conceptual. As a result, these students will find the conceptual component difficult but approachable while remaining apprehensive of the mathematics. If you fall in this group, you might want to check out the Prologue, which contains a gentle review of basic mathematics, before tackling the rest of the book.

Statistics as an area of study is therefore unusual in that it combines the abstract reasoning of a more conceptual course (like business administration or human resources) with the concrete mathematics of a more technical course (like accounting or finance). If you approach it with an open mind, I'm confident that you'll see the union is a happy one.

Regardless of your intended speciality, you're likely to see statistics again in your advanced courses and later, on the job. For example, accountants use statistical sampling techniques to conduct large-scale account reviews. Human resource managers use sampling and correlational analyses to explore and predict employee behaviour. Marketers are increasingly turning to large-scale data collection from social media to assess campaign success. Economists use statistical forecasting to predict the future of economies or economic indicators. Wherever you go, you'll find that statistics is critical to understanding the world of business.

This text is divided into three parts. In Part 1: Descriptive Statistics, you'll learn about the foundational concepts of statistics: how to describe and summarize data. For example, if you were to conduct a survey, how would you meaningfully describe the results of that survey to someone else? In Part 2: Inferential Statistics, you'll learn about how to use the data you have to make decisions about data you wish you had. For example, if you were to ask questions of 20 customers, how could you meaningfully draw conclusions about *all* of your customers? Finally, in Part 3: Wrap-Up, you'll combine everything you learned in the previous two units to produce meaningful answers to the sort of ambiguous business questions you are likely to face in the real world.

Good luck with your studies, and thanks for reading!

PROLOGUE

REVIEW OF ESSENTIAL MATHEMATICS

WHAT YOU WILL LEARN FROM THIS PROLOGUE

- How to add, subtract, multiply and divide positive and negative numbers
- How to read order of operations from formulas and calculate using powers and exponents
- How to think about and work with numbers

This prologue provides material to refresh yourself with the mathematics necessary to calculate basic statistics. You have probably learned most, if not all, of this material at some point before in your schooling. If it's all very familiar to you, you might even consider skipping this section. But if you didn't, or if that time of your life is a bit hazy in retrospect, you might find this review useful.

Before we dig in, it's important to think for a moment about why fluency in mathematics is important, for both this text and your life in general. In short, mathematics forms the foundation of everything. Really, everything. Nature, science, business and art all, at their cores, rely upon mathematics. That's not to say that your skill level solving quadratic equations will necessarily be valuable to you a few years from now. Instead, what's important is that you develop a comfort and ease reasoning through numerical relationships and working with numbers. This is a skill called numeracy. It doesn't come naturally to just about anyone, but it is something you develop with time. The first step to building numeracy skills is building a fluency in the most core mathematical concepts, so that's the purpose of this prologue.

If you're feeling a bit nervous because it's been a few years since you've done anything maths-related, don't worry. In the grand scheme of mathematics, you will need less mathematics when learning basic statistics than you'd get in a single refresher college maths course. The skills themselves aren't very complicated, and you probably already have them from earlier schooling. So what you need to focus on instead is recognizing when to use those skills. That's numeracy.

P.1 ADDING, SUBTRACTING, MULTIPLYING AND DIVIDING

The most basic mathematical operations are addition, subtracting, multiplication and division. Each corresponds to an even more basic concept in terms of numeracy. We'll cover each in turn.

1   The mathematical concept of addition reflects the bringing of two smaller groups together to create a larger one. If I have two apples, and you hand me five more, I now have seven $(2 + 5 = 7)$.

2   The mathematical concept of subtraction reflects the reduction of a larger group by a smaller group. If I have seven apples and you take away three, I now I have four $(7 - 3 = 4)$.

3   The mathematical concept of multiplication reflects the end result of collecting multiple groups of the same size. If apples are sold in baskets of ten and I buy six baskets, I now have sixty $(10 * 6 = 60)$.

4   The mathematical concept of division reflects the end result of breaking apart a larger group into smaller portions of the same size. If I have twelve apples and want to split them into two portions for you and for me, each portion will have six apples $(12/2 = 6)$. If you find you can't split the larger group into equally smaller-sized groups, you first create as many smaller-sized groups as you can and then note somehow how many members of your original group you have left over. If I had thirteen apples instead and wanted to split them between you and me, each portion would still have six apples, but I'd also have one extra apple, leaving me both six complete groups of two apples as well as a partial group of two containing only one apple $(13/2 = 6½)$. When calculating statistics, we usually express this remainder as groups of tens (or hundreds, thousands, etc.), which we call decimals $(6 ½ = 6$ and $5/10 = 6.5)$.

Before now, you might have seen multiplication written as an asterisk (*) or a cross (×), so $10 * 6$ and $10 × 6$ are the same. We'll use asterisks in this book. There are more options for division, in which you might see a forward slash (/) or an obelus (÷), also called a division sign. You might also see division written as a horizontal line (–) with numbers above and below it. That means $10/6$, $10 ÷ 6$ and $^{10}/_6$ are also all the same.

The four numeracy concepts above – bringing groups together, reducing them, collecting multiples of them, and dividing them into portions – are the basis of all calculations in statistics. The problem that many people have is that they forget this when actually running the calculations. It's far easier, in the moment, to simply try to work through the formula by rote, step by step, instead of thinking about what is happening to all the groups you are working with.

To see why this can be a problem in the real world, consider the jewellery wholesaler who has just been called by a client on her smartphone while riding a metro. She's a little flustered but excited about the sale, and she doesn't have time to consult her spreadsheets or she could lose the sale. The client says, 'I want to buy fifty-five emerald necklaces at £525 each, so how much will that run?' She pulls up a calculator on her smartphone and quotes the client £11,550. Thrilled with the price, the client agrees. It's only after ending the call that the wholesaler realizes that she keyed in the price wrong – the real value is £28,875! But now she has only two options: either call the client back to change the price or absorb a £17,325 loss. Neither is a good option.

Numeracy in this situation – specifically, a little mental math and the willingness to use it – would have helped immensely. As soon as the client said fifty-five at five hundred, a wholesaler more comfortable with numbers might have thought, 'Fifty-five is a little more than fifty, and £525 is close to £500 – and $50 * 500$ is around 25,000. So the price I quote should be around that too!' This illustrates how relying on a calculator alone is a risky proposition. Even the experts press the wrong key sometimes, and numeracy helps them catch those little mistakes before making big ones.

Having said all that, most people starting to learn about statistics can already add, subtract, multiply and divide. The calculation and execution of statistics involve the use of mathematics in quite concrete ways, so you won't need to remember many of the abstract rules that you might need when learning algebra or geometry. Yet there are a few places where students tend to get tripped up, which will be the focus of the next two sections.

To refresh yourself with basic addition, subtraction, multiplication and division, try out the practice problems below – without a calculator!

TEST YOURSELF

1	5 + 9	8	2 * 6
2	13.1 + 10.5	9	16.4 * 12
3	54.1 + 12.95	10	110.21 * 65.90
4	107.61 + 499.42	11	24/12
5	16 – 7	12	144/10
6	100 – 95.4	13	144.5/10
7	325.23 – 114.76	14	11/4.4

ANSWERS

1	14	8	12
2	23.6	9	196.8
3	67.05	10	7262.839
4	607.03	11	2
5	9	12	14.4
6	4.6	13	14.45
7	210.47	14	2.5

P.2 NEGATIVE NUMBERS AND COMBINING THEM (FIGURE P.01)

Addition	Subtraction	Multiplication	Division
6 + 3 = 9	6 – 3 = 3	6 * 3 = 18	6/3 = 2
6 + (– 3) = 3	6 – (– 3) = 9	6 * (– 3) = – 18	6/(– 3) = – 2
(– 6) + 3 = – 3	(– 6) – 3 = – 9	(– 6) * 3 = – 18	(– 6)/3 = – 2
(– 6) + (– 3) = – 9	(– 6) – (– 3) = – 3	(– 6) * (– 3) = 18	(– 6)/(– 3) = 2

FIGURE P.01   Combining negative numbers

Negative numbers are abstract; they are more of an *idea* than something you can count, because they seem to represent something being missing. Positive numbers represent presence; you can easily count five apples. Those five apples are very real whereas negative five apples – well, what exactly are negative five apples? Isn't that just zero apples?

Importantly, the answer to that question is no. Negative five apples are precisely negative five apples. An easier way to think about this is to imagine numbers as part of a payment process. If I have negative five apples, it's because I am missing five apples. I am *owed* five apples – not quite the same as zero. Thus, negative numbers are in fact presence – they represent the presence of debt.

So how do we consider debt when conducting basic mathematical operations on negatives? In addition and subtraction, it's quite easy. Just remember that subtraction is really a sneaky negative. For example, $12 - 5$ can also be written $12 + (-5)$. In both cases, we could say 'start with 12, and then add a debt of 5'. Since we have 12 but owe 5, we really have 7, so $12 - 5 = 7$. If we start with a debt of 6 and add a debt of 5, we end up with a debt of 11, so $-6 + -5 = -6 - 5 = -11$.

For multiplication, it's a bit more complicated. When multiplying by a negative, you're adding debt several times. So $-6 * 10 = -60$ to indicate the total owed as a result of 10 sets of a debt of 6. When multiplying two negatives together, you are *removing debts*. $-3 * -4 = 12$ because you start with a debt of 3 and then removed that debt 4 times. Thus, you end up with a positive number. The simple rule to remember here is that two negative numbers multiplied together result in a positive number.

For division of negatives, remember first that division is really multiplication of an inverse. For example, $10/6$ is the same as $10 * 1/6$. Given that, the rules are the same as multiplication. Removal of debts results in a positive number, so if both numbers are negative, the result will be positive. If only one number is negative, the result will be negative (a debt). If both numbers are positive, the result will be positive too.

TEST YOURSELF

1	$12 + -5$		6	$4 * -12$
2	$-16 + -12$		7	$-11 * -11$
3	$-13 - 6$		8	$-11/-11$
4	$6 - (-2)$		9	$14/-2$
5	$-4 * 12$		10	$-63/-9$

ANSWERS

1	7		6	-48
2	-28		7	121
3	-19		8	1
4	8		9	-7
5	-48		10	7

P.3 POWERS, INDICES AND EXPONENTS

Depending upon your country, you may use any or several of these three terms to describe the multiplication of a number by itself: powers, indices and exponents. They all refer to the same mathematical procedure: the number of times that a number is to be multiplied by itself, represented by a number above another number and to the right. For example, four raised to the power of five (or 'raised to the fifth power') looks like:

$$4^5 = 4*4*4*4*4 = 1024$$

In this case, the five is referred to as either an exponent or an index.

In the type of statistics you'll be using in this book, you will usually only need to raise a number to the second power (i.e., an exponent/index of two), which is called squaring. Occasionally, you'll need to raise a number to the third power, which is called cubing.

Three squared $= 3^2 = 3 * 3 = 9$
Two cubed $= 2^3 = 2 * 2 * 2 = 8$

So, what do we do with negative numbers when calculating powers? The answer is that it depends on where the negative sign is. This is particularly important when using calculators, because it is easy to key formulas into calculators such that the calculator doesn't know where the negative sign is supposed to be, which can give you an incorrect answer. When the negative sign is within parentheses, you will be multiplying a negative number by itself. When the negative sign is outside of parentheses, you will be multiplying a positive number by itself and then making it negative. Depending upon your exponent, this could result in either positive or negative answers. Several such situations are shown in Figure P.02.

Even exponents/indices	Odd exponents/indices
$2^2 = 2 * 2 = 4$	$2^3 = 2 * 2 * 2 = 8$
$-2^2 = -(2 * 2) = -4$	$-2^3 = -(2 * 2 * 2) = -8$
$-(2)^2 = -(2 * 2) = -4$	$-(2)^3 = -(2 * 2 * 2) = -8$
$(-2)^2 = -2 * -2 = 4$	$(-2)^3 = -2 * -2 * -2 = 4 * -2 = -8$

FIGURE P.02   Powers and negative symbols

In statistics, we also commonly want to know the reverse of square – what number squared would have led to a particular answer? This is referred to as a square root, represented by a symbol called a radix ($\sqrt{\ }$). Thus, $\sqrt{6.5}$ asks us to determine what number squared would result in 6.5. Square roots are generally a task best left to calculators. In this case, the answer is 2.55, rounded to two decimal places.

As you test your skills with powers in the next section, challenge yourself by only using a calculator when square roots are required.

TEST YOURSELF

1 3^2

2 15^3

3 10.2^2

4 -5.2^2

5 $-(2.65)^2$

6 $(-7.6)^3$

7 -3.3^3

8 $(-3.3)^3$

9 $\sqrt{16}$

10 $-\sqrt{38}$

ANSWERS

1 9

2 3375

3 104.04

4 -27.04

5 -7.0225

6 -438.976

7 -35.937

8 -35.937

9 4

10 -6.164414

P.4 WORKING WITH PARENTHESES/BRACKETS AND ORDER OF OPERATIONS

Statistics involves a lot of formulas, and some of these formulas are pretty intimidating at first glance. In this book, I've broken down every statistical formula step by step so that you can see how it's calculated. But in addition to that, you will want to be familiar with why I follow the order I do, a concept called order of operations.

Order of operations is important because it ensures that every person looking at a particular mathematical formula goes about calculating it the same way. This order of operations goes by many acronyms to make it easier to remember, but you've probably heard of either PEMDAS or BIDMAS depending upon the country where you learned it:

1 Parentheses/Brackets

2 Exponents/Indices

3 Multiplication and Division

4 Addition and Subtraction

A common mistake with PEMDAS/BIDMAS is to think that the acronym specifies six distinct stages because it has six letters, but this is incorrect. Multiplication and division should be evaluated at the same time whereas additional and subtraction should also be evaluated at the same time. Otherwise, always move left to right. To illustrate why this is important, consider the following problem:

$10 - 5 + 3$

The correct procedure here involves two steps. First, subtract 5 from 10 to get 5. Second, add 3 to 5 to get 8. Step by step, the calculation looks like this:

$10 - 5 + 3$

$5 + 3$

8

If you evaluated the addition *then* the subtraction, you would have ended up with 2, which is incorrect. If we wanted to create a formula where addition occurred first despite being further to the right, the formula would need to look like this:

$10 - (5 + 3)$

In this case, we evaluate $5 + 3$ first because it is inside parentheses/brackets, creating a three-step process:

$10 - (5 + 3)$

$10 - (8)$

$10 - 8$

2

So always remember that MD go together, as do AS, to make four steps: P E MD AS or B I DM AS. Within each category, evaluate left to right.

Of these four steps, the most complicated is the first: parentheses/brackets are processed from the innermost sets to the outermost sets. Consider the following formula:

$12 - ((24 - 34) + 12)$

To work this problem, we must progress from the innermost parentheses first. Here is the solution, step by step:

$12 - (24 - 34) + 12)$

$12 - ((- 10) + 12)$

$12 - (- 10 + 12)$

$12 - (2)$

$12 - 2$

10

Once we combine this with exponents, we see the full complexity of order of operations. Consider the following formula, which you'll encounter much later in this book:

$$\sqrt{(3-1)^*1.645}\sqrt{12^*\left(\frac{1}{4}+\frac{2}{5}\right)}$$

First, we'll place this entirely on one line to make it a little easier to read. We'll also add the implied multiplication between the two radixes and the implied brackets beneath the radixes. Numbers above and below horizontal division lines should be placed inside brackets.

$$\sqrt{((3-1)^*1.645)}^*\sqrt{(12^*((1)/(4)+(2)/(5)))}$$

First, we have several numbers that are by themselves inside brackets. That means the brackets no longer serve any purpose, so we'll remove them:

$$\sqrt{((3-1)^*1.645)}^*\sqrt{(12^*(1/4+2/5))}$$

Within the next set of innermost brackets, there is only one calculation, so that's easy:

$$\sqrt{((2)^*1.645)}^*\sqrt{(12^*(1/4+2/5))}$$

Within the second set, we need the remainder of order of operations. There are no powers to worry about, so we skip that. But there is division and addition. Given the order of operations, we should tackle them in that order:

$$\sqrt{((2)^*1.645)}^*\sqrt{(12^*(0.25+0.40))}$$
$$\sqrt{((2)^*1.645)}^*\sqrt{(12^*(0.65))}$$

Now that we've simplified all of our innermost brackets as much as possible, we can remove them:

$$\sqrt{(2^*1.645)}^*\sqrt{(12^*0.65)}$$

We have two more sets of brackets again to process, but both involve only one calculation. I'll do both at the same time in this next line:

$$\sqrt{(3.29)}^*\sqrt{(7.8)}$$

Once again, we have simplified brackets as much as possible, so we can remove them:

$$\sqrt{3.29}^*\sqrt{7.8}$$

On the outermost level, we have three calculations left: two exponents and one multiplication. Remember that square roots are evaluated with exponents, so they come first. I'll calculate each to six decimal places, which will be the convention in this book:

$$1.813836*2.792848$$

Finally, multiply.

$$5.065768$$

Try out your order of operations skills with the following problems. Avoid using your calculator except when absolutely necessary.

TEST YOURSELF

1. $\dfrac{(12-6)^2}{8}$

2. $\dfrac{((12-3)+(16-3))^2}{16-1}$

3. $\sqrt{\dfrac{(17-3)^2}{10}}$

4. $\sqrt{\dfrac{5^2-\dfrac{4.5^2}{2}}{6-1}}$

5. $\dfrac{(3-1)-(5-4)}{\sqrt{12^2\left(\dfrac{1}{4}+\dfrac{2}{5}\right)}}$

ANSWERS

1. 4.5

2. 11.866667

3. 4.427189

4. 1.724819

5. 0.103362

P.5 STATISTICS AND NUMERACY

One of the most important skills that you should work on developing when learning statistics is a sense of approximately what sort of number to expect after you finish working through a formula. For example, in Chapter 3, you'll learn how to calculate two statistics called variance and standard deviation. If you really learn those concepts when you get to them in the book, you'll learn these two facts about them:

1 Standard deviations are always smaller than variances.

2 Both standard deviations and variances are always positive numbers.

With that information, you can then look out while running calculations to ensure that those two things are always true. Even right now, without knowing how to calculate variance and standard deviations, you know a few things to be true based upon the two facts above. For example, if you calculate a standard deviation or variance that's negative, something must've gone wrong. If you calculate a standard deviation that is larger than the variance it is based upon, something must've gone wrong. For every statistical test covered in this book, you should think about what is *always true*, what is *usually true*, and what is *never true*. Then, if you find yourself violating one of the truth rules you created, you know to double-check your work to figure out why it's happening.

One rule that applies across all of statistics: you'll never need to calculate the square root of a negative number. Because statistics deals with real quantities, you'll never need to deal with 'imaginary' numbers when running through statistical formulas. If you ever find yourself needing to calculate the square root of a negative number, you've violated a truth rule – something must have gone wrong somewhere earlier in your calculations. Now you just need to find where!

STATISTICS IN THE REAL WORLD

If you hate maths, see these six high-energy TED talks explaining why you shouldn't: www.ted.com/playlists/251/talks_for_people_who_hated_mat.

Math educator Dan Meyer describes how maths education is often designed poorly to teach people how to understand maths: www.ted.com/talks/dan_meyer_math_curriculum_makeover.

How did the way you learn maths affect how you feel about it now?

SCHOLARSHIP FOR ADVANCED LEARNERS

This research study revealed that business owners' lack of financial literacy was associated with financial difficulties for their businesses: http://scholarcommons.usf.edu/cgi/viewcontent.cgi?article=1146&context=numeracy.

How could your business suffer if you don't learn these skills?

PART 1
DESCRIPTIVE STATISTICS

Part 1 explores Descriptive Statistics. These are the building blocks of statistics, focusing on how to describe, illustrate and explain data. Each chapter builds on its predecessor, so it is strongly recommended that you read them in the order provided. And if you don't remember maths, I'd strongly recommend you review the Prologue before getting started.

In Chapter 1, we follow the story of Ben, a small business owner who has hired a consultant to investigate the problem of slowing sales. By reading The Language of Statistics with Ben, you'll learn how to accurately describe the data his consultant collected and the ways that data are created.

In Chapter 2, we read the story of Jamal, the owner of a small online retail business. He hopes to use website usage data to improve the functioning of his business, but he's not sure how to interpret the vast piles of data he has acquired. By reading Working with Numbers and Data Display with Jamal, you'll learn how to describe and summarize data with both tables and graphics.

In Chapter 3, we hear about Sue's business which conducts taste-testing research for restaurants. While Sue knows how to chart and visualize data from Chapter 2, she wants more accurate summary numbers for her survey data. By reading Central Tendency and Variability with Sue, you'll learn how to summarize several aspects of numerical datasets with single numbers.

In Chapter 4, we learn about Jill's used vehicle shop. Jill is worried about the sales performance of her employees and seeks to meaningfully compare their individual figures. By reading Probability Distributions with Jill, you'll learn how to describe patterns of data and meaningfully compare one dataset with another.

In Chapter 5, we read the story of Alex, general manager of a local branch office of a paper product sales company. Alex wants to meaningfully compare sales at his branch with those across the company but is not sure of the best way to do so. By reading Sampling Distributions with Alex, you'll learn how data selected from larger collections of data can meaningfully represent those larger collections.

1 THE LANGUAGE OF STATISTICS

WHAT YOU WILL LEARN FROM THIS CHAPTER

- How to describe data in a spreadsheet
- How to categorize variables by their scale of measurement
- How to identify whether variables are continuous or discrete, quantitative or qualitative
- How to identify a Likert-type scale
- How to specify a population and produce a sample from it
- How to identify constructs of interest and operationalize them
- How to identify experiments, quasi-experiments and correlational studies

DATA SKILLS YOU WILL MASTER FROM THIS CHAPTER

- Creating a dataset
- Identifying a dataset
- Navigating a dataset
- Specifying variable characteristics (SPSS only)

CASE STUDY   WHAT DO I DO WITH THIS SPREADSHEET?

Ben is the owner of Scoops, a local frozen yogurt chain with five locations. Sales have been slumping at some of these locations, and Ben wants to determine the cause. He suspects that some of his store managers have been letting customer satisfaction slip, but he needs a stronger case than a gut feeling to convince them to change their ways. He decides that the first step in getting this evidence will be to assess customer satisfaction at each location and see if it's affecting sales.

Because Ben doesn't have a background in statistics, he runs a search on the Internet for a consultancy that can help him answer his questions. He contacts one of the results from his search, Surveys 1-2-3, because they promise to use 'data-driven techniques to answer any question you have about your business' for a reasonable fee.

(Continued)

(Continued)

After a six-month data collection effort by Surveys 1-2-3, the hired consultant calls Ben to tell him that his data have been collected and his questions answered. He says, 'Decreased customer satisfaction does not lead to decreased sales at Scoops.' Ben is surprised, and asks him if he can get more detail or a second opinion. The consultant says, 'I'll send you the data so you can see for yourself.'

So now Ben is staring at a spreadsheet full of numbers. There are several rows across several columns of numbers, and he has no idea what any of them mean. He could send the spreadsheet to another consultant, but that's just going to cost more time and money. And even if he does, what does he do if they disagree? How does he know who to trust – Surveys 1-2-3 or someone else?

Take a look at Ben's spreadsheet of customer satisfaction data for yourself in chapter1.xls (Excel) or chapter1.sav (SPSS) online.

Although for-profit organizations have always focused on the bottom line, there is increasing pressure to collect data from all areas of the organization in order to stay competitive. Simply producing a good product or delivering excellent customer service is often not enough; the owners of a competitive business must constantly conduct research on their own organizations to identify weak points and repair them.

As a result, the case study described above is common in growing small businesses. Suddenly finding themselves needing to conduct such research, many small business owners simply do not have the skills to do so. Like Ben, many recognize this need but do not even fully understand the results of research conducted on their behalf. Learning statistics and research methods are the keys to preventing this from happening to you.

In this chapter, you will take the first step toward understand statistics: learning the language of statistics. This is an especially important chapter because everything else you'll learn about statistics builds on these concepts. So take your time and make sure you understand them completely before moving on to the next chapter.

1.1 DESCRIBING NUMBERS

In the first half of this chapter, we'll explore ways to talk about numbers in spreadsheets.

If you find the idea of numbers – with or without spreadsheets – a little intimidating, or if it's been a while since you took a maths class, now would be a good time to take a look at this book's Prologue: Review of Essential Mathematics. In that prologue, I refresh you with basic mathematical operations, order of operations, powers and exponents. I also help you start to think with numbers. This is a vital skill as you learn statistics, because it develops your sense of 'that doesn't look right'. Developing a 'that doesn't look right' sense helps you avoid making silly mistakes, and silly mistakes with statistics can eventually be very costly for you and your business. So start early by reviewing the Prologue now if you haven't already!

1.1.1 DATUM, DATA AND DATASETS

The general term for a single value collected in the context of research is a datum. A datum might be a number, letter or word. For example, a '2' is a datum, but so is 'yellow' or 'tall' or even a 'p'. When you are referring to more than one datum, you are referring to data. You might say, 'take a look at this datum' or 'these data are interesting'.

When multiple related data are collected in one place, a dataset is created. In our case study example, the spreadsheet that Ben received was a dataset, as it contained a great deal of data collected for a single purpose. A small piece of that dataset might have looked something like Figure 1.01.

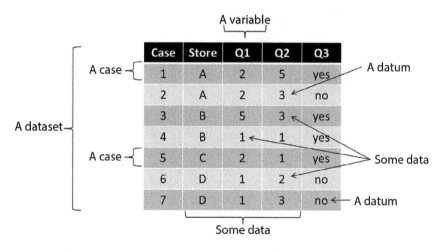

FIGURE 1.01   Sample dataset with illustration of important chapter terms

This dataset contains many data. In the Q2 column in Figure 1.01, the first '3' is a datum, but if we referred to both that 3 and the 3s below it, we are talking about data.

In fact, you can get a sense of whether or not someone is accustomed to working with real data themselves by whether or not they say 'data is' or 'data are'. People that say 'data is', such as 'the data is incoming', think about data as a single thing, a resource to be utilized. These people rarely work with actual data, so you should interpret their perspective accordingly. People that actually work with data tend to say 'data are', such as 'the data are complex', because they think of each number, each letter, or each word of data as a unique piece of information that contributes to a larger complete picture. So that means as a business statistician-in-training, you should say 'data are'.

Datasets can be further described with two other terms appearing in Figure 1.01: cases and variables. A variable is a collection of data with different values based upon its source, represented in a dataset as a column. For example, if you measured your height and the height of all of your friends, you have measured height as a variable. In Figure 1.01, Store, Q1, Q2 and Q3 are all variables.

If you remember anything from secondary/high school algebra and geometry, you probably remember the value called pi. This value is equal to 3.14159 …, with infinitely more numbers after the decimal. Pi is always this value. It never changes. Any time you see the word 'pi' or the symbol π, you know this is what it means. That is what makes pi a constant. If a value is not constant – or in other words, if it varies – it is a variable. When you see the word 'height', it could refer to your height, your friend's height, the height of a building, or any height at all. That means height is a variable. In statistics, constants are generally used in formulas, and variables are usually parts of datasets.

So now that we have all these variables, how do we know which values were collected from the same source? A case is a group of data, collected across one or more variables from one source, represented in a dataset as a complete row. In Figure 1.01, Case 1 contains four data: an 'A' for the Store variable, a '2' for the Q1 variable, a '5' for the Q2 variable and a 'yes' for the Q3 variable.

In summary, a dataset is a collection of data linked together in some meaningful way. A dataset is a spreadsheet containing variables as columns and cases as rows. Each variable represents a collection of a single type of data, while a case represents all of the data on all variables in the dataset from a single source.

1.1.2 SCALES OF MEASUREMENT

Once we have a dataset, we need terms to describe the kinds of data we're looking at. This is important because different kinds of data call for different kinds of analysis (more on this in later chapters). So, what really is the difference between a '3' and a 'yes'?

The most basic categorization of data is quantitative versus qualitative data. Quantitative data are quantities (usually represented as numbers), while qualitative data are labels or qualities (usually represented as words or letters). In our case study dataset, Q3 is clearly qualitative because 'yes' and 'no' are labels. Q1 and Q2 are probably quantitative because they are represented by numbers.

You might have noticed the word 'probably' in my previous sentence. This is where things get a little tricky! Some numbers are quantitative and others are qualitative. The difference is driven by what those numbers represent – see Figure 1.02.

For example, consider the number on a footballer's shirt. This number is not a quantity because higher numbers do not represent 'more' of anything. A player with a 12 is not

Examples of Data	
Quantitative	Qualitative
Numeric survey responses (1,2,3,4,5)	Opinions from focus groups
Sales in euros € 10000 per year)	Product preferences, ('Version A' ('I liked it') 'version B')
Turnover rate (25 employees per year)	Rankings ('1st , '2nd, '3rd')
Counts (2000 Twitter followers)	Verbal approximations ('high', 'low')

FIGURE 1.02   Examples of quantitative and qualitative data

necessarily more skilled, more respected or even taller than a player with a 5. If 'shirt number' were a variable in a dataset, it would be a qualitative variable.

Another way to conceptualize data is by considering scale of measurement. There are four scales of measurement: nominal, ordinal, interval and ratio. Each in this order is more specific (has more requirements) than the one before – see Figure 1.03. For example, all ordinal scales can also be considered nominal scales, but only some ordinal scales are also interval. To illustrate the differences between these categories, we'll cover each scale of measurement in turn, considering the following four variables as we go, each with three cases:

1 Opinions from focus groups: 'I liked it', 'I'm not sure if I liked it', 'I didn't see it'.

2 Ranked product preferences: 1st, 2nd, 3rd.

3 Employment test ranging from 10 to 30: 10, 20, 30.

4 Sales in euros: €10000 per year, €20000 per year, €30000 per year.

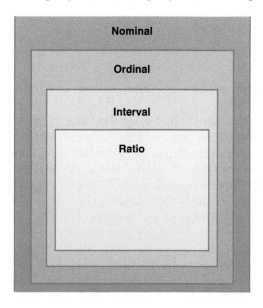

FIGURE 1.03   Relationship between the scales of measurement

DETERMINING SCALE OF MEASUREMENT

When you need to figure out what the scale of measurement is for a particular variable, work your way up, asking yourself the questions from Figure 1.04 in order.

	If you answer...	
	Yes	No
1. Are the labels meaningful?	Go to Question 2.	There's no measurement!
2. Do the labels have an order?	Go to Question 3.	It's nominal.
3. Are the distances between values meaningful?	Go to Question 4.	It's ordinal.
4. Is there a meaningful zero?	It's ratio.	It's interval.

FIGURE 1.04   Step by step process for identifying scale of measurement

Nominal data are data with meaningful labels – that is, the symbols used as data represent something in the real world. Nominal data are qualitative. If you can derive a value and put it in a dataset, it's at least nominal. Common examples of nominal variables are sex, gender and race. Results from focus groups, rankings, hiring tests and sales are all meaningful labels, so all of our demonstration variables meet this requirement and are therefore at least nominal measurements. A special type of nominal data are dichotomous data – these are data with only two possible values (for example, 'male' and 'female').

Ordinal data are nominal data with a meaningful order; that is, they have all the properties of nominal data (meaningful labels) plus ordering. Ordinal data are qualitative. Some values are clearly 'higher', 'more' or 'greater' than others. A common example of an ordinal variable is rank data. Let's examine each of our demonstration variables:

1 Opinions from focus groups: The responses here ('I didn't see it' and 'I liked it', for example) do not have a clear order. This variable is not ordinal. It is nominal only.

2 Ranked product preferences: 1st is always better than 2nd, and 2nd is always better than 3rd. These rankings are at least ordinal.

3 Employment tests ranging from 10 to 30: 30 is always a higher score than 20, and 20 is always a higher score than 10. This test is at least ordinal.

4 Sales in euros: More money is always more money. At least ordinal again.

Interval data are ordinal data with meaningful distances between values; that is, they have all the properties of ordinal data (meaningful labels that are ordered) plus meaningful distances. Interval data are quantitative. For example, the distance between '1' and '2' is equal to the distance between '3' and '4'. A classic example of an interval scale is temperature in degrees Celsius. The difference between 50 and 60 degrees is the same amount 'hotter' as the difference between 90 and 100 degrees. Back to our three remaining examples (we already identified focus group opinions as nominal):

1 Ranked product preferences: A person who rates Product A as '1st' and Product B as '2nd' may still like both products. The relative standings don't tell us anything across persons. Ranker A might love both products and Ranker B might hate both products, but each respond with the same '1st' and '2nd'. The differences between ranks are therefore not meaningful. Ranked product preferences are not interval. They are ordinal only.

2 Employment test ranging from 10 to 30: A person with a 30 is always 10 points better than a person with a 20. A person with a 20 is always 10 points better than a person with a 10. This test is at least interval.

3 Sales in euros: €30000 is always €10000 more than €20000. €20000 is always €10000 more than €10000. Sales in this scale are also at least interval.

Ratio data are interval data with a meaningful zero point; that is, they have all the properties of interval data (meaningful ordered labels with consistent distances between values) plus a meaningful zero. Ratio data are quantitative. An easy way to figure out if a scale has a meaningful zero is to figure out if multiplying two by a value really results in 'twice' as many of that value. For example, a common example of a ratio scale is temperature in degrees Kelvin. Zero degrees Kelvin is called absolute zero and can be thought of as the *absence* of temperature (i.e., molecular movement). Ten degrees Kelvin is double the temperature (molecular movement) of five degrees Kelvin. Thus, the zero on this scale is meaningful and degrees Kelvin is a ratio scale. Let's consider our two remaining examples:

1 **Employment test ranging from 10 to 30:** A person with a 20 is not necessarily 'twice' as employable as a person with a 10. On top of that, the scale only goes down to 10. This employment test is not ratio. It is interval measurement only.

2 **Sales in euros:** €0 really is 'no sales'. We can also think about it by saying that €20000 is double €10000. This scale passes both tests; it is ratio measurement.

Scale of measurement has a lot of implications, as it determines what kind of mathematics (and, ultimately, which statistics) you can use on the values from that scale. Interval scales allow you to use addition and subtraction, while ratio scales allow you to use multiplication and division. For example, it doesn't make sense to divide temperature in degrees Celsius; 100 degrees is not twice as hot as 50 degrees. So any statistical procedure that would require you to multiply or divide those values could not be used on that scale. These requirements are called assumptions, and they are different for every test. We'll cover assumptions for each test in detail as we get to them.

There is one exception to the procedure described here, and that has to do with survey data. Surveys often contain a particular type of question called a Likert-type item, which is often combined with other Likert-type items into a Likert-type scale. Figure 1.05 is an example of a two-item Likert-type scale for product satisfaction.

	Strongly disagree	Disagree	Neither	Agree	Strongly agree
I enjoyed this product.	1	2	3	4	5
I would use this product again	1	2	3	4	5

FIGURE 1.05   Sample Likert-type survey items

With which scale of measurement would you describe the items in Figure 1.05? Let's go through our list:

1 **Are the labels meaningful?** Yes, agreement is a meaningful concept.

2 **Do the labels have an order?** Yes, strongly agree is certainly 'more' than strongly disagree, and this order is consistent.

3 **Are the distances between values meaningful?** Sort of. A five is certainly one point greater than a four, but what about the labels themselves? Is the distance between strongly agree and agree really the same as the distance between agree and neither?

Whether to consider Likert-type data ordinal or interval is a matter of some disagreement among statisticians. The advantage to considering it interval is that this enables you to run more interesting and powerful statistical procedures on the data. The disadvantage is that using these procedures may not result in accurate conclusions if the data really are ordinal. Some fairly complicated arguments have been made in the scientific research literature on both sides.

For the purposes of this text, we will be considering survey data to be interval. But if you are using this text for a course, you should ask your instructor for his or her opinion, just to be safe.

1.1.3 DISCRETE VS CONTINUOUS DATA

In addition to scale of measurement, there is one other important distinction when talking about what data look like.

Continuous data can be subdivided infinitely without losing their meaning. For example, you can add an infinite number of decimal points to a temperature, and it is still a meaningful value. 25.123 degrees is a specific temperature; 25.123623 is, too. We can subdivide smaller and smaller portions, but these values continue to have meaning. Money is typically considered continuous; even fractions of pence are meaningful (just ask a bank manager!).

In contrast, discrete data have only specific meaningful values. For example, the number of applicants for a particular position is discrete, because you can't have a fraction of a person.

In general, qualitative (nominal and ordinal) data are always discrete, while quantitative (interval and ratio) data may be discrete or continuous.

1.1.4 DETERMINING THE CHARACTERISTICS OF VARIABLES

At this point in the text, you should be able to consider any variable and label it with the terms we've covered so far. Let's consider our case study from the beginning of the chapter (Figure 1.06).

Case	Store	Q1	Q2	Q3
1	A	2	5	Yes
2	A	2	3	No
3	B	5	3	Yes
4	B	1	1	Yes
5	C	2	1	Yes
6	D	1	2	No
7	D	1	3	No

FIGURE 1.06   Case study dataset

You can see the first problem our owner, Ben, is facing. Without more information, there's no way to even know the scale of measurement of these values! Fortunately, that can be fixed with another e-mail to the consultant asking some pointed questions like 'What do these variables represent?' and 'What do these values mean?' The consultant adds a little more information in his reply to Ben:

> After customers purchased something at each location, we asked them several ques-
> tions and recorded it in this spreadsheet. I coded the five locations of Scoops as A
> through E in the Store variable. Question 1 (Q1) was a five-point Likert-type ques-

tion to customers, 'Do you like this store?', with values 'Dislike much', 'Dislike', 'Neither', 'Like' and 'Like much'. Q2 was a question to customers, 'How many times have you been to this Scoops in the last six months?' Q3 was a question to customers, 'Did you receive excellent customer service?'

We can approach each variable using the same procedures as before. Try to figure out the answers to these questions for yourself before looking at Figure 1.07: 'Is this variable quantitative or qualitative?', 'Is this variable discrete or continuous?' and 'What is this variable's scale of measurement?'

	Store	Q1	Q2	Q3
Quantitative or qualitative?	Qualitative	Quantitative	Quantitative	Qualitative
Discrete or continuous?	Discrete	Discrete	Discrete	Discrete
Scale of measurement	Nominal	Interval	Ratio	Nominal
1 Are the labels meaningful?	Yes	Yes	Yes	Yes
2 Do the labels have an order?	No	Yes	Yes	No
3 Are the distances between values meaningful?	–	Yes	Yes	No
4 Is there a meaningful zero?	–	No	Yes	–

FIGURE 1.07   Determining meaningful labels for the variables in the case study dataset

1.2 NUMBERS IN THE REAL WORLD

In the second half of this chapter, we'll consider how to describe the relationship between these numbers and the real world. Remember that a dataset is not just a collection of numbers. Those numbers all have a context – they came from somewhere specific, and that context gives those numbers meaning.

1.2.1 POPULATIONS VS SAMPLES

When we want to answer a question using data, we rarely have all of the information we want. In the case of Ben's business, Scoops, there is no way for Ben to ask questions of every past, current and future customer in order to assess customer satisfaction. Ben wants to draw conclusions about 'customers' in general, which makes 'customers' the population he is interested in.

Populations are the theoretical group that you want to draw conclusions about. If you were interested in people's opinions, your population would be made up of people. If you were interested in organizational success, your population would be made up of organizations. Populations are generally not measurable directly because they are too large, they are too unwieldy or it would otherwise be too impractical to do so. Yet we want to make a conclusion about these groups! So what do we do?

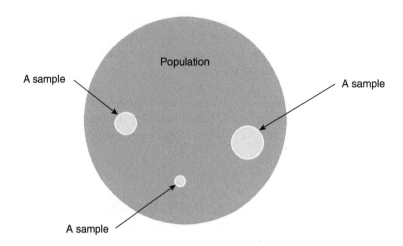

FIGURE 1.08   Relationship between samples and the population from which they are drawn

The answer: we get a sample. Samples are groups of subjects drawn from a population at random – see Figure 1.08. Because samples are much smaller than populations, we can more realistically collect measurements from those samples. In our case study, Ben is interested in all 'customers' (the population), but because it is unrealistic to assess *every* customer, the consultants asked only those who had just purchased something at Scoops. The customers that were asked questions are the sample.

So how do we know that conclusions drawn from our sample reflect the conclusions we would have drawn if we had the population? If Ben concludes 'customer satisfaction is lowest at Store D', how do we know that's really because customer satisfaction is lowest at Store D (a question about the population) or because the people that by chance were shopping that day at Store D were less satisfied (a problem with the sample)?

Unfortunately, we can never know for sure! This is a question of how representative the sample is of the population. If the sample is highly representative, conclusions drawn from the sample are likely to reflect conclusions that would have been drawn from the population. If the sample is not representative, conclusions drawn from the sample are unlikely to reflect the population.

Representativeness can never be assessed with numbers. It is a rational argument. For example, Ben might realize that the sample taken from Store D was taken during a rush period, yet the samples taken from the other stores were taken during slow periods. Customer service will generally be poorer during the rush period, because there are more customers with less individual attention, but this does not mean that Store D is poorer in customer service than any other store. Instead, Ben is making an argument that a sample of customers purchasing during the rush period is not representative of a population of all customers. Given that, conclusions from that sample cannot be used to make conclusions about the population.

When trying to address a research question, you must decide on the population you are interested in, and then identify a sample you can reasonably approach that should represent that population. There are ways to increase the representativeness of a sample – larger samples, for example – but we'll get to this topic in more detail in Chapter 5: Sampling Distributions.

1.2.2 CONSTRUCTS VS OPERATIONAL DEFINITIONS

Just as we need to worry about how our samples represent the populations we wish we could study, we must also consider how the numbers we collect represent the concepts we wish we could study.

In Ben's case, he is really interested in a hypothetical idea called 'customer satisfaction'. There is no way to measure customer satisfaction directly. We can't, for example, walk up to a customer with a ruler and assess their satisfaction. That means customer satisfaction is a construct, which can be defined as a characteristic or property of interest in a population that cannot be measured directly.

When we have specific beliefs about what might be true in the relationship between constructs, we have a theory. In our case study, Ben has a theory that customer satisfaction is different between different stores. Because customer satisfaction is a construct, there's no way to measure it – but that doesn't make the theory any less interesting.

Now that we have a theory linking several constructs, we need a way to test this theory in the 'real world'. The first step is to identify an operational definition for each of our constructs. An operational definition is the way we represent a construct in a dataset, and we sometimes refer to this definition as the operationalization of a construct. The link between a construct and operational definition, just like the link between a population and a sample, cannot be demonstrated with numbers. It too is a rational argument.

In our case study, 'customer satisfaction' was operationalized with Questions 1 through 3 (Q1–Q3), and the identity of the store was operationalized as a letter (A–E). In each of these cases, Ben left it to the consultant to determine what the best operationalization might be. If this operational definition doesn't make sense, it might explain why the results were not as Ben expected. Is a Likert-type question the best way to assess customer satisfaction? Is a simple yes/no question about customer service better? There is no clear 'right answer' here. The only way to show that this is a good operationalization is for Ben or the consultant to make a solid argument as to what makes the most sense given his theory.

After deciding on operationalizations of each of our constructs, we can now test our theory by creating a hypothesis, which is a testable relationship between operational definitions that reflects a theory. Because we can never actually test a theory, because constructs can never be measured, we can only create a set of operational definitions and test the relationships between them. If all of our rational arguments make sense (if our operationalizations reflect our constructs, and if our sample represents our population), then we have built a case to say: 'If we find evidence supporting our hypothesis, our theory is probably true.' We will get into the specifics of this argument in later chapters.

In Figure 1.09, you can distinguish between hypotheticals and the 'real world' by looking at the dotted line. Anything above or that crosses that line is theoretical and can only be 'proven' by making a rational argument that it is true. Anything below that line can be demonstrated with numbers (measured).

1.2 .3 EXPERIMENTS, QUASI-EXPERIMENTS AND CORRELATIONAL STUDIES

Now that we have a hypothesis, we need to test it in a way that tells us something interesting. Just because we have numbers doesn't mean they're telling us the truth – this depends upon how the data are collected and analysed.

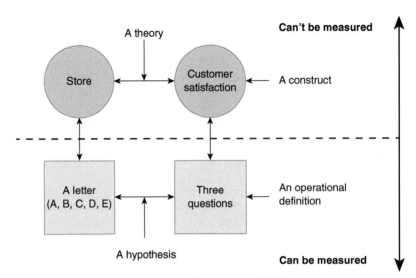

FIGURE 1.09   Relationship between constructs and operational definitions

There are three major approaches to testing a hypothesis in a business context: an experiment, a quasi-experiment or a correlational study – see Figure 1.10. Each brings different advantages and disadvantages.

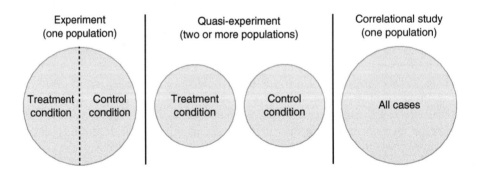

FIGURE 1.10   Comparison of how samples are drawn in experiments, quasi-experiments and correlational studies

The most rigorous approach is an experiment. This is the only approach that allows you to conclude something causes something else. For example, if our hypothesis was 'increased customer satisfaction causes sales', the only way to demonstrate this would be with an experiment. Unfortunately, an experiment is the most difficult approach to implement.

To run an experiment, you split a sample randomly into two or more groups called conditions, a process called random assignment. You can then treat each condition differently and observe any resulting differences between the groups. Because you assigned the people to each group at random, the only difference between the two groups should be the way you treated them differently.

For example, imagine that you were considering a new training programme for your employees. You need to pay for each trainee, so you'd like to know if the training works before you purchase it for everyone. You decide to run an experiment. You randomly pick half of your employees to receive the training (the treatment condition), while the other half will receive nothing (the control condition). A few months after the training, you check to see if job performance is higher for the group that received the training. If so, you can conclude that the training caused the higher level of performance (and purchase it for everyone!).

As you can see, the restrictions and planning required for an experiment are rather extensive. There are many situations where experimentation is not realistic or is downright impossible. For example, consider our original question: does increased customer satisfaction cause increased sales? We cannot randomly assign customer satisfaction, so an experiment is not possible here.

When an experiment is not possible, a researcher often uses a correlational study. A correlational study is any study where multiple variables are measured at the same time without special treatment by the researcher. We can never make conclusions about causality from correlational studies. For example, we could see if there are differences in customer satisfaction by store. We can't randomly assign stores, so we can never conclude that the management, employees, or anything else about those stores *causes* those differences in satisfaction. While the store might cause these differences, there is no way to support this theory with a correlational study. Despite this, determining if there is a relationship between two variables may be a valuable piece of a puzzle to be solved.

One type of correlational study is worth special discussion, and this is the quasi-experiment. Quasi-experiments look like experiments on the surface, but lack random assignment of subjects. For example, consider our training programme above. Instead of randomly picking half of your employees to receive the training, you ask for volunteers. Now, instead of drawing from a single population (employees) and randomly assigning them to conditions, you are drawing from two populations (volunteers and non-volunteers) and letting them choose their own conditions. This is a problem, because if the trainees ended up performing better, you would have no way to know if this was because the training works for all employees or only for enthusiastic volunteers.

It's also important to note that random assignment must take place at the level of the subject, or it is still a quasi-experiment. Consider our training example. Instead of randomly assigning all employees to either training or no training, what happens if you randomly assign the day shift to training and the night shift as the control? Despite having a treatment and control condition, this is still a quasi-experiment, because these are two different populations. There is no way to know if any observed differences were caused by the treatment (getting training) or instead because of pre-existing differences between the people working in those shifts.

If experimentation is possible, you always want to conduct an experiment, because it will give you the highest quality answer to your questions. Quasi-experiments and correlational studies are always a backup choice. But sometimes, they're the only choice.

1.2.4 DETERMINING THE CHARACTERISTICS OF STUDIES

Now that we have all these terms to describe study design, can we apply these terms to help Ben figure out if he should trust the consultant's conclusion: 'Decreased customer satisfaction does not lead to decreased sales at Scoops'? Let's return to the first line of that follow-up e-mail from the consultant:

> After customers purchased something at each location, we asked them several questions and recorded it in this spreadsheet.

That's relevant to the sample and population. The sample assessed appears to be made up of customers that have purchased something and elect to complete a survey afterwards. Does this reflect a population of customers in general? Maybe, maybe not. But that's something Ben needs to decide for himself.

What constructs and operational definitions are we talking about? Did at least these operationalizations make sense? It's not clear which questions the consultant used to make these conclusions. Our constructs of interest are 'customer satisfaction' and 'sales'. So which questions were used to assess these?

Q2 was 'How many times have you been to this Scoops in the last six months?' and is the closest we have to 'sales'. Q3 was 'Did you receive excellent customer service?' and is the closest we have to 'customer satisfaction'. Are these reasonable operational definitions for these constructs? Again: maybe, or maybe not. A customer may not be able to remember how many times he's been to a particular location over six months. Number of visits rather than money spent may not be the best way to assess sales. A single question about customer service might not include all aspects of customer satisfaction: satisfaction with employees' attitudes, satisfaction with employee speed, satisfaction with employee attention, and so on. None of these criticisms necessarily condemn this study, but they are things that Ben needs to consider. Does he believe these operational definitions really represent the constructs they are designed to represent? If not, then this study is not credible.

When the consultant concluded that 'Decreased customer satisfaction does not lead to decreased sales at Scoops', he made a conclusion about causality. *Lead to* implies that satisfaction *caused* sales. Is that conclusion justified? The consultant did not create conditions and assign people to them; he passively collected information from customers as they left. This is a correlational study; any conclusions about causality are not justified. This conclusion cannot be made from this study.

With weaknesses in the population being sampled, the study design and the operational definitions of the constructs, Ben should conclude that this study (and this consultancy) is not credible. Even though they collected data, they are not drawing appropriate conclusions from those data. Collecting numbers is not enough to tell a credible story; the source of those numbers must also be sound.

1.3 APPLYING THE LANGUAGE OF STATISTICS

To apply what you've learned from this chapter, consider the following case study, questions posed about that case study, and discussion of those questions.

1.3.1 APPLICATION CASE STUDY

Maya is a manager for We Get You There, a small travel agency that arranges family vacations. Each of the agents at her agency is assigned clients by alphabetical rotation – that is, when a new client contacts the agency, that client is assigned to the next agent down the list, repeating from the beginning. As a result, clients are shared equally among all the agents, ensuring that no one agent is favoured above any other. This creates a very friendly work environment, but Maya is concerned that it is hurting agency profits. After all, skill as a travel agent varies a great deal, and her less skilled agents work with as many clients as her most skilled agents.

1 If Maya is interested in examining whether or not agent skill is affecting company profits, what variables could she examine?

2 Pick a few variables of interest for Maya. What are their scales of measurement? Are they discrete or continuous?

3 How could Maya examine these variables? What research design is most appropriate?

1.3.2 APPLICATION DISCUSSION

The path from research question to research study is one of the most difficult we face as managers and owners. In Maya's case, there are many possible ways to answer her question, and the ones you come up with are probably not the one we will discuss here. However, this will serve as a reasonable prototype.

Maya is interested in the relationship between agent skill and company profits. That means agent skill and profits are her two constructs of interest. When we seek to create variables, we are really creating new operationalizations of those constructs. There are an infinite number of ways to do this. However, we might operationalize agent skill with a test. For example, Maya might ask her agents to run through a sales simulation to gauge their effectiveness. Alternatively, Maya might conduct surveys of clients, asking them about their experiences with their agent. To operationalize the effect on company profit, Maya could examine the total amount of sales over some period of interest.

Scale of measurement will change dramatically depending on what Maya chooses. A simulation test could produce many types: a 'pass/fail' test would be nominal (and discrete), but a test that produced a score would be interval or ratio (and could be discrete or continuous, depending on the specific scoring technique). If she chose a survey, this could be anything, depending on the types of questions asked. Total sales might be computed in British pounds of services sold per month, which would be continuous and ratio. However, it could be computed as a total count of sales, in which case it would be discrete and ratio. It all depends on what Maya chooses.

For research design, we face a common problem in business: there is no way to randomly assign agents to be 'good' or 'bad'. As a result, Maya most likely needs to passively measure her variables and compare them: a correlational design.

EXPLORING THE LANGUAGE OF STATISTICS IN EXCEL AND SPSS

EXCEL

Download the Excel dataset for the demonstration below as **chapter1.xls** from the book's website. As you read this section, try to apply the terms you've learned in this chapter to the dataset and follow along with Excel on your own computer.

You can also get a video demonstration of the section below under **Excel Videos: Chapter 1**.

Excel is a very flexible spreadsheet program, but it is not principally designed for computing and analysing statistics. As a result, it doesn't have quite the power of SPSS to answer statistical questions. Despite this, it is advantageous to learn Excel for analysing statistics because it is a much more common program than SPSS; you can find Excel and similar spreadsheet programs like OpenOffice.org Calc on computers throughout the world.

A dataset in Excel is saved in a worksheet, which you can access via the tabs at the bottom. Otherwise, it's very similar to Figure 1.01 earlier in this chapter – compare Figures 1.01 1.11. To enter data, just click and type.

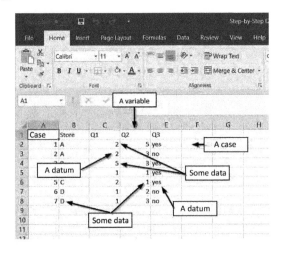

FIGURE 1.11   A dataset as shown in Excel

SPSS

Download the SPSS dataset for the demonstration below as **chapter1.sav** from the book's website. As you read this section, try to apply the terms you've learned in this chapter to the dataset and follow along with SPSS on your own computer.

You can also get a video demonstration of the section below on the book's website under **SPSS Videos: Chapter 1**.

Because it is specifically designed for computing and analysing statistics, SPSS is a very powerful program for computing a wide variety of statistics. With increased flexibility, however, comes increased complexity. Working with data in SPSS requires a bit more work up front than in Excel.

There are two views of interest in SPSS. The first is the **Data View**, which displays your dataset. It looks a lot like Figure 1.01 earlier in this chapter – compare Figures 1.01 and 1.12. The biggest difference is that SPSS automatically creates a column of case numbers, so you don't need to add them yourself. Cases with data in them appear with black text, while empty cases appear with grey text.

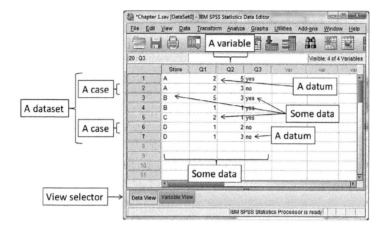

FIGURE 1.12   A dataset as shown in SPSS Data View

Using the view selector at the bottom, you can also gain access to the **Variable View**, which allows you to set the properties of your variables. The settings you choose here help SPSS to decide how to treat your variables in analyses.

	Name	Type	Width	Decimals	Label	Values	Missing	Columns	Align	Measure
1	Store	String	5	0		None	None	6	Left	Nominal
2	Q1	Numeric	2	0	Do you like this store?	{1, Dis...	None	6	Right	Scale
3	Q2	Numeric	2	0	How many times have y...	None	None	6	Right	Scale
4	Q3	String	3	0	Did you receive excellen...	None	None	6	Left	Ordinal
5										

FIGURE 1.13   A dataset as shown in SPSS Variable View

In the Variable View, you can see the same four variables we saw in the Data View, but with a lot of extra settings for each one (see Figure 1.13).

■ **Name**: This is the word used at the top of the column in your Variable View. You can't start a variable name with a number, spaces or special characters.

(Continued)

(Continued)

- **Type**: This is the general format for the data contained in this variable. The two options you'll use most often are Numeric (for numbers) or String (for text).
- **Width**: This is the number of characters recorded for each datum. For example, if you have a string of Width 2 and try to enter 'Yes', it will be truncated to 'Ye'.
- **Decimals**: When using numeric data, this determines how many numbers after the decimal place will be displayed. It does not affect how many numbers are stored. For example, if you stored 12.3456 in a variable with 2 for Decimals, you would see '12.35' in the Data View, even though 12.3456 would be used in statistics calculations.
- **Label**: These are the words you'll see in place of the variable name when running statistical analyses. For example, if we computed an average for 'Q1', the results would label it, 'Do you like this store?' This is only used to make output more readable, and has no effect on the results.
- **Values**: These are the words you'll see in place of the numbers used for each datum in analyses. In this example, clicking on the […] button brings up the panel shown in Figure 1.14

With this set of values, 1 through 5 will be replaced with these words to make the output more readable. This also has no effect on results.

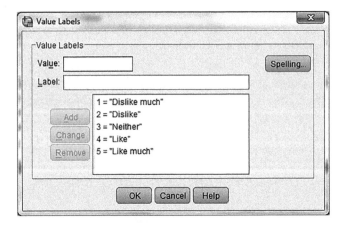

FIGURE 1.14   The values dialogue in SPSS

- **Missing**: This allows you to set missing values. This is an important component of statistical analyses in the real world, but involves a lot of complicated decisions you'll talk about more in a research methods class. In this statistics text, we'll just be leaving this unset.
- **Columns**: This sets how wide the variable appears in the Data View. You can change this manually by click-dragging the width of the columns in the Data View.
- **Align**: This sets the text alignment of each variable in the Data View. This has no effect on results.
- **Measure**: This is one of the most important parts of the Variable View. Setting this tells SPSS which scale of measurement your variable is, which in turn tells it which analyses are appropriate for that variable. There are three options. Select *Nominal* for nominal variables and *Ordinal* for ordinal variables. Select *Scale* for both interval and ratio variables.

STATISTICS IN THE REAL WORLD

 These web links can be accessed directly from the book's website.

Philip Evans, senior partner of Boston Consulting Group, describes how data are transforming the business world: www.ted.com/talks/philip_evans_how_data_will_transform_business.

How has the increasing availability of data fundamentally changed business? Can a business ignore data and still be successful?

National Numeracy, a UK charity, explains why fluency with numbers and statistics is critical to our futures as world citizens: www.nationalnumeracy.org.uk/why-numeracy-important.

What are the costs of ignoring numbers in the modern economy?

TEST YOURSELF

 After you've completed the questions below, check your answers online.

1 Sally, the owner of Two Pi Are Pizza, decides to conduct a research study to determine if adding double cheese free of charge to pizza orders improves customer satisfaction. Sally adds a customer satisfaction survey with Likert-type scales to every pizza box. She randomly assigns her stores on the west side of the city to change their procedures to use extra cheese and plans to compare these with stores on the east side of the city, where nothing will change.

   a Is this an experiment, quasi-experiment or correlational study, and why?

   b Can Sally provide evidence that extra cheese *causes* increased customer satisfaction using this design? If not, how could she change this design so that she can?

   c What is the treatment and what is the control condition?

   d What is a possible hypothesis for Sally's study?

   e Is Sally drawing her participants from a sample or a population?

   f What constructs are being assessed, and how are they being operationalized?

   g Are the addition of a free extra cheese variable and the Likert-type scales collected here quantitative or qualitative?

   h Are the addition of a free extra cheese variable and the Likert-type scales collected here discrete or continuous?

   i What are the scales of measurement of the addition of a free extra cheese variable and Likert-type scales as assessed here?

2 Ben, the owner of Scoops, decides to hold a frozen yogurt eating contest to promote the opening of a new store. He decides to collect some data about the contestants in the contest to include on his website. Identify the scale of measurement for each of the variables he measured:

   a Age.

   b Favourite flavour of frozen yogurt.

   c Order of finish in the contest (i.e., 1st place, 2nd place, 3rd place).

   d How much the contestant reported liking frozen yogurt on a 1–5 scale.

   e The number of eating contests the contestant had previously participated in.

   f Where the contestant lives.

(Continued)

(Continued)

3 Produce an operationalization of 'successful online social media strategy'. Describe this operationalization in the terms we've used here to describe variables.

DATA SKILL CHALLENGES

 After you've completed the questions below, check your answers online.

1 Five people completed a five-item Likert-type scale. Here are their scores:

George: 1, 2, 3, 4, 5
Bill: 2, 2, 3, 3, 3
Amy: 5, 5, 4, 5, 5
Jonathan: 4, 3, 2, 1, 1
Stephanie: 3, 3, 2, 2, 5

Place these scores into a dataset, organizing it into rows and columns as appropriate. Remember to include the person's name in your dataset as appropriate.

2 Here are data for the top three finishers in Ben's frozen yogurt eating contest (see Test Yourself Question 2 above):

Anton: 16, Vanilla, 1st, 4, 5, Newton.
Jemia: 37, Chocolate, 2nd, 5, 0, Blackwell.
Harry: 22, Strawberry, 3rd, 3, 21, Newton.

Place these scores into a dataset, organizing it into rows and columns as appropriate. Remember to include the person's name in your dataset as appropriate.

3 Here are data for Sally's first four deliveries:

Customer 1:   Large, 1, Thursday, 2 km, evening, £2.
Customer 2:   Medium, 2, Thursday, 4 km, evening, £3.
Customer 3:   Small, 1, Friday, 3 km, afternoon, £1.
Customer 4:   Extra Large, 2, Friday, 1 km, evening, £4.

Place these scores into a dataset, organizing it into rows and columns as appropriate. Remember to include the customer number in your dataset as appropriate.

4 Here are sales data for the branch offices of a large sales organization:

Branch 1:   West region, 20 units sold, €34000.
Branch 2:   West region, 40 units sold, €50000.
Branch 3:   East region, 16 units sold, €35000.
Branch 4:   East region, 93 units sold, €85000.

Place these scores into a dataset, organizing it into rows and columns as appropriate. Remember to include the branch number in your dataset as appropriate.

NEW TERMS

case: conditions: constant: construct: continuous: control condition: correlational study: data: Data View: dataset: datum: dichotomous: discrete: experiment: hypothesis: interval: Likert-type item: Likert-type scale: nominal: operational definition: operationalization: ordinal: population: qualitative: quantitative: quasi-experiment: random assignment: ratio: representative: sample: scale of measurement: subject: theory: treatment condition: variable: Variable View:

Visit https://study.sagepub.com/landers2e **for free additional online resources related to this chapter.**

2 WORKING WITH NUMBERS AND DATA DISPLAY

WHAT YOU WILL LEARN FROM THIS CHAPTER

- How to choose an appropriate translation for your data
- How to avoid misleading others with your own translations
- How to identify misleading translations
- How to identify and interpret frequencies, relative frequencies and cumulative frequencies
- How to distinguish between fractions, proportions and percentages
- How to read formulas with subscripts
- How to specify sample size in a formula

DATA SKILLS YOU WILL MASTER FROM THIS CHAPTER

- Creating a frequency table
- Creating a bar chart
- Creating a pie chart
- Creating a histogram
- Creating a frequency polygon
- Creating a scatterplot

CASE STUDY HOW CAN THESE NUMBERS TELL A STORY?

Jamal is the owner of DropIt, a company specializing in online retailing. Jamal's company does not actually stock any products. Instead, Jamal's business model is based on dropshipping; that is, when an order comes in from a customer on one of his websites, Jamal places a mirror order with a wholesaler, who then ships the product directly to the customer. This means that the success of Jamal's business is based almost entirely on his ability to attract customers to his website to make a purchase.

Jamal's website portfolio is fairly large; he currently runs ten websites, each with a different focus. For example, one of his websites sells women's clothing and another sells jewellery. Each website is designed to attract customers that would be likely to purchase something there. For example, the women's clothing website provides fashion advice; the jewellery website has an interactive app where customers can upload a photo and virtually try items on. Jamal spends a lot of his time working on these extra features to attract customers.

Recently, Jamal has begun to wonder if this effort has been a waste of time. He's not quite sure how to answer this question, but he knows that the website usage and sales data should hold the answer, and asks his website manager to e-mail it to him.

Having read Chapter 1 of this text, he at least knows what he's looking at – a dataset containing one case for each person to visit his website and three variables: which of the ten websites they visited (represented as numbers), the number of minutes they spent on that website, and the number of items they purchased when they were there. Because these are data that have been passively collected, he also correctly identifies it as a correlational study.

So, although he understands the dataset, he's a bit overwhelmed. What does he do with it now? How can he translate all of these numbers into something useful that will help answer his question? How can he tell the story of his business through this dataset?

Take a look at Jamal's website usage data for yourself in chapter2case.xls (Excel) or chapter2case.sav (SPSS) online.

Humans are not very good at interpreting large amounts of raw data. It's simply overwhelming. Our brains have a hard time keeping track of hundreds of numbers at the same time in order to identify patterns, and patterns are exactly what we want to know about.

In this chapter's case study, Jamal needs to translate the many numbers he received into a meaningful story about his business. There are two ways to do this:

1 Translate many numbers into fewer numbers. We'll begin to cover this here when discussing frequency tables, but we will cover this in much more depth in Chapters 3 and 4.

2 Translate many numbers into illustrations, pictures and graphics. This will be the focus of most of this chapter.

In this chapter, you'll learn about several possible translations for data and when they are appropriate. As you read, consider how you might choose to translate Jamal's data into something more understandable.

2.1 CHOOSING THE RIGHT CHART OR GRAPHIC TO REPRESENT YOUR DATA

FOUNDATION CONCEPTS

A **qualitative variable** is a variable containing data about qualities, in either a nominal or an ordinal scale of measurement. Examples: favourite colours, gender. See Chapter 1, p. 6.

A **quantitative variable** is a variable containing data about quantities, in either an interval or a ratio scale of measurement. Examples: survey data, counts. See Chapter 1, p. 6.

One of the most common ways that people mislead with statistics and are misled by statistics is through inappropriate translations of numbers. Just as humans are not very good at interpreting large amounts of raw data, we are easily misled by a pretty picture. While learning to use statistics for business, this is important for three reasons:

1 **You could be fooled by others with their poor translations.** When someone unethical is trying to sell you something, they may torture their data so that it tells the story they want it to tell. They do not need to tell outright untruths. Instead, they take advantage of your ignorance to convince you of something that is only half true. Understanding how to translate data helps you recognize when someone is trying to trick you.

2 **You could fool others with your poor translations.** Even with the best intentions, ignorance of proper technique could lead you to produce translations that don't tell the whole truth. As your customers begin to realize this, you will lose their business – and word-of-mouth spreads quickly.

3 **You could fool yourself with your poor translations.** Even if you only run statistics to improve processes internal to your own organization, you want to base your decisions upon accurate information. Otherwise, what's the point? You want to make data-driven decisions because these are the decisions that will improve your business. Basing decisions on faulty translations is no better than guessing.

One of the most basic questions we must ask, then, is: what kind of translation will be best for my data? The answer, as with many issues you will discover throughout this textbook, is: it depends. And in this case, it depends on what kind of data you want to translate.

Qualitative and quantitative variables are treated differently because they contain different types of information, and any translations of such data should reflect those differences. Qualitative variables can be translated with either summaries (translating many numbers into fewer numbers) or illustrations (translating many numbers into pictures). Quantitative variables are best translated with illustrations. We'll cover each in turn.

2.2 WORKING WITH NUMBERS

As we begin our discussion of how best to translate variables, it's important to first take a step back to ensure we are all speaking the same language. Statistics can become very complicated (not for several chapters though!), so statisticians use a sort of shorthand when representing complicated concepts. This shorthand is used in formulas, which is how statistical concepts are concisely represented.

If you recall your primary school mathematics, you probably remember fractions, which are a common way of representing portions of wholes. For example, if we wanted to represent 'one half' as a fraction, we'd write it as ½. In formulas, fractions are used to illustrate algebraic relationships between variables instead of portions of wholes. This is because using fractions in this way would be very confusing. Consider the well-known formula for the quadratic equation shown in Figure 2.01.

$$x = \frac{-b \pm \sqrt{b^2 - 4ac}}{2a}$$

FIGURE 2.01   A sample formula

If you don't remember the purpose of this formula, that's okay – it's not important right now. But you probably did know it in secondary school! For now, consider if we used fractions to represent all of the variables in that formula (Figure 2.02).

$$x = \frac{-\frac{1}{2} \pm \sqrt{\frac{1}{2}^2 - 4\left(\frac{3}{8}\right)\left(\frac{1}{8}\right)}}{2\left(\frac{3}{8}\right)}$$

FIGURE 2.02   A sample formula using fractions

Ugh – that just looks terrible, doesn't it? The logical relationships in the first formula become confused when we fill it up with lots of fractions – it becomes unnecessarily complex. I even had to add parentheses so that you didn't get confused about what those numbers meant – 'four and three eighths' and 'four multiplied by three eighths' are very different!

To avoid this confusion, statisticians writing formulas represent most fractions as proportions, which are the decimal equivalents of those values. For example, ½ becomes .5. Consider that formula again, with proportions – Figure 2.03.

$$x = \frac{-.5 \pm \sqrt{.5^2 - 4(.375)(.125)}}{2(.375)}$$

FIGURE 2.03   A sample formula using proportions

Although there are a lot of numbers in there, the interrelationships between the numbers are much clearer in this version. And as an added bonus, it's much more obvious how to key this into a calculator.

You are probably also already familiar with a cousin of the proportion: the percentage, which is the value of a proportion multiplied by 100, followed by a percentage symbol (%). That means ½ and .5 can both be represented as the percentage 50%.

While the relationships between fractions, proportions and percentages may seem straightforward, it's easy, mid-computation, to forget to move the decimal over by the correct number of places. Study Figure 2.04, and double-check that you have things right.

Fraction	Proportion	Percentage
0	.0	0%
1/10	.1	10%
1/5	.2	20%
1/3	.333333	33.3333%
1/2	.5	50%
5/8	.625	62.5%
1	1	100%

FIGURE 2.04   Common values and their representation as fractions, proportions and percentages

Different statistical analyses call for different types of values, depending on the goal of the procedure. Almost all formulas take proportions, but their result may be most clearly expressed as a percentage. Ensure you pay attention to the requirements and description of each formula you encounter so that you use the correct version.

MISLED BY PERCENTAGES

Percentages and proportions alone are often used to mislead the statistically unsophisticated. For example, consider this report from the videogame industry:

> Sales of retail videogames this year only represented 50% of videogame sales in comparison to last year when retail made up 75% of videogame sales. This indicates a decrease in the viability of the videogame market and we recommend investors react accordingly.

When someone reports a percentage alone, it's important to ask (at least to yourself) what 'real' numbers underlie those percentages. Yes, retail videogame sales make up a lower percentage of total sales this year in comparison to last year, but does that necessarily mean fewer videogames were sold? What if the real data looked like Figure 2.05?

	Retail sales (in billions)	Retail sales (percentage of total sales)	Downloads (in billions)	Downloads (percentage of total sales)
Last year	15.0	15/20 =75%	5.0	5/20 =25%
This year	20.0	20/40 = 50%	20.0	20/40= 50%
Change by year	+5.0	50%–75% = –25%	+15.0	50% 25% = +25%

FIGURE 2.05   Videogame sales data illustrating misleading percentages

Despite having a smaller percentage of total sales, retail sales actually grew in the last year! The real cause of the relative percentage drop is the massive increase in game downloads. But in contrast to the report's recommendation, the videogame industry is booming – and certainly worth investment. The report could have avoided this problem by reporting raw numbers (an increase from 15 to 20 billion) rather than percentages (a decrease from 75% to 50% of total sales).

The use of percentages here only adds to confusion about the real underlying data. Whether interpreting or creating your own percentages, be careful to avoid this pitfall. Always check to make sure the story the data are really telling is the story you are translating from them.

2.3 PUTTING NUMBERS INTO FORMULAS

FOUNDATION CONCEPTS

A **sample** is a group gathered at random from a population. Example: a focus group randomly selected from a larger population of customers. See Chapter 1, p. 11.

Now that we have some ground rules, what's our first bit of statistical shorthand? Fortunately, it's quite easy: the capital letter N. This represents the population size, which is the total number of cases within a particular population. If our population contained 5000 businesses, we would say $N = 5000$.

We can contrast this with sample size, which is the number of cases in a particular sample (or dataset). We represent this with a lower-case n. So if our sample was made up of 40 people, we would say $n = 40$.

This creates some strange-sounding sentences. For example, when discussing studies, a researcher might ask, 'What was the n?' What this researcher is really asking is, 'What was the sample size?'

Formulas are usually written quite generally because they can be used in many different settings. For example, I can compute n for a sample I collected from a correlational study, and another n for a sample I collected from an experiment. After I've computed these two n, I need some way to keep track of which n came from which sample in my notes.

To do this, we typically use subscripts, which are smaller letters used beneath terms in formulas to denote where a variable came from. For example, I might refer to $n_{\text{Experiment}}$ and $n_{\text{Correlational}}$ so that I can keep track of which n is which. The specific labels aren't important, although you don't want to pick anything with too many letters. As long as you can keep them straight in your mind, you might label these sample sizes as n_{E} and n_{C}. When computing your own statistics, it's up to you to pick clear subscripts.

We'll take a look at how you might use this new shorthand – both n and subscripts – in the next section.

2.4 SUMMARIZING QUALITATIVE VARIABLES

When summarizing qualitative data, you display all of your original data to the person looking at your summary, but reorganized into an easier-to-understand form. This means that the person viewing your translation can come to his or her own conclusions about what the data imply. Instead of scrolling through 500 cases of nominal responses, your reader will see counts of how many nominal responses are contained in those 500 cases. It is much simpler to view a summary than to view a large dataset.

In comparison with illustrations, there is a greater burden on the person viewing the summary, as it is generally more difficult to look at tables of numbers than pictures representing those numbers. For this reason, if you are trying to translate data for a client or customer, you will usually choose to illustrate the data rather than to summarize them. If you want to include summaries anyway, because a client requests them or just to be thorough, you will typically place them in an appendix. But if you are creating the summary for yourself, the information it provides is invaluable.

2.4.1 DESCRIBING THE FREQUENCY OF DATA

There are several major ways to summarize qualitative data.

The first is a frequency, which is a count of how many times a value appears in a variable within a dataset (see Chapter 1, p. 30). Frequencies are symbolized with an italicized *f*. They are sometimes called 'simple frequencies'.

Consider Figure 2.06, which contains the first 12 sales of the day at Marv's Muffin Stand. Each value in this table can be represented by a frequency. For example, of the first 12 sales, only one was a bran muffin, so we would say $f = 1$ for bran muffins. Apple cinnamon muffins (my favourite!) were sold four times, so $f = 4$.

Multi purchases
Chocolate
Chocolate
Banana Nut
Apple Cinnamon
Chocolate
Banana Nut
Apple Cinnamon
Apple Cinnamon
Chocolate
Bran
Apple Cinnamon
Banana Nut

FIGURE 2.06 Sample sales data from Marv's Muffin Stand

Frequencies by themselves are interesting but potentially misleading. For example, what if I told you that the frequency of bran muffin sales at Martha's Muffin Stand (next door to Marv's – they are bitter enemies) was $f = 5$! Martha sold five times as many bran muffins and therefore must be much better at selling them, right? Not so fast! Martha didn't report the first 12 sales – she reported her first 60 sales. For both Martha and Marv, the proportion of their muffins sold that were bran was .083 (8.3%). This proportion is a relative frequency, which is represented by the term rel.f, and will be your very first formula (see Figure 2.07).

$$\text{rel.} f = \frac{f}{n}$$

FIGURE 2.07   Relative frequency formula

We can plug in the values for f and n into this formula for each of the examples above, as shown in Figure 2.08.

$$\text{rel.} f_{\text{Marv}} = \frac{f}{n} = \frac{1}{12} = .083$$

$$\text{rel.} f_{\text{Martha}} = \frac{f}{n} = \frac{5}{60} = .083$$

FIGURE 2.08   Sample calculations for relative frequencies

Each of these proportions represents the bran portion of total muffin sales for each store. Together with frequencies, this gives a very clear picture of what information your dataset really contains without taking up too much space. Or at least it will, once we organize it all into a well-designed table.

2.4.2 FREQUENCY TABLES

Frequency data are typically organized in a common table format. This certainly isn't the only way to organize frequency data, but it is the way that most people will expect. Figure 2.09 provides an example, using the Muffin Purchases dataset above.

Value	f	rel.f	Cum.f	cum.%
Apple Cinnamon	4	4/12 = .33	4	4/12 = 33%
Banana Nut	3	3/12 = .25	4+3 = 7	7/12 = 58%
Bran	1	1/12 = .08	4+3+1 = 8	8/12 = 67%
Chocolate	4	4/12 = .33	4+3+1+4 = 12	12/12 =100%

FIGURE 2.09   Frequency table from Figure 2.06 data

We wouldn't normally put computation inside our table – that's here just to make it clearer how each cell of the table was calculated.

To create this table, you must first get a list of every unique value in your qualitative variable and put them in order.

If your data are text based (e.g. Apple Cinnamon, Banana Nut), this should be alphabetical order.

Once you have your list of values in a meaningful order, determine the frequencies and relative frequencies of each of those values, using the techniques described above, and enter them into your table.

You probably noticed two new statistics in this table – cum.*f* and cum.%. These are the cumulative frequency and cumulative percentage which represent the number and percentage of cases, respectively, with that value or values higher in the table, based upon the order you have chosen. In this example, Bran's cum.*f* represents the number of Apple Cinnamon (4) plus the number of Banana Nut (3) plus the number of Bran (1) muffins sold: 4 + 3 + 1 = 8. In turn, cum.% = 67% because 8/12 = .67.

There are two things about cumulative frequencies that you should remember. First, a common mistake when calculating cumulative percentages occurs if you try to sum the relative frequencies instead of summing the frequencies themselves and dividing by the total. This mistake occurs because relative frequencies in frequency tables are often rounded. For example, the relative frequency of Apple Cinnamon, .33, is in fact .33333333 and so on, with 3 repeating infinitely. Because of rounding like this, if you try to sum the three values for Bran to calculate cum.%, you will produce a slightly incorrect answer: .33 + .25 + .08 = .66 = 66%. This value, as explained earlier, should be 67%. You can (and should) avoid this problem by always calculating cum.% from the *f* values directly, as shown here.

Second, the cum.*f* and cum.% in the first row of your table will always be the same as the *f* and rel.*f* (expressed as a percentage) for that row, since those are the only numbers at or above that point in the table – in this case, both *f* and cum.*f* for Apple Cinnamon are 4, whereas rel.*f* and cum.% are .33 and 33%, respectively. In contrast, the last cum.*f* in your table should always be equal to *n*, and the last cum.% should always be 100%, because 100% of the data are at or above that row – in this case, the cum.*f* for Chocolate is 12: 4 Apple Cinnamon + 3 Banana Nut + 1 Bran + 4 Chocolate sold. Thus, in that last row, 12 out of 12 total muffins appear at or above that row in the table, a cum.% of 100%, as shown in Figure 2.10.

$$\text{cum.}f_{chocolate} = 4 + 3 + 1 + 4 = 12$$

$$\text{cum.\%}_{chocolate} = \frac{(4+3+1+4)}{12} = \frac{12}{12} = 1$$

FIGURE 2.10   Sample calculation for cumulative frequency

If your data are numeric (e.g. 1st, 2nd, 3rd), you should use numeric order, and you should not generally skip numbers. For example, if you were tracking the ranks of your products in various competitions and only had 1st, 3rd and 4th place awards (Figure 2.11), you would still want to include '2nd' in your table – the frequency would simply be 0 (Figure 2.12).

Win record
1st
3rd
4th
4th

Win record
4th
1st
3rd
3rd
1st
1st

FIGURE 2.11   Sample product ranks data

Value	F	rel. f	cum.f	cum.%
1st place wins (Golds)	4	4/10 = .40	4 = 4	4/10 = .40
2nd place wins (Silvers)	0	0/10 = .00	4 + 0 = 4	4/10 = .40
3rd place wins (Bronzes)	3	3/10 = .30	4 + 0 + 3 = 7	7/10 = .70
4th place + (Consolation)	3	3/10 = .30	4 + 0 + 3 + 3 = 10	10/10 = 1.00

FIGURE 2.12   Frequency table from Figure 2.11 data

2.5 ILLUSTRATING A QUALITATIVE VARIABLE

While summaries give a lot of useful information about a variable, they can be quite complicated. Often, you want to simply deliver a clear, powerful message about a variable, and that is where illustrations are most useful.

There are two common illustrations for qualitative data. The specific type of illustration depends on what message you want to convey.

2.5.1 BAR CHARTS

A bar chart illustrates data by displaying categories on the x-axis as independent bars and simple frequencies on the y-axis. Bar charts are the most common illustration for qualitative data. They represent simple frequencies as the height of a bar.

The person reading this bar chart (Figure 2.13) can easily determine n, the number of categories of responses, and f for each of those categories. In this case, it is clear that $f_{apple} = 4$, $f_{banana} = 3$, $f_{bran} = 1$ and $f_{chocolate} = 4$.

There are several rules for creating bar charts that make them easily interpretable. Ensure all of your bar charts have these attributes:

- General Chart Characteristics
    - The chart is a bit wider than it is tall (roughly a 4:3 ratio).
    - The chart is descriptively titled at the top.
- *x*-Axis (across the bottom of the chart)
    - The axis label is centred and is the name of the variable being illustrated.
    - The category labels are informative for each category (try to avoid abbreviations).

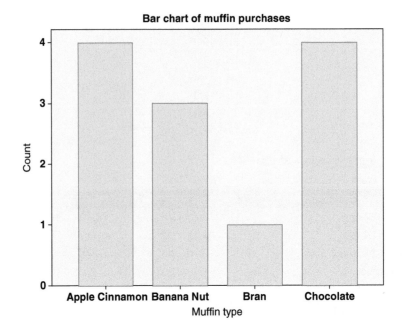

FIGURE 2.13   Bar chart of data in Figure 2.06

■ *y*-Axis (up the left side of the chart)
  ○ The axis label is centred in the chart and reads 'Count' or 'Frequency'.
  ○ The largest value is at the top of the chart and is the largest frequency in the dataset (or is slightly larger).
  ○ The smallest value is at the bottom of the chart and is zero (0).
  ○ Values appear at regular intervals between these two values, but not so densely as to make them difficult to read.
■ Bars
  ○ Each bar represents one category.
  ○ Each bar is the same colour as every other bar.
  ○ All categories in the variable are represented in the chart. Never skip categories.
  ○ There are gaps between the bars. (This is super important! I'll explain why in the Histograms section later in this chapter).

2.5.2 BEING MISLED WITH BAR CHARTS

Why are there so many rules regarding bar charts? Remember that humans are easy prey for a pretty picture. We tend to believe what we see. Consider the two graphics shown in Figure 2.14.

In which of these bar charts are there bigger differences between regions? Neither! These two charts were created from the same dataset.

These bar charts demonstrate one of the most common ways to mislead people with graphics. Look at the *y*-axis on the chart on the right – it doesn't start with zero, which exaggerates the differences between regions. Even though the data itself is a nominal scale of measurement, the counts are ratio-level, and that zero is meaningful.

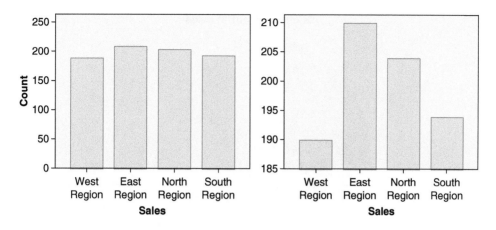

FIGURE 2.14 Comparison of two bar charts from the same dataset following different display rules

Most people who saw the chart on the left would see small differences, while those who saw the chart on right would see large differences. But you know better! The creator of the chart on the right didn't follow the rules; the left chart best represents the real data.

This is why we have so many rules. They create a common set of expectations about what data should look like so that our initial impressions from charts are correct. But as long as you know those rules and check to make sure they haven't been violated whenever you see a new data illustration, you can't be misled either!

2.5.3 PIE CHARTS

A pie chart illustrates data by displaying frequencies and relative frequencies or percentages as portions of a circle. Unless you specifically want this feature of a pie chart, you should stick with a bar chart. For example, if I was interested in illustrating each type of muffin sale as a portion of total muffin sales, I would use a pie chart. If I just wanted to illustrate muffin sales generally, I would use a bar chart.

In the pie chart shown in Figure 2.15, each number on a pie slice represents f while the percentage represents rel.f expressed as a percentage. Like bar charts, there are several rules governing pie charts:

- General Chart Characteristics
  - The pie is round, but the chart itself should be slightly wider than it is tall (again, roughly 4:3).
  - The chart is descriptively titled at the top.
  - The chart contains a **legend** illustrating the colours for the pie slices.
  - If colour can't be used, use patterns (for example, dots, horizontal lines or hatch marks) to distinguish slices. Be careful when printing colour charts to black and white printers!
- Slices
  - Each slice should be labelled with both a frequency and relative frequency (expressed as either a proportion or a percentage).
  - The pie slices should be sufficiently dissimilar colours so that they are not easily confused (for example, don't use navy and midnight blue together).

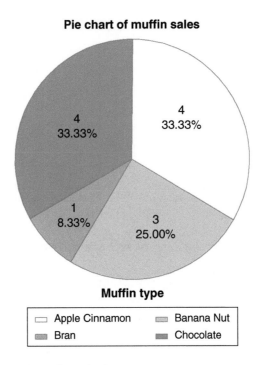

Pie chart of muffin sales

4
33.33%

4
33.33%

1
8.33%

3
25.00%

Muffin type

| | Apple Cinnamon | | Banana Nut |
| | Bran | | Chocolate |

FIGURE 2.15   Pie chart from data in Figure 2.06

2.6 ILLUSTRATING A QUANTITATIVE VARIABLE

Because quantitative variables do not have simple categorical labels, they must be illustrated differently. Imagine a bar chart for a sales office with 100 salespersons where everyone has slightly different sales numbers. There would be 100 bars in a bar chart illustrating those data! As a result, different illustrations are used for quantitative variables, the two most common of which we'll cover here.

2.6.1 HISTOGRAMS

Histograms are the most common illustration for a single quantitative variable. They strongly resemble bar charts, but with one key difference: there are no gaps between bars.

There are no gaps between bars because each bar does not represent a unique, discrete value. Instead, it represents a range of values, which is called a bin. For example, in the histogram in Figure 2.16, 73 employees sold between 17500 and 20000 euros worth of product (the bin is 12500 euros wide). But there is no way to know the exact sales figures for those individual employees.

This is a trade-off common when translating data – a simpler illustration results in a more powerful message, but with less secondary information. This histogram clearly illustrates that the company's star performers are selling more than 27500 euros worth of product, while the employees that may need a new line of work are selling less than 12500.

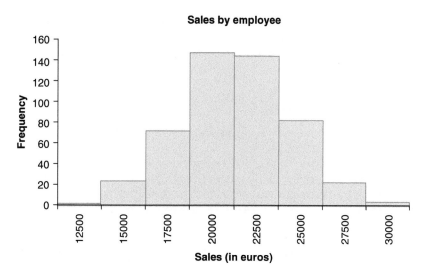

FIGURE 2.16 Sample histogram

As before, there are several rules for the creation of histograms, which you should find quite familiar:

- General Chart Characteristics
  - The chart is a bit wider than it is tall (roughly a 4:3 ratio).
  - The chart is descriptively titled at the top.
- *x*-Axis (across the bottom of the chart)
  - The axis label is centred and is the name of the variable being illustrated.
  - Numbers are evenly spaced, aligned with the bars, and easy to read.
- *y*-Axis (up the left side of the chart)
  - The axis label is centred in the chart and reads 'Count' or 'Frequency'.
  - The largest value is at the top of the chart and is the largest frequency in the dataset (or is slightly larger).
  - The smallest value is at the bottom of the chart and is zero (0).
  - Values appear at regular intervals between these two values, but not so densely as to make them difficult to read.
- Bars
  - Each bar represents a consistent quantity of scores (for example, each bar represents a gap of 12500 in Figure 2.16).
  - Each bar is the same colour as every other bar.
  - All data in the variable are represented in the chart.
  - There are no gaps between bars.

The easiest way to tell the difference between a histogram and a bar chart are the gaps between the bars. Bar charts have gaps because the data they represent are discrete, unique values. Each bar represents one level of the variable – for example, Apple Cinnamon or Bran. Histograms do not have gaps because each bar represents all of the values contained within the bin – for example, all values between 12500 and 15000.

This is useful from the perspective of someone reading graphs as well. If the bars aren't touching, you can generally assume that every category you see is a category that was measured. If the bars are touching, you know the data have been grouped together somehow.

BEING MISLED BY HISTOGRAMS

Histograms can be used to distort the real message the data are telling in the same ways as bar graphs, but with one added twist: bin size.

In the histograms shown in Figure 2.17, an employer worried about office productivity has tracked the average number of minutes per day that employees spend using the social networking website Facebook. He has created two histograms of his data. That's right – the data used to make each of these histograms are identical. The only difference is the bin size.

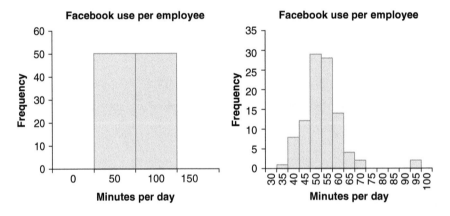

FIGURE 2.17   Comparison of two histograms from the same dataset following different display rules

In the histogram on the left, the bin size is 50. From this, it appears that the employees are evenly distributed. Half spend less than 50 minutes per day, while the other half spend between 50 and 100 minutes per day.

In the histogram on the right, the bin size is 5. This makes a dramatic difference in the impression the histogram makes. Now we can see a great deal of variety in Facebook usage among employees – and two employees spending between 90 and 95 minutes per day – much more than every other employee! But this information would have been lost if the bin size had been too large.

Any time you create a histogram, try several different bin sizes to see which one translates the data most appropriately. The first one you try is rarely the best.

2.6.2 FREQUENCY POLYGONS

Frequency polygons are similar to histograms in that they contain the same information – frequencies are represented on the *y*-axis and bins are computed to group the data into manageable chunks. But instead of using bars to represent frequencies within bins, a line is drawn, as shown in Figure 2.18.

FIGURE 2.18   Frequency polygon of sales data

Polygons do not illustrate the data as clearly as histograms, so unless you have a specific reason to use a polygon, you should use a histogram. What is the specific reason that would drive you to use a polygon? To compare two frequency distributions – see Figure 2.19.

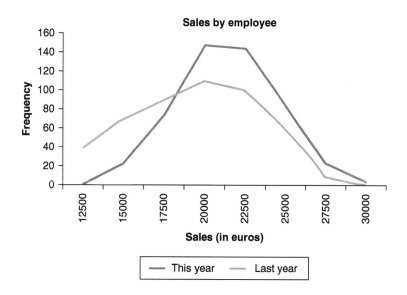

FIGURE 2.19   Frequency polygon comparing two years of sales

The rules governing polygons are identical to those for histograms, except that you are drawing lines instead of bars.

There is also a general preference to represent actual frequencies in frequency polygons instead of bins, but this is ultimately up to you.

2.7 COMPARING TWO VARIABLES GRAPHICALLY

All of the illustrations we've covered earlier in this chapter are ways to translate single variables for easier viewing. But what if you wanted to compare two variables, to consider how one variable behaves in relation to another? For this, we use a scatterplot.

2.7.1 SCATTERPLOTS

Scatterplots place one variable of interest on the *x*-axis and a second variable of interest on the *y*-axis. This allows the viewer to *see* the relationship between the two variables. For example, as one variable increases, what does the other do? Each point in a scatterplot represents the scores of two variables for a single case.

In Figure 2.20, we can see individual employees represented as individual points in the plot. For example, the employee represented by the point furthest to the left in this figure had roughly 12000 in sales last year but 27000 in sales this year. The employee represented by the point furthest to the right had roughly 28000 in sales last year but 39000 this year. As with the other illustrations, some precision is lost when representing the data graphically.

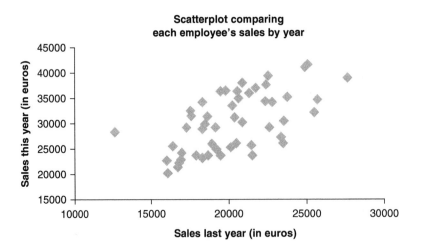

FIGURE 2.20   Scatterplot contrasting sales year over year

Scatterplots have similar rules to other charts:

- General chart characteristics
    - The chart is a bit wider than it is tall (roughly a 4:3 ratio).
    - The chart is descriptively titled at the top.
- Both axes
    - Numbers are evenly spaced and easy to read.
    - The axis labels are centred and are the names of the variables being illustrated.

- The largest values are at the end of each axis and are slightly larger than the largest values in the variable.
  - The smallest values are at the origin of the chart (bottom left corner) and are slightly smaller than the smallest values in the variable.
  - Values appear at regular intervals between these two values, but not so densely as to make them difficult to read.
- Data points
  - All points are the same colour, shape and size.

Scatterplots can be used to examine qualitative or quantitative data, and can even be used to compare qualitative and quantitative data with each other. However, the lower the scale of measurement for the variables being analysed, the less informative the scatterplot will be.

2.8 CREATING THE BEST TRANSLATION FOR DATA

Let's return to our case study to explore which translations would be best for Jamal at DropIt. The first step in determining appropriate translations for data is simply to write out descriptions of your variables and what you know about them. Here's a start:

- Name of the website visited: qualitative, nominal.

- Number of minutes spent on the website: quantitative, ratio.

- Number of items purchased: quantitative, ratio.

We always want to start with a simple translation of each of our variables. Because our first variable is qualitative, we'll create a frequency table and a bar graph to explain it. Because our second and third variables are quantitative, we'll use histograms.

Figures 2.21 and 2.22 alone tell us interesting information about the variables in the dataset.

From the frequency table and bar chart, Jamal can see that most sales come from the Electronics store, while the fewest sales come from Men's Fashion, with Discount Clothing and Video Games not far behind. Whether Jamal should emphasize his strengths by working more heavily on the Electronics store or bolster his weaknesses by focusing on Men's Fashion, Discount Clothing and Video Games is a decision for later.

From the right-hand histogram in Figure 2.22, we can see that most people browsing the websites don't spend very much time before making a purchase. Most spend less than ten minutes! But if they're spending less than ten minutes, are they even taking the time to use the special features that Jamal spends so much time creating?

From the left-hand histogram, we can see that most customers purchase two items, followed by three, followed by one. Very few visitors to the website purchase nothing. But why? Shouldn't there be plenty of visitors just browsing? Perhaps that means most customers are referrals – they already know what they want to buy when they get to his website. Or perhaps it means that his website is so effective, visitors are driven to purchase!

Website visited

		Frequency	Percent	Cumulative Percent
Valid	Art Supplies	148	11.1	11.1
	Discount Clothing	44	3.3	14.4
	Electronics	309	23.2	37.6
	Household Goods	118	8.8	46.4
	Jewellery	123	9.2	55.6
	Men's Fashion	37	2.8	58.4
	Sporting Goods	151	11.3	69.7
	Vehicle Parts	125	9.4	79.1
	Video Games	48	3.6	82.7
	Women's Fashion	231	17.3	100.0
	Total	1334	100.0	

FIGURE 2.21   Frequency table of purchases by store

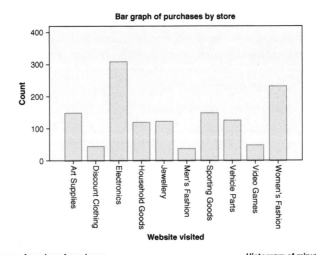

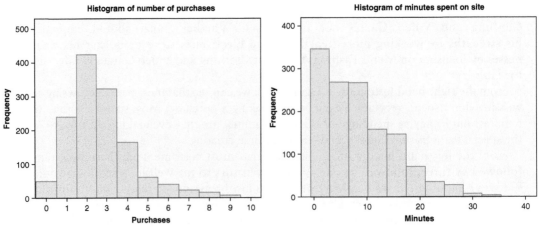

FIGURE 2.22   Graphs of purchases by store, minutes spent on site, and number of purchases

Given all of this information about the variables themselves, Jamal now wants to address his original question: are the website features he's creating worth the effort? If we put that in terms of the dataset, it's a slightly different question: do users that spend more time on the website make more purchases? For this, he creates the scatterplot shown in Figure 2.23.

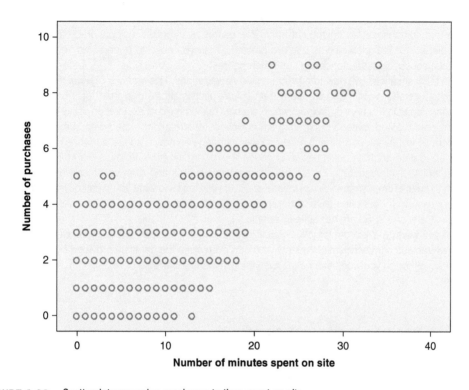

FIGURE 2.23   Scatterplot comparing purchases to time spent on site

It looks like Jamal's work might have paid off. While there are many customers clustered at the bottom left corner – those that didn't spend much time and also didn't make many purchases – virtually all of the customers that purchased more than four items spent a lot of time on the site. So even if the features he's building don't work for everyone, they seem to be keeping the attention of many.

But, as with every research study, Jamal must consider alternate explanations. This is not an experiment, so we can't conclude that greater time on the website *causes* increased sales. Instead, something else might have caused this apparent relationship. Perhaps visitors looking for more products naturally spend more time on the site, and Jamal's website features have nothing to do with their behaviour.

Let's not forget Chapter 1, either – is 'number of minutes' even the best operational definition of what Jamal is really after? Would the results be different if he could capture the number of minutes spent using his specially developed online tools? What is the real construct of interest here?

Thus, as often happens with research, this study creates more questions than it answers. But at least it gives Jamal a little more direction as to which questions to ask next.

VISUALIZING DATA WHEN THEY GET 'BIG'

In the real world, carefully crafted datasets like Jamal's are not the only kind you'll see. If you keep electronic records of any type, you'll sooner or later encounter 'big data'. Big data can be truly huge, with millions or more cases, and visualization is often the only way to holistically understand them. For example, imagine that you had access to the entire purchasing history of every person that had ever purchased any product from the global retailer, Amazon.com. Such a dataset, which would contain billions of cases, would be impossible to simply poke around in. You cannot open these data in a spreadsheet and glance at them. You cannot even create a single graph to capture the complexities of the relationships that are present; when you need to understand 10000 variables simultaneously, a scatterplot doesn't do much good.

In such situations, we now turn to interactive visualizations. This sort of tool is not found in SPSS or Excel; instead, you'll need to use a data visualization platform designed for this purpose. An industry leader in this area is Tableau, which enables real-time visual exploration of live data sources as they are created. Instead of creating static pictures of already-collected data, the visualizations you create in Tableau and other similar programs change as new data are added, enabling you to stay up to date on most cutting-edge changes in your organization. Perhaps the most compelling aspect of Tableau is that it's fun to use; you can literally click and drag variables where you want them to create new, dynamic visualizations at will. If you don't like what you created, Tableau makes it very easy to try out alternative visualizations until you find something you like. As you'll notice below, Excel and SPSS are not quite so simple.

If you want to explore interactive visualizations yourself, Tableau offers a free student version at www.tableau.com/academic/students. You can even open the datasets provided by this book in Tableau, although you won't see nearly everything Tableau is capable of.

2.9 APPLYING DATA DISPLAY

To apply what you've learned from this chapter, consider the following case study, questions posed about that case study, and discussion of those questions.

2.9.1 APPLICATION CASE STUDY

Dakota is the manager and coordinator of Fluffy Paws, a small pet-grooming service operating out of a major pet supply store. Each day, Dakota contacts past clients to schedule new appointments with both clients and her staff. Up to this point, Dakota has randomly assigned groomers to clients as they made appointments. Recently, a handful of customer complaints have demonstrated to her that her groomers are not equally skilled across animals. Some do better work on cats and others on dogs. However, she doesn't have any easy way to know which groomers are most skilled at which animal. To answer her question, she conducts a survey of her past clients and collects 20 sets of surveys on each of her groomers. She also looks in their personnel files and collects various pieces of information she thinks are relevant to her question. Her dataset reads like this:

- Variable 1: Name of groomer.

- Variable 2: Total number of months of pet grooming experience.

- Variable 3: Stated animal preference (cat or dog).

- Variable 4: Average 'cat effectiveness' rating by clients on a five-point Likert-type scale.

- Variable 5: Average 'dog effectiveness' rating by clients on a five-point Likert-type scale.

- Variable 6: Average number of minutes spent when grooming cats.

- Variable 7: Average number of minutes spent when grooming dogs.

As a first step, Dakota wants to translate all of the variables she has collected into something more interpretable. What should she do for each variable, and why? She also wants to examine the relationship between effectiveness and time spent. How should she represent this relationship?

2.9.2 APPLICATION DISCUSSION

Although we've passed the difficult first step of research study design as we discussed in Chapter 1, Dakota is faced with the next problem we face with new data: appropriate translation to make data more meaningful. The type of translation is directly driven by the variable type, so we'll approach each one at a time.

Variable 1 is the name of the groomer. Because each groomer will have a different name, no translation is necessary – this is simply an identifier (like a case number) for each person.

Variable 2 is a total number of months of pet grooming experience. Months of experience is ratio-level scale of measurement, so a histogram is appropriate. Depending on how widely months of experience vary, Dakota might also consider a frequency table. For example, if every employee has between 0 and 5 months experience, a frequency table will separate out these groups very clearly. However, if every employee has between 0 and 120 months experience, she probably doesn't have enough data for a frequency table to be very helpful.

Variable 3 is stated animal preference. This is nominal-level scale of measurement, so a bar chart or pie chart would be most appropriate. A bar chart would enable viewers to see at a glance whether dogs or cats are more popular, so this seems the best choice. A frequency table would also summarize this quite clearly.

Variables 4 and 5 are survey results, which we treat in this text as interval-level data. As a result, a histogram is appropriate for each. However, since Dakota wants to compare dogs with cats, a frequency polygon displaying both simultaneously might be a good choice.

Variables 6 and 7 are ratio-level, which again would make histograms appropriate. However, as with Variables 4 and 5, a display of both on a frequency polygon is worth exploring too.

To compare each pair of effectiveness and time spent (once for cat and once for dog), she would need a scatterplot. We can only create a scatterplot if both variables are interval or ratio; in this case, one is interval and the other is ratio, so this is a great choice.

EXPLORING FREQUENCIES, GRAPHS AND PLOTS IN EXCEL AND SPSS

FREQUENCIES IN EXCEL

Download the Excel dataset for the demonstration below as **chapter2freq.xls**. As you read this section, try to apply the terms you've learned in this chapter to the dataset and follow along with Excel on your own computer.

You can also get a video demonstration of the section below under **Excel Videos: Chapter 2**.

There are two worksheets in this dataset, which you can navigate between using the tabs at the bottom, as shown in Figure 2.24.

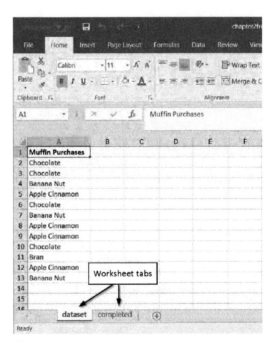

FIGURE 2.24   How to switch between worksheets in Excel

In Excel, each worksheet generally contains a unique dataset. In this case, the **dataset** worksheet contains the raw muffin purchase data from earlier in this chapter while the **completed** worksheet contains the raw data plus a completed frequency table (the goal of this exercise). You should try to follow along in the book to create your own frequency table in the **dataset** worksheet, and then check this against the completed frequency table in the **completed** worksheet to ensure you followed the instructions correctly.

To create your frequency table, you should first create the framework for your table – columns and rows. Columns are easy – a few rows to the right of your data, create the four-column frequency table format discussed earlier: Value, f, rel.f, and cum.f. The rows are a little more complicated.

There are ways to have Excel automatically produce a list of all unique values in your dataset, but it is generally easier to sort the column so that you can see them for yourself. Click on the **Muffin**

Purchases column, click on the **Data** ribbon at the top, then click on the **Sort A to Z** button. This will work for alphabetical or numeric data. At this point, your screen should look like Figure 2.25.

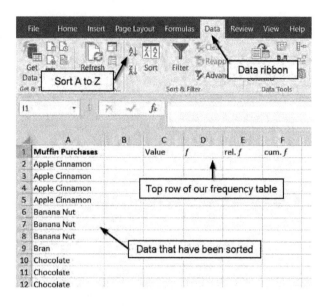

FIGURE 2.25   Aspects of the Excel interface relevant to sorting

With the data sorted, you can clearly see each unique value in the dataset: Apple Cinnamon, Banana Nut, Bran and Chocolate. Copy/paste each of these into the columns below **Value**. Copy/paste is important because you want to make sure that the spelling and capitalization of these entries is identical to what is contained in your dataset. You should end up with the table shown in Figure 2.26, ready for values.

C	D	E	F
Value	f	rel. f	cum. f
Apple Cinnamon			
Banana Nut			
Bran			
Chocolate			

FIGURE 2.26   Preparing your frequency table in Excel

In Excel, functions are used to compute values automatically. To compute f automatically, we'll need to learn the COUNTIF() function. There are several sections to COUNTIF(), as shown in Figure 2.27.

(Continued)

(Continued)

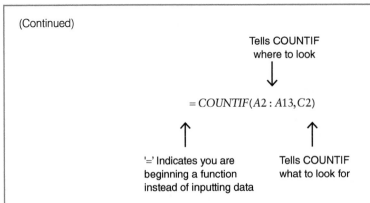

FIGURE 2.27   Important sections of the COUNTIF function in Excel

Type this formula into cell D2 – the cell where you want $f_{\text{AppleCinnamon}}$ to appear. This tells Excel to look in all cells between A2 and A13 (that's the dataset) and look for the value found in C2 (which is 'Apple Cinnamon'). In this case, Apple Cinnamon appears four times, so the number 4 will appear.

You'll continue this pattern for the remaining three cells – see Figure 2.28.

In cell	Formula
D2	=COUNTIF(A2:A13, C2)
D3	=COUNTIF(A2:A13, C3)
D4	=COUNTIF(A2:A13, C4)
D5	=COUNTIF(A2:A13, C5)

FIGURE 2.28   Formulas to display frequencies (f) in Excel

If you need to change a formula, simply click on the cell to make the formula reappear at the top of the screen. Formulas are never lost; if you change the data at this point, your COUNTIFs will all update themselves automatically to account for that change.

In the next column, you'll use simple division to compute relative frequencies. Remember that relative frequencies are simple frequencies divided by n. Here, n is 12, so we'll divide each frequency by 12, as shown in Figure 2.29.

In cell	Formula
E2	=D2/12
E3	=D3/12
E4	=D4/12
E5	=D5/12

FIGURE 2.29   Formulas to display relative frequencies (rel.f) in Excel

In the final column, you'll need to do a little more legwork to compute cumulative frequencies. Remember that cumulative frequencies are the sum of the simple frequencies in that row of the table and all rows above it. The first cum.f is always equal to the relative frequency of that row, so that part's easy. But the rest of the rows become increasingly complicated – see Figure 2.30.

In cell	Formula
F2	=D2
F3	=D2+D3
F4	=D2+D3+D4+D5
F5	=D2+D3+D4+D5
G2	=F2/12
G3	=F3/12
G4	=F4/12
G5	=F5/12

FIGURE 2.30   Formulas to display cumulative frequencies (cum.f) and percentages (cum.%) in Excel

Notice the pattern – we are adding together the f on the current row and all previous rows for cum.f, then dividing by n for cum.%. When creating your own frequency tables, this also enables you to easily check that you have n correct. If your final cum.% doesn't equal 100%, something's wrong!

At this point, your frequency table is done! Check it against the table in the **completed** worksheet to check your answers.

GRAPHS AND PLOTS IN EXCEL

Download the Excel dataset for the demonstration below as **chapter2case.xls**. As you read this section, try to apply the terms you've learned in this chapter to the dataset and follow along with Excel on your own computer.

You can also get a video demonstration of the section below under **Excel Videos: Chapter 2**.

QUALITATIVE VARIABLES

Bar charts and pie charts in Excel both start with frequency tables (see p. 47 for instructions on how to create frequency tables in Excel). The **store** variable in this dataset, despite being qualitative, is represented with numbers, so you'll need a key to translate between the two. And here it is:

1 Art Supplies store
2 Discount Clothing store
3 Electronics store
4 Household Goods store
5 Jewellery store
6 Men's Fashion store
7 Sporting Goods store
8 Vehicle Parts store
9 Video Games store
10 Women's Fashion store

Using this, you can create a frequency table. Add a new column to the left with the labels above. Your final product should look like Figure 2.31.

(Continued)

(Continued)

Label	Value	f	rel.f	cum.f	Cum.%
Art Supplies	1	148	0.11	148	11%
Discount Clothing	2	44	0.03	192	14%
Electronics	3	309	0.23	501	38%
Household Goods	4	118	0.09	619	46%
Jewellery	5	123	0.09	742	56%
Men's Fashion	6	37	0.03	779	58%
Sporting Goods	7	151	0.11	930	70%
Vehicle Parts	8	125	0.09	1055	79%
Video Games	9	48	0.04	1103	83%
Women's Fashion	10	231	0.17	1334	100%

FIGURE 2.31   A complete frequency table with a key in Excel

To create your bar or pie chart, (1) click on a blank cell in the worksheet, (2) click to open the **Insert** ribbon, (3) click the **Column** button, and then (4) click the very first button – see Figure 2.32.

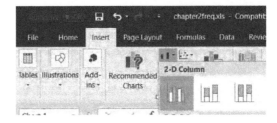

FIGURE 2.32   Step 1 of how to create a bar chart in Excel

This will open a big blank white rectangle that will eventually become your chart. You can drag this rectangle wherever you want. Right-click on this rectangle and click on **Select Data** (Figure 2.33).

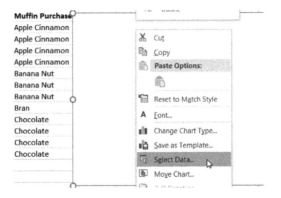

FIGURE 2.33   Step 2 of how to create a bar chart in Excel

Next, click the **Add** Button to add a new data series (Figure 2.34).

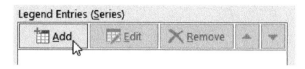

FIGURE 2.34   Step 3 of how to create a bar chart in Excel

This screen is where you specify the source of the data. In the first row, you'll enter the name of the variable *as a formula*, which will become the title of your chart. In this case, the variable is **Website Visited**, so type: ="Website Visited".

In the second row, you'll specify where the data are. The easiest way to do that is to click the button shown in Figure 2.35.

FIGURE 2.35   Excel button to specify a cell range

You can then click-drag across the values in the *f* column of your frequency table. If you do everything correctly, it should look something like Figure 2.36.

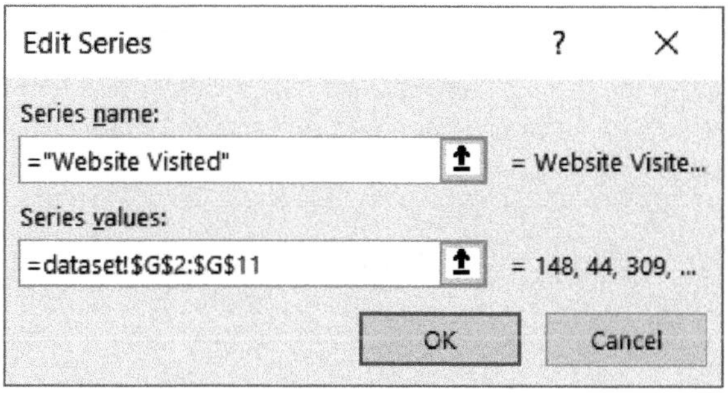

Edit Series	?	✕
Series name:		
="Website Visited" ↑	= Website Visite...	
Series values:		
=dataset!$G$2:$G$11 ↑	= 148, 44, 309, ...	
	OK	Cancel

FIGURE 2.36   Completed Excel dialogue to specify series

Note that my frequencies were listed between G2 and G11, so that's what I selected. This formula tells Excel to look in the cells between G2 and G11 in the worksheet called 'dataset'. If you put your frequencies elsewhere, those cell names should point there instead. After you have everything correct, click **OK**.

Excel automatically creates *x*-axis labels for your dataset, but we want labels that are a little more descriptive. Click **Edit** on the right side to change them (Figure 2.37).

(Continued)

(Continued)

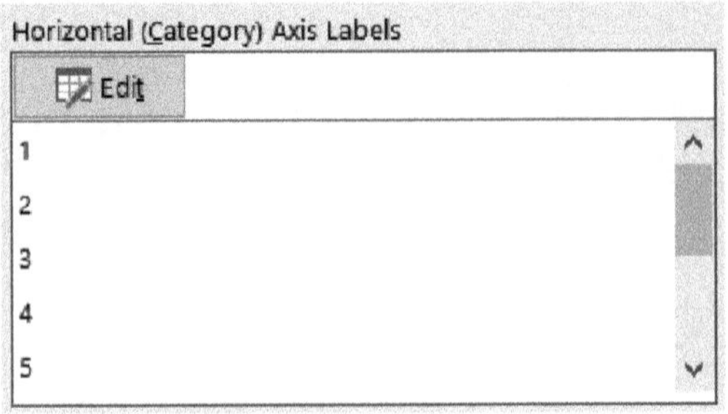

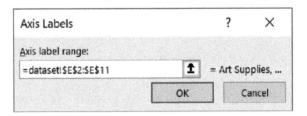

FIGURE 2.37   Excel x-axis label specification area

Like last time, use the selection button to highlight the labels you already created, hopefully something like Figure 2.38 (my labels were between E2 and E11).

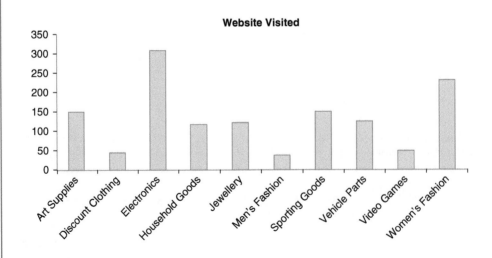

FIGURE 2.38   Completed x-axis label selection dialogue box

Hit **OK** twice to close the editing dialogues and take a look at your new bar chart! Because there's only one variable, we don't need a legend, so click on it and press the delete key. You should end up with something like Figure 2.39.

FIGURE 2.39   Excel bar chart with updated labels

There's only one thing missing at this point – the axis titles!

For the x-axis, with the chart selected, click on the **Design** ribbon (under **Chart Tools**) to bring up chart options. Click **Add Chart Element**, then click **Axis Titles**, and then click **Primary Horizontal** (see Figure 2.40). This will create a new x-axis title.

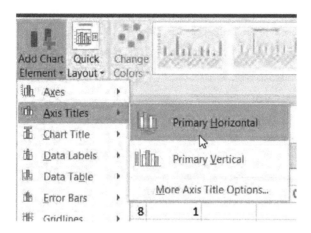

FIGURE 2.40   Selection of x-axis label in Excel

For the y-axis, with the chart selected, click on the **Design** ribbon (under **Chart Tools**) to bring up chart design options. Click **Add Chart Element**, then click **Axis Titles**, and then click **Primary Vertical**, in order to add a vertical axis title rotated by 90 degrees (Figure 2.41).

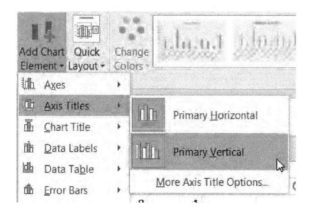

FIGURE 2.41   Selection of y-axis label in Excel

For each of these titles, click once on the axis title itself to enable editing and then type whatever you want. Remember that the y-axis should generally read 'Count' or 'Frequency', and the x-axis should be the name of the variable. You can also use this technique to rename the title. You can also now drag the chart to a 4:3 ratio. Hopefully you'll end up with something like Figure 2.42.

(Continued)

(Continued)

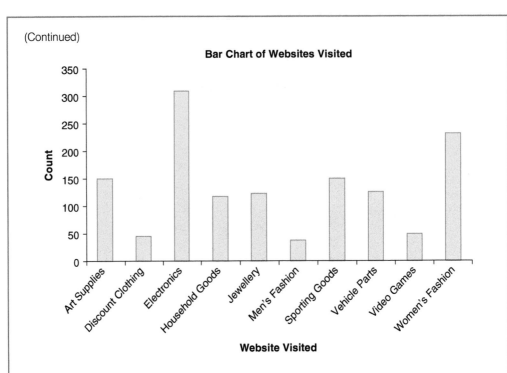

FIGURE 2.42   Completed bar chart in Excel

That's it! You've created a bar chart!

Pie charts are created the same way, except that instead of initially choosing **Column**, you should choose **Pie** and the first option there – see Figure 2.43.

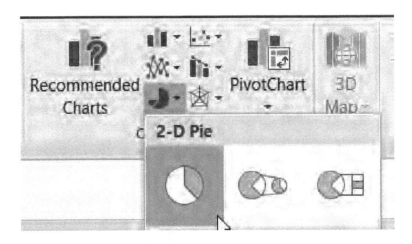

FIGURE 2.43   Selection of a pie chart in Excel

Hopefully you'll end up with something like Figure 2.44.

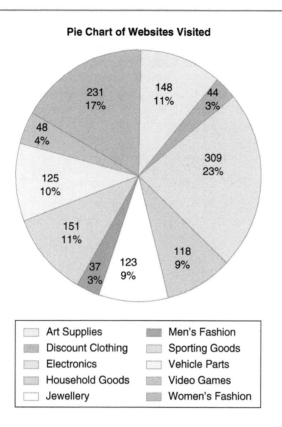

Pie Chart of Websites Visited

Art Supplies	Men's Fashion
Discount Clothing	Sporting Goods
Electronics	Vehicle Parts
Household Goods	Video Games
Jewellery	Women's Fashion

FIGURE 2.44   Completed pie chart in Excel

For instructions on including data labels within the chart, as well as video demonstrations of how to create each of these chart types from scratch, don't forget to check out the book's website.

QUANTITATIVE VARIABLES

Quantitative variables are, unfortunately, a bit difficult in Excel because you need to create the bins yourself for histograms and polygons. This requires a special feature of Excel called formula arrays. Instead of entering a formula for a single cell, you'll enter a formula for a range of cells simultaneously.

To do this, first determine the maximum and minimum values in your dataset. We'll use the **minutes** variable, which is in column B. So in F1, I'll type =MIN(B:B) and in F2, I'll type =MAX(B:B). In E1 and E2, I'll type simple descriptive labels. You should end up with something like Figure 2.45.

E	F
min(minutes)	0
max(minutes)	35

FIGURE 2.45   Minimum and maximum values in Excel

(Continued)

(Continued)

With these numbers in mind, you can create some reasonable bins for your histogram. You'll want to have around ten bins in a typical histogram, but you'll experiment a bit with this after making your histogram to find an ideal bin size (see the online video for more detail).

In this case, we'll use eight bins because it creates a convenient five-point bin size. Type each number, 0 to 35, in five-point increments in E5 to E12. Each number will represent the lower boundary of a bin. With labels, you should end up with Figure 2.46.

	E	F
4	Bins	Count
5	0	
6	5	
7	10	
8	15	
9	20	
10	25	
11	30	
12	35	

FIGURE 2.46   Bins specified in Excel to define a histogram

The count will contain the number of cases larger than that bin size but lower than the next bin. For example, F5 will contain a count of all cases greater than 0 but less than or equal to 5 (which also means it will include 5).

To create the formula array, click-drag to highlight F5 to F12. Type this formula but *don't hit enter yet*: =FREQUENCY(B:B,E5:E12).

This tells Excel to use the data in Column B to complete a chart of bin counts as specified in E5 to E12. To convert this formula to a formula array, hold both the **Control** and **Shift** keys and press **Enter**. On MacOS, hold ⌘ and press Return.

If the conversion went correctly, the formula will now have curly braces around it like this: {=FREQUENCY(B:B,E5:E15)}.

If you don't see curly braces, delete the formula and try again. You should also see different values in each cell, as in Figure 2.47.

	E	F
4	Bins	Count
5	0	88
6	5	436
7	10	365
8	15	230
9	20	132
10	25	53
11	30	25
12	35	5

FIGURE 2.47   Completed bin specifications for a histogram in Excel

If you were creating bins for your own data, now would be the time to experiment with different bin settings. What looks best? What illustrates the data most clearly? Different bin sizes can produce dramatically different impressions.

Next, create a chart using the F5:F12 data as the series and the E5:E12 data as the legend in the same way that you did for the bar chart (see above). You should end up with Figure 2.48.

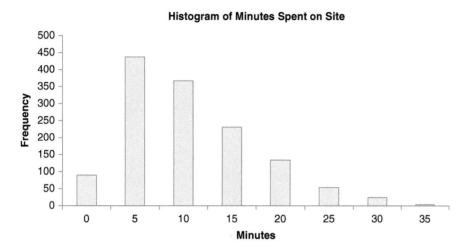

FIGURE 2.48   Almost completed histogram in Excel

There's only one thing wrong with this illustration – it's not a histogram! Remember that the defining feature of a histogram is that the bars touch. Right now, this graph is a bar chart!

To convert it to a histogram, right-click on a bar (⌘-click on Mac OS) and select **Format data series** (Figure 2.49). If it says **Format Chart Area** or **Format Plot Area** instead, you didn't click in the right place.

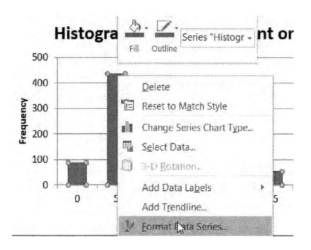

FIGURE 2.49   Right-click dialogue when right-clicking on bins

(Continued)

(Continued)

On the right side of the screen, the **Format data series** dock will appear. Click on the little bar chart icon under **Series Options** and decrease the **Gap Width** to '0%', as shown in Figure 2.50.

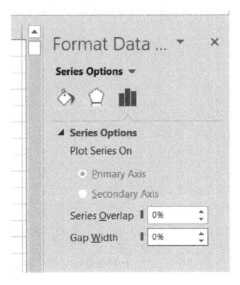

FIGURE 2.50   Visual bin size specification dialogue in Excel

Without gaps, the bars are difficult to tell apart, so also click on the paint can icon, then open the **Border** submenu, then click on **Solid line**, and select the colour black, as shown in Figure 2.51.

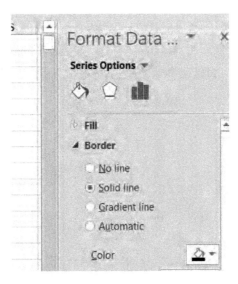

FIGURE 2.51   Border colour specification dialogue in Excel

Click **Close** and admire your new histogram (Figure 2.52)!

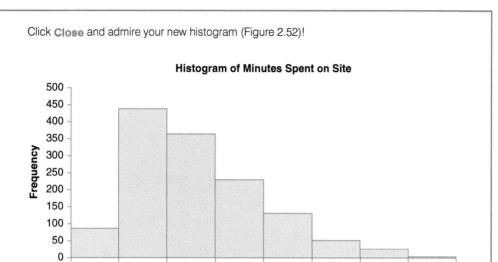

FIGURE 2.52   Completed histogram in Excel

To create a frequency polygon instead of a histogram (Figure 2.54), simply select **Line** instead of **Column** in the first step (Figure 2.53).

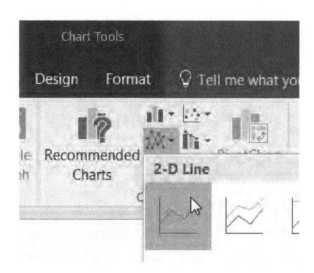

FIGURE 2.53   Menu option to create a frequency polygon in Excel

To add a second line to your frequency polygon, add a second series of frequencies after right-clicking on the chart and then clicking **Select Data**.

(Continued)

(Continued)

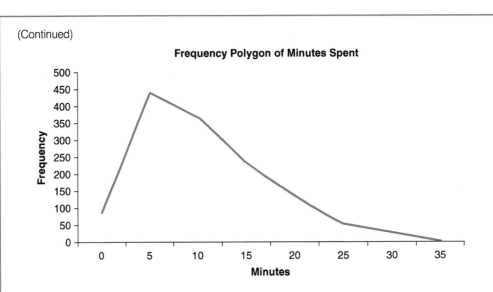

FIGURE 2.54   Completed frequency polygon in Excel

SCATTERPLOTS

To create a scatterplot, click on a blank cell, then click on the **Insert** ribbon, then click on **Scatter**, then click on the top left option – see Figure 2.55.

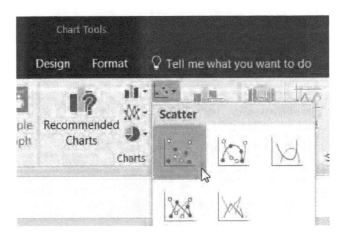

FIGURE 2.55   Menu option to select a scatterplot in Excel

Right-click on the chart, click **Select Data**, and click **Add**, exactly as you would do for any of the other chart types we've looked at.

This screen is a little different from before, but that's because we're telling Excel to graph two variables instead of one. Using the techniques described before, select each series of data – one for the *x*-axis and the other for the *y*-axis. The series title will be used as the chart title. You should end up with Figure 2.56.

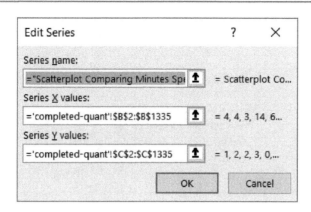

FIGURE 2.56   Series dialogue with scatterplot data entered in Excel

Click **OK** twice. As with the other charts, you'll next need to add axis titles, ultimately producing the scatterplot shown in Figure 2.57.

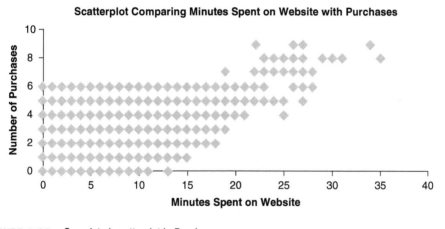

FIGURE 2.57   Completed scatterplot in Excel

FREQUENCIES IN SPSS

Download the SPSS dataset for the demonstration below as **chapter2freq.sav**. As you read this section, try to apply the terms you've learned in this chapter to the dataset and follow along with SPSS on your own computer.

You can also get a video demonstration of the section below under **SPSS Videos: Chapter 2**.

Because SPSS is a program designed to conduct statistical analyses, creating frequency tables is quite easy. With the dataset open, click **Analyze**>**Descriptive Statistics**>**Frequencies** (see Figure 2.58).

(Continued)

(Continued)

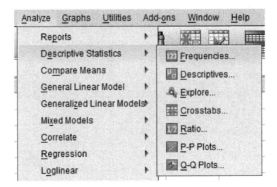

FIGURE 2.58   How to access the Frequencies option in SPSS

The list of variables on the left contains all the variables in your dataset, while the list on the right contains the variables to be analysed. Click on **Muffin Purchases** to select it, followed by the right arrow, to move the Muffin Purchases variable to the list on the right, as shown in Figure 2.59.

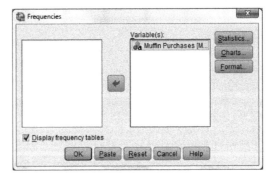

FIGURE 2.59   Selecting your variable for a frequency table in SPSS

Each of the buttons on the right allows you to make changes to the analysis. For example, if you click on the **Format** button, you can change the sort options – see Figure 2.60.

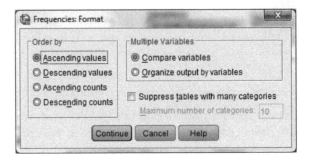

FIGURE 2.60   Changing the format for a frequency table in SPSS

The **Ascending values** option is exactly what we want – it will order the frequency table in ascending alphanumeric order. Click **Continue** then **OK** to run the analysis.

Analyses in SPSS appear in a separate window called the Output Pane. Any time you run an analysis, this window will appear containing the results of your analysis (although you may need to wait a second for the analysis to finish). Frequency tables are easy for the computer, so you should see this quite quickly, as shown in Figure 2.61.

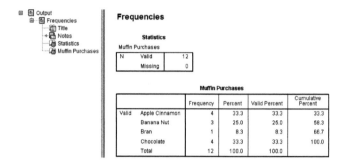

FIGURE 2.61   A frequency table displayed in the Output Pane in SPSS

On the right, you'll see the results of any analyses you have conducted. In this case, two tables were created – a small table summarizing *N* as well as a frequency table. Although we'd normally recognize a capital *N* as a population size, SPSS uses *N* to represent the count of whatever data you have inputted, whether you are analysing a population or a sample. Thus, in this case, SPSS's *N* represents the sample size.

Note that the frequency table is not the standard type – the labels are different. That's because SPSS reports **relative frequencies** as **percentages**, which appear in the **Percent** column. **Cumulative frequencies** are reported as **cumulative percentages** and appear in the **Cumulative Percent** column. SPSS also adds a 'Total' row in which the frequency is always equal to *N*.

On the left, you'll see an outline of the results from your analysis. You can click on any of these items to jump down to that part of the analysis. This will be more useful when you conduct several analyses on the same dataset.

GRAPHS AND PLOTS IN SPSS

Download the SPSS dataset for the demonstration below as **chapter2case.sav**. As you read this section, try to apply the terms you've learned in this chapter to the dataset and follow along with SPSS on your own computer.

You can also get a video demonstration of the section below under **SPSS Videos: Chapter 2**.

SPSS is built for data analysis, so graphing is quite straightforward.

QUALITATIVE VARIABLES

To create a bar chart, click on **Graphs**, then **Legacy Dialogs**, then **Bar** (Figure 2.62).

(Continued)

(Continued)

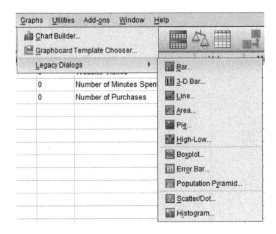

FIGURE 2.62 Menu option for creating a bar chart in SPSS

Click **Define** on the next dialogue – don't worry about these settings.

Click on the variable you want to graph first – in this case, **Website Visited**. Then click on the right arrow by **Category axis** (Figure 2.63).

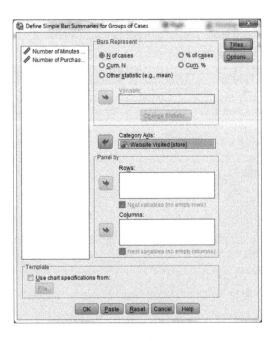

FIGURE 2.63 Dialogue for specifying a bar chart in SPSS

Next, click on **Titles** and type 'Bar Chart of Website Visited' for Line 1 of the Title, which will add this as the title of the chart. Click **Continue**, then click **OK**.

The output pane will pop up with your bar chart (Figure 2.64)!

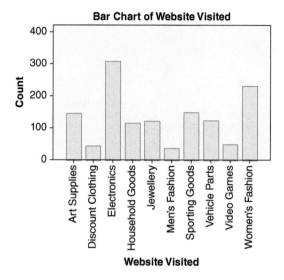

FIGURE 2.64   Completed bar chart in SPSS

To create a pie chart, click **Graphs**, then click **Legacy Dialogs**, then click **Pie** (Figure 2.65).

FIGURE 2.65   Menu option to create a pie chart in SPSS

Again, click **Define** on the next dialogue – don't worry about these settings for now.

Click on the variable you want to graph first – in this case, **Website Visited**. Then click on the right arrow by **Define Slices By.** The right arrow will become a left arrow if you've done this correctly (Figure 2.66).

(Continued)

(Continued)

FIGURE 2.66   Dialogue to specify a pie chart in SPSS

Next, click on **Titles** and type 'Pie Chart of Website Visited' for Line 1 of the Title, which will add this as the title of the chart. Click **Continue**, then click **OK**.

The output pane will pop up with your pie chart (Figure 2.67). For instructions on how to add data labels (and you always should), see the online video for pie charts.

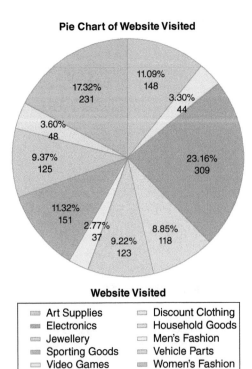

FIGURE 2.67   Completed pie chart in SPSS

QUANTITATIVE VARIABLES

To create a histogram, click on **Graphs**, then click **Legacy Dialogs**, then click **Histogram** (Figure 2.68).

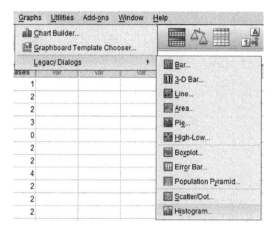

FIGURE 2.68   Menu option to create a histogram in SPSS

Click on the variable you want to graph – in this case, **Number of Minutes**. Then click on the right arrow by **Variable** (Figure 2.69).

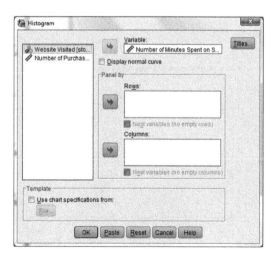

FIGURE 2.69   Dialogue to specify a histogram in SPSS

Next, click on **Titles** and type 'Histogram of Minutes Spent on Website' for Line 1 of the Title, which will add this as the title of the chart. Click **Continue**, then click **OK**.

The output pane will pop up with your histogram (Figure 2.70)!

(Continued)

(Continued)

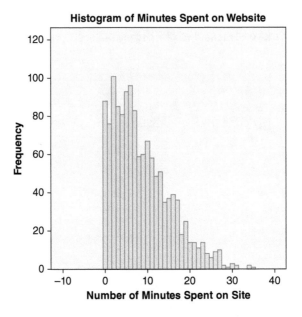

FIGURE 2.70   Almost completed histogram in SPSS

Right now, this histogram has far too many bars. Each bin is only one minute wide! To make this histogram more interpretable by widening the bins, double-click on the chart itself to open the chart editor. Within the chart editor, click once on the bars so that a faint outline appears around them – see Figure 2.71.

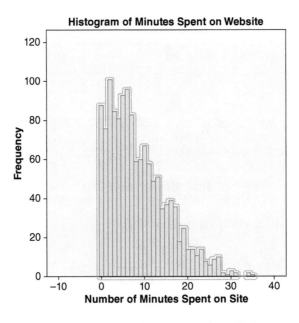

FIGURE 2.71   Selecting bars to edit their properties (note the faint outline)

That faint outline is very important. When you edit chart settings, they will apply to whatever the outline surrounds. If the line surrounds the wrong part of the chart, you won't be able to change the bins. Next, double-click on the bars to open the **Properties** window. Click on the **Binning** tab at the top.

Here, you can choose the width of your x-axis bins. Select **Custom**, change the number of intervals to **10**, and click **Apply** (Figure 2.72).

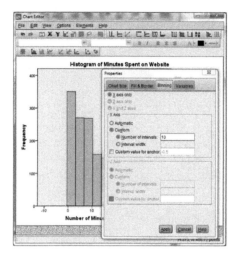

FIGURE 2.72   Specifying bin size for histogram in SPSS

If you created a histogram for your own data, experiment with a variety of settings until you find one that illustrates the data clearly. Click **Close** and your histogram is done (Figure 2.73)!

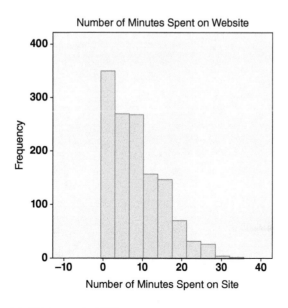

FIGURE 2.73   Completed histogram in SPSS

(Continued)

(Continued)

To create a frequency polygon, click on **Graphs**, then click on **Legacy Dialogs**, then click on **Line** (Figure 2.74).

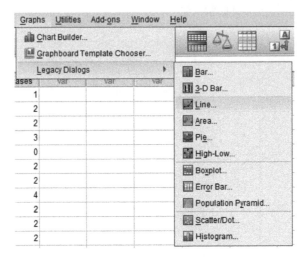

FIGURE 2.74   Menu option to create a frequency polygon in SPSS

Again, click **Define** on the next dialogue – don't worry about these settings for now.

Click on the variable you want to graph – in this case, **Number of Minutes**. Then click on the right arrow by **Category Axis**, which will become a left arrow if you've done this correctly (Figure 2.75).

FIGURE 2.75   Dialogue to specify options for a frequency polygon in SPSS

Next, click on **Titles** and type 'Frequency Polygon of Minutes Spent on Website' for Line 1 of the Title, which will add this as the title of the chart. Click **Continue**, then click **OK**.

The output pane will pop up with your polygon (Figure 2.76)! Note that SPSS does not bin polygons. If you want to use binning, you'll need to create a histogram or work in Excel.

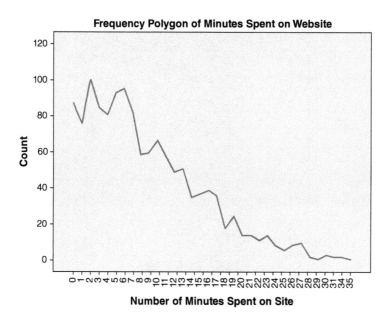

FIGURE 2.76   Completed frequency polygon in SPSS

SCATTERPLOTS

To create a scatterplot, click on **Graphs**, then click on **Legacy Dialogs**, then click on **Scatter/Dot** (Figure 2.77).

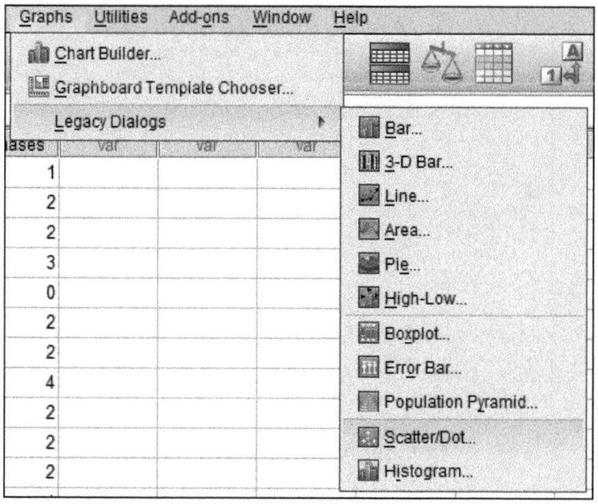

FIGURE 2.77   Menu option to create a scatterplot in SPSS

(Continued)

(Continued)

Again, click **Define** on the next dialogue – don't worry about these settings for now.

On this panel, click on the variables you want to include one at a time, followed by the right arrow pointing at the desired axis – see Figure 2.78 for what this will look like when you're ready for the next step.

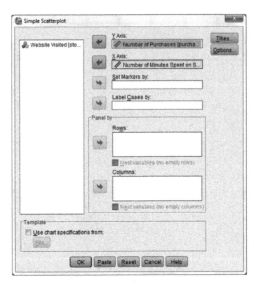

FIGURE 2.78   Dialogue to specify options for a scatterplot in SPSS

Next, click on **Titles** and type 'Scatterplot Comparing Minutes Spent on Websites with Purchases' for Line 1 of the Title, which will add this as the title of the chart. Click **Continue**, then click **OK**.

The output pane will pop up with your scatterplot (Figure 2.79).

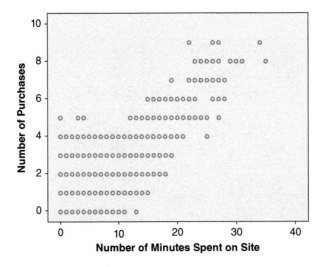

FIGURE 2.79   Completed scatterplot in SPSS

STATISTICS IN THE REAL WORLD

 These web links can be accessed directly from the book's website.

Data journalist David McCandless describes how design is the key to making meaningful, compelling visualizations of complex data: www.ted.com/talks/david_mccandless_the_beauty_of_data_visualization.

Why are images representing data so much more convincing than data themselves?

Wes O'Donnell explains how visualizations are perhaps the most important outcome of data: www.youtube.com/watch?v=J2v23amv-IA.

What sorts of insights can you get from data visualizations that you cannot gain from data alone? How can these insights be misleading?

TEST YOURSELF

After you've completed the questions below, check your answers online.

1 Convert each of the following into a fraction, a proportion, and/or a percentage as appropriate:

a 5/4.

b .20.

c 5%.

2 The frequency distribution in Figure 2.80 represents how often customers purchased shirts in red, green, blue and purple. Based on this distribution, identify the following:

a Frequency of red shirts purchased.

b Total number of shirts purchased.

c Relative frequency of a green shirt being purchased.

d Cumulative percentage of a blue shirt being purchased.

Value	f
Red	4
Green	3
Blue	2
Purple	1

FIGURE 2.80 Frequency distribution of shirts for Test Yourself Question 2

3 For each of the following variables/situations, which illustration would be most appropriate, and why?

a A sales manager wants to compare car sales levels for all of his salespeople as a portion of total sales company-wide. Each sale is recorded as a new row in a sales chart.

b A human resources manager deploys a psychological survey to assess current employee satisfaction.

c Worried that low-paid employees are taking advantage of petty cash to make up for their low salaries, a company accountant wants to compare wages and petty cash reimbursements.

(Continued)

(Continued)

 d A marketing manager wants to prepare a report for the executive team illustrating the number of ads placed on different television channels, newspapers and websites. She has counts for each location.

 e An executive wants to examine spending on R&D across the company. He has a list of how much money has been spent on each R&D initiative for the past two years, and would like to compare spending in Year 1 with spending in Year 2.

4 Why are there gaps in bar charts but not in histograms?

DATA SKILL CHALLENGES

 After you've completed the questions below, check your answers online.

Consider the following datasets and create appropriate translations using SPSS or Excel.

1 **Drink Preferences**: Cola, Water, Water, Cola, Juice, Cola, Water, Juice, Cola, Cola, Water, Cola.

2 **Sales by Salesperson**: Jim, Sue, Sue, Al, Jim, Jim, Sue, Jim, Al, Jim, Sue, Jim, Jim, Sue, Al, Al, Sue.

3 **Sales in Chinese Yuan**: 200000, 125000, 180000, 170000, 210000, 190000, 220000, 1800000.

4 **Survey Results**: 2.1, 3.0, 2.7, 2.6, 1.5, 1.2, 3.0, 3.6, 2.8, 2.7.

NEW TERMS

bar chart: bin: cumulative frequency: cumulative percentage: formula: fraction: frequency (or simple frequency): frequency polygon: frequency table: histogram: percentage: pie chart: proportion: relative frequency: sample size: subscript:

NEW STATISTICAL NOTATION AND FORMULAS

N: population size.
n: sample size.
f: frequency.
rel.f: relative frequency.
cum.f: cumulative frequency.
cum.%: cumulative percentage.

$$rel.f = \frac{f}{N}$$

FIGURE 2.81 Formula for relative frequency

Visit https://study.sagepub.com/landers2e **for free additional online resources related to this chapter.**

3 CENTRAL TENDENCY AND VARIABILITY

WHAT YOU WILL LEARN FROM THIS CHAPTER

- How to identify the normal distribution
- How to identify positively and negatively skewed data
- How to distinguish between parameters and statistics
- How to interpret the central tendency and variability of a variable
- How to identify the balance between robustness and precision and its effect on estimates of central tendency
- How to identify when it is appropriate to use the mean vs median vs mode to assess central tendency
- How to identify when it is appropriate to use the range vs standard deviation vs variance to assess variability

DATA SKILLS YOU WILL MASTER FROM THIS CHAPTER

- Computing the mode, median and mean
- Computing the range, variance and standard deviation

CASE STUDY   ARE THESE GROUPS DIFFERENT?

Often, restaurant diners leave no feedback on the food they eat. With politeness in mind, dissatisfied diners often do not mention their dissatisfaction to their servers. Their impressions and opinions are instead reflected in return visits. If they liked the food, they are likely to come back. If they didn't like the food, they are unlikely to come back, and are also likely to speak badly of their experience to all their friends.

(Continued)

(Continued)

To address this problem, Sue opened Tastetastic, a B2B company that performs taste testing research for restaurants. When a chef wants to introduce a new menu, he takes his dishes to Tastetastic, who will gather diner focus groups to share their opinions. Too spicy, too bland, too creamy, too heavy – these are the opinions that can really make a difference for a small, growing restaurant's bottom line.

With what she learned from Chapter 1, Sue has carefully designed her approach to conducting this research. She pays random groups of theoretical restaurant-goers to taste the food, ensuring her sample represents her population of interest. She asks each participant to eat each dish from the chef's new menu. Afterwards, she collects survey measures assessing one construct per dish: overall flavour. It is on a scale of 1 to 7, where 1 = 'worst I've ever had' and 7 = 'best I've ever had'.

With what she learned from Chapter 2, Sue has correctly produced several histograms that illustrate her interval-level data clearly for her clients. But one of her current clients wants a little more detail. 'Graphs are pretty,' he says, 'but we have many dishes, and many of the graphs look similar. The graphs seem to cluster around the same values. So how can we tell the dishes apart? And some of these graphs are much wider than others – what does that mean?'

📊 Take a look at Sue's survey data for yourself in chapter3.xls (Excel) or chapter3.sav (SPSS) online.

Although graphing and illustrating data makes them more easily interpretable, sometimes we need precision. In Chapter 2, we learned that the trade-off when graphing is often between precision and simplicity of message. A bar graph is a much clearer message than a frequency table, but that frequency table contains a lot more information.

So far, we've only summarized qualitative data with numbers, and we did so by creating a large, complex table. We have not summarized quantitative data at all; we have only used illustrations. But the problem in this case study is one that can't be solved by graphing alone. While we could create a unique histogram for every dish, we are then left with the problem of comparing those histograms. If two histograms are visually similar, it can be difficult to determine just how similar the underlying data really are.

This is exactly the problem Sue faces. She has created histograms for each dish individually, but she still doesn't have the answer the client wants – all she has is a big pile of histograms and doesn't know how to compare them. Where exactly is the middle of a histogram? Does it matter where the ends of the histogram fall? She needs more precision to draw the conclusions the client is looking for.

In this chapter, you'll learn about the tools that can be used to produce precise measurements that summarize both qualitative and quantitative data. As you read, consider how you might apply the concepts you learn to solve Sue's problem.

3.1 THE SHAPE OF DATA

In order to achieve more precision with our descriptions of data, we need a way to refer to the shape of that data. In Chapter 2, we looked at histograms of many shapes. Some had data clustered on the left, others had data clustered on the right, and still others took the shape of a small hill or bell.

These shapes change how precise we can be. If we're trying to capture the 'centre' of a dataset, that means different things for different shapes. The most straightforward of these is the hill-shaped distribution of data. Figure 3.01 gives an example.

There are two parts to this histogram. The first is the data itself, which ranges from 1 to 5. The bars represent the actual data – nothing has changed from Chapter 2. But we've added a bell-shaped curved line to this graph. This represents a common shape that data take and is called the normal distribution.

It's important to notice that the real data graphed here does not perfectly follow the curve. This is, pardon the pun, *normal*. In Figure 3.01, you can see that the real data are not in the shape of a perfect curve, but if you squint a bit you can see how it mimics the bell shape of the solid line. For now, this is sufficient visual evidence that the underlying data come from a normal distribution.

WHAT ABOUT THE ABNORMAL DISTRIBUTION?

The normal distribution is not normal because other distributions are abnormal. Instead, it is called the normal distribution because it is so common. Most data follow the normal distribution because of what that distribution represents.

Imagine that we were to create a histogram of customer satisfaction ratings on a scale of 1 to 5. Imagine further that the population's (see Chapter 1, p. 11) customer satisfaction level was 2.5. That doesn't mean that every customer's satisfaction is 2.5. Some customers will be a bit higher and others will be a bit lower, but most customers will fall pretty close to 2.5. A few customers might be pretty far away from 2.5, but there won't be as many of these as there are customers close to 2.5. This tendency is what gives the normal distribution its bell shape. We'll cover this in more detail in Chapters 4 and 5.

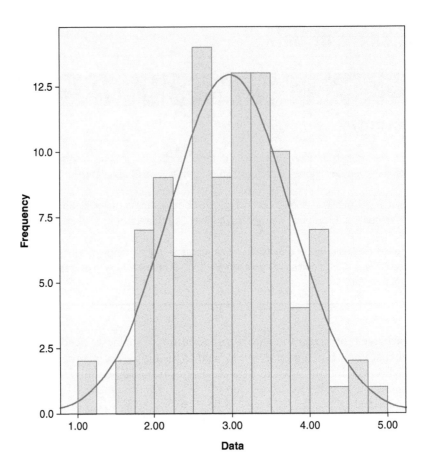

FIGURE 3.01   Example of normally distributed data (shaped like a hill or bell)

In the two graphs shown in Figure 3.02, we see common variants of the normal distribution – skewed data. Data with skew are data that deviate from the normal distribution. The graph either trails off to the left, which is called negative skew, or it trails off to the right, which is called positive skew.

The words 'positive' and 'negative' are confusing to some. Remember it this way: the skew is defined by which direction the 'tail' of the graph points. If the tail points toward positive numbers, it's positive skew. If the tail points toward negative numbers, it's negative skew.

Skewed data can be found throughout business research. For example, negatively skewed data are fairly common in human resources research on job performance. Many supervisors, knowing their employees could lose their jobs if their ratings are too low, rate their employees artificially highly, creating skew as in the graphic on the left of Figure 3.02. This has some important implications for data analysis, which we'll discuss later in this chapter.

3.2 A NEW SYMBOL FOR FORMULAS

Before we get into the next section, we need to talk about a new symbol that will be used in most of the formulas we'll use from now on. This is the capital Greek letter sigma:

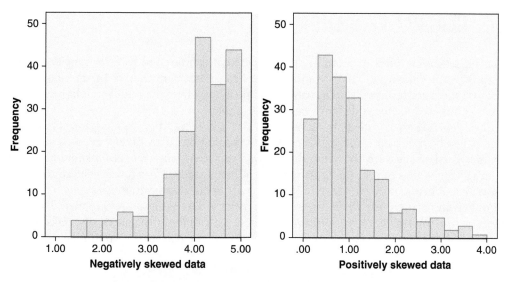

FIGURE 3.02   Examples of negatively and positively skewed data

When learning new formulas, your first goal should be to speak that formula aloud. For example, consider this formula:

$$y = \sum x$$

The Greek capital sigma character is pronounced 'sum of' because it indicates that we should take all the values to the right of it and add them together. This formula is therefore pronounced: 'y equals sum of x'.

To calculate, simply take all values of x and add them together. Consider the dataset shown in Figure 3.03.

x
2
5
1
3

FIGURE 3.03   Sample dataset for summing

For this dataset, $\sum x = 2 + 5 + 1 + 3 = 11$.

It's also important to note that we often use the character x to denote 'values of a single variable of interest in a dataset'. The variable does not need to be called 'x' for the formula to apply to that data. For example, if the dataset above was named 'customer service ratings', it would still be equal to 11.

3.3 CENTRAL TENDENCY

Central tendency refers to a family of statistics that can be used to determine where the 'middle' of a dataset is. That's a more complicated problem than it might first appear because there are several different ways to think about where the middle might be, and the approach that you choose depends on the data's shape.

This dependency is called an assumption. For a statistic to be meaningful, its assumptions must be met. Some statistics have fewer assumptions than others, even though they are designed to measure the same thing. For example, many statistics assume that your data's shape is that of a normal distribution. When a statistic has fewer assumptions, it is described as being more robust than statistics with more assumptions.

You always want to use the most precise statistics whose assumptions are met. There are three major ways to compute central tendency, with different balances of precision and robustness. For our exploration of all three, we'll use the dataset shown in Figure 3.04.

Customer satisfaction survey			
Question 1	Question 2	Question 3	Question 4
4	3	1st	Pat
4	2	3rd	Jen
3	3	1st	Pat
3	2	2nd	Al
3	3	1st	Pete
3	3	1st	Jen
3	2	2nd	Pat
2	4	4th	Al
3	2	3rd	Pat
2	2	4th	Jen
2	1	2nd	Al
3	4	1st	Pat

FIGURE 3.04   Dataset for exploration of central tendency

Here's what the questions represent:

■ Question 1: How satisfied were you with your experience today? (1 to 4, very dissatisfied to very satisfied).

■ Question 2: How satisfied were you with your salesperson? (1 to 4, very dissatisfied to very satisfied).

■ Question 3: Of the last four stores you have visited, rank your customer service experience today.

■ Question 4: Who was your salesperson?

3.3.1 MODE

Our first measure of central tendency, the mode, is the most common value in a variable. The mode is the most robust but least precise measure of central tendency, and is appropriate for all scales of measurement.

Q1		Q2		Q3		Q4	
Value	f	Value	f	Value	f	Value	f
1	0	1	1	1st	5	Al	3
2	3	2	5	2nd	3	Jen	3
3	7	3	4	3rd	2	Pat	4
4	2	4	2	4th	2	Pete	1

FIGURE 3.05   Frequencies for dataset in Figure 3.04 used to determine modes

The mode is quite easy to calculate: create a frequency table (at least the f column) and name the most common value you find.

In the dataset from Figure 3.04, we can create the lists of f shown in Figure 3.05.

From this, we can conclude that the mode of Q1 is 3, the mode of Q2 is 2, the mode of Q3 is 1st, and the mode of Q4 is Pat.

What do we do if two values are both the most common? Consider this dataset: 1, 2, 2, 2, 3, 3, 3, 4.

Both 2 and 3 appear three times. Which one is the mode? The answer: both. This dataset has two modes, 2 and 3.

Computing the mode on interval- and ratio-level data can be problematic if the data are continuous, as there may not be many repeated values. For example, this dataset would make computing the mode difficult: 1.23, 1.52, 2.12, 3.40, 3.50. In these cases, the mode should not be used as a measure of central tendency.

3.3.2 MEDIAN

FOUNDATION CONCEPTS

A nominal variable has meaningful labels (for example, 'male' or 'female'). See Chapter 1, p. 8.

An ordinal variable has the characteristics of a nominal variable, but also with meaningful order (for example, '1st', '2nd', '3rd'). See Chapter 1, p. 8.

An interval variable has the characteristics of ordinal data, but also with meaningful distances between values (for example, temperature in degrees Celsius). See Chapter 1, p. 8.

A ratio variable has the characteristics of an interval variable, but also with a meaningful zero point (for example, sales in euros). See Chapter 1, p. 8.

Our second measure of central tendency, the median, is the middlemost value in a variable. The median is less robust than the mode, but more precise. While the mode determines central tendency by count, the median focuses on order. It is inappropriate to use the median with nominal data, because nominal data have no order.

To determine the median, put all of the values of the variable into ascending order and count to the middle.

For example, let's look at this small dataset: 2, 4, 3, 1, 5.

When we put this dataset in order, we end up with 1, 2, 3, 4, 5.

3 is the middlemost value; therefore, 3 is the median of this variable.

Things get more complicated when we don't have a middle value. Let's look at Q1. It contains the following values: 4, 4, 3, 3, 3, 3, 3, 2, 3, 2, 2, 3.

If we put these in ascending order, we end up with this list: 2, 2, 2, 3, 3, 3, 3, 3, 3, 3, 4, 4.

Uh-oh – there's a problem. As we can see in Figure 3.06, there are two middlemost values!

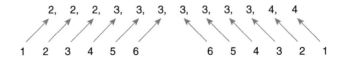

FIGURE 3.06   Counting values for Q1 to determine the median

Fortunately, they're the same! So we can safely conclude that 3 is the median. But will it be so easy for Q2 (Figure 3.07)?

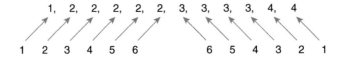

FIGURE 3.07   Counting values for Q2 to determine the median

This time they are different! The solution? Take an average: $(2 + 3)/2 = 2.5$. The median of Q2 is 2.5.

Although Q3 contains rank (ordinal) data, the process is the same. Try it on your own – you should find the median is 2nd.

Because Q4 is nominal measurement, the assumptions of the median are not met – a median assumes ordinal-level measurement or higher. We cannot compute a median for Q4.

3.3.3 MEAN

Our third and final measure of central tendency, the mean, is the arithmetic average of the values in a variable. The mean is the least robust but most precise of the central tendency measures. For a mathematical average to be meaningful, the distances between numbers must be meaningful. For that reason, the mean assumes the data to be interval- or ratio-level measurements. A mean should not be calculated for ordinal-level data.

The sample mean is represented as $\bar{x}$ (pronounced 'x bar') and is calculated with the formula shown in Figure 3.08.

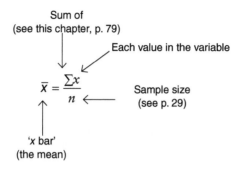

FIGURE 3.08   Annotated formula for calculating the mean

We can pronounce this formula as: 'x bar equals the sum of x divided by n'. We could further break it down by saying 'the mean equals the sum of all values in the variable divided by the number of cases in the variable'.

We can compute the mean only for Q1 and Q2 (Figure 3.09), since Q3 is ordinal-level measurement and Q4 is nominal.

$$\bar{x}_{Q1} = \frac{\sum x}{n} = \frac{4+4+3+3+3+3+3+2+3+2+2+3}{12} = \frac{35}{12} = 2.92$$

$$\bar{x}_{Q2} = \frac{\sum x}{n} = \frac{3+2+3+2+3+3+2+4+2+2+1+4}{12} = \frac{31}{12} = 2.58$$

FIGURE 3.09   Step by step calculations of the mean for Q1 and Q2

Thus, the mean of Q1 is 2.92, and the mean of Q2 is 2.58.

3.3.4 COMPARING THE CENTRAL TENDENCY MEASURES

Figure 3.10 summarizes a lot of the above information, stating when it is appropriate to consider each type of central tendency measure.

	Nominal	Ordinal	Interval	Ratio
Mode	Yes	Yes	Yes, if Discrete	Yes, if Discrete
Median	No	Yes	Yes	Yes
Mean	No	No	Yes	Yes

FIGURE 3.10   Appropriateness of central tendency measures given scale of measurement

We can also summarize the precision–robustness relationship – see Figure 3.11.

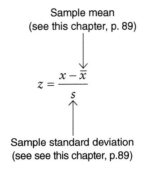

Sample mean
(see this chapter, p. 89)

$$z = \frac{x - \bar{x}}{s}$$

Sample standard deviation
(see see this chapter, p.89)

	Robustness	Precision
Mode	Highest	Lowest
Median	Middle	Middle
Mean	Lowest	Highest

FIGURE 3.11   Relationship between precision and robustness

So, since the mean is the most precise, does that mean we should always use the mean with interval- and ratio-level data? Not necessarily. The mean also assumes that the data are normally distributed. So what happens to our central tendency measures if the data they describe are skewed?

Visually, from Figure 3.12 we might conclude that the bulk of the data are around the mode and median. The mean is fairly far from this 'middle'. The positive skew has pulled the mean away from the apparent centre of the data. This is because the mean is less robust than the other two central tendency statistics. The median is less robust than the mode, but more robust than the mean, so it doesn't get pulled as far toward the tail of the data. If your data are skewed, take a look at the histogram to determine which of the three measures of central tendency would be best – in most cases, the balance in precision and robustness provided by the median makes it a preferred choice.

If the data were normally distributed, the mode, median and mean would be roughly the same, although we'd expect the mean to be the most precise.

3.4 VARIABILITY

Now that we can identify the 'middle' of the distribution, we need a way to refer to its width. The two histograms in Figure 3.13 are quite different, although they have identical means and sample sizes ($x = 2.6$ and $n = 50$ for each).

The width of these graphs represents variability, which is a general term referring to the degree to which scores within a single variable are different from one another. In the graph on the left, scores are much more similar – everything falls between 2.0 and 4.0. In the graph on the right, scores vary a great deal, ranging from .5 up almost to 5.0. Thus, the variable on the right has a great deal more variability than does the variable on the left.

How can we capture this numerically? We'll cover each technique in turn.

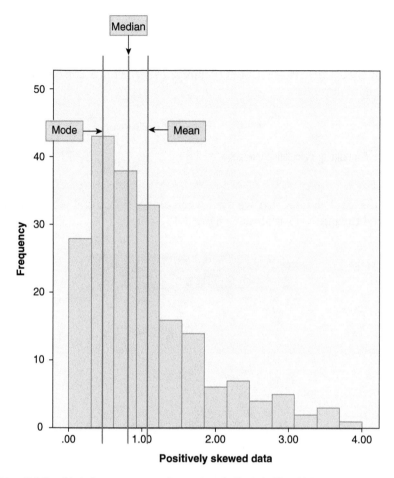

FIGURE 3.12   Relationship between mean, median and mode illustrated in a histogram

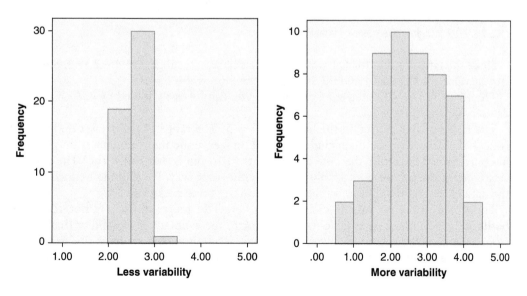

FIGURE 3.13   Comparison of two variables: one with little variability and one with much variability

3.4.1 RANGE

The simplest measure of variability is the range, which refers to the distance between the largest and smallest scores in the dataset (Figure 3.14). The range can be used to summarize interval- or higher-level data.

$$\text{range} = x_{\text{largest}} - x_{\text{smallest}}$$

FIGURE 3.14   Formula for calculating the range

We'll use the same dataset that we used when exploring central tendency, although we now only need the interval variables – Figure 3.15.

Customer satisfaction survey	
Question 1	Question 2
4	3
4	2
3	3
3	2
3	3
3	3
3	2
2	4
3	2
2	2
2	1
3	4

FIGURE 3.15   Quantitative variables from Figure 3.04

Since the largest value for Q1 was 4 and the smallest 2, $\text{range}_{Q1} = 4 - 2 = 2$. Since the largest value for Q2 was 4 and the smallest 1, $\text{range}_{Q2} = 4 - 1 = 3$.

The range is a very limited statistic because you can be easily fooled by it. Consider the datasets shown in Figure 3.16.

The range of the dataset on the left is $5 - 0 = 5$. The range of the dataset on the right is $20 - 0 = 20$. We would conclude from the ranges alone that the dataset on the right has much more variability than the dataset on the left. But is that really true? The data are clustered on the left on both graphs in exactly the same way. We shouldn't conclude that the data on the right are more variable just because of one tricky case.

This lonely unusual case is called an outlier. The range statistic is not robust to outliers. If even one case is far outside the norm, the estimate of variability that we get from a range will be dramatically over-inflated. While it is obvious from this graph that the outlier is dramatically increasing this range estimate, there are many situations where it is less clear.

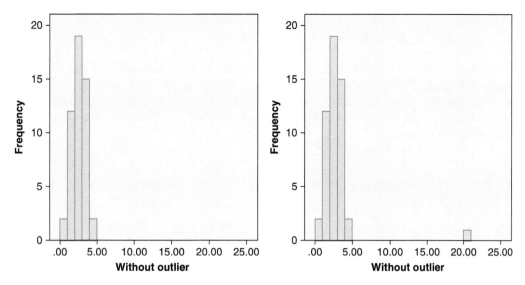

FIGURE 3.16   Comparison of dataset without outliers to a dataset with one outlier

Because it is driven entirely by the value of two scores, regardless of how unusual those scores might be, the range is generally not a good way to assess variability. We need something else.

3.4.2 STATISTICS VS PARAMETERS

FOUNDATION CONCEPTS

A **population** is a theoretical group that you want to draw conclusions about. See Chapter 1, p. 11.

A **sample** is a group gathered from a population. See Chapter 1, p. 12.

We're temporarily going to talk about variability in populations, and hold back for a bit on talking about variability in samples. This is because variability in samples is a little more complicated, and it's easier to learn about variability in populations first.

This also changes the formulas a bit. When we calculate numbers to summarize populations, we are computing parameters, while numbers calculated to summarize samples are called statistics. We represent these values differently in formulas.

For example, the population size (N) is a parameter, while the sample size (n) is a statistic.

This can be applied to almost any measurement. The mean we learned earlier, $\bar{x}$, is a statistic. There is also a mean that is a parameter, but it is represented by the lower-case Greek letter mu (μ, pronounced 'mew').

Therefore, if you saw $\bar{x} = 1$, you would pronounce this as 'the sample mean equals 1' or 'x bar equals 1'. If you saw $\mu = 1$, you would pronounce this as 'the population mean equals 1' or 'mu equals 1'.

Although you could calculate the population mean in the same way that you calculate the sample mean (but with population data), in the real world you will rarely work with population data. Most of the time, you'll want to make conclusions about parameters you can't measure based upon statistics you can measure. We'll return to this concept in much more detail in Chapter 6.

3.4.3 AVERAGE DEVIATION

What we really want to know when assessing variability is how far away the scores are from the mean. If these deviations are large, we should conclude that there is a lot of variability. If these deviations are small, we should conclude that there is not much variability. So why not take the average of the deviations?

The formula for deviation from a population mean is: deviation $= x - \mu$.

If the mean was 1, and a score was 2, the deviation would be $2 - 1 = 1$. Therefore, that score is 1 point above the mean.

If the mean was 1, and a score was .5, the deviation would be $.5 - 1 = -.5$. Therefore, that score is .5 points below the mean.

Let's apply this logic to a sample variable from a population which is summarized in Figure 3.17. For this example, the five scores printed in the table are the only five scores we'd ever been interested in (a population). We'll compute the mean of those scores, as well as the deviations.

Population variable (x)	Population Mean (μ)	Deviation (x-μ)
2	3.4	$2 - 3.4 = -1.4$
2	3.4	$2 - 3.4 = -1.4$
4	3.4	$4 - 3.4 = 0.6$
4	3.4	$4 - 3.4 = 0.6$
5	3.4	$5 - 3.4 = 1.6$

FIGURE 3.17   Population of five scores, the mean of those five scores, and deviation scores from each

Now that we have deviations, we should be able to calculate an average to get an estimate of variability, right? But there's a problem. Let's go ahead and calculate it (Figure 3.18) and see what happens.

$$\mu_{Deviations} = \frac{-1.4 - 1.4 + .6 + .6 + 1.6}{5} = \frac{0}{5} = 0$$

FIGURE 3.18   Step by step calculation of the mean of the deviations

What happened? Why is the value zero? Remember what we did – we computed the deviations from the mean, and then took the average of those deviations. The mean is, by definition, the mathematical centre of the data! So the average deviation is *always* zero. If we want to use deviations to understand variability, we'll need to find another way. Simply calculating the mean of the deviations won't work.

3.4.4 POPULATION STANDARD DEVIATION AND VARIANCE

The most common way to deal with this problem is to compute the square of each deviation (multiplying each value by itself) and then to take the average of those values. Then we can calculate the square root of our final answer to get back to what we're really interested in: the average distance that scores are from the mean.

Fortunately, we're already part of the way there. We already have the deviations, $x - \mu$. Now, we need to add the squared deviations: $(x - \mu)^2$ – see Figure 3.19.

		Population	
x	Mean (μ)	$(x - \mu)$	$(x - \mu)^2$
2	3.4	−1.4	$(-1.4)^2 = 1.96$
2	3.4	−1.4	$(-1.4)^2 = 1.96$
4	3.4	.6	$(.6)^2 = 0.36$
4	3.4	.6	$(.6)^2 = 0.36$
5	3.4	1.6	$(1.6)^2 = 2.56$

FIGURE 3.19   Population of five scores, mean of those scores, deviations from that mean, and squared deviations

We've now created a list of squared deviations. If we compute the average of these values, we'll end up with something meaningful – the variance of the population, as shown in Figure 3.20.

$$\sigma^2 = \frac{(1.96 + 1.96 + .36 + .36 + 2.56)}{5}$$

$$= \frac{7.2}{5}$$

$$= 1.44$$

FIGURE 3.20   Step by step calculation of population variance

The variance is represented here as the symbol σ^2, which is the lower-case Greek character sigma, squared. Remember that capital sigma (Σ) means 'sum of' – be careful not to confuse them.

Thus, we could pronounce $\sigma^2 = 1.44$ as either 'sigma squared equals 1.44' or 'the population variance is 1.44'.

All the work we just did is summarized in the conceptual formula for σ^2 shown in Figure 3.21.

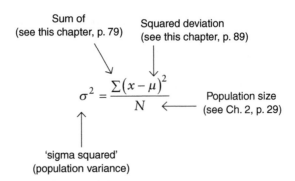

FIGURE 3.21   Annotated conceptual formula for the variance

We could pronounce this as 'sigma squared equals the sum of the squared deviations divided by the population size'.

That 1.44 is not very easily interpretable. Because we squared each deviation, 1.44 equals the average squared deviation. We need to take the square root of that to get back to an interpretable result – the standard deviation (SD) of the population (Figure 3.22).

$$\sigma = \sqrt{\sigma^2} = \sqrt{1.44} = 1.2$$

FIGURE 3.22   Step by step calculation of the standard deviation from the variance

We could pronounce $\sigma = 1.2$ as either 'sigma equals 1.2' or 'the population standard deviation is 1.2'.

We could add a square root to our variance formula to get the conceptual formula for σ in Figure 3.23.

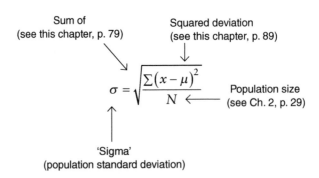

FIGURE 3.23   Annotated conceptual formula for the population standard deviation

Because we've taken the square root to get back to our original scale, this is interpretable. A standard deviation of 1.2 means that, on average, scores differ from the mean by 1.2 points.

Together, the variance and standard deviation form a much more accurate picture of variability in a variable. They both take into account all of the individual deviations (instead of only the most extreme scores), and the standard deviation is interpretable in terms of the original measurement. If the original variable captured 'sales in £', the standard deviation is in £, too.

Ultimately, this section can be summarized as: the 'average' deviation always equals zero, but by computing squared deviations, averaging them, and then computing the square root, we can produce the 'standard' deviation, which gives us the average distance that scores fall from the mean.

3.4.5 SAMPLE STANDARD DEVIATION AND VARIANCE

As we discussed in Chapter 1, measuring populations is typically not feasible. We want to make conclusions about 'customers' or 'employees', not the handful of people we actually have access to or who are willing to complete our surveys. As a result, we typically measure samples of those populations instead, measuring statistics rather than parameters.

Statisticians who have researched variability have found that variances and standard deviations calculated from samples systematically underestimate population variances and standard deviations. In other words, they are predictably smaller than they should be. This predictable difference between sample statistics and the population parameter they are supposed to be estimating is called bias. Fortunately, those same researchers identified a way to 'fix' the sample estimates of variance and standard deviation that's not very difficult – instead of dividing by n, we use $n - 1$. We'll discuss the reason for this in more detail in Chapter 6.

This changes our conceptual formulas from before, just a little bit, as shown in Figures 3.24 and 3.25.

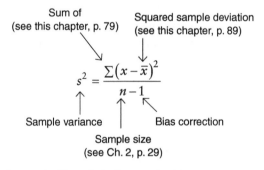

FIGURE 3.24   Annotated conceptual formula for the sample variance

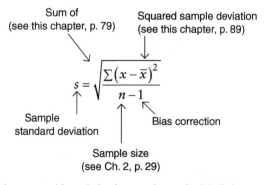

FIGURE 3.25   Annotated conceptual formula for the sample standard deviation

The differences between the sample and population formulas are summarized in Figure 3.26.

	Measures...	In a...	Using this mean...	With a square root?	With a bias correction?
σ	Standard deviation	Population	μ (mu)	Yes	No
σ^2	Variance	Population	μ (mu)	No	No
S	Standard deviation	Sample	$x-$ (x bar)	Yes	Yes
s^2	Variance	Sample	$x-$ (x bar)	No	Yes

FIGURE 3.26 Summary of differences between sample and population formulas for variance and standard deviation

3.4.6 CONCEPTUAL VS COMPUTATIONAL FORMULAS

So far, we've been looking at the conceptual formulas, so named because they illustrate the underlying relationships between variables implied by a statistic or parameter. When we look at the formula for the standard deviation, we can easily see from the conceptual formula itself that it measures the average (bottom of the formula) deviation from the mean (top of the formula).

But this approach is very clunky in practice. Creating a table to compute each deviation creates many opportunities for error, especially when working with numbers with many decimal places. Fortunately, each of these formulas can be mathematically manipulated into something easier to calculate, which are called the computational formulas – see Figures 3.27 and 3.28. Whether you use the conceptual or the computational formula, you'll end up with the same answer – the computational formulas are just simpler when using a calculator. That means, in practice, calculating something both ways is a useful way to check the accuracy of your work. If the results don't agree, you did something wrong in at least one of them.

$$s = \sqrt{\frac{\sum x^2 - \frac{(\sum x)^2}{n}}{n-1}}$$

Sample size (see Ch. 2, p. 29)   Bias correction

FIGURE 3.27 Annotated computational formula for the sample standard deviation

$$s^2 = \frac{\sum x^2 - \frac{(\sum x)^2}{n}}{n-1}$$

Sample size (see Ch. 2, p. 29)   Bias correction

FIGURE 3.28 Annotated computational formula for the sample variance

In our computational formulas, two terms look very similar: Σx^2 and $(\Sigma x)^2$. It's very important that you don't confuse these terms. They mean very different things.

To compute Σx^2, square each value, and add those squared values together. To compute $(\Sigma x)^2$, add all the values together, and square the result.

Thus, if your dataset was 1, 2, 3, the results would be as shown in Figure 3.29.

$$\Sigma x^2 = 1^2 + 2^2 + 3^2 = 1 + 4 + 9 = 15$$
$$(\Sigma x)^2 = (1 + 2 + 3)^2 = 6^2 = 36$$

FIGURE 3.29   Step by step calculation of Σx^2 and $(\Sigma x)^2$

3.4.7 STEP BY STEP EXAMPLE OF CALCULATING VARIANCE AND STANDARD DEVIATION

Let's step through computation of a standard deviation and variance given a particular dataset. Here's the dataset: 1, 4, 2, 4, 2, 5.

First, create a table with your x values (Figure 3.30).

x
1
4
2
4
2
5

FIGURE 3.30   Dataset for Section 3.4.7

Second, add a column with the squared values in it (Figure 3.31).

x	x^2
1	1
4	16
2	4
4	16
2	4
5	25

FIGURE 3.31   Step by step calculation of the variance, step 1

Third, with these values, look at the formula and determine what numbers you need: n, Σx^2 and $(\Sigma x)^2$ (Figure 3.32).

$$n = 6$$

$$\Sigma x^2 = 1 + 16 + 4 + 16 + 4 + 25 = 66$$

$$(\Sigma x)^2 = (1 + 4 + 2 + 4 + 2 + 5)^2 = 18^2 = 324$$

FIGURE 3.32   Step by step calculation of the variance, step 2

Fourth, plug these values into the variance formula (Figure 3.33).

$$s^2 = \frac{\Sigma x^2 - \dfrac{(\Sigma x)^2}{n}}{n-1}$$

$$= \frac{66 - \dfrac{324}{6}}{6-1}$$

$$= \frac{66 - 54}{5}$$

$$= \frac{12}{5}$$

$$= 2.4$$

FIGURE 3.33   Step by step calculation of the variance, step 3

Now you've calculated the variance! Take the square root to determine the standard deviation (Figure 3.34). Carry out your computation to at least two decimal places.

And now you've calculated the standard deviation too!

$$s = \sqrt{s^2} = \sqrt{2.4} = 1.55$$

FIGURE 3.34   Step by step calculation of the standard deviation from the variance.

3.5 APPLYING CENTRAL TENDENCY AND VARIABILITY

To apply what you've learned from this chapter, consider the following case study, questions posed about that case study, and discussion of those questions.

3.5.1 APPLICATION CASE STUDY

Farris is a family doctor. He maintains personal relationships with each patient and finds this personally fulfilling. He abides carefully by the Hippocratic Oath to do no harm. He believes strongly that in order to do no harm, he should be constantly learning and improving upon his personal skills, in terms of both technical proficiency and bedside manner. While he strives for perfection in his work, he's noticed that many of his patients are seemingly not as committed to their own health as he is. While he prescribes courses of action that should improve their lives, like better diet and more exercise, many patients simply don't comply with his recommendations. Curious about how widespread this is, he sends out an informal survey to his past patients, asking them several questions:

1 How often do you comply with the behavioural recommendations I provide you? (1 = Never, 2 = Sometimes, 3 = Often, 4 = Always).

2 Do you trust the behavioural recommendations I provide you? ('Yes' or 'No').

3 How many days in the past year have you complied with the behavioural recommendations I provided you? Please respond with a number from 0 to 365.

When Farris gets back his survey, what type of summary statistics will he be able to use, and why? Which won't he be able to use, and why not? What information will these statistics tell him, and what information will still be missing?

3.5.2 APPLICATION DISCUSSION

Farris's data have the potential to influence him to change the way he practises medicine. Because of this, he should be very cautious to appropriately summarize and interpret the data he collects. We'll cover each of the three variables he has measured separately.

The first variable ranges from 1 to 4, with labels Never, Sometimes, Often and Always. This is an ordinal measure. As a result, the mean will not be a meaningful summary of its central tendency, although he can calculate the median and mode. For variability, without a meaningful mean, he cannot calculate the variance or standard deviation – only the range is available.

The second variable includes 'Yes' and 'No' only, making it a nominal variable. This time, only the mode will meaningfully summarize central tendency, and none of the variability statistics covered here will be useful.

The third variable is a number from 0 to 365, and it is ratio-level scale of measurement. All the statistics covered in this chapter are appropriate, and the mean and standard deviation are preferred.

For each of these variables, measures of central tendency and/or variability are available, and they all provide useful information about the centre and spread of the data contained in each. However, it's important to remember that such statistics can be distorted by outliers and peculiar shapes of data. Farris should also remember to create visual data displays – in this case, two bar charts and a histogram – to complement the numerical summaries he has created. This will provide a more complete picture of the data from which to make important decisions.

EXPLORING CENTRAL TENDENCY AND VARIABILITY IN EXCEL AND SPSS

EXCEL

Download the Excel dataset for the demonstration below as **chapter3.xls**. As you read this section, try to apply the terms you've learned in this chapter to the dataset and follow along with Excel on your own computer.

You can also get a video demonstration of the section below under **Excel Videos: Chapter 3**.

In our case study dataset, Sue at Tastetastic collected survey data from her research participants. Since this is discrete interval-level data, we can use any of the three measures of central tendency.

Because we want to calculate means, medians and modes for all eight of our variables, we'll add a new column to contain titles. Right-click on the head of Column A and select **Insert** (Figure 3.35). This will move all of your data one column to the right and insert a blank column in A.

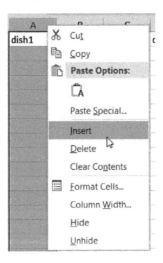

FIGURE 3.35   Right-click menu enabling insertion of a new column in Excel

Once your data have moved to the right, enter the words 'Mode', 'Median' and 'Mean' in A23, A24 and A25 respectively. You'll put the actual values for each variable in the columns to the right. We put a blank row between the data and our statistics so that it remains obvious where the data end and our work begins (Figure 3.36).

18		4	1	2
19		2	3	4
20		2	2	2
21		1	1	4
22				
23	Mode			
24	Median			
25	Mean			
26				
27				

FIGURE 3.36   Labels for computing central tendency statistics in Excel

The Excel formulas for these three statistics are pretty straightforward.

1 **Excel 2010 or later:** In B23, type: =MODE.SNGL(B2:B21).
2 **Excel 2007 or earlier:** In B23, type =MODE(B2:B21).
1 In B24, type: =MEDIAN(B2:B21).
2 In B25, type: =AVERAGE(B2:B21).

You should end up with the mode, median and mean for Dish #1. Note that for datasets with multiple modes, only the first mode will be displayed. Fortunately for us, none of the case study variables have multiple modes. Click and drag to highlight B23 to B25. It should look like Figure 3.37.

22		
23	Mode	2
24	Median	3
25	Mean	2.7

FIGURE 3.37   Central tendency statistics for the first variable

We'll use the small black box on the bottom right corner to **fill the formulas** to the right. This will automatically copy/paste your formulas in all of the other cells, but will update the formula references as it goes. Click-drag the little black box, and drag it to the bottom right corner of I25, as in Figure 3.38.

22		
23	Mode	2
24	Median	3
25	Mean	2.7

FIGURE 3.38   Filling central tendency formulas to the right for other variables

Once you let go, you'll see modes, medians and means for all eight of your variables (Figure 3.39). If your data have multiple modes, this technique will only display the lowest mode.

22								
23	Mode	2	2	3	2	3	3	2	3
24	Median	3	2	2.5	3	3	3	2	3
25	Mean	2.7	2.4	2.45	2.75	2.7	2.6	2.3	2.65
26								

FIGURE 3.39   Completed central tendency computations in Excel

Based on the means, it looks like Dishes #1 and #5 have the highest ratings, while Dish #7 has the lowest.

Since this is interval-level data, we can calculate the range, variance and standard deviation as estimates of variability.

Since we've already added a blank column for labels, we'll now just add three more: range, variance and standard deviation, in A27, A28 and A29 respectively (Figure 3.40).

(Continued)

(Continued)

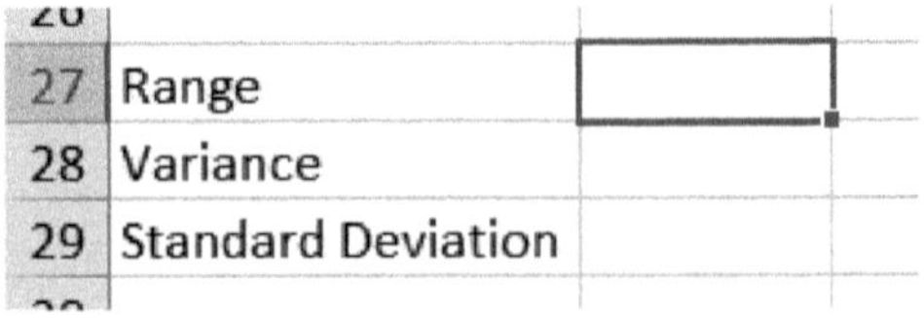

26		
27	Range	
28	Variance	
29	Standard Deviation	
30		

FIGURE 3.40   Labels for variability statistics in Excel

The range is the difference between the maximum and minimum values in a dataset, so that's exactly what we'll tell Excel to do. In B27, type: =MAX(B2:B21)-MIN(B2:B21).

Because Sue has only collected a random group of taste perceptions from a larger population of possible tastes, we are analysing a sample.

1 **Excel 2010 or later:** To compute the sample variance, in B28, type: =VAR.S(B2:B21). If you wanted to compute the population variance instead, you would use =VAR.P().
2 **Excel 2007 or earlier:** To compute the sample variance, in B28, type: =VAR(B2:B21). If you wanted to compute the population variance instead, you would use =VARP().

We could compute the standard deviation in two different ways. Since we already have the variance, we could use the =SQRT() function to compute a square root. For example, in B29, we might type =SQRT(B28)

If we didn't already have the variance, it would be a waste to compute the variance first. Instead, there are formulas available to compute the standard deviation directly.

1 **Excel 2010 or later:** To compute the sample standard deviation, in B29, type: =STDEV.S(B2:B21). If you wanted to compute the population standard deviation instead, you would use =STDEV.P().
2 **Excel 2007 or earlier:** To compute the sample standard deviation, in B29, type: =STDEV(B2:B21). If you wanted to compute the population standard deviation instead, you would use =STDEVP().

If all goes well, you should end up with three scores. Click-drag to highlight all three, as you did for central tendency (Figure 3.41).

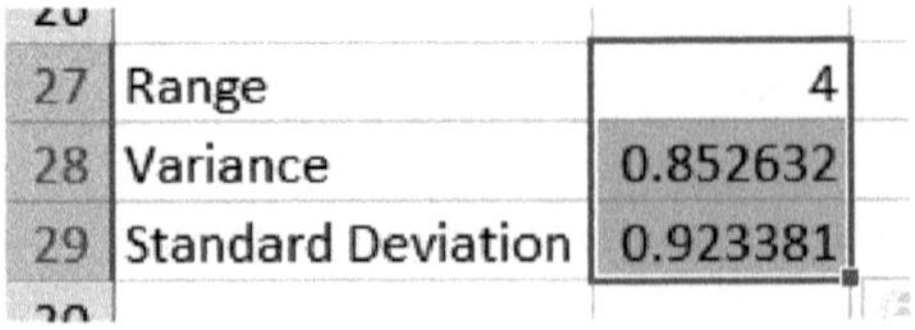

26		
27	Range	4
28	Variance	0.852632
29	Standard Deviation	0.923381
30		

FIGURE 3.41   Variability statistics for the first variable

Click-drag the small black box on the bottom right corner of the selected cells over to I29 (Figure 3.42). This will fill the cells to the right with the formulas you've already written, but updated to reference each column they are underneath.

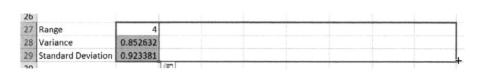

26									
27	Range	4							
28	Variance	0.852632							
29	Standard Deviation	0.923381							

FIGURE 3.42   Filling variability formulas to the right for other variables

If all goes well, you've just computed the range, variance and standard deviation for all eight variables – see Figure 3.43.

26									
27	Range	4	4	4	4	4	3	3	3
28	Variance	0.852632	1.305263	1.313158	1.460526	0.852632	1.094737	0.852632	0.871053
29	Standard Deviation	0.923381	1.142481	1.145931	1.208522	0.923381	1.046297	0.923381	0.933302

FIGURE 3.43   Completed variability statistics in Excel

From this, we can see that Dish #4 has the most variability, while Dishes #1, #5 and #7 have the least. To Sue, this means that diners have more widely varying opinions about the quality of Dish #4, while they are more in agreement for the others. What to do with this information is up to her client.

SPSS

Download the SPSS dataset for the demonstration below as **chapter3.sav**. As you read this section, try to apply the terms you've learned in this chapter to the dataset and follow along with SPSS on your own computer.

You can also get a video demonstration of the section below under **SPSS Videos: Chapter 3**.

In our case study dataset, Sue at Tastetastic collected survey data from her research participants. Since this is discrete interval-level data, we can use any of the three measures of central tendency.

We'll collect central tendency information the same way we produced frequency charts: open **Analyze**, then **Descriptive Statistics**, then **Frequencies** – see Figure 3.44.

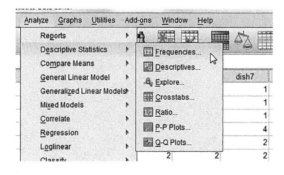

FIGURE 3.44   Menu option to create frequency tables in SPSS

(Continued)

(Continued)

Click the **Statistics** button on the top right (Figure 3.45).

FIGURE 3.45   Button to open Statistics dialogue within frequency dialogue in SPSS

In the Frequencies:Statistics panel that opens, check 'Mean', 'Median' and 'Mode' (Figure 3.46), then click **Continue**.

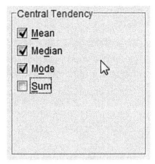

FIGURE 3.46   Central tendency options within the frequency table analysis in SPSS

Back at the Frequencies dialogue, move the variables of interest to the right by clicking on them, followed by the right arrow, as we've done before. Also uncheck the 'Display frequency tables' option, since we don't need them (Figure 3.47). Finally, click **OK**.

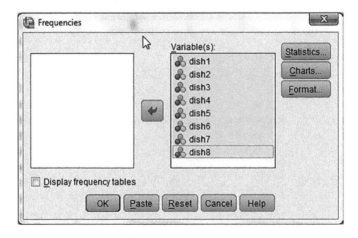

FIGURE 3.47   Frequencies dialogue ready to conduct analysis on case study dataset in SPSS

In the output pane (which should pop up), you'll see the means, medians and modes (Figure 3.48). If a variable has multiple modes, only the smallest will be shown.

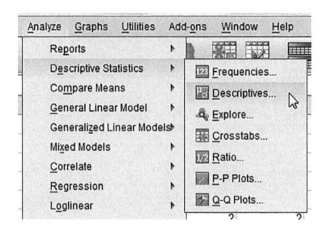

Statistics

		dish1	dish2	dish3	dish4	dish5	dish6	dish7	dish8
N	Valid	20	20	20	20	20	20	20	20
	Missing	0	0	0	0	0	0	0	0
Mean		2.70	2.40	2.45	2.75	2.70	2.60	2.30	2.65
Median		3.00	2.00	2.50	3.00	3.00	3.00	2.00	3.00
Mode		2[a]	2[a]	3	2[a]	2[a]	3	2	2[a]

a. Multiple modes exist. The smallest value is shown

FIGURE 3.48　Central tendency summary statistics output from frequencies dialogue in SPSS

Based on the means, it looks like Dish #4 has the highest ratings, while Dish #7 has the lowest. We'll collect variability information with a new area of SPSS: open **Analyze**, then **Descriptive Statistics**, then **Descriptives** – see Figure 3.49.

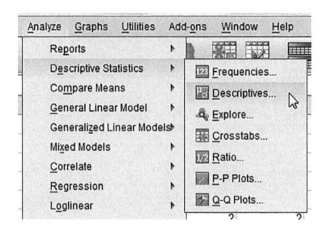

FIGURE 3.49　Menu option to output descriptive statistics in SPSS

Click the **Options** button on the right (Figure 3.50).

FIGURE 3.50　Options button within Descriptives tool

Check 'Standard Deviation', 'Variance' and 'Range' (Figure 3.51). Note that you can also get the mean using this tool.

(Continued)

(Continued)

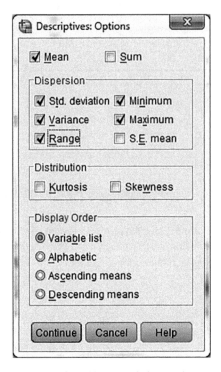

FIGURE 3.51   Options to display variability within Descriptives tool

Click **Continue**, and move all variables to the right, as we have several times before now – either click-drag each variable to the right, or click each variable and then the right arrow (Figure 3.52).

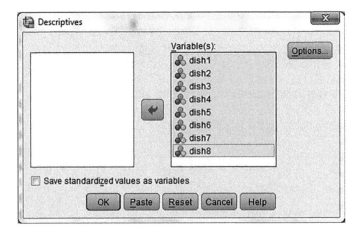

FIGURE 3.52   Descriptives dialogue ready to run on case study data

Click **OK**, and the output pane will pop up with your variability estimates – see Figure 3.53.

Descriptive Statistics

	N	Range	Minimum	Maximum	Mean	Std. Deviation	Variance
dish1	20	4	1	5	2.70	.923	.853
dish2	20	4	1	5	2.40	1.142	1.305
dish3	20	4	1	5	2.45	1.146	1.313
dish4	20	4	1	5	2.75	1.209	1.461
dish5	20	4	1	5	2.70	.923	.853
dish6	20	3	1	4	2.60	1.046	1.095
dish7	20	3	1	4	2.30	.923	.853
dish8	20	3	1	4	2.65	.933	.871
Valid N (listwise)	20						

FIGURE 3.53   Output from descriptive statistics analysis in SPSS

From this, we can see that Dish #4 has the most variability, while Dishes #1, #5 and #7 have the least. To Sue, this means that diners have more widely varying opinions about the quality of Dish #4, while they are more in agreement for the others. What to do with this information is up to her client.

STATISTICS IN THE REAL WORLD

  These web links can be accessed directly from the book's website.

Data visualization editor Alan Smith discusses the power of basic summary statistics: www.ted. com/talks/alan_smith_why_we_re_so_bad_at_statistics.

How does your understanding of and familiarity with basic summary statistics, like medians, influence how you view the world?

Investment firm The Motley Fool explains how standard deviation in stock performance is related to portfolio risk: www.fool.com/knowledge-center/how-to-calculate-the-volatility-for-a-portfolio-of. aspx.

What advantages does an analyst who understands variability have over analysts who don't?

TEST YOURSELF

☑ **After you've completed the questions below, check your answers online.**

1 Is the graph in Figure 3.54 normally distributed or skewed? If it is skewed, how is it skewed?

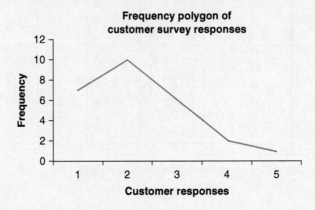

FIGURE 3.54   Graph for Test Yourself Question 1

2 For the data provided – X: 3, 1, 4, 4, 2, 3, 4
   a Identify if the data are normally distributed, positively skewed or negatively skewed.
   b Calculate ΣX.
   c Calculate the mode.
   d Calculate the range.

3 Pronounce the formula shown in Figure 3.55.

$$z = \frac{X - \bar{X}}{s}$$

FIGURE 3.55   Formula to be pronounced for Test Yourself Question 3

4 For each of the following scenarios, identify the scale of measurement for the variable and the most appropriate measure of central tendency:
   a Age.
   b Favourite colour.
   c Military rank.

5 For the sample data provided – X: 4, 6, 2, 8
   a Calculate the median.
   b Calculate the mean.
   c Calculate the variance.
   d Calculate the standard deviation.

6 Interpret the following as you would to someone unfamiliar with statistics: $\mu = 3$, Range = 20.

DATA SKILL CHALLENGES

 After you've completed the questions below, check your answers online.

1 Compute all appropriate central tendency and variability statistics for the dataset shown in Figure 3.56. Do so both by hand and by using the statistics program of your choice; the answers should agree. When calculating statistics by hand, carry out all calculations to at least six decimal places. Otherwise, your final answers may be slightly inaccurate.

These scores are from an employee performance appraisal; responses are given by supervisors. Each case is a unique employee. Each dimension of employee behaviour is assessed on a scale of 1 to 7.

Job knowledge	Customer service	Attitude	Discipline
2	3	1	3
3	2	4	6
4	4	4	3
5	4	6	7
7	6	5	7
7	6	6	7
3	7	2	1

FIGURE 3.56 Dataset for Data Skill Challenge 1

2 Current employee gender, employee salary, sales by employee and productivity ratios (sales divided by salary) appear in Figure 3.57. Compute all appropriate central tendency and variability statistics.

Gender	Salary	Sales	Productivity
M	30000	160000	5.33
F	19000	90000	4.74
M	22000	102000	4.64
M	28000	131000	4.68
F	17000	97000	5.71
F	22000	110000	5.00
M	23000	148000	6.43

FIGURE 3.57 Dataset for Data Skill Challenge 2

3 Jamal from Chapter 2 is interested in numerically summarizing the variables from his research on his business's website. Open the **chapter2case** dataset and produce meaningful central tendency and variability statistics for the **minutes** and **purchases** variables.

4 Ben from Chapter 1 is interested in numerically summarizing the results of his survey. Open the **chapter1** dataset and produce meaningful central tendency and variability statistics for the **Q1**, **Q2** and **Q3** variables.

(Continued)

(Continued)

NEW TERMS

assumption: bias: central tendency: deviation: fill: mean: median: mode: negative skew: normal distribution: outlier: parameter: positive skew: precision: range: robustness: skew: standard deviation: statistic: variability: variance:

NEW STATISTICAL NOTATION AND FORMULAS

Σ: capital Greek letter sigma, pronounced 'sum of' in formulas

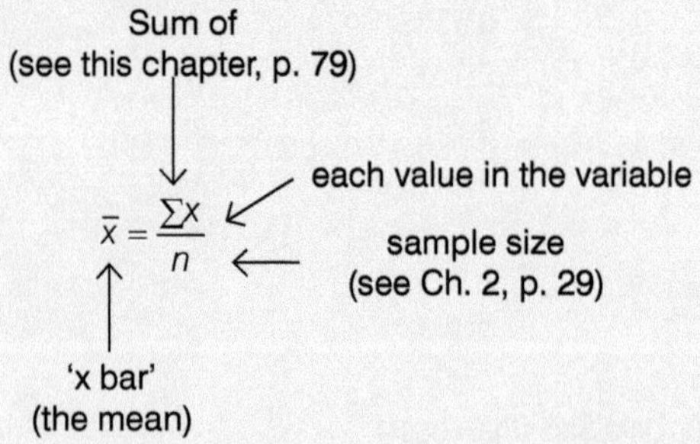

$$\bar{x} = \frac{\sum x}{n}$$

Sum of
(see this chapter, p. 79)

each value in the variable

sample size
(see Ch. 2, p. 29)

'x bar'
(the mean)

FIGURE 3.58   Annotated formula for sample mean

$$\text{range} = x_{\text{largest}} - x_{\text{smallest}}$$

FIGURE 3.59   Formula for range

$$\text{deviation} = x - \mu \frac{1}{2}$$

FIGURE 3.60   Formula for deviation

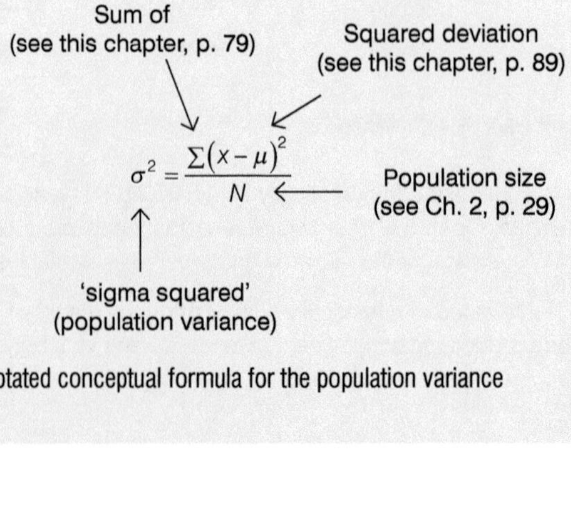

$$\sigma^2 = \frac{\sum (x - \mu)^2}{N}$$

Sum of
(see this chapter, p. 79)

Squared deviation
(see this chapter, p. 89)

Population size
(see Ch. 2, p. 29)

'sigma squared'
(population variance)

FIGURE 3.61   Annotated conceptual formula for the population variance

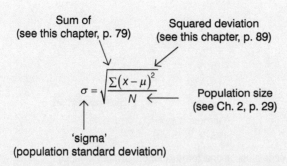

FIGURE 3.62   Annotated conceptual formula for the population standard deviation

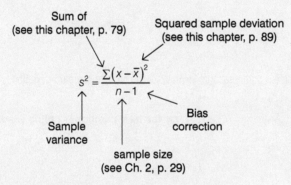

FIGURE 3.63   Annotated conceptual formula for the sample variance

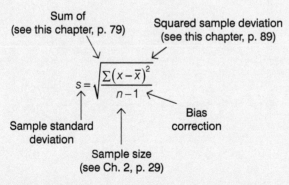

FIGURE 3.64   Annotated conceptual formula for the sample standard deviation

(Continued)

(Continued)

$$s^2 = \dfrac{\Sigma x^2 - \dfrac{(\Sigma x)^2}{n}}{n-1}$$

Bias correction

Sample size
(see Ch. 2, p. 29)

FIGURE 3.65   Annotated computational formula for the sample variance

$$s = \sqrt{\dfrac{\Sigma x^2 - \dfrac{(\Sigma x)^2}{n}}{n-1}}$$

Bias correction

Sample size
(see Ch. 2, p. 29)

FIGURE 3.66   Annotated computational formula for the sample standard deviation

Visit https://study.sagepub.com/landers2e **for free additional online resources related to this chapter.**

4 PROBABILITY DISTRIBUTIONS

WHAT YOU WILL LEARN FROM THIS CHAPTER

- How to work with and interpret probabilities
- How to distinguish between normal, uniform and Poisson distributions
- How to predict the probability of cases based upon the normal distribution
- How to round appropriately so as to minimize errors
- How to convert between raw data, z-scores and proportions
- How to identify when it is appropriate to convert between raw data, z-scores and proportions

DATA SKILLS YOU WILL MASTER FROM THIS CHAPTER

- Computing z-scores
- Computing the mean of variables
- Computing percentiles

CASE STUDY   WHO NEEDS EXTRA TRAINING?

Jill is the owner of Jill's Used Cars, a used vehicle business with a staff of 55 salespeople. With her new-found knowledge from previous chapters of this text, Jill decided it would be useful to analyse sales to see how well her employees were performing relative to each other. Because she wanted to examine employees' previous patterns of sales, and based upon reading Chapter 1, she decided to use a correlational design. Because part of her organization's mission

(Continued)

(Continued)

was to sell 'the best car for the customer', she decided to operationalize monthly sales as number of vehicles sold instead of the value of those vehicles.

This didn't require much additional effort on Jill's part, because she'd already been recording monthly sales for each employee and writing them on a whiteboard in the break room. This, she hoped, would motivate her salespeople to sell more. If the poorer-performing sellers could see how much the top sellers were bringing in, and they knew how much commission those sellers were earning for their increased sales, they might be motivated to sell a bit more. But in watching sales from month to month, Jill has noticed that her salespeople tend to stay around the same performance level relative to their peers.

Most of her salespeople have been working for her for three or more years. Jill believes the interrelationships between her team members are important, so she wants to keep as many

employees as she can. She doesn't want to let anyone go unless there's no other option. But some of her employees definitely need help to perform at a satisfactory level.

Last week, Jill received an e-mail from an online training provider offering an intensive online sales seminar. It looks very promising, but it's expensive. Jill only wants to provide training to those who will benefit most from it. From reading Chapter 3, she has identified the mean and variability of the monthly sales numbers for the past six months. There is quite a bit of variability, as she suspected, and sales month-to-month are often quite different. But that doesn't tell her anything about individual employees. Just how different are each of their sales numbers? What's the best way to compare employees with each other across months?

Take a look at Jill's employee sales data for yourself in chapter4.xls (Excel) or chapter4.sav (SPSS).

Jill's problem is a common one. Although employee success varies, it's not immediately clear just how meaningful that variance is when considering the success of individuals. As we learned in Chapter 3, measures of central tendency and variability are excellent ways to precisely consider the quantitative characteristics of a group in aggregate. But those statistics alone don't tell us much if we need to make judgements about individuals within those groups.

In this case study, to compare employees, Jill's only option so far is to compare the raw numbers of sales between employees. But if one employee sells 10 vehicles and another sells 11 vehicles, is the one that sold 11 vehicles really a 'better' seller? Or is it, perhaps, that the seller was just lucky? In statistics, we refer to luck as chance, and one of the major goals of statistics is to explore and explain the effects of chance.

We began our exploration of chance in Chapter 3 by learning about the normal distribution. But why do data tend to be normally distributed? Are there other common distributions of data? In this chapter, we will begin our exploration of chance by considering several common shapes of data and why we tend to see these shapes. As you read, consider how knowledge of these distributions can help Jill understand the relative performance of her employees.

4.1 PROBABILITY

To identify why data typically appear in the various shapes they appear in, we first need to explore the concept of probability. Probability, broadly, refers to how likely a specific event is to occur. It is typically expressed as a proportion (see Chapter 2, p. 27) and ranges from .00 (a specific event will never occur) to 1.00 (a specific event will always occur). One of the major purposes of statistics is to accurately assess probabilities associated with data.

In some cases, probability is very easy to compute. For example, consider a coin – one side is heads; the other is tails. Any time you toss the coin in the air and let it fall, it will land either heads-up or tails-up. If there's nothing strange about the coin, it will fall heads-up about half of the time and tails-up the other half of the time. Thus, the probability of heads is .50. The probability of tails is also .50.

As we add more possible outcomes, the probabilities become more complex. Next consider a five-sided die with the numbers 0, 1, 2, 3 and 4 on its sides. The probability that any particular number will land facing up when rolling that die is 1/5, which we can express as a probability as .20. Thus, the probability of a 0 is .20, 1 is .20, 2 is .20, 3 is .20 and 4 is .20. All together, these numbers add up to 1.00, since with any given roll of the die, one of these numbers will appear 100% of the time.

If we didn't know ahead of time the probabilities associated with this, we could use a process called the classical method of assigning probability. The classical method involves simply doing the thing you're curious about many, many times, and then calculating how many times each outcome occurred relative to the total. For example, let's roll our five-sided die 10000 times. In doing so, you might end up with 1942 rolls of 1, 2029 rolls of 2, 2013 rolls of 3, 2038 rolls of 4, and 1978 rolls of 5. By calculating relative frequencies (for example, 1942/10000 = .1942), you can see that each is very close to .2. If I were really going to assign a probability to each size using this method, I'd want to collect many more than 10000 cases to make those numbers more stable and closer to .2.

An alternative way to assign probabilities is the relative frequency of occurrence method of assigning probability in which historical data are consulted. For example, if we want to know the probability that the person we just hired will quit within six months, we could consult our company's human resources records to determine the relative frequency of newly hired employees that quit within six months. If we found that 56 out of the 178 people we've ever hired had quit in the last six months, we could conclude that the probability of the new hire quitting is also 56/178 = .31, or a 31% chance.

In organizational research, probability is much more complicated, because we typically don't know the total number of possibilities. In our case study, how likely is it that an employee will sell ten cars in any particular month? What about six or 30? Should we consider 100? We could use the relatively frequency of occurrence method, but how do we know if last month's sales or this month last year's sales is a better choice? These are the problems that keep statisticians up at night. Without a list of every possibility, we cannot compute a specific, precise probability that any of these events will occur.

Fortunately, data typically take one of several common shapes, and we can compute the probability of data occurring within any of these shapes. The next sections will explore what these shapes look like and the relative probabilities of the data they contain.

COMBINING PROBABILITIES

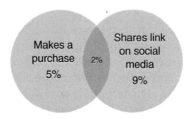

FIGURE 4.01   Unions and intersections

Sometimes you need to think and talk about probabilities in relation to one another. In these cases, probability often does not work the way that people intuitively think it should. In Figure 4.01, I've depicted three relative frequencies reported by a marketing department related to the performance of a product on their sales website. 5% of customers viewing the product purchase it. 9% of customers viewing it share a link to it on social media. 2% of customers do both. Implied by this diagram then is that 100% − 5% − 9% − 2% = 84% of customers viewing this product neither purchase it nor share a link. We can utilize the relative frequency of occurrence method to convert these numbers into probabilities; for example, the probability of a customer viewing this page making a purchase is .05.

So what is the probability that a customer will make a purchase *or* share a link? Combining probabilities this way is called union and is signified by the word 'or'. To calculate this probability, we need to *add together* all of the component probabilities. In this case, 5% + 2% + 9% = 16%. Thus, the probability of a customer seeing this webpage making a purchase or sharing a link is .16.

But what if we want to know the probability a customer will make a purchase *and* share a link? Combining probabilities is called intersection and is signified by the word 'and'. To calculate this probability, we need to simply look at the intersection point alone: 2%. Thus, the probability of a customer seeing this webpage making a purchase and sharing a link is .02.

If making a purchase and sharing a link were unrelated events, which is to say if we assumed the occurrence of one does not affect the other and that nothing externally affects them together, we'd expect the probability of intersection to be the value of the two component probabilities multiplied together. In this case, we'd expect a probability of .05 * .09 = .0045 for people to both make a purchase and share a link. Because the observed value, .02, is much higher than that, we could conclude that they probably are related. This is the basic logic of hypothesis testing, which we'll explore in much greater detail starting in Chapter 7.

4.2 DISTRIBUTIONS OF DATA

Data take different shapes, called distributions. There are several common distributions, three of which we'll cover in this chapter. It's important to realize that distributions are prototypes; 'real' data never conform perfectly to any prototype. You've already seen several examples of this in the previous chapter; although the normal distribution is a nice, predictable bell-shaped curve, the data you examined in the examples and case study created only a vaguely bell-shaped histogram.

Most statistical tests (especially the ones we cover in this book) are fairly robust (see Chapter 3, p. 80) to small variations from prototype distributions. For example, in the last chapter we learned that the mode and median reflect central tendency even if the data are skewed. So don't worry too much that the data you collect to answer your organization's research questions don't perfectly represent the prototypes. You just need to know which distribution to expect given your data and take a look at a histogram to verify that it is roughly the shape you're expecting.

4.2.1 UNIFORM DISTRIBUTION

The simplest data distribution is the uniform distribution. In a uniform distribution, every possibility is equally probable. We don't see this distribution very much among organizational data, but it is easy to interpret, so it's a good place to start.

Let's return briefly to die-rolling, this time with a ten-sided die with sides numbered from 1 to 10. If we were to roll our ten-sided die 50 times, we'd expect each number to appear five times. This is because each side is equally probable: each roll, the probability of any particular side appearing on the top of the die is .10. A bar graph of our expectations appears in Figure 4.02.

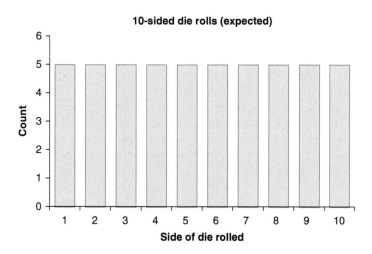

FIGURE 4.02   Expected sample of n = 50 die rolls drawn from a uniform distribution

If we were to actually roll a ten-sided die 50 times, it's very unlikely we'd see such a perfect distribution. However, you can easily see why the distribution is called 'uniform' – all options are equally probable. With real data, we'd be more likely to see something like the two samples in Figure 4.03.

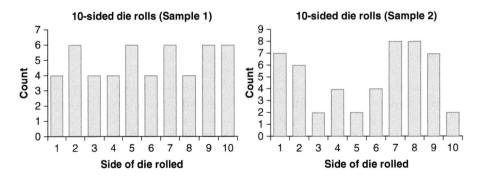

FIGURE 4.03   Examples of observed samples (*n* = 50) drawn from a uniform distribution

Both of these figures show data from 50 rolls of a 10-sided die. Yet, they look dramatically different from our expected distribution. This is because of chance. Although we expect a perfectly uniform distribution, real data are typically messy, as we see here, and luck alone can lead to substantial variation from the expected distribution. The more that data deviate from an expected distribution, the more sceptical we must be when interpreting statistics that expect that distribution. Fortunately, there's a fairly easy way to get closer-to-expected distributions of real data: large samples. We'll discuss this principle in much more detail in the next chapter.

4.2.2 POISSON DISTRIBUTION

The Poisson (pronounced: pwah-SAHN) distribution describes data containing small numbers of independent counts. It typically occurs when there are a small number of observations for a relatively large number of opportunities for those observations to occur. Like the normal distribution, it is a spread of random data.

Consider an example of how a Poisson distribution might appear in an organizational context. In a call centre, employees are rarely asked by the people they are calling to escalate the call to a supervisor. Every customer has the power to ask this, but relatively few actually do. On average, the call centre handles two elevated calls per day. This creates the Poisson distribution in Figure 4.04.

Thus, on roughly 13.5% of days, the call centre has no escalated calls. On 27% of days, the call centre has one escalated call. On 27% of days, the call centre has two. On 18% of days, the call centre has three. On 9% of days, the call centre has four (and so on).

This distribution thus appears similar to the skewed normal distribution we discussed in Chapter 3, with one key difference: it only applies to discrete, nominal data (counts; see Chapter 1, p. 8).

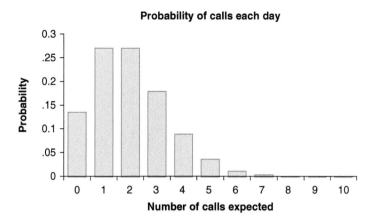

FIGURE 4.04   Example of a Poisson distribution from a call centre

4.2.3 NORMAL (AND STANDARD NORMAL) DISTRIBUTIONS

FOUNDATION CONCEPTS

A **normal distribution** is a common shape in which data are found resembling a bell or hill. See Chapter 3, p. 77.

The **standard deviation** is the average distance between all scores in a variable and their mean, represented in a population as σ (sigma) and in a sample as s, and is also the square root of the variance. See Chapter 3, p. 90.

Normal distributions are the most common shape of data you are likely to see, especially if you ask many organizational questions with surveys. We learned a bit about these distributions in Chapter 3. When data are normally distributed, cases are more likely to occur close to the mean and increasingly unlikely to appear the further we move away from the mean in either direction. This is what creates the bell shape.

We sometimes refer to the standard normal distribution, which is a perfectly normal distribution with a mean of zero and a standard deviation of one ($\mu = 0$; $\sigma = 1$). This is also called a z-distribution. You can see a z-distribution in Figure 4.05.

The standard normal distribution is useful because it is defined in terms of standard deviations. When looking at a standard normal distribution, -2 is two standard deviations below the mean, -1 is one standard deviation below the mean, 0 is the mean, $+1$ is one standard deviation above the mean, and $+2$ is two standard deviations above the mean. These numbers are called z-scores. They don't need to be whole numbers; for example, $z = -1.29$ describes a score 1.29 standard deviations below the mean. A z-score can be calculated from the scores in any dataset.

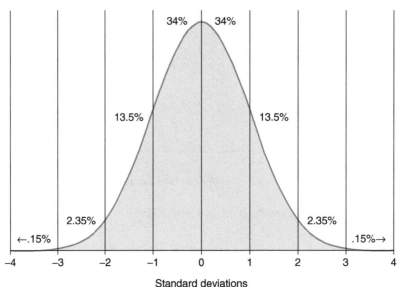

Standard normal (z) distribution

FIGURE 4.05   Normal (z) distribution and percentage of cases under the curve divided between standard deviations

WHY MIGHT DATA THAT WE EXPECT TO BE NORMAL BE SKEWED?

When there is some restriction that prevents normally distributed data from moving away from the mean in both directions, it bunches up wherever it is blocked, creating skew. This creates a problem in organizational research because skew distorts the results of many common statistical tests.

For example, the collection of supervisory ratings of job performance is often tricky for organizational researchers because many supervisors rate their direct reports (the employees that report to them) very highly. There are many reasons for this. Some supervisors don't want to expose their direct reports to the risk of layoffs. Others have personal relationships with their direct reports and don't want to rate them poorly regardless of their actual performance. Still other supervisors have a difficult time assessing the job performance of others so, to be safe, they rate every direct report identically.

Regardless of the reason, when responding to a five-point survey question about employee job performance where five is the strongest response, the mode will often be a five. Although we'd expect these data to be normally distributed, because there are no options higher than five, the data will be negatively skewed.

When analysing organizational data, z-scores are helpful because they can be **standardized** from **raw data**. Raw data are data as they are collected and thus cannot be compared across dissimilar variables. For example, it is impossible to directly compare 18 sales with a rating of '4' from a supervisor. However, each of these values can be standardized so that they are comparable. For example, 18 sales may be $z = 1.1$ (1.1 standard deviations above the mean) while '4' is $z = -.2$ (.2 standard deviations below the mean). Therefore, this employee is above average in sales but slightly below average in supervisory ratings.

By standardizing, we can compare these numbers directly with one another (below average in one regard; above average in another regard).

In our case study, standardization is critical because sales fluctuate radically by month, regardless of employee performance. Consider an employee whose raw sales in July and December are 10 and 10. Doesn't look bad, right? But if we convert these values to z-scores, we find that this employee's July sales were $z = -.10$, whereas his December sales were $z = -1.15$. From these standardized scores, we can conclude that this employee was slightly below average in July and very below average in December. This information was not obvious from the raw data alone. Car sales are simply higher in some months than others. By converting monthly sales to z-scores, we can therefore more accurately assess how well employees are doing relative to their co-workers.

4.3 PROPORTIONS OF CASES WITHIN NORMALLY DISTRIBUTED DATA

FOUNDATION CONCEPTS

A **proportion** is a portion of a whole represented as a decimal. For example, .35 is a proportion indicating 35 for every 100. See Chapter 2, p. 27.

A **percentage** is a portion of a whole represented as its share of 100. For example, 35% is a percentage indicating 35 for every 100. See Chapter 2, p. 28.

One of the advantages to collecting and analysing data that conform to a normal distribution is that the normal distribution is highly predictable. If we collected a large amount of normally distributed data, we would expect that:

- .15% (.0015) of cases fall below −3 standard deviations.

- 2.35% (.0235) of cases fall between −3 and −2 standard deviations.

- 13.5% (.1350) of cases fall between −2 and −1 standard deviations.

- 34.0% (.3400) of cases fall between −1 standard deviation and the mean (0).

- 34.0% (.3400) of cases fall between the mean (0) and +1 standard deviation.

- 13.5% (.1350) of cases fall between +1 and +2 standard deviations.

- 2.35% (.0235) of cases fall between +2 and +3 standard deviations.

- .15% (.0015) of cases fall above +3 standard deviations.

We also have some broader expectations:

- 50% (.50) of cases fall above the mean (0).

- 50% (.50) of cases fall below the mean (0).

You can actually *see* these percentages in Figure 4.05 above. Since the distribution represents 100% of the data, we can cut it up and look at the area under the curve to identify what percentage of cases fall between any two particular points of interest.

For example, if an employee's job performance was $z = +1$, that employee's performance would be higher than roughly 84% of her fellow employees. I got this number by adding the percentage of cases falling below the mean (50%) and the percentage of cases between 0 and +1 standard deviations (34%). That employee's performance would also be below approximately 16% of employees (13.5% + 2.35% + 0.15%).

By converting between raw scores, z-scores and the proportion of cases associated with particular z-scores, we can make many meaningful conclusions about the frequency of values relative to their populations. Exploring this concept mathematically will make up the remainder of this chapter.

4.3.1 CONVERTING FROM RAW DATA TO Z-SCORES

ACCOUNTING FOR ROUNDING ERROR

If you are using this textbook as part of a course, and you haven't talked about it already, this is an excellent point at which to talk to your instructor about measurement precision. Calculation in statistics often involves working with very small numbers, and the computations you'll be doing with z-scores are no exception. Every time you round a value, you lose a little bit of precision, which can lead to your final answer being incorrect.

To account for this, this text recommends carrying out all computations to six decimal places mid-computation, only then rounding the final answer to two decimal places. All computations displayed in this text from this point forward will adopt this strategy. However, if you are using this text for a course, your instructor may want your final answers to be more or less precise; if you don't know your instructor's expectation on this yet, you should ask as soon as possible.

To convert a raw score to a z-score, you must know the mean and standard deviation of the sample or population you want to compare it with. You might calculate this yourself from a dataset, or you might be given this information.

If you were analysing data from within your own organization, you would probably have access to the raw data and would therefore be able to compute the mean and standard deviation for yourself. But there are times when you might not have access to this information, or you might want to compare it with population data. Whichever mean and standard deviation you choose, this will be the comparison group for your z-scores.

For example, if you were worried about the attitudes toward customer service shown by some of your employees, you might hire a consultant to administer a customer service survey to them to assess this. After getting the results, you don't necessarily want to know how your employees compare with each other – instead, you want to know how they compare with customer service employees *in general*. In this case, you might ask the consultant to provide the mean and standard deviation of their survey across all employees they've ever assessed. Any z-scores computed with this mean and standard deviation will be in reference to that group. A $z = -1$ in this context would indicate an employee with customer service attitudes one standard deviation below employees *in general*.

Regardless of the source of your comparison group, the formulas for converting a raw score to a z-score are similar whether you have samples or populations for comparison – see Figures 4.06 and 4.07.

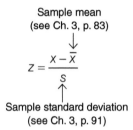

Sample mean
(see Ch. 3, p. 83)

$$z = \frac{X - \bar{X}}{S}$$

Sample standard deviation
(see Ch. 3, p. 91)

FIGURE 4.06   Annotated z-score formula for a sample

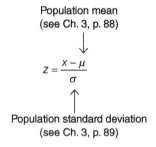

Population mean
(see Ch. 3, p. 88)

$$z = \frac{X - \mu}{\sigma}$$

Population standard deviation
(see Ch. 3, p. 89)

FIGURE 4.07   Annotated z-score formula for a population

Take a moment to think about why the z-score formula is constructed this way. In each formula, we first subtract the sample or population mean from the value we're interested in. This results in a difference score representing the distance between the score and the mean. In the second step, we divide this difference by the standard deviation to convert the difference to standard deviation units.

As an example, consider the value of '15' sales from our case study dataset, coming from November sales. The mean of November sales is 12.327272, while the standard deviation of November sales is 4.830668. In the first step of the computation, we calculate $15 - 12.327272$, which gives us 2.672728. This number indicates the difference in sales between the case and the mean; in other words, 15 sales is 2.672728 sales higher than the mean. In the second step of the computation, we divide 2.672728 by the standard deviation, 4.830668, which gives us .553283. Therefore, the score is .55 standard deviations above the mean, and $z = .55$.

If we think about the relationship between these two numbers, this should seem obvious. 2.672728 is roughly half of 4.830668, so a z of .55 makes sense – the score (15) and the mean (12.327272) are roughly half of one standard deviation apart. We can see the steps of this computation in Figure 4.08, broken down step by step.

4.3.2 CONVERTING FROM Z-SCORES TO RAW DATA

To convert a raw score to a z-score, use the formula in Figure 4.08 in reverse. The formula solves for z, but we want to solve for x. Fortunately, as you can see from Figure 4.09, it's quite easy to convert.

$$z = \frac{x - \bar{x}}{s}$$

$$= \frac{15 - 12.327272}{4.830668}$$

$$= \frac{2.672728}{4.830668}$$

$$= .553283 = .55$$

FIGURE 4.08   Step by step calculation of a z-score from a sample

From this, you can see that converting a z-score back to a raw score requires you to know three pieces of information: the z-score, the standard deviation and the mean. This formula, like the one before, can be expressed in terms of either samples or populations (Figures 4.10 and 4.11).

Here's the starting formula:

$$z = \frac{x - \bar{x}}{s}$$

Next, we multiply both sides by s: $\quad zs = x - \bar{x}$

Finally, we add $\bar{x}$ to both sides: $\quad zs + \bar{x} = x$

FIGURE 4.09   Algebraically modifying z-score formula to solve for a raw score

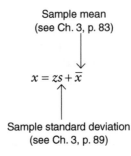

Sample mean
(see Ch. 3, p. 83)

$$x = zs + \bar{x}$$

Sample standard deviation
(see Ch. 3, p. 89)

FIGURE 4.10   Annotated formula to calculate a raw score from a sample z-score

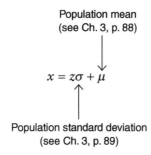

Population mean
(see Ch. 3, p. 88)

$$x = z\sigma + \mu$$

Population standard deviation
(see Ch. 3, p. 89)

FIGURE 4.11   Annotated formula to calculate a raw score from a population z-score

In our case study dataset, imagine that Jill wanted to reward every employee selling more than +2 standard deviations of vehicles in November. What score would she look for? We'll use the same values from the example in the previous section: the mean of November sales is 12.327272, while the standard deviation of November sales is 4.830668 – see Figure 4.12.

$$x = zs + \bar{x}$$
$$= 2(4.830668) + 12.327272$$
$$= 9.661336 + 12.327272$$
$$= 21.988608 = 21.99$$

FIGURE 4.12   Step by step calculation of a raw score from a sample z-score

Thus, Jill would reward anyone selling 22 or more vehicles in November.

4.3.3 CONVERTING FROM Z-SCORES TO PROPORTIONS

Although conversions between raw scores and z-scores are interesting, the most useful information is when we then convert those z-scores to proportions. We've already done some simple conversions using the proportions associated with $z = -3, -2, -1, 0, 1, 2$ and 3 shown in the normal distribution in Figure 4.05 above. For example, 84% of cases fall above $z = -1$ (50% + 34%). But what if we want proportions for other z-scores? For that, we must reference the z-table, which appears in Appendix A1 (see p. 424).

In the z-table, you'll see columns and rows representing z-scores. To find the value in the table corresponding to any particular z-score, add the numbers you find at the top of the table with the numbers you find on the left side of the table. For example, if you want to find $z = 2.36$, look for the row labelled 2.3 and the column labelled .06. The value where these two numbers intersect is .0091 (Figure 4.13).

z	0	0.01	0.02	0.03	0.04	0.05	0.06	0.07	0.08	0.09
2	0.0228	0.0222	0.0217	0.0212	0.0207	0.0202	0.0197	0.0192	0.0188	0.0183
2.1	0.0179	0.0174	0.0170	0.0166	0.0162	0.0158	0.0154	0.0150	0.0146	0.0143
2,2	0.0139	0.0136	0.0132	0.0129	0.0125	0.0122	0.0119	0.0116	0,0113	0.0110
2.3	0.0107	0.0104	0.0102	0.0099	0.0096	0.0094	0.0091	0.0089	0.0087	0.0084
2.4	0.0082	0.0080	0.0078	0.0075	0.0073	0.0071	0.0069	0.0068	0.0066	0.0064
2.5	0.0062	0,0060	0.0059	0,0057	0.0055	0.0054	0,0052	0.0051	0.0049	0.0048
2.6	0.0047	0.0045	0.0044	0.0043	0.0041	0.0040	0.0039	0.0038	0.0037	0.0036
2.7	0_0035	0,0034	0.0033	0,0032	0.0031	0.0030	0.0029	0.0028	0.0027	0.0026
2.8	0.0026	0,0025	0.0024	0.0023	0.0023	0.0022	0.0021	0.0021	0.0020	0.0019
2.9	0.0019	0.0018	0.0018	0.0017	0.0016	0.0016	0.0015	0.0015	0.0014	0.0014

FIGURE 4.13 Locating a z-score in the z-table (Appendix A1)

So what does this value mean? This is the proportion of cases falling *above* this positive z-score. Thus, .91% of cases fall above $z = 2.36$. To determine how many cases fall *below* this point, subtract it from 1. In this example, $1 - .0091 = .9909$. Therefore, 99.09% of cases fall below $z = 2.36$. You can see this graphically in Figure 4.14.

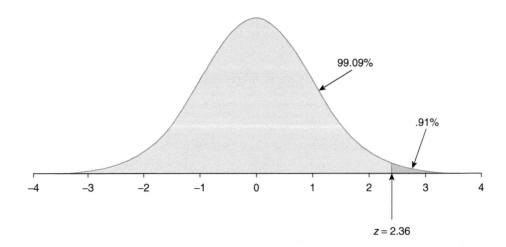

FIGURE 4.14 z-distribution and percentage of cases falling above $z = +2.36$, based upon the z-table

We sometimes refer to the smaller portion of this graph as the positive 'tail' of the distribution. So what do we do if our z is negative? The process is exactly the same – because the z-distribution is symmetrical, the proportions are the same on the negative tail. Simply look up the value associated with the positive z-score (Figure 4.15).

So given this, what's the proportion of values *outside* z ±2.36? Just add them together: .91% + .91% = 1.82%. We can then compute the remainder (the values *inside* z ±2.36) as $1 - .0182 = 98.18\%$ (Figure 4.16). The distribution always contains a total of 100% of all values. In this case, .91% + 98.18% + .91% = 100%.

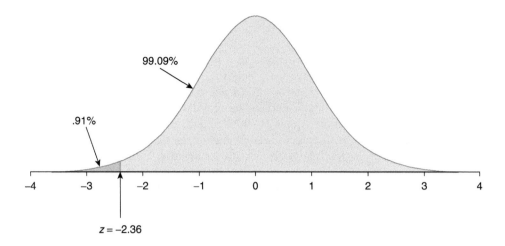

FIGURE 4.15   z-distribution and percentage of cases falling below z = −2.36, based upon the z-table

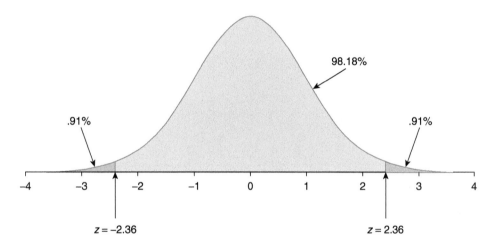

FIGURE 4.16   z-distribution and percentage of cases falling outside of z = ±2.36, based upon the z-table

WHY DOES THE Z-TABLE END AT 3.59?

Sometimes, when looking at the z-table, students conclude that z must always be between −3.59 and +3.59. This is not true! In fact, a z-score can be absolutely any value from negative infinity to positive infinity. Values below −3.59 or above 3.59 are simply extremely uncommon.

For example, if we look in Appendix A1, we see that the proportion associated with 3.59 is .0002. That means that only 0.02% of cases fall above 3.59 or below −3.59 (or .04% of cases beyond both). That is, we'd expect only four cases per 10000 to be this or more extreme. That doesn't mean these scores don't exist; in fact, you'll find these in your own data from time to time if you work with statistics long enough. It just means that you don't see them very often!

4.3.4 CONVERTING FROM PROPORTIONS TO Z-SCORES

Just as we might need to convert a *z*-score into a proportion, we might need to convert a proportion into a *z*-score. To do this, we simply follow the procedure above in reverse.

We need to do this most often when we are interested in percentiles. A percentile represents the point at which a particular percentage of a dataset falls below a specific point. For example, if the 90th percentile equals 10, 90% of data are smaller than 10 and 10% of data are bigger than 10. The 50th percentile is the median (see Chapter 3, p. 81) – the point at which 50% of data are bigger and 50% of data are smaller. You might see a percentile expressed as a proportion (e.g. the 30th percentile might be represented as .30).

So when converting between proportions and *z*-scores, you might see a question like this: 'What *z*-score corresponds to the 63rd percentile?' When trying to answer such questions, draw it to help yourself visualize what the question is asking. The 63rd percentile is greater than the median (the 50th percentile), so the dividing line will be somewhere on the right side of the distribution. 63% of scores fall below the point you're interested in, which means that 37% (100% − 63%) fall above it. It doesn't matter exactly where you draw the line, as long as it's on the correct side of the median. What you draw should look something like Figure 4.17.

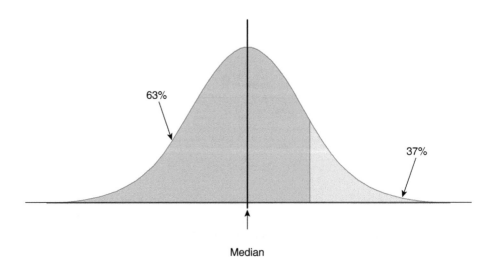

63%

37%

Median

FIGURE 4.17 The 63rd percentile of a *z*-distribution

Although the question asks about the '63rd percentile', the *z*-table only contains information about the tails. So instead of 63%, you'll be looking up 37%.

Next, scan the *z*-table in Appendix A1 until you find the two proportions that surround .37 – one bigger and one smaller. In this case, the two closest proportions are .3707 and .3669. The cell we will concentrate on will be .3707, as it is closer to .37. As before, add together the column and row headings to determine the associated *z*-score. In this case, .3707 is in row .3 and column .03 (Figure 4.18). Thus, the *z*-score we're looking for is .3 + .03 = .33. The 63rd percentile corresponds to *z* = .33.

z	0	0.01	0.02	0.03	0.04	0.05	0.06	0.07	0.08	0.09
0	0.5000	0.4960	0.4920	0.4880	0.4840	0.4801	0.4761	0.4721	0.4681	0.4641
0.1	0.4602	0.4562	0.4522	0.4483	0.4443	0.4404	0.4364	0.4325	0.4286	0,4247
0.2	0.4207	0.4168	0.4129	0.4090	0.4052	0.4013	0.3974	0.3936	0.3897	0.3859
0.3	0.3821	0.3783	0.3745	0.3707	0.3669	0.3632	0.3594	0.3557	0.3520	0.3483
0.4	0.3446	0.3409	0,3372	0.3336	0.3300	0.3264	0,3228	0.3192	0.3156	0.3121
0.5	0.3085	0.3050	0.3015	0.2981	0.2946	0.2912	0.2877	0,2843	0.2810	0,2776
0.6	0.2743	0.2709	0.2676	0.2643	0.2611	0.2578	0.2546	0,2514	0.2483	0.2451

FIGURE 4.18 Identifying the z-score corresponding to the 63rd percentile

If the z-score we were looking for was on the left side of the median, we'd simply use a minus sign with that value to reflect the negative z-score. You can use this general procedure for any type of conversion between a proportion and a z-score.

4.3.5 CONVERTING BETWEEN PROPORTIONS AND RAW DATA

When converting between raw data, z-scores and proportions, you will always use some combination of the tools listed above. These relationships are illustrated in Figure 4.19.

FIGURE 4.19 Illustration of necessary conversions between raw data and proportions/percentiles

You can consult Figure 4.19 whenever asked to make a conversion. For example, imagine you were provided a proportion and asked to identify the raw score at which that proportion would be found. Since you can never convert directly from a proportion, you must convert to a z-score first.

For example, in our case study, what would Jill do if she wanted to identify how many cars an employee would have sold in August if that employee was performing at the 20th percentile. From the data, we know that the mean of August sales is 9.727273 and its standard deviation is 2.805118.

First, Jill needs to draw it out (Figure 4.20).

This time, 20% of values fall in the tail, so that's the number we'll look up. When looking in the z-table (Appendix A1), the two closest values we can find are .2005 and .1977. The closer is .2005, so we'll use that – its associated z-value is .84 (Figure 4.21). Because the tail is on the left side of the distribution, we know that the z-score is negative; thus, the z-score associated with the 20th percentile is $z = -.84$.

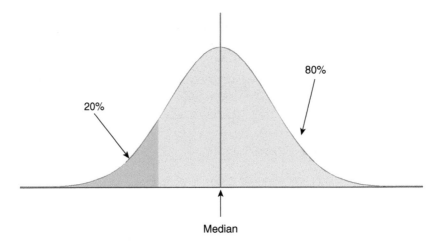

FIGURE 4.20   Drawing of 20th percentile with relevant percentages

z	0	0.01	0.02	0.03	0.04	0.05	0.06	0.07	0.08	0.09
0	0.5000	0.4960	0.4920	0.4880	0.4840	0.4801	0.4761	0.4721	0.4681	0.4641
0.1	0.4602	0.4562	0.4522	0.4483	0.4443	0.4404	0.4364	0.4325	0.4286	0,4247
0.2	0.4207	0.4168	0.4129	0.4090	0.4052	0.4013	0.3974	0.3936	0.3897	0.3859
0.3	0.3821	0.3783	0.3745	0.3707	0.3669	0.3632	0.3594	0.3557	0.3520	0.3483
0.4	0.3446	0.3409	0,3372	0.3336	0.3300	0.3264	0,3228	0.3192	0.3156	0.3121
0.5	0.3085	0.3050	0.3015	0.2981	0.2946	0.2912	0.2877	0,2843	0.2810	0,2776
0.6	0.2743	0.2709	0.2676	0.2643	0.2611	0.2578	0.2546	0,2514	0.2483	0.2451
0.7	0.2420	0,2389	0,2358	0.2327	0.2296	0.2266	0.2236	0.2206	0.2177	0,2148
0.8	0.2119	0,2090	0.2061	0.2033	0.2005	0,1977	0.1949	0.1922	0.1894	0,1867
0.9	0.1841	0.1814	0.1788	0.1762	0.1736	0.1711	0.1685	0.1660	0.1635	0.1611

FIGURE 4.21   Looking up the 20th percentile in the z-table (Appendix A1)

Next, we need to use the formula above to convert z-scores to raw data. The mean and standard deviation are provided in the question, so we'll use those values in the formula (Figure 4.22).

$$x = zs + \bar{x}$$
$$x = -.84 * 2.805118 + 9.727273$$
$$x = -2.356299 + 9.727273$$
$$x = 7.370974 = 7.37$$

FIGURE 4.22   Step by step calculation of raw score from a percentile

Thus, the 20th percentile is associated with 7.37 cars sold.

SUMMARY OF CONVERSIONS WITH Z-SCORES

Conversion from	Information needed	Procedure/formula used
Raw data to z-score	A score, the mean, and the standard deviation. You may need to calculate the mean and standard deviation or they may be provided for you.	Sample mean (see Ch. 3, p. 83) $$z = \frac{x - \bar{x}}{s}$$ Sample standard deviation (see Ch. 3, p. 89) Population mean (see Ch.3, p. 88) $$z = \frac{x - \mu}{\sigma}$$ Sample standard deviation (see Ch. 3, p. 89)
z-scores proportion/ percentile	A z-score and a z-table (found in Appendix A1).	Find the z-score in the z-table by scanning across columns and down rows, adding the column head and row head together. For example, column .03 and row 1.0 intersect at z =.03. The number you find there is the proportion of values found in the tail. It you are interested in the proportion of values in the tail, use this value. If you are interested in the proportion of values in the rest of the distribution, subtract this value from 1.
Proportion/ percentile to z-score	A proportion! percentile and a z-table (found in Appendix A1).	Find the proportion in the z-table by looking for the closest value to the proportion you are looking for. Next, add the numbers found at the left of the row and the top of the column to compute the z-score. For example. the closest proportion to .01 is .0099, which corresponds to $z = 2.33$. If you are identifying a proportion in the lower tail (left side of the distribution), your z-score will be negative.
z-score to raw data	A z-score, the mean, and the standard deviation. You may need to calculate the mean and standard deviation or they may be provided for you.	Sample mean (see Ch. 3, p. 83) $$x = zs + \bar{x}$$ Sample standard deviation (see Ch. 3, p. 89) Population mean (see Ch.3, p. 88) $$x = z\sigma + \mu$$ Sample standard deviation (see Ch. 3, p. 89)

FIGURE 4.23   Summary table of conversions involving z-scores

4.4 APPLYING PROBABILITY DISTRIBUTIONS

To apply what you've learned from this chapter, consider the following case study, questions posed about that case study, and discussion of those questions.

4.4.1 APPLICATION CASE STUDY

Raphael is head sales agent of Where the Heart Is, a residential estate agency. He is responsible for tracking sales for the entire firm. One of the owner's goals is for Where the Heart Is to sell across the full spectrum of the housing market, from the smallest flat to the largest mansion. This, the owner believes, will make the broadest impression on potential clients through word-of-mouth, improving the overall number of clients.

What statistical approach might Raphael use to ensure this goal is being met? He has access to the full list of houses put on the market over the past year, as well as the list of houses managed by Where the Heart Is. What statistics could he use to ensure that the owner's goal is being met?

4.4.2 APPLICATION DISCUSSION

Like most real business scenarios calling for statistics, there are multiple ways to approach Raphael's problem. However, an obvious approach here would be to use z-scores.

Raphael actually has a population – the current housing market. Since the owner's goal is for house values from Where the Heart Is to match those of the market, we can examine the z-score of each house represented by Where the Heart Is in relation to that market.

For example, if houses for Where the Heart Is were $z = +.5$, $z = +1.0$ and $z = +1.3$, we'd know from the mean of these z-scores ($z = +.93$) that the houses Where the Heart Is tends to sell are above average for the current housing market. We could further conclude from that average that houses sold were one standard deviation above the average house sold in the population, which is around the 84th percentile. If the owner's goal was being met, the average z-score should be close to zero, because the average house sold by Where the Heart Is should be approximately equal to the average house on the overall market.

EXPLORING PROBABILITY DISTRIBUTIONS IN EXCEL AND SPSS

EXCEL

Download the Excel dataset for the demonstration below as **chapter4.xls**. As you read this section, try to apply the terms you've learned in this chapter to the dataset and follow along with Excel on your own computer.

You can also get a video demonstration of the section below under **Excel Video: Chapter 4**.

In our case study, Jill is trying to identify which employees are consistently weak in sales. She has collected data on employee sales for the months July through December. Try using the techniques you learned in Chapter 3 to identify the mean and standard deviation of each month. You'll find that there is quite a bit of variation from month to month (if you don't find the values given in Figure 4.24, review Chapter 3's lesson on Excel).

	July	August	Septembe	October	Novembe	December
Mean	9.75	9.73	10.04	10.36	12.33	15.20
SD	2.65	2.81	2.98	3.42	4.83	4.53

FIGURE 4.24 Means and standard deviations from case study dataset in Excel

If we look at any one month, we may not get the whole story; perhaps an employee was simply having a bad month, but it doesn't reflect their overall performance. But if we add all sales across all months for each employee, we may miss patterns of poor performance. For example, what if an employee does well during the December rush, but is consistently poor during all other months? To address this problem, we will convert each month's sales for each employee to z-scores, so that we can identify how well each employee was doing each month relative to his or her co-workers.

First, create six new columns to represent where our new z-values will go (Figure 4.25).

G	H	I	J	K	L
zJuly	zAugust	zSeptemb	zOctober	zNovemb	zDecembe

FIGURE 4.25 Six new column labels for z-scores in Excel

In G2, we want the number we find to represent the z-score for the first employee's July sales. We'll create this formula just like we would if we were doing it by hand: a z-score equals the score minus the mean, all divided by the standard deviation. We'll use the mean and standard deviation formulas we learned in Chapter 3.

1 **Excel 2010 or later:** To compute the z-score in G2, type: =(A2-AVERAGE(A:A))/STDEV.S(A:A).
2 **Excel 2007 or earlier:** To compute the z-score in G2, type: =(A2-AVERAGE(A:A))/STDEV(A:A).

You should end up with something like Figure 4.26.

G2			fx	=(A2-AVERAGE(A:A))/STDEV(A:A)		
	A	B	C	D	E	F	G
1	July	August	Septembe	October	Novembe	December	zJuly
2	12	9	13	15	16	18	0.851647

FIGURE 4.26 Computed z-scores for first case's data in Excel

(Continued)

(Continued)

This formula is a little different than the ones we've used before now. Instead of naming specific cells – like A2:A56 – we've named an entire column. Excel will ignore cells with text in them, like the word 'July'.

This is an important change because it changes how Excel fills formulas. Do you remember the fill from Chapter 3? We did a fill when we clicked on the little black box at the bottom-right corner of a cell and dragged it right to copy the content of the cells we'd highlighted. When you run a fill, Excel automatically updates the references of all cells copied to match wherever you copied them. For example, if you filled one cell right from a cell that referenced A2, the new cell's formula would reference B2 instead (because B2 is one cell to the right of A2).

When filling down, this becomes a problem if we've named specific cells. For example, if we'd named A2:A56 and filled down, the next cell would contain A3:A57, the next would contain A4:A58, and so on. We want our fill to always reference the entire column, so this is incorrect. By referencing A:A instead, Excel will simply copy A:A in every cell. When we fill right, Excel will still know to convert our A:A to B:B.

Do this now – fill down from G2 by highlighting G2 and click-dragging the little black box down to G56. Once at G56, click-drag again to the right to L56. You should now have a new table of values with z-scores for every employee for every month, as in Figure 4.27.

	A	B	C	D	E	F	G	H	I	J	K	L
1	July	August	Septembe	October	Novembe	Decembe	zJuly	zAugust	zSeptemb	zOctober	zNovemb	zDecembe
2	12	9	13	15	16	18	0.851647	-0.25927	0.994109	1.356605	0.760294	0.618472
3	13	13	12	12	12	18	1.229393	1.166699	0.658674	0.478802	-0.06775	0.618472
4	10	10	12	10	10	16	0.096154	0.097225	0.658674	-0.1064	-0.48177	0.176706
5	11	11	11	11	11	14	0.4739	0.453716	0.323238	0.186201	-0.27476	-0.26506
6	3	5	7	6	5	8	-2.54807	-1.68523	-1.0185	-1.27681	-1.51682	-1.59036
7	10	10	10	9	10	12	0.096154	0.097225	-0.0122	-0.399	-0.48177	-0.70683
8	8	9	11	11	15	16	-0.65934	-0.25927	0.323238	0.186201	0.553283	0.176706
9	9	8	9	9	9	13	-0.28159	-0.61576	-0.34763	-0.399	-0.68878	-0.48594
10	10	11	11	14	15	19	0.096154	0.453716	0.323238	1.064004	0.553283	0.839355
11	9	9	10	10	9	12	-0.28159	-0.25927	-0.0122	-0.1064	-0.68878	-0.70683
12	10	10	14	14	13	15	0.096154	0.097225	1.329545	1.064004	0.139262	-0.04418

FIGURE 4.27   Dataset with z-scores filled down in Excel

Now that we have z-scores for every month, we can more meaningfully compute a mean. Create a new column M with the mean of scores in columns G through L. If you aren't sure how to do this, review the Excel portion of Chapter 3 (see p. 96). You should end up with something like Figure 4.28.

G	H	I	J	K	L	M
zJuly	zAugust	zSeptemb	zOctober	zNovemb	zDecembe	zMean
0.851647	-0.25927	0.994109	1.356605	0.760294	0.618472	0.72031
1.229393	1.166699	0.658674	0.478802	-0.06775	0.618472	0.680715
0.096154	0.097225	0.658674	-0.1064	-0.48177	0.176706	0.073431
0.4739	0.453716	0.323238	0.186201	-0.27476	-0.26506	0.149539
-2.54807	-1.68523	-1.0185	-1.27681	-1.51682	-1.59036	-1.60597
0.096154	0.097225	-0.0122	-0.399	-0.48177	-0.70683	-0.2344
-0.65934	-0.25927	0.323238	0.186201	0.553283	0.176706	0.05347
-0.28159	-0.61576	-0.34763	-0.399	-0.68878	-0.48594	-0.46978
0.096154	0.453716	0.323238	1.064004	0.553283	0.839355	0.554958
-0.28159	-0.25927	-0.0122	-0.1064	-0.68878	-0.70683	-0.34251
0.096154	0.097225	1.329545	1.064004	0.139262	-0.04418	0.447002

FIGURE 4.28   Mean calculated from six z-scores in Excel

Now that we have mean z-scores for each employee, we should convert them to percentiles to make the z-scores more interpretable. Create a new column N labelled 'Percentile'.

1 **Excel 2010 or later:** To compute the percentile in N2, type: =NORM.S.DIST(M2, TRUE).
2 **Excel 2007 or earlier:** To compute the percentile in N2, type: =NORMSDIST(M2).

You should end up with percentiles as shown in Figure 4.29.

f_x	=NORM.S.DIST(M2, TRUE)

L	M	N
zDecembe	zMean	Percentile
-1.59036	-1.89153	0.029277
-2.25301	-1.88564	0.029672
-1.36947	-1.7429	0.040675
-1.36947	-1.68357	0.046132
-1.59036	-1.60597	0.054141
-1 14859	-1 49201	0 067849

FIGURE 4.29   Percentiles computed from mean z-scores

Sort the data in column N in ascending order to see the lowest-ranking employees first. If you don't remember how to sort, see Chapter 2 (p. 47).

Now the situation is a bit clearer. Roughly a dozen employees stand out as particularly low sellers, month over month. Their z-scores are always negative (they are always below average), and there's a fairly steep decline in percentiles down to this lower group. While other employees may have good months and bad months, these employees are consistently poor. That means these employees are definitely the ones that Jill should target. But what to do with them is up to her.

SPSS

Download the SPSS dataset for the demonstration below as **chapter4.sav**. As you read this section, try to apply the terms you've learned in this chapter to the dataset and follow along with SPSS on your own computer.

You can also get a video demonstration of the section below under **SPSS Videos: Chapter 4**.

In our dataset, Jill is trying to identify which employees are consistently weak in sales. She has collected data on employee sales for the months July through December. Try using the techniques you learned in Chapter 3 to identify the mean and standard deviation of each month. You'll find that there is quite a bit of variation from month to month (if you don't find the values shown in Figure 4.30, review Chapter 3's lesson on SPSS).

(Continued)

(Continued)

Descriptive Statistics

	N	Mean	Std. Deviation
July	55	9.75	2.647
August	55	9.73	2.805
September	55	10.04	2.981
October	55	10.36	3.418
November	55	12.33	4.831
December	55	15.20	4.527
Valid N (listwise)	55		

FIGURE 4.30   Descriptive statistics from case study dataset in SPSS

If we look at any one month, we may not get the whole story; perhaps an employee was simply having a bad month, but it doesn't reflect their overall performance. But if we add all sales across all months for each employee, we may miss patterns of poor performance. For example, what if an employee does well during the December rush, but is consistently poor during all other months? To address this problem, we will convert each month's sales for each employee to z-scores, so that we can identify how well each employee was doing each month relative to his or her co-workers.

In SPSS, we do this with a tool we first tried in Chapter 3 – Descriptives. Open **Analyze**, then **Descriptive Statistics**, then **Descriptives** (Figure 4.31).

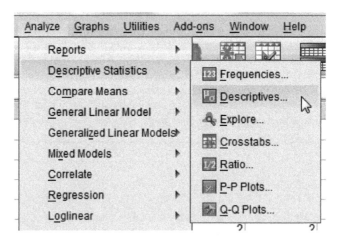

FIGURE 4.31   Menu option to run Descriptive statistics in SPSS

Move all of your variables to the right (again, see Chapter 3 if you've forgotten how).

This time, we're going to change one little thing – the checkbox that says 'Save standardized values as variables'. By checking this box, we tell SPSS not only to compute descriptives, but also to create new variables containing z-scores for each variable we are looking at. You should end up with something like Figure 4.32.

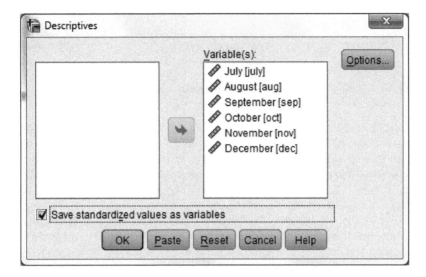

FIGURE 4.32   Descriptive statistics dialogue with option to save z-scores selected in SPSS

Click OK. The output pane will pop up as usual, but we're not worried about that this time. Instead, turn back to your raw data. You'll see six new variables containing z-scores (Figure 4.33).

	july	aug	sep	oct	nov	dec	Zjuly	Zaug	Zsep	Zoct	Znov	Zdec
1	12	9	13	15	16	18	.85165	-.25927	.99411	1.35661	.76029	.61847
2	13	13	12	12	12	18	1.22939	1.16670	.63267	.47880	-.06775	.61847
3	10	10	12	10	10	16	.09615	.09722	.65867	-.10640	-.48177	.17671
4	11	11	11	11	11	14	.47390	.45372	.32324	.18620	-.27476	-.26506
5	3	5	7	6	5	8	-2.54807	-1.68623	-1.01850	-1.27681	-1.51682	-1.59036
6	10	10	10	9	10	12	.09615	.09722	-.01220	-.39900	-.48177	-.70683
7	8	9	11	11	15	16	-.65934	-.25927	.32324	.18620	.55328	.17671
8	9	8	9	9	9	13	-.28169	-.61576	-.34763	-.39900	-.68878	-.48594

FIGURE 4.33   Dataset with new z-score variables in SPSS

Each set of z-scores has been calculated exactly as we would calculate it by hand.

Now that we have z-scores for every month, we can more meaningfully compute mean performance across months. To do this, we'll use a new tool called Compute. Open the **Transform** menu and select **Compute Variable** at the top (see Figure 4.34).

(Continued)

(Continued)

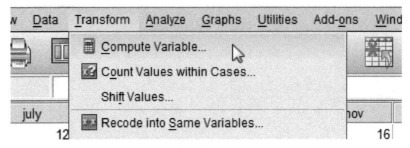

FIGURE 4.34   Menu option to compute values for new variables from current variables

You might be wondering why we're using a different tool to compute a mean. The difference is the type of mean. Before, we were interested in computing the mean score within a variable, so we used Descriptives. This time, we're interested in *creating a new variable* that is the mean of other variables. Any time you need to create a new variable, you'll generally use Compute.

If you've done this successfully, the Compute dialogue box will pop up. This looks fairly complicated, but we don't need to worry about anything here for now except the Target Variable and Numeric Expression sections. The Target Variable section lets you specify the name of your new variable. This can be whatever you want, as long as it doesn't start with a number or contain spaces and inappropriate symbols (SPSS will tell you if you try to name it something inappropriate, and it's easy to change). In our case, we want to compute the mean z-score, so we'll just call it zMean.

In the Numeric Expression section, we provide code to SPSS to tell it what to put into the new variable. In this case, we want the mean of the six new z-score variables we just created.

In the Numeric Expression section, type: MEAN(Zjuly, Zaug, Zsep, Zoct, Znov, Zdec).

If you don't trust yourself to spell the variable names correctly, you can also click-drag the variables or use the arrow button, just like we've been doing in other SPSS dialogue boxes. You should end up with something like Figure 4.35.

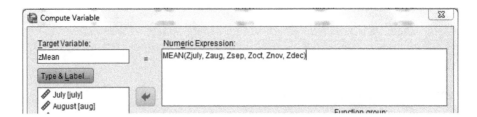

FIGURE 4.35   Compute variable dialogue in SPSS, with expression to compute new variable with mean of the six z-score variables

Click OK. Once again, the output pane will pop up, but we're interested in the dataset itself. Click back over to the main dataset, and you should now have a new column of mean z-scores at the far right (you may need to scroll to see them) (see Figure 4.36).

	Znov	Zdec	zMean
661	.76029	.61847	.72
880	-.06775	.61847	.68
640	-.48177	.17671	.07
620	-.27476	-.26506	.15
681	-1.51682	-1.59036	-1.61
900	-.48177	-.70683	-.23
620	.55328	.17671	.05
900	-.68878	-.48594	-.47
400	.55328	.83936	.55

FIGURE 4.36   Newly computed mean variable in SPSS

Now that we have mean z-scores for each employee, we should convert them to percentiles to make the z-scores more interpretable. Once again open the Compute dialogue, but this time, change two things:

In the Target Variable section, type: Percentile.

In the Numeric Expression section, type: CDF.NORMAL(zMean,0,1).

Remember to change the Target Variable name, or you could overwrite your other variables instead of creating a new one!

Once ready, the dialogue box should look like Figure 4.37.

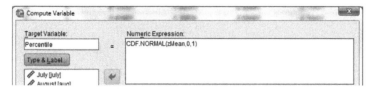

FIGURE 4.37   Compute variable dialogue in SPSS, with expression to compute new variable with percentile conversions of dataset z-scores

This formula is a little denser than the others we've covered, so let's break it down – see Figure 4.38.

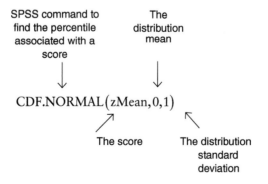

FIGURE 4.38   Annotated SPSS computation formula to convert z-scores to percentiles

(Continued)

(Continued)

In this case, we have a distribution of z-scores, so we want to know the percentile associated with a standard normal distribution – this distribution has a mean of 0 and standard deviation of 1. By including 'zMean' as the score, SPSS uses the 0 and 1 for every calculation but changes each zMean for each row of data.

You should end up with Figure 4.39 (you may need to scroll further right).

	Zdec	zMean	Percentile
)29	.61847	.72	.76
'75	.61847	.68	.75
I77	.17671	.07	.53
I76	-.26506	.15	.56
;82	-1.59036	-1.61	.05
I77	-.70683	-.23	.41
}28	.17671	.05	.52
}78	-.48594	-.47	.32
}28	.83936	.55	.71

FIGURE 4.39   Final dataset in SPSS with percentile conversions from zMean variable

Sort the data in the Percentile column in ascending order to see the lowest-ranking employees first. To do this, click on **Data** and then **Sort Cases** (Figure 4.40).

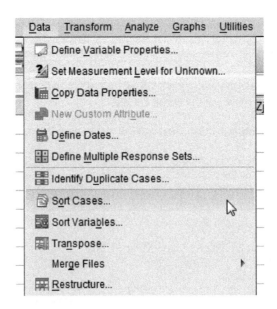

FIGURE 4.40   Menu option to sort data in SPSS

In the next dialogue, scroll down and drag Percentile to the right or use the arrow button. Ensure that 'Ascending' is selected so that the scores are ordered from smallest to largest (Figure 4.41).

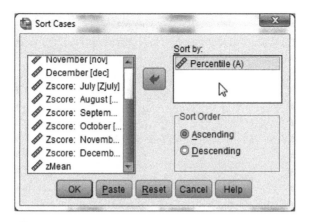

FIGURE 4.41   Dialogue to sort cases in SPSS

Click OK. At the top of your dataset, you'll see the lowest-performing sellers. Now the situation is a bit clearer. Roughly a dozen employees stand out as particularly low sellers, month over month. Their z-scores are always negative (they are always below average), and there's a fairly steep decline in percentiles down to this lower group. While other employees may have good months and bad months, these employees are consistently poor. That means these employees are definitely the ones that Jill should target. But what to do with them is up to her.

STATISTICS IN THE REAL WORLD

 These web links can be accessed directly from the book's website.

YouTube channel Numberphile gives an example of how probability doesn't always work the way you intuitively think it should, which could lose you money on a game show: https://ed.ted.com/featured/PWb09pny.

A demonstration from the National HE STEM Programme shows how normal distributions occur naturally given randomness alone using a real-life Galton Board: www.youtube.com/watch?v=6YDHBFVlvls.

How do you see normal distributions of data in your everyday life?.

TEST YOURSELF

☑   **After you've completed the questions below, check your answers online.**

1   What distribution would you expect and why for each of the following situations?
   a   Tossing a coin.
   b   Counting employee absences.
   c   Collecting survey data.

(Continued)

(Continued)

2 Using appropriate rounding as described in this chapter, what is the final answer for each of these computations?

   a   4.12 * 2.64.

   b   (7.1/2.31)/4.1.

   c $2.5^2 + 3.33^2$.

3 If $\bar{x} = 5$ and $s = 2$, calculate x for the following z-scores:

   a $z = 1.5$.

   b $z = -3$.

   c $z = 2.25$.

4 Without referencing a z-table, determine what proportion of cases we would expect to fall

   a Between $z = -3$ and $z = 1$.

   b Below $z = -1$.

   c Below $z = 2$.

DATA SKILL CHALLENGES

 After you've completed the questions below, check your answers online.

Remember to try these calculations by hand and in the statistical program of your choice; the answers should agree.

1 Given this dataset: 1, 3, 2, 5, 4, 3, 2

   a Convert each of these values to a z-score.

   b What percentage of cases would you expect to fall above 2.5?

   c What score would be at the 20th percentile?

2 Given this dataset: 3, 6, 2, 1, 2, 3, 4

   a Convert each of these values to a z-score.

   b What percentage of cases would you expect to fall below 2?

   c What score would be at the 90th percentile?

3 Given this dataset: 5, 5, 7, 2, 3, 4, 4

   a Convert each of these values to a z-score.

   b What percentage of cases would you expect to fall above 4?

   c What score would be at the 75th percentile?

4 Given this dataset: 2, 3, 3, 1, 4, 2, 3

   a Convert each of these values to a z-score.

   b What percentage of cases would you expect to fall below 3?

   c What score would be at the 40th percentile?

NEW TERMS

area under the curve: chance: classical method of assigning probability: distribution: intersection: percentile: Poisson distribution: probability: raw data: relative frequency of occurrence method of assigning probability: standard normal distribution: standardization (or standardized): uniform distribution: union: z-distribution: z-score:

NEW STATISTICAL NOTATION AND FORMULAS

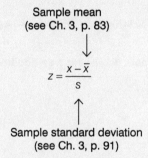

Sample mean
(see Ch. 3, p. 83)

$$z = \frac{x - \bar{x}}{s}$$

Sample standard deviation
(see Ch. 3, p. 91)

FIGURE 4.42   Annotated formula to compute a z-score from sample data

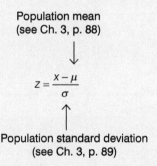

Population mean
(see Ch. 3, p. 88)

$$z = \frac{x - \mu}{\sigma}$$

Population standard deviation
(see Ch. 3, p. 89)

FIGURE 4.43   Annotated formula to compute a z-score from population data

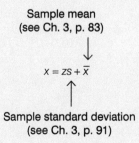

Sample mean
(see Ch. 3, p. 83)

$$x = zs + \bar{x}$$

Sample standard deviation
(see Ch. 3, p. 91)

FIGURE 4.44   Annotated formula to compute a raw score from a sample z-score

(Continued)

(Continued)

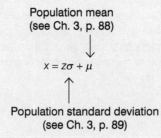

FIGURE 4.45   Annotated formula to compute a raw score from a population *z*-score

Visit https://study.sagepub.com/landers2e **for free additional online resources related to this chapter.**

5 SAMPLING DISTRIBUTIONS

WHAT YOU WILL LEARN FROM THIS CHAPTER

- How to identify when sampling is appropriate
- How to create and measure a sampling distribution with a simple population
- How to interpret the standard error of the mean
- How to describe the central limit theorem and its importance in statistics
- How to infer the mean and standard deviation of a theoretical sampling distribution

DATA SKILLS YOU WILL MASTER FROM THIS CHAPTER

- Drawing a sample from a population
- Computing the standard error of the mean

CASE STUDY   WHO DO I SURVEY?

Alex is the general manager of the local branch office of TrebhamBogg, a mid-sized company that sells paper products to other organizations. Alex is concerned that sales at his location last quarter were low relative to other branches. He's contacted corporate headquarters to get company-wide sales numbers and confirmed his suspicions: his branch is toward the bottom of the list.

'Perhaps that isn't so bad,' thinks Alex. 'Perhaps TrebhamBogg branches are all strong performers!' To investigate this, he hunts down publicly available income statements for other paper organizations. He discovers that TrebhamBogg is quite typical; it reports total income from sales at a similar level to many of its competitors.

Eager to correct his branch's low numbers, Alex examines last quarter's sales numbers in a bit more detail. Much like Jill in Chapter 4, Alex's salespeople vary a great deal in their

(Continued)

(Continued)

success rates. Some are strong sellers; some are not. But does this single quarter of numbers really represent his employees' relative strengths? For that matter, does a single quarter of poor sales for his office really mean that his branch is weaker than others? How does he know which differences are real and which are just chance?

Alex is also curious about his employees' opinions on this matter, and he wants to interview them to find out. But he also doesn't want to interview everyone – that seems like a huge waste of time and money. So how many employees does he need to interview to get a good picture of what everyone thinks? How does he know he is capturing the thoughts of the entire branch? Right now, all he has is a list of employee ID numbers and their demographics.

Take a look at Alex's list of employees for yourself in chapter5.xls (Excel) or chapter5.sav (SPSS) online.

Making conclusions about a large group based upon a small group is at the very heart of statistics. In the case study above, Alex wants to make conclusions about the strength of his sales team, but he is unsure if numbers from a single quarter really represent their true skill. He wants to make conclusions about the success of individual salespeople, but the problem remains – how does he know if low sales numbers are because the salesperson is a poor performer or just unlucky?

We tend to think about luck and chance as being chaotic: 'Anything could happen!' When we roll a die, whether for our own amusement or to win big at the casino, there's no way to know for certain which side will land face up. Statistics cannot help us with this problem.

However, statistics *can* help us understand how luck behaves in the aggregate. Although we can never know which side of a six-sided die will turn up on any particular toss, we know that across 60 throws of that die, we'd expect to see each number approximately ten times. It probably won't be perfectly 10-10-10-10-10-10, but it'll be fairly close. We saw some examples of this when discussing the uniform distribution in Chapter 4 (see p. 113).

Although Alex's sales numbers are a bit more complicated than the simple rolling of a die, the same basic principles apply. In the aggregate, we can make fairly accurate judgements of what the population Alex is interested in probably looks like. As you read Chapter 5, consider how the concepts of samples and sampling can help Alex understand his dilemma.

5.1 WHEN SHOULD YOU SAMPLE?

FOUNDATION CONCEPTS

A **population** is a theoretical group that you want to draw conclusions about. See Chapter 1, p. 11.

A **sample** is a group gathered at random from a population. See Chapter 1, p. 12.

A **parameter** is a numeric summary of a population, for example, a population mean μ (mu). See Chapter 3, p. 87.

A **statistic** is a numeric summary of a sample, for example, a sample mean (x bar). See Chapter 3, p. 87.

If populations give you all the information that you want, why don't we just measure parameters instead of statistics? The answer is quite simple: we do if we can. Measuring a parameter is always preferable if it's feasible, because then you are measuring *exactly* who or what you want to get more information about.

We can measure parameters in situations where we are only interested in the group of people we have access to, at this point in time. For example, suppose we wanted to ask the question, 'Are my current employees satisfied?' Sampling is not, strictly speaking, necessary. Instead, we could simply provide a survey to every employee asking about their job satisfaction. But if you instead wanted to know, 'Are employees of my organization satisfied?', you might consider your current employees a sample of that larger population of 'all employees I have had, currently have, and will have'. If you want to know, 'Do employees of my organization have a typical level of satisfaction in comparison to all those in my country?', you might consider your employees to be a sample of the larger population of all employees nationwide. Thus, whether or not a particular dataset is a sample or a population depends upon what you intend to do with that dataset and who you want to draw conclusions about. Most of the time, you'll find that a sample is all you have access to.

To this point, we've talked about the noun 'sample', which refers to a group gathered at random from a population. But we can also use 'sample' as a verb. When we talk about sampling, we are referring to different methods of identifying samples. As you will discover, there are many different ways to 'gather at random' from a population.

5.2 A SAMPLE OF SAMPLING

To make the issue of sampling clearer, let's first consider a really, really small and easy-to-remember population: four puppies. Four puppies are an unusual example, but they will make the rest of this section a little easier to remember and to visualize. The puppies in this population only come in two colours: grey and red. In fact, there are two grey puppies and two red puppies – see Figure 5.01.

FIGURE 5.01 A population of four puppies, labelled P1–P4

This is the population. If you wanted to know 'what proportion of my four puppies are grey?', you could simply count them: two puppies divided by four puppies equals .5. Thus, .5 (50%) of this population of puppies are grey. This is the population mean (see Chapter 3, p. 88), and thus $\mu = .5$.

But suppose this entire population was not available to you. Instead, imagine that you could only pick two puppies at random from these four – without looking at them – and use that to make a judgement about the colour composition of the group. What might happen?

Note that the puppies in this figure are labelled P1, P2, P3, P4. How many possible draws of puppies are there?

1	P1, P2.	7	P3, P1.
2	P1, P3.	8	P3, P2.
3	P1, P4.	9	P3, P4.
4	P2, P1.	10	P4, P1.
5	P2, P3.	11	P4, P2.
6	P2, P4.	12	P4, P3.

There are 12 different combinations of puppies when selecting two of the four. You have an 8.33% chance of any of these draws (1/12). How many colour possibilities? There are four. Since you are drawing a sample of two from this population of four, one of the following will happen:

1 First you pick a grey puppy, then another grey puppy (G+G).

2 First you pick a grey puppy, then a red puppy (G+T).

3 First you pick a red puppy, then a grey puppy (T+G).

4 First you pick a red puppy, then another red puppy (T+T).

So if P1/P2 are grey and P3/P4 are red, what proportion of grey puppies is drawn in each of these 12 possibilities?

1	P1, P2 (G+G; 100%).	7	P3, P1 (R+G; 50%).
2	P1, P3 (G+R; 50%).	8	P3, P2 (R+G; 50%).
3	P1, P4 (G+R; 50%).	9	P3, P4 (R+R; 0%).
4	P2, P1 (G+G; 100%).	10	P4, P1 (R+G; 50%).
5	P2, P3 (G+R; 50%).	11	P4, P2 (R+G; 50%).
6	P2, P4 (G+R; 50%).	12	P4, P3 (R+R; 0%).

Since you are only drawing two puppies, there is an 8.33% chance for each of the options above to occur. However, 2 of these 12 draws are 100% grey, 8 of these 12 draws are 50% grey, and 2 of these 12 draws are 0% grey. So if you were to collect only one sample, what would you conclude?

■ There is a 16.67% (2/12) chance that you would conclude that the population was 100% grey ($\bar{x} = 1.0$).

■ There is a 66.66% (8/12) chance that you would conclude that the population was 50% grey ($\bar{x} = .5$).

■ There is a 16.67% (2/12) chance that you would conclude that the population was 0% grey ($\bar{x} = .0$).

Although you have the greatest chance of discovering the correct proportion (the population is 50% grey and so is your sample 66.66% of the time), you also have a 33.33% chance of making an incorrect conclusion (that the population is either 100% grey or red).

This is the power of sampling. Although we only have access to half the population, most of the time we will still make an accurate conclusion. The larger our sample, the better it will represent the population it is drawn from. We can quantify this in this example by computing the population standard error of the mean, which is the standard deviation of all possible sample means. This is often shortened to simply 'population standard error', and we could also call it the standard error parameter. We represent this standard error with the symbol $\sigma_{\bar{x}}$, pronounced 'sigma-sub-x-bar'.

WHY SIGMA-SUB-X-BAR?

The statistical notation for the population standard error may look like a strange collection of symbols at first, but each piece is meaningful and something you've seen before. Let's take it piece by piece.

The σ (sigma) symbol represents a population standard deviation. This should make sense, since the standard error is itself a standard deviation.

The next part of the formula is a subscript (see Chapter 2, p. 29), which indicates that what follows makes sigma more specific. In Chapter 2, we talked about $N_{Experiment}$ representing the sample size *of an experiment*, but that the subscript could be anything. The same principle applies here: it's not just a regular population standard deviation; it's a specific type of sigma.

$\bar{x}$, which appears in the subscript, is a sample mean. Thus, the type of sigma is one that describes sample means.

Now put it all together: we call it sigma-sub-x-bar because the standard error is the standard deviation (sigma) of (sub) the sample means (x-bar). If you always remember to break down symbols like this, you'll never forget what they mean.

Let's examine the population standard errors from our example above. You can compute these values for yourself by using the population standard deviation formula from Chapter 3 on the data in Figure 5.02.

Two puppies drawn from four
Population: 50% grey
Possible sample means: 0%, 0%, 50%, 50%, 50%, 50%, 50%, 50%, 50%, 50%, 100%, 100%
Mean of all possible sample means: 50.0% grey
Standard deviation of all possible sample means (population standard error): 28.87%

FIGURE 5.02   Summary of population and sampling for a sample of two puppies drawn from a population of four

The population standard error is 28.87%. Thus, on average, two puppies drawn from four will vary from the mean by 28.87% greyness.

What would we expect to happen if we had drawn three puppies instead of two? Because more draws means that we are sampling a larger proportion of our population, our standard error would decrease! If you try this out yourself (there are 24 possibilities this time, instead of 12), you'll find the standard error decreases to 16.67% whereas the mean remains the same (50.0%).

Samples of three puppies are *more accurate*, on average, than samples of two puppies, in estimating the mean greyness of the population of four puppies. We can convert that idea into a bigger one: a larger sample (increasing n) means greater accuracy when estimating a population.

In our case study, Alex asked, 'Does a single quarter of poor sales for my office really mean that my branch is weaker than others?' The answer is 'no'. Because Alex only has numbers from a single quarter, pure chance potentially plays a large role in the precise value of that number. Alex could be much more confident in his performance numbers if he collected a larger sample and computed the mean – for example, by collecting sales numbers over multiple quarters.

It's important to note that increasing sample size does not *ensure* an accurate sample from the population. In the real world, we only collect a single sample, and we don't typically know what the population actually looks like. In these cases, our single sample mean will differ from the population mean by some unknown degree. We refer to this difference as sampling error. In our example, if we drew a sample of two puppies and found a sample mean of 0%, we'd have a sampling error of 50% (population mean μ– sample mean = 50% − 0% = 50%).

Sampling error exists with all types of sample statistics. Imagine you were measuring the satisfaction of your customers by asking each customer that comes into your store: 'How satisfied are you with your experience today?' You ask this on a scale of 1 to 5, with 1 indicating 'very dissatisfied', 3 indicating 'neither dissatisfied nor satisfied' and 5 indicating 'very satisfied'.

Next, imagine that in the population, if you were to measure customer satisfaction of every current and possible customer, you'd compute a mean of 4.10. In real life, you can't do this. But that population mean still exists, and your sample is a reflection of it. By measuring the sample mean you're hoping to estimate the population mean.

Given this, no sample will ever perfectly reflect the population. Instead, individual scores will vary around the population mean. Since the population mean represents the central tendency of the population, most sample mean statistics will be close to the mean parameter. Fewer values will be far from this parameter. And although the population mean in our example is 4.10, it's unlikely that the sample mean will ever be exactly 4.10 too.

WHY IS IT CALLED 'ERROR'?

When we hear the word 'error', we typically think of it as if someone made a mistake. But error in a statistical sense is not necessarily 'bad'. Here, error refers to the degree to which a sample value misrepresents a population value. While we certainly want our sample mean to be as close as possible to our population mean, a large sampling error does not necessarily mean we did anything wrong. Instead, the sample mean will almost always misrepresent the population mean purely by chance – even if we did everything perfectly. The only way to eliminate sampling error is to measure the population itself.

In our case study, the population sales level of Alex's branch could be any number. For this example, let's imagine that the population mean of Alex's branch's sales is £25000. In other words, for the entire lifetime of this branch, we would expect an average of £25000 each quarter. Last quarter, the branch only sold £21000 worth of product. We thus have a sampling error of £25000 − £21000 = £4000. The quarter sales number is 'correct' in that it accurately represents sales this quarter. Alex did nothing wrong acquiring this value. Instead, sampling error is a natural by-product of the act of sampling. While we want to minimize sampling error, it does not necessarily mean we did anything 'wrong'.

5.3 METHODS FOR SAMPLING

There are many ways to draw a sample from a population. In the remainder of this chapter, we'll cover three of the most common. Of these three, two are probabilistic (simple random sampling and stratified random sampling) and one is not (convenience sampling). Probabilistic sampling is always preferable to non-probabilistic sampling because it allows us to carefully control who our sample contains so that the sample represents a particular population of interest. Unfortunately, probabilistic sampling is not always possible. We'll discuss each of these approaches, and their relative value, in turn.

5.3.1 SIMPLE RANDOM SAMPLING

The example above described simple random sampling, which occurs when everyone or everything in the population has an equal chance of being drawn. When we were picking puppies, every puppy had an equal chance to be picked.

Simple random sampling is ideal if you have complete access to your population and if that population contains no subgroups of interest (we'll return to this concept in the next section). For example, in our case study, Alex wants to get his current employees' opinions about the branch's low performance. Since he has access to every employee, he could utilize simple random sampling to pick a subset of employees to interview. But how does he pick them?

In the days before computers, this was done with a random number table, which looked something like Figure 5.03.

34121	64756	14499	83346	82590	47126	82956
50513	40641	81764	44563	35420	79392	31080
04560	14568	67599	77150	07620	75578	51767
16811	78705	09796	92509	66259	19163	60964
17356	18661	45897	30186	50954	49983	66267
77788	71611	61264	05535	51056	83877	47733
54452	83406	36934	84254	37418	77126	13440

FIGURE 5.03   Random number table

You could then manoeuvre around the random number table using whatever made-up scheme you thought made sense. In Alex's case, he has 125 employees, so he might assign each of those employees a number 1 through 125. He might next pick a random point in the random number table to start – let's say 44563. Perhaps next he would simply read the numbers he encountered moving left to right, top to bottom. So for his sample, he'd first pick 44, then 56, then 33, then 54, then 20, then 79, then 39, then 23, then 108, then 45 – and so on. If it doesn't seem like there's any good reason for picking those numbers specifically, you are correct, and that is the purpose of this exercise. It's *random*.

However, this process is time-consuming, and it can be frustrating to keep track of all the numbers and the pattern you're using. Additionally, once you've used a random number table a few times, you are likely to develop patterns of picking numbers without even realizing it, making it not-so-random anymore. Fortunately, both Excel and SPSS have random number generators built in, making this process easier, less biased, and essentially instantaneous. We'll explore this process at the end of this chapter.

5.3.2 STRATIFIED RANDOM SAMPLING

While simple random sampling is excellent when you have a single group of interest, sometimes we want to balance some characteristic of interest across our sample so we are certain that subgroups are represented. For example, in our case study, Alex has a mixture of men and women working at his branch. If he relied on simple random sampling, it might simply be his poor luck to get 100% men or 100% women. To ensure that men and women are equally represented, Alex could use stratified random sampling with women and men. Each group of interest in stratified random sampling is called a stratum, and together they are called strata. After appropriate strata are identified, simple random sampling is used within those subgroups.

For example, if Alex's employees were 50% men and 50% women and he wanted a total sample of 40, he might split his employees into two strata (women and men) and then use simple random sampling within each group to pick 20 women and 20 men.

If his organization was not 50% men and 50% women, he would create strata of sizes representative of his organization. Imagine that Alex wants to draw a stratified random sample of 40 employees from his branch, which is made up of 75 women and 50 men. First, he identifies the relative frequency (see Chapter 2, p. 31) of each stratum in his population. Next, he multiplies that relative frequency by his total desired sample size to identify the number of people within each sample stratum – see Figure 5.04.

Stratum	Population *f*	rel.*f*	Desired sample	Sample stratum *f*
Men	50	50 / 125 = .4	40	.4 * 40 = 16
Women	75	75 / 125 = .6	40	.6 * 40 = 24

FIGURE 5.04   Example of calculations to compute sample strata sizes given a particular population

Thus, to ensure his sample represents the gender breakdown of his employees, Alex should interview 16 men and 24 women for their opinions (Figure 5.05).

There is also a sampling technique similar to stratified random sampling common to marketing called cluster sampling. In this approach, the population is divided into strata based upon naturally occurring groups, and simple random sampling is used within each stratum. However, the purpose of this approach is to compare the clusters with each other. In stratified random sampling, we are trying to minimize the effects of underrepresented groups within our sample. In cluster sampling, we are trying to form a sample so that we

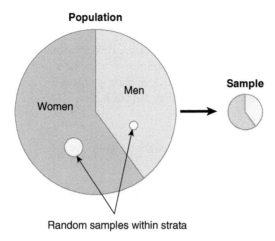

Random samples within strata

FIGURE 5.05   Visualization of stratified random sampling

can compare particular groups of interest directly with one another. If you need this technique, you are likely to learn more about it in an advanced marketing course.

5.3.3 CONVENIENCE SAMPLING

Although simple random sampling and stratified random sampling are ideal methods for picking cases at random from a population, these methods are often not possible. Instead, we often rely on convenience samples, so named because they are not drawn randomly, instead being picked because they are conveniently accessible. This is a common method used when surveying customers.

Why can't we randomly sample customers? Because they wouldn't do it! Imagine the business that collected information about each and every customer that ever walked in its door in order to randomly survey those customers later. What a hassle for the customers! And even if you did collect this information, you'd be unlikely to get a true random sample anyway due to angry customers. Instead, many organizations put invitations to complete surveys at the end of receipts, offering customers some sort of reward for doing so. If they find the reward suitably attractive, they complete the survey. If they don't find the reward attractive, they ignore the survey invitation.

This is not random sampling; it is convenience sampling. You can never be quite sure that your sample represents your population. In the example above, customers who are willing to respond to a survey in exchange for a reward may not be the same sorts of customers that you are interested in. What if these customers tend to be happier and more satisfied with your organization than those that don't respond? You would never know! You can only hope, making a well-reasoned argument that the sample you conveniently have access to is random 'enough'.

In the calculation of statistics, we assume our variables were randomly sampled; if they were not randomly sampled, our conclusions are suspect. For example, if you found a particular mean satisfaction level for your customers using a convenience sampling method like the receipt approach above, and later discovered that only satisfied customers took your survey, your mean would be meaningless.

If this reminds you of the discussion of experiments versus quasi-experiments in Chapter 1, you're right! Just as we never use quasi-experiments unless situation constraints require us to do so, we never want to use convenience sampling unless it is the only practical choice – when our choice is 'convenience sampling or nothing'.

5.4 SAMPLING DISTRIBUTIONS AND SAMPLING ERROR

Let's briefly return to our over-the-top puppy example from before. Recall that we used simple random sampling to identify all possible samples of two puppies and three puppies from a population of four puppies, and we used our samples to try to make conclusions about our population. With larger samples, we decreased the population standard error, which is the standard deviation of all possible sample means.

When we create a bar chart of all possible sample means given a particular sample size, we produce what's called a sampling distribution and, as we discussed before, its standard deviation is called the population standard error. We know already that the standard error can be different even with the same population mean; it changes mostly as a function of sample size (*n*). Therefore, sampling distributions are also different for different sample sizes. Figure 5.06 shows the two quite different sampling distributions for the two puppy examples (same population mean, same population standard deviation, different sample sizes and different standard errors).

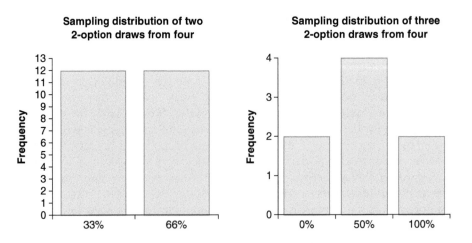

FIGURE 5.06   Two sampling distributions with identical means and standard deviations, but different sample sizes and standard errors

Because we know every possible draw from the population, we can create bar charts that represent the sampling distribution entirely and precisely. We can also compute the population standard error by computing the standard deviation of the values within these charts.

When facing real business questions, this situation is fairly uncommon. We rarely know the standard deviation of the population or of the sampling distribution. Instead, we only have our sample. For example, imagine if you were conducting market research and wanted to get a better sense of typical per-employee training costs in your industry. You collect a convenience sample of all the training cost documentation that is available to you from publicly filed documents and other public statements. You compute a sample mean, and it's your best guess as to the population mean. But just how accurate would we expect that mean to be?

Fortunately, there is a relationship between the standard deviation, sample size and sampling error that allows us to calculate the standard error even without measuring the sampling distribution directly – see Figure 5.07.

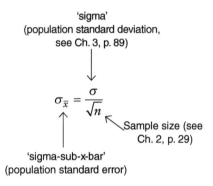

FIGURE 5.07   Annotated formula for population standard error

The full name for this statistic, which we shorten to 'population standard error', is the 'population standard deviation of the sampling distribution of the sample means'. Instead of calculating a single piece of information about the population or about the sample, we're calculating what the variability would be in a *population of samples*, all of the same sample size. If that doesn't blow your mind, I don't know what will.

We can also calculate an estimate of the population standard error with a similar formula, substituting *s* for σ, as shown in Figure 5.08.

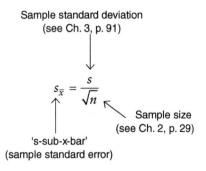

FIGURE 5.08   Annotated formula for sample estimate of standard error

We call this the sample standard error of the mean, sometimes called simply the 'standard error', and it is our best guess as to the value of the population standard error without being able to measure the population directly. We interpret this value as 'the average distance sample means fall away from the population mean' – or, more simply, 'the average sampling error'.

For example, imagine that instead of interviews, Alex conducts a survey. He picks 25 of his 125 employees to complete a survey with a single question asking, 'How do you think we are doing in comparison to other branches?' For a scale, 1 indicates 'worse', 2 indicates 'about the same', and 3 indicates 'better'. He finds a mean of 2.1, with a standard deviation of 0.5. How accurate is this 2.1?

To determine this, he calculates the standard error, as shown in Figure 5.09.

$$s_{\bar{x}} = \frac{s}{\sqrt{n}} = \frac{.5}{\sqrt{25}} = \frac{.5}{5} = .1$$

FIGURE 5.09   Step by step calculation of sample estimate of standard error

Thus, on average, mean scores from surveys of 25 people (like the one that Alex conducted) with a standard deviation of 0.5 fall within 0.1 points of the population mean. Since this is the standard deviation of the sampling distribution, we can use the rules of thumb regarding standard deviations that we learned in Chapter 4.

If the population mean really is 2.1 (right now, we only have a sample mean, but this is the best guess we have):

- 68% (34% + 34%) of the time, sample means will fall within ±0.1 of that value (±1 SD).

- 95% (13.5% + 34% + 34% + 13.5%) of the time, sample means will fall within ±0.2 of that value (±2 SD).

We sometimes talk about accuracy this way as 'margin of error'. If you're not sure where I'm getting these numbers, reread the section on the z-distribution in Chapter 4 (p. 115). We will return to the concept of margin of error in greater detail in Chapter 6.

With these formulas, we no longer need to determine every possible value of a sampling distribution to measure its standard error. Instead, we only need our sample standard deviation to estimate the population standard error. *That makes this a very valuable formula.* But how can we know that almost any sampling distribution will have a meaningful standard deviation without measuring it directly? If a sampling distribution was skewed, the standard deviation would not be meaningful. Doesn't that mean that sampling distributions must be normally distributed for this statistic to make any sense?

Yes – it does! Fortunately, most sampling distributions are normally distributed regardless of what the population looks like. The reason is the central limit theorem. This is a statistical principle stating that when sample means of a particular sample size are infinitely drawn from a particular population, the sampling distribution of those means will be approximately normally distributed.

So regardless of whether your population distribution is normal, uniform, Poisson or anything else, with a sufficient sample size, its sampling distribution will be approximately normal. Again, this demonstrates the power and value of sampling – it helps us find order and predictability in apparent chaos.

One caveat: with extremely small sample sizes ($n < 5$), sampling distributions aren't always normal. Easy solution: always get as large a sample as you can!

5.5 COMPARING ALL THREE TYPES OF DISTRIBUTIONS

We've talked about three distributions to this point – sample distributions, population distributions and sampling distributions. But how are they related to one another?

Let's consider this question by walking through Figure 5.10. At the top, you have a population of interest. This is the group that you want to make conclusions about. If you're conducting background market research, this might be a population of yearly sales from all the businesses in the area where you are considering opening your new business. You want to know the mean yearly sales for every business. Unfortunately, you can't get access to all those numbers; most businesses don't share in-depth sales information. Instead, you can only locate a sample.

The accuracy of your sample mean depends on how many cases you can find. The more cases you find, the more accurate your sample mean will be. However, in the population, there are only so many possible combinations of businesses that you could ever identify. For example, if there were 500 businesses you were interested in comparing with (the population), there are only so many possible combinations of $n = 30$. All of these possible means appear in a single sampling distribution, given a particular n, shown in the middle level of Figure 5.10. On average, sample means will fall one standard error away from the population mean. Larger n will result in smaller standard errors.

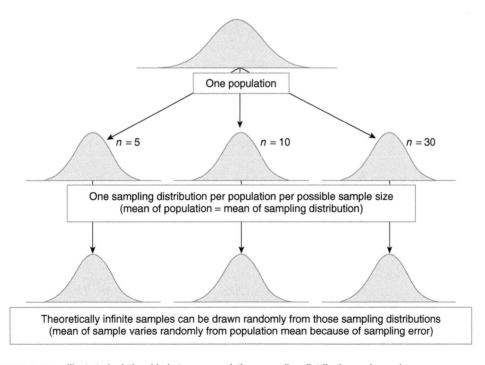

FIGURE 5.10   Illustrated relationship between population, sampling distribution and samples

When you actually collect your sample, you only end up with one sample. The members of this sample come from the population (top line of the chart) but their means form the shape of a sampling distribution (middle line of the chart). Thus, there's no way to know how accurate the mean of your particular sample really is. All you can make conclusions about is what happens to samples on the average. On the bottom row, we see the single sample we actually draw from the many possible samples in the sampling distribution. While we know that there is a sampling distribution and a population distribution that this sample came from, it's unlikely we will ever be able to measure either one.

If we return to our case study, we can see how these issues help Alex understand his measurement concerns. His branch is toward the bottom of the sales number list. What kind of distribution this sales number list is depends on what Alex wants to know. If his research question is, 'Did my branch perform more poorly last quarter?', then his population of interest is the list he's staring at. He doesn't need to calculate sampling error or worry about sampling distributions in this case, because he has the population data in his hand. His branch is toward the bottom of the list – end of story.

However, if his question is, 'Does my branch perform more poorly than other branches in general?', the set of numbers he's looking at is just a sample. There's no way to know from a single sample if his branch is poorer or not. In fact, even if he gets more samples, his population is theoretically infinite; he really wants to know, 'Is my branch worse than all branches previously, all branches now, and all branches in the future?' He can never actually know the population. He can only make inferences about it – essentially, educated guesses.

What Alex can do is make some assumptions and examine how well his branch matches those assumptions. For example, perhaps he could assume that the mean of all the other branches is 'good enough' and see how unusual his branch is in comparison to those other branches. This approach would involve a calculation similar to a z-score, but it would be calculated with a sampling distribution instead of with a sample. This approach is called hypothesis testing, and it is the focus of Part 2 of this textbook. We'll return to the concept of sampling distributions in much more detail there. If Alex wants to know how to solve his problem, he'll just have to read faster!

5.6 APPLYING SAMPLING DISTRIBUTIONS

To apply what you've learned from this chapter, consider the following case study, questions posed about that case study, and discussion of those questions.

5.6.1 APPLICATION CASE STUDY

Naomi is shop manager at Magic Spanner, a car service centre. She is responsible for ordering parts to meet customer orders quickly, meeting with irate customers and managing the overall flow of vehicles in and out of her workshop. The business is quite busy; her mechanics worked on 200 vehicles last month.

Because her workshop is so busy, Naomi is interested in improving the turnaround time of vehicles in her service bays. If vehicles get out of the workshop more quickly, her business earns more money. She comes up with an idea to improve service: she wants to keep a larger stock on hand of the items typically needed by her customers.

In the past, this has been a big problem for Magic Spanner. Because each make of car requires different parts to other makes, vehicles often get put in the service bay, tested to identify the problem they are having, removed from the service bay to wait for a part to arrive, and then put back in the service bay to have that part installed. If more parts were on hand, this process would take less time, improving customer satisfaction and profit.

But how does she know which parts to order? She can't afford to stock *every* part that might be needed. There simply isn't enough space, and the overhead would be too big. How does she select the parts she needs most often?

5.6.2 APPLICATION DISCUSSION

Naomi is facing a problem of sampling. She needs to identify the parts most needed by her mechanics in order to keep them in stock, reducing the total amount of time wasted by waiting for delivery.

Convenience sampling is the first choice that Naomi would be likely to consider – simply look at the last month of part needs and order whatever was needed most. The problem with this approach is that there is no way to know from this alone if anything unusual happened this month that would have led to unusual part needs. Instead, Naomi would be better served by stratified random sampling. For example, because car wear and tear is largely driven by the time of year (winter needs are quite different from summer needs), she might look at parts needed seasonally over the last several years.

Alternatively, Naomi might look at the list of regular clients that come in for repairs. Given a list of makes and models typically coming into the workshop, Naomi might use simple random sampling to pick the most-needed parts among those models.

Whichever approach she takes, the overall goal is the same: find a well-reasoned way to ensure that what she picks for her sample represents what she expects from her population.

EXPLORING SAMPLING IN EXCEL AND SPSS

EXCEL

[icon] Download the Excel dataset for the demonstration below as **chapter5.xls**. As you read this section, try to apply the terms you've learned in this chapter to the dataset and follow along with Excel on your own computer.

[icon] You can also get a video demonstration of the section below under **Excel Video: Chapter 5**.

One problem of Alex's that we *can* solve is his need to randomly pick 25 of his 125 employees. Instead of using a random number table, like the one shown in this chapter, Excel can assign random numbers to each employee, which you can then use to sort them.

(Continued)

(Continued)

In the dataset, you'll see a list of employee ID numbers from 1 to 125. Create a new column called 'random'.

In B2, type =RAND().

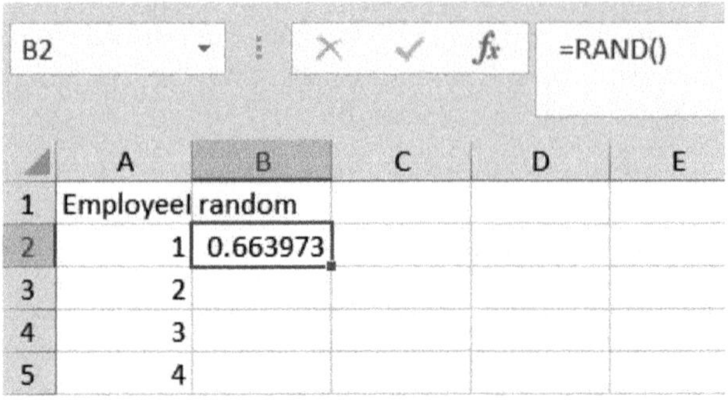

B2	=RAND()				
	A	B	C	D	E
1	Employeel	random			
2	1	0.663973			
3	2				
4	3				
5	4				

FIGURE 5.11 Random number produced by Excel

This will create a random number between 0 and 1 (see Figure 5.11). Using the fill box at the bottom right corner of the cell, fill down to B126 – see Figure 5.12. As a shortcut, you can just double-click the little box.

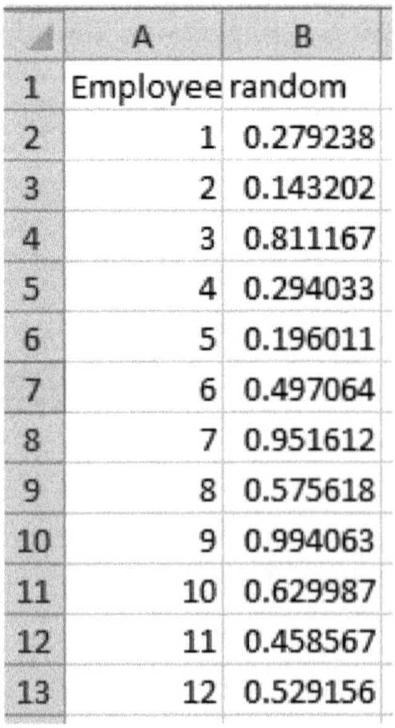

	A	B
1	Employee	random
2	1	0.279238
3	2	0.143202
4	3	0.811167
5	4	0.294033
6	5	0.196011
7	6	0.497064
8	7	0.951612
9	8	0.575618
10	9	0.994063
11	10	0.629987
12	11	0.458567
13	12	0.529156

FIGURE 5.12 Random numbers produced by Excel, filled down

Notice that when you filled down, Excel recalculated the random value in B2. Every time you edit the worksheet, these random numbers will change.

Now that every employee has a random number, sort on column B (Figure 5.13). If you don't remember how to sort, see Chapter 2 (p. 47).

	A	B	C
1	Employee	random	
2	71	0.536562	
3	105	0.429759	
4	41	0.787375	
5	113	0.062115	
6	53	0.033077	
7	21	0.381556	
8	46	0.405955	
9	87	0.047673	
10	118	0.446396	
11	34	0.817806	
12	26	0.913084	
13	70	0.302541	
14	119	0.914625	

FIGURE 5.13   Employees sorted randomly

Now the employee ID numbers are sorted randomly. To pick 25 employees, simply pick the first 25 employee IDs in your new list. In my dataset, this would include all employees from Row 2 to Row 26 (71, 105, 41, 113, 53, etc.), but the employees you choose are likely to be different.

SPSS

Download the SPSS dataset for the demonstration below as **chapter5.sav**. As you read this section, try to apply the terms you've learned in this chapter to the dataset and follow along with SPSS on your own computer.

You can also get a video demonstration of the section below under **SPSS Videos: Chapter 5**.

One problem of Alex's that we *can* solve is his need to randomly pick 25 of his 125 employees. Instead of using a random number table, like the one shown in this chapter, SPSS can identify any number of random cases that you specify, which you can then use to sort them.

In the dataset, you'll see a list of employee ID numbers from 1 to 125. In the **Data** menu, select **Select Cases** (Figure 5.14).

(Continued)

(Continued)

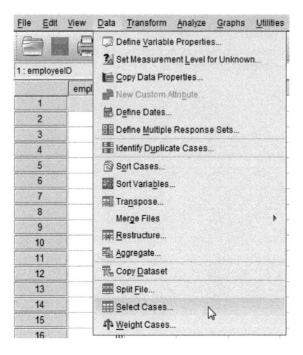

FIGURE 5.14   Menu option to select subset of cases for further analyses in SPSS

When the Select Cases dialogue pops up, click on 'Random Sample of Cases' and click the **Sample** button (Figure 5.15).

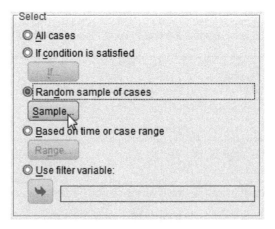

FIGURE 5.15   Select cases dialogue, random sample selected

Since we want to select 25 employees of the 125 available, enter those values on the next screen (Figure 5.16).

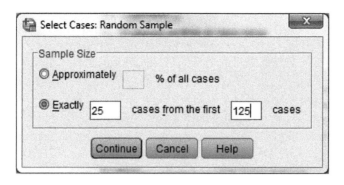

FIGURE 5.16   Subdialogue to specify random sample

Click **Continue** then **OK**.

If you look at your dataset now, you'll notice that two things have changed. First, a new variable called filter_$ has been created. Second, on the left side of the screen, many of the case numbers have slashes drawn through them – see Figure 5.17.

	employeeID	filter_$
1	1	0
2	2	0
3	3	0
4	4	0
5	5	0
6	6	1
7	7	0
8	8	1
9	9	0
10	10	0

FIGURE 5.17   Randomly selected cases in SPSS (6 and 8 selected; others not selected)

The slash indicates that any analyses you run right now will **not** include the slashed cases. Since we selected 25 cases, 100 cases should have slashes through them. The new filter_$ variable reflects this: any case with a 0 is not being included, while any case with a 1 is being included. To get a convenient list, sort your dataset by the filter_$ variable in descending order. This will put all cases with a '1' for filter_$ at the top of your dataset – see Figure 5.18. For more detail on sorting, see Chapter 4, p. 47.

(Continued)

(Continued)

	employeeID	filter_$
1	6	1
2	8	1
3	12	1
4	17	1
5	21	1
6	22	1
7	32	1
8	33	1
9	36	1
10	52	1

FIGURE 5.18   Randomly selected cases sorted to top of dataset

My dataset shows these interviewees: 6, 8, 12, 17, 21, etc. Yours is probably different.

STATISTICS IN THE REAL WORLD

These web links can be accessed directly from the book's website.

Nate Silver, an American statistician specializing in predicting government elections, describes how complex sampling becomes within real-world constraints, and how margin of error doesn't always tell the whole story: https://fivethirtyeight.com/features/what-the-hell-is-happening-with-these-alabama-polls.

What types of response biases can result in inaccurate election polling? How do these same response biases influence sampling accuracy with organizational problems?

Michael Li, Founder of Data Incubator, writes in *Harvard Business Review* about how data analysts sometimes don't explain the uncertainty underlying their analyses, and how understanding sampling and error can help you better understand decision risk for your organization: https://hbr.org/2015/10/the-two-questions-you-need-to-ask-your-data-analysts.

When you are trying to interpret your own data or the work of your data analyst, what pitfalls should you look out for?

TEST YOURSELF

☑   **After you've completed the questions below, check your answers online.**

1   When do we use …
   a   Simple random sampling?
   b   Stratified random sampling?
   c   Convenience sampling?

2 If we were randomly drawing a sample of two marbles from a population of five, where three are blue and two are red, how many possible draws are there?

3 Amar's customer base is about 80% female and 20% male. He is interested in collecting a sample of customers where men and women are appropriately represented. If he wants a sample of 50, how many men and women should he seek? What type of sampling should he use?

4 How many sampling distributions are possible given a particular population and $n = 15$?

5 The standard error estimated from a sample is 1. What's the population standard error?

DATA SKILL CHALLENGES

 After you've completed the questions below, check your answers online.

1 Draw five numbers randomly from this set: 1, 2, 3, 4, 5, 6, 7, 8, 9, 10. It is recommended you do this in Excel or SPSS.

2 Estimate the population standard error from this sample: 5, 2, 7, 3, 4, 8, 2, 3.

3 John is a manager interested in assessing customer satisfaction at his store. However, he is only able to get surveys back from five customers. The values he gets are 4, 1, 5, 2 and 1. From this, he computes a mean. How accurate is this mean in representing the population? Compute a statistic appropriate to address this question and interpret it.

4 Estimate the population standard error from these sample means: 6, 5, 2, 4, 1, 6, 5, 2, 7, 8, 9.

NEW TERMS

convenience sampling: population standard error of the mean: sample standard error of the mean: sampling: sampling distribution: simple random sampling: strata: stratified random sampling: stratum:

NEW STATISTICAL NOTATION AND FORMULAS

$\sigma_{\bar{x}}$: population standard error (or: standard error parameter), pronounced 'sigma-sub-x-bar'.

$s_{\bar{x}}$: sample standard error (or: standard error statistic), pronounced 's-sub-x-bar'.

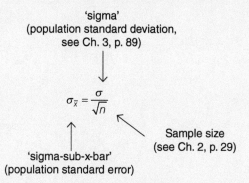

FIGURE 5.19 Annotated formula for population standard error

(Continued)

(Continued)

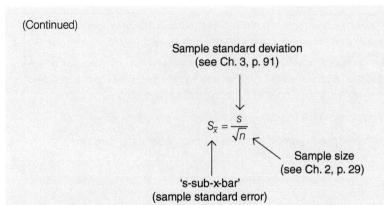

FIGURE 5.20   Annotated formula for sample estimate of standard error

Visit **https://study.sagepub.com/landers2e** **for free additional online resources related to this chapter.**

PART 2

INFERENTIAL STATISTICS

Part 2 explores Inferential Statistics. These chapters introduce a process for using samples to ask meaningful questions about populations. Like Part 1, each chapter builds on the preceding chapter, so it is strongly recommended that you read them in the order provided.

In Chapter 6, we follow the story of Chaitra, a regional manager for a major steel manufacturer. Chaitra has been tasked with providing an executive summary on the performance of her branch and wants to find the best way to broadly summarize her branch's performance. By reading Estimation and Confidence Intervals with Chaitra, you'll learn the differences between the various techniques for estimating parameters and their calculation.

In Chapter 7, we read the story of Jesse, the owner of a non-profit think tank. He hopes to use the results of his think tank thus far to make a conclusion about the quality of their solutions. By reading Hypothesis Testing with Jesse, you'll learn a formal process for using samples to answer questions about populations. The process introduced in this chapter will be used in each chapter in the remainder of Part 2.

In Chapter 8, we hear about Grace, manager of a small tutoring company. To produce marketing materials, Grace wants to statistically demonstrate that her employees are above average in comparison to the competition. By reading z-Tests and One-Sample t-Tests with Grace, you'll learn how to compare samples against given populations and draw meaningful conclusions about how well your samples represent those populations.

In Chapter 9, we learn about Diego's work as a placement manager at an employment agency. Diego wants to improve the quality of people hired and needs to answer several questions about the types of people brought in. By reading Paired- and Independent-Samples t-Tests with Diego, you'll learn how to test for mean differences over time and between groups.

In Chapter 10, we read the story of Colleen, marketing manager of an online entertainment company that collects viral videos from the Internet. Colleen wants to compare website designs to maximize revenues from advertisers paying when visitors come to her website. By reading Analysis of Variance (ANOVA) with Colleen, you'll learn how to test for differences in means between three or more groups and look for similar sets within your groups.

In Chapter 11, we examine the story of Maria, head of research and development for a chewing gum manufacturer. Maria has collected focus groups, hoping to identify flavour preferences that will help her identify which flavours will be most profitable. By reading Chi-squared Tests of Fit with Maria, you'll learn how to produce and test how well your ideas about nominal data match the observed realities.

In Chapter 12, we work with Ryan, marketing manager for a business intelligence provider. He is interested in predicting the success of prior projects based upon the number of hours put into them. By reading Correlation and Regression with Ryan, you'll learn how to summarize the relationship between two quantitative variables and predict one from the other.

6 ESTIMATION AND CONFIDENCE INTERVALS

WHAT YOU WILL LEARN FROM THIS CHAPTER

- How to distinguish between point estimates and interval estimates and their relative value
- How to interpret confidence intervals
- How to choose an appropriate confidence interval given the data available
- How to interpret margin of error

DATA SKILLS YOU WILL MASTER FROM THIS CHAPTER

- Computing the confidence interval of the mean when the population standard deviation is known (by hand and Excel only)
- Computing the confidence interval of the mean when the population standard deviation is not known
- Computing the margin of error when the population standard deviation is known (by hand and Excel only)
- Computing the margin of error when the population standard deviation is not known

CASE STUDY   WHICH NUMBER DO I USE?

Chaitra is a regional manager at Prettva Steel Manufacturing, an international manufacturer of small steel products. Their lines include nuts, bolts, screws, pins, washers, anchors and rivets. Chaitra is responsible for plants in Asia, where she oversees 12 separate facilities. Each facility manufactures all seven products, and uses the same industrial processes to do so.

(Continued)

(Continued)

As part of a report to be shared at an upcoming executive meeting, Chaitra has pulled production records from her 12 facilities. She needs to report the production level of her plants. She has captured daily production logs (nuts produced per day, screws per day, pins per day, etc.) for each facility. From Chapter 1, Chaitra knows she is conducting a correlational study of her plants. She also knows that these plants have a population mean production level; if she knew the production level of her plants every day that they ever have or will exist, she could compute this value. Unfortunately, she has no way to collect that information. As she learned from Chapter 5, although she wants to know the mean production level of each item in the population, she must instead rely on samples of those production levels that she can realistically collect. The daily production is likely to vary randomly away from the population mean; in other words, just because Chaitra finds a production rate of 15000 bolts per day at one plant does not necessarily mean this one measurement is representative of all her plants, in general.

So which of these numbers will help her produce her report? She has different measurements for each of the seven products produced at each of her 12 plants, along with daily production records for the last month. She knows from Chapter 3 that computing means will give her a better estimate of the central tendency of her daily production records. But then what? Are the means the best number she has available?

That doesn't seem right either. Although she can determine the mean production level of her samples, her plants vary a great deal. If she reports a single value, doesn't that mean she's telling upper management that her plants are precisely that efficient? Wouldn't a range of values be more appropriate? If so, what range should she use?

Take a look at Chaitra's mean daily production data for yourself in chapter6.xls (Excel) or chapter6.sav (SPSS) online.

Chaitra's choice of summary statistic and how to report it highlights a key issue we face in the study of statistics. *What represents what?* While we can generally say that samples represent populations, the issue is more complex than it initially appears. How do you choose your population, and how does this choice affect the kinds of sample that are appropriate? And what kinds of conclusion can you really make from a single sample?

In Chapter 5, we learned that sample means vary randomly from the population mean. Although we may be pulling samples from a single population, those sample means are going to be different. Fortunately, sampling error should be normally distributed across those samples. While some sample means will be high, others will be low and, on average, they will be zero. That means that we can calculate the sample standard error as an estimate of the population standard error.

6.1 POINT VS INTERVAL ESTIMATES

FOUNDATION CONCEPTS

A **population** is a theoretical group that you want to draw conclusions about. See Chapter 1, p. 11.

A **sample** is a group gathered at random from a population. See Chapter 1, p. 12.

A **parameter** is a numeric summary of a population, for example, a population mean μ(mu). See Chapter 3, p. 87.

A **statistic** is a numeric summary of a sample, for example, a sample mean x (x bar). See Chapter 3, p. 87.

The **sampling distribution** is the distribution of all possible sample means given a particular sample size. See Chapter 5, p. 150.

The **standard error** is the standard deviation of the sampling distribution. See Chapter 5, p. 145.

Until now, we've been referring to sample statistics as our 'best guesses' of the values of population parameters. But there is a more precise word for this: point estimates. A point estimate is your single best sample estimate of a parameter. It is a 'point' because it is a single value. Up to this point in this book (pardon the pun), we have talked exclusively about point estimates. For example, is a point estimate of μ. If you were asked to give your best guess as to the value of μ, you would provide the sample mean as your answer.

Point estimates can give us a false sense of security. When we compute the mean of a sample, it can lead us to believe that this single value is an accurate representation of the parameter it is sampled from – population mean. Unfortunately, this is often not true. The accuracy of point estimates is described by the standard error. Consider the two sampling distributions in Figure 6.01.

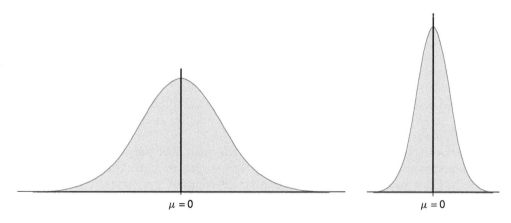

$\mu = 0$ $\mu = 0$

FIGURE 6.01 Two sampling distributions with different standard deviations

Although both of these sampling distributions have identical means, their standard deviations (that is, the standard errors) are quite different. When sampling from the first distribution, our sample mean is more likely to be further away from our population mean than when sampling from the second distribution. We would expect the point estimate derived from the first distribution to be more accurate than the point estimate drawn from the second distribution. However, this is not at all obvious from the point estimate alone.

In our case study, Chaitra is currently considering only point estimates – means. While this will give the executives her 'best guess' as to her production numbers, this does not capture the day-to-day or month-to-month variation in production, nor does it capture her confidence in that estimate. If she reports only means, the executives might expect her plants to consistently produce at that rate, in which case her estimate may be inaccurate.

To address this problem, interval estimates contain information about both the sample mean and the sampling distribution from which it was drawn. They provide a range of realistic values for a particular parameter, given the sample that was used to estimate it. This provides more information about the parameter than a point estimate alone.

Different methods are used to compute interval estimates depending on what information you have available about the sample and population. In this chapter, we'll focus on two ways to compute the most common type of interval estimate for means: the confidence interval.

6.2 CONFIDENCE INTERVALS (CI)

A confidence interval is a range of values within which we would expect sample statistics to fall, given a particular sample size, a particular parameter and a particular level of confidence. We often abbreviate them as 'CI'. Confidence refers to a chosen level of probability that defines the width of the range; for example, with 95% confidence, we determine the range of values in which 95% of sample statistics should fall.

The most typical levels of confidence that we see when computing confidence intervals are 95% (CI_{95}) and 99% (CI_{99}). So what do these levels imply?

- 95% confidence interval: The means of 95% of samples of the same size drawn from a population with the given mean will fall between these two values.

- 99% confidence interval: The means of 99% of samples of the same size drawn from a population with the given mean will fall between these two values.

How do the sizes of these intervals compare with each other? If we include 99% of samples, we'll be including the first 95% of samples plus an additional 4%. So the 99% interval will always be bigger.

The choice of these values (95% vs 99%) is *traditional*. The only reason we use these values is because, in the past, an intelligent statistician thought '95% is sufficiently accurate to get a good picture of the sampling distribution'. Another statistician said '95% is optimistic, because we ignore 5% of samples! We should use 99%! That better represents reality!' But that's the entire reason. There is no other rationale for these specific numbers. You can actually compute a confidence interval of any size. 99.99%,

80%, 50%, 10.25% – these are all valid confidence intervals, although we rarely see anything other than 95% or 99%.

Confidence intervals are very commonly misinterpreted. Pay very close attention to the difference between these two statements:

- ■ Correct: The means of 95% of samples of the same size drawn from a population with the given mean will fall between these two values.

- ■ Incorrect: There is a 95% chance that the population mean is between these two values.

The second of these statements is logically impossible. The population mean either is or is not within that interval. This is a fact, although we don't know which. That population mean exists regardless of whether or not we measure it, and the probability of its existence does not change because we measured it. Unfortunately, we have no way to know whether it really is in that interval, given only a sample. All we can conclude is that 95% of samples drawn from a population with that mean will fall between those two values.

IF 99%, WHY NOT 100%?

You might think that a 100% confidence interval would be more accurate than a 99% confidence interval, so we should use the 100% confidence interval instead. And you're right – a 100% confidence interval would contain every sample possible drawn from the parameter's sampling distribution that we are interested in. Unfortunately, a 100% confidence interval would also not be very useful for that same reason: because it would contain every possible mean. CI_{100} for a five-point survey (with scores ranging from 1 to 5) doesn't tell us much: $CI_{100} = [1,5]$.

The only way to avoid this problem is to measure the population itself; then you can be 100% confident in a particular point estimate. But if you can measure the population itself, you no longer need a point or interval estimate – you don't need any estimates at all because you already have the precise parameter you want.

We report confidence intervals as a pair of two values, which we call the upper and lower bounds. The centre of the confidence interval is always a sample statistic (usually the mean), although we don't typically report that statistic when reporting the confidence interval. We place the bounds inside brackets to indicate that they are a pair. For example, a 95% confidence with a lower bound of 1.5 and an upper bound of 2.5 computed from a sample of ten would be reported as $CI_{95} = [1.5, 2.5]$.

Because a confidence interval is always centred on the mean, we know that the mean is 2.0. So how do we interpret this interval? Again, pay close attention to the difference between these two sentences:

- ■ Correct: 95% of $n = 10$ sample means drawn from a population with a mean of 2.0 will fall between 1.5 and 2.5.

- ■ Incorrect: There is a 95% chance that the population mean is between 1.5 and 2.5.

Remember, the population mean either is or is not between 1.5 and 2.5. Computing a confidence interval does not change that, so the second sentence here is incorrect. The only conclusion we can make is the first sentence.

While that may seem like a limited definition, it still gives us a lot of useful information. For example, imagine that in our case study, Chaitra found these confidence intervals for her daily production counts:

Nuts CI_{95} = [1500, 2500]

Bolts CI_{95} = [1000, 3000]

While the mean (point estimate) of both is 2000 units (2000 is at the centre of both of these intervals), the estimate of the population mean of nut production is more precise than the estimate of bolt production. If we were to assume that the population means were 2000 units, we would expect 95% of samples of this size drawn from the nut production population to fall between 1500 and 2500. In contrast, we would expect 95% of samples of this size drawn from the bolt population to fall between 1000 and 3000.

This demonstrates the value of confidence intervals: they communicate, at a glance, the precision of a point estimate as a measure of its parameter.

WHAT IF I WANT TO KNOW THE LOGICALLY IMPOSSIBLE?

At this point you might be thinking to yourself, 'why is concluding that there's a 95% chance that the mean is between two numbers logically impossible?' The reason is that everything we're discussing in this textbook is based upon something called **frequentism**. Frequentism is a philosophical point of view about probability. It suggests that all events in the world have a true frequency (i.e., a parameter) and that the purpose of statistics is to estimate these frequencies. Thus, 'a 95% chance that the mean is between 1 and 2' is a nonsense statement to a frequentist; the mean exists, and the purpose of your analysis is to give your best estimate as to what that mean is.

An alternative philosophy is **Bayesianism**, named after Thomas Bayes, the English statistician who created it in the 1700s. For a Bayesian, parameter estimates themselves are less interesting than our certainty about them, so Bayesians have developed an entire system of statistical analyses with an alternative set of assumptions that allows them to estimate certainty directly. Within Bayesian statistics, you *can* calculate the probability that a mean exists between two numbers. However, the cost of being able to conclude something like that is that there are more assumptions you must make in comparison to frequentist statistics. Because of those extra assumptions, and because the maths is a bit more difficult, Bayesianism is still relatively uncommon in comparison to frequentism. Thus, this book focuses on frequentist approaches. But you should still be aware of Bayesianism in case it comes up when speaking with professional statisticians and analysts!

6.3 HOW TO CALCULATE CONFIDENCE INTERVALS

Now that we've learned what confidence intervals are and why they are important, we'll learn how to compute them. There are two major types of confidence interval that you should be familiar with. The appropriateness of each depends on if you have one key piece of information: the population standard deviation (or standard error). Although you rarely have this piece of information in the real world, going through its computation will make clearer why confidence intervals are calculated the way they are calculated – see Figure 6.02.

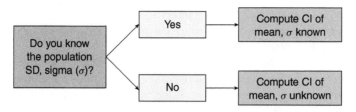

FIGURE 6.02 Decision tree when a confidence interval of the mean is needed

6.3.1 CI OF A MEAN WITH A KNOWN POPULATION STANDARD DEVIATION/ STANDARD ERROR

6.3.1.1 THEORETICAL BASIS

When σ is known, the two bounds of a confidence interval are determined by three parts: a statistic (the mean), its standard error and a z-score. The formula incorporating these three parts appears in Figure 6.03.

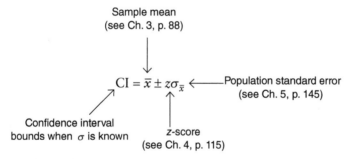

FIGURE 6.03 Annotated formula for calculating the confidence interval bounds when the population standard deviation/error is known

Since we need to identify both an upper and lower bound for the confidence interval, we actually calculate this formula twice, adding or subtracting the second portion of the formula depending on which bound we want to know (subtract for the lower bound; add for the upper bound), as demonstrated in Figure 6.04.

$$CI_{LB} = \bar{x} - z\sigma_{\bar{x}}$$
$$CI_{UB} = \bar{x} + z\sigma_{\bar{x}}$$
$$CI = \left[\bar{x} - z\sigma_{\bar{x}}, \bar{x} + z\sigma_{\bar{x}}\right]$$

FIGURE 6.04 Variations on the confidence interval formula when σ is known: lower bound, upper bound and both bounds

Each part of the formula serves a particular purpose. The sample mean, $\bar{x}$, is the centre of the interval, so we always start with that. Since we'll be adding and subtracting the same amount to identify the two bounds, the mean will always stay at the mathematical centre of the interval.

By putting the mean at the centre of the interval, we are saying, 'This is our best guess as to the population parameter. And if this were the parameter, what range of sample means would we expect to be drawn from this population?'

Next, we create a cross-product of a z-statistic and the standard error. Remember z-scores? They represent how many standard deviations from a sample or population mean a particular value is. For example, $z = -1$ represents a value that is one standard deviation below the mean. If this doesn't seem familiar, this would be a good time to review Chapter 4.

The same principle applies here, but instead of identifying a z-score for a sample, we are identifying a z-score for a sampling distribution. Does the formula in Figure 6.05 look familiar?

$$x = zs + \bar{x}$$

FIGURE 6.05   Formula to convert a z-score into a raw value (from Chapter 4)

We used this formula to convert a z-score into a raw value in Chapter 4. We multiplied a z-score by a standard deviation and added the mean to determine what the raw value originally was. *Computing the bounds of a confidence interval is essentially the same.* We're really trying to determine 'between which two values would we expect 95% of sample means?' Since the standard deviation of the sampling distribution is the standard error, we simply replace the standard deviation in our z-score formula with the standard error to create our confidence interval formula.

6.3.1.2 STEP BY STEP COMPUTATION

So let's try it. Imagine that Chaitra (from our case study) was interested in identifying the confidence interval surrounding daily bolt production at her 12 plants. She recently received a report from corporate HQ that, on average, daily bolt production at each plant company-wide varies by 2000 bolts. Hopefully you recognize this as the definition of standard deviation; if not, review Chapter 3 (see p. 89).

Since production techniques are for the most part standardized across her organization, Chaitra believes the standard deviation provided by corporate HQ will be a better estimate of the population standard deviation than she could identify from her sample alone. So if Chaitra wants to get an estimate of mean bolt production, this value (2000) must be a population standard deviation. In real life, it's fairly unusual that you'd be able to identify a population standard deviation, so this isn't a situation you're likely to encounter very often. But just bear with me! This will help you understand the more realistic scenario coming up in the next section, when things get a little more complicated.

WHY SAMPLING TECHNIQUE IS CRITICAL

In the last chapter, we learned about three sampling techniques: random, stratified random and convenience sampling. The decision on sampling technique has important implications for the conclusions Chaitra can draw from her dataset. In this chapter, Chaitra has a sample of mean daily production rate (over one month) at her 12 plants, and from that she wants to draw conclusions about her plants in general. So what kind of sample is this, and how does that affect her conclusions?

This is a *convenience sample*. Chaitra wants to draw conclusions about her plants *in general*. If she were collecting a random sample, she would need to locate data randomly drawn from the past, present and future. That way, even if she didn't collect data from every time point, she could at least be sure that she was getting a good representation of how her plants produce. Unfortunately, this is impossible – a convenience sample is the best option available.

Sometimes the *problems brought* about by convenience sampling are obvious and sometimes they are more subtle. An obvious problem here is that the particular month chosen may influence the mean daily rates observed within that month. What if Chaitra routinely hired college students looking for summer work to boost her production rates each summer? If this sample was collected during the summer, it would be much more unlikely to reflect the population value in general. Less-obvious problems might be employee vacation patterns, the frequency of equipment breakdowns, changes in managers, or any other factor that might make a particular month unusual. It is ultimately your responsibility as the creator of these numbers to identify any possible confounding factors, to ensure your point and interval estimates reflect what you claim them to represent. The only way to avoid this is to use random sampling – but in business, this usually isn't a realistic option.

When Chaitra measures the mean of bolt production in her plants, she finds that her plants, on average, produce about 14000 bolts each day. She calculates this from the data she collected, using the tools we covered in Chapter 3. Thus, 14000 is her sample mean. The only piece of the formula she is missing is the *z*-score.

Fortunately, the *z*-score is the easiest part of this formula! Remember that the confidence interval formula operates very similarly to our original *z*-score-to-raw-score conversion formula. In the problems we covered in Chapter 4, we solved problems just like this one. For a 95% confidence interval, we want to identify the two outer values between which 95% of sample means will fall. Just like in Chapter 4, let's draw it out first – you should end up with something like Figure 6.06.

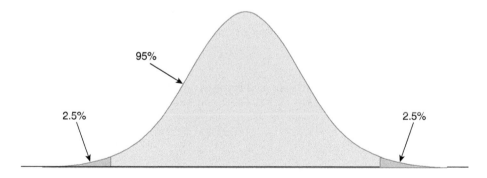

FIGURE 6.06   95% confidence interval bounds of a sampling distribution

When computing the boundaries of a 95% confidence interval, we need to identify at what *z*-score 2.5% of the distribution lies in the tail. Find this value in Appendix A1 using the techniques you practised in Chapter 4, as shown in Figure 6.07.

From this, we can conclude that the *z*-score associated with a 95% confidence interval is 1.96. *This will always be true.* 95% confidence intervals will always use 1.96 as their associated *z*-score, so if you memorize that value, you won't need to look it up in Appendix A1 ever again.

z	0	0.01	0.02	0.03	0.04	0.05	0.06	0.07	0.08	0.09
t	0.1587	0.1562	0.1539	0.1515	0.1492	0.1469	0.1446	0.1423	0.1401	0.1379
1.1	0.1357	0.1335	0.1314	0.1292	0.1271	0.1251	0.1230	0.1210	0.1190	0.1170
1.2	0.1151	0.1131	0.1112	0.1093	0.1075	0.1056	0.1038	0.1020	0.1003	0.0985
1.3	0.0968	0.0951	0.0934	0.0918	0.0901	0.0885	0.0869	0.0853	0.0838	0.0823
1.4	0.0808	0.0793	0.0778	0.0764	0.0749	0.0735	0.0721	0.0708	0.0694	0.0681
1.5	0.0668	0.0655	0.0643	0.0630	0.0618	0.0606	0.0594	0.0582	0.0571	0.0559
1.6	0.0548	0.0537	0.0526	0.0516	0.0505	0.0495	0.0485	0.0475	0.0465	0.0455
1.7	0.0446	0.0436	0.0427	0.0418	0.0409	0.0401	0.0392	0.0384	0.0375	0.0367
1.8	0.0359	0.0351	0.0344	0.0336	0.0329	0.0322	0.0314	0.0307	0.0301	0.0294
1.9	0.0287	0.0281	0.0274	0.0268	0.0262	0.0256	0.0250	0.0244	0.0239	0.0233

FIGURE 6.07   Looking up Appendix A1 for the critical z-score in the confidence interval formula

To test yourself, see if you can identify the z-score associated with a 99% confidence interval. If you do it correctly, you should find that it is 2.575.

Now we have almost everything we need to compute the bounds of the CI. All that's remaining is the standard error. We know that the population standard deviation is 2000 because it was provided, and we also know that Chaitra has collected a sample of 12 plants. Calculation of the standard error based upon this information appears in Figure 6.08.

$$\sigma_{\bar{x}} = \frac{\sigma}{\sqrt{n}} = \frac{2000}{\sqrt{12}} = \frac{2000}{3.464102} = 577.350205$$

FIGURE 6.08   Computing the standard error for the case study dataset when the population standard deviation is provided

Since we'll be using the computed standard error in new formulas, we'll keep it rounded to six digits. Don't ever round early. We'll next compute the actual bounds of the 95% confidence interval separately. These calculations appear in Figures 6.09 and 6.10.

$$CI_{95LB} = \bar{x} - z\sigma_{\bar{x}}$$

$$= 14000 - 1.96(577.350205)$$

$$= 14000 - 1131.606402$$

$$= 12868.393598$$

$$= 12868.39$$

FIGURE 6.09   Step by step calculations for the lower bound of a 95% confidence interval when σ is known

$$\text{CI}_{95\text{UB}} = \bar{x} + z\sigma_{\bar{x}}$$

$$= 14000 + 1.96(577.350205)$$

$$= 14000 + 1131.606402$$

$$= 15131.606402$$

$$= 15131.61$$

FIGURE 6.10   Step by step calculations for the upper bound of a 95% confidence interval when σ is known

From this, we can make a more formal statistical conclusion about the confidence interval:

$$\text{CI}_{95} = [12868.39, \ 15131.61]$$

We can then also interpret this interval: if '14000 bolts' is truly the population mean, 95% of samples drawn from that population would fall between 12868.39 and 15131.61.

Each of these statements – a formal statistical conclusion and an interpretation – is required when reporting a confidence interval.

6.3.2 CI OF A MEAN WITH AN UNKNOWN POPULATION STANDARD DEVIATION/STANDARD ERROR

6.3.2.1 THEORETICAL BASIS

As mentioned earlier, it is fairly unusual to know the population standard deviation or standard error. Instead, we typically only have access to the sample standard deviation. You might think that we could use the same formula as in the previous section, replacing the population standard error with the sample standard error in order to compute the bounds of the confidence interval. Unfortunately, it's not quite so simple, because the z-distribution can be biased when considering samples.

You might remember reading about bias in standard deviations in Chapter 3 (see p. 89). When computing the sample standard deviation, if we put n in the bottom of the formulas, we'd end up with estimates of the population standard deviation that were too large. Instead, we use $n − 1$. The reason for this is that when a sample is small, extreme scores become relatively more important in the calculation than when a sample is large. Consider these two samples with identical means:

Sample 1: 1, 5, 9

Sample 2: 1, 4, 5, 6, 9

Although the means of both of these distributions are 5, they differ dramatically in their variability. Both have relatively extreme scores (1 and 9), but the slightly larger sample provides more opportunity for scores to fall close to the mean (4 and 6). That means that in small samples, scores tend to fall in the tails more often. This bias is the reason for $n - 1$; we're trying to get as accurate a point estimate of the population standard deviation as possible, and we need to account for extreme scores when doing so.

Around 1930, a statistician working for the Guinness Brewery in Dublin named William Sealy Gosset noticed the same problem in sampling distributions. Because extreme scores are more influential in small samples, the z-distribution is inaccurate in describing the sampling distribution when samples are small. When n is smaller than N, sample means tend to fall further from the population mean than the z-distribution would suggest, leading to an underestimation of the population standard error.

To solve this problem, Gosset mathematically derived what sampling distributions look like when sample sizes are small. But because Gosset couldn't publish his work with his name on it (think of it as an early intellectual property conflict), he published this finding under the name 'Student'. Thus was born the student's t-distribution, often shortened to simply *t-distribution*.

The t-distribution is quite a bit different from the z-distribution because it is a different shape depending on the sample size. In this way, the 't-distribution' is really an entire set of distributions. You can see the differences between some of these shapes in Figure 6.11.

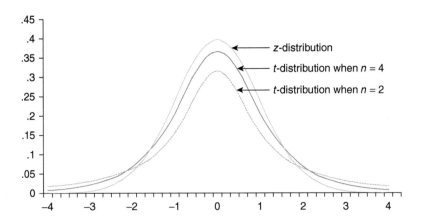

FIGURE 6.11   Comparing the shape of the z-distribution and t-distribution with varying sample sizes

The difference between the z-distribution and the t-distribution gets smaller as sample sizes get larger. When $n > 30$, the z-distribution and t-distribution are very similar. When n is much smaller, they are quite different, as can be seen in Figure 6.11. The smaller n is, the thicker the tails of the sampling distribution.

When σ is unknown and therefore a t-distribution better reflects the sampling distribution, a confidence interval is created with three parts: a statistic (the mean), its standard error and a t-score – see Figure 6.12.

There are two major changes to this formula from the first we learned. First, since we don't know the population standard deviation or standard error, we must now compute the *sample* standard error. Second, since we are using the sample standard error, we must use scores from the t-distribution.

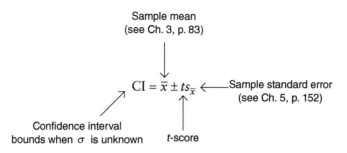

FIGURE 6.12   Annotated formula for calculating the bounds of a confidence interval when the population standard deviation/error is not known

We again need to identify both an upper and lower bound for the confidence interval, so we still calculate this formula twice, adding or subtracting the second portion of the formula depending on which bound we want to know (subtract for the lower bound; add for the upper bound) – see Figure 6.13.

$$\text{CI}_{\text{LB}} = \bar{x} - ts_{\bar{x}}$$

$$\text{CI}_{\text{UB}} = \bar{x} + ts_{\bar{x}}$$

$$\text{CI} = \left[\bar{x} - ts_{\bar{x}}, \bar{x} + ts_{\bar{x}}\right]$$

FIGURE 6.13   Variations on the confidence interval formula when σ is unknown: lower bound, upper bound and both bounds

Nothing changes in the interpretation of this confidence interval in comparison with the confidence interval we calculated when we knew the population standard deviation. The only difference is that this interval should be more accurate.

6.3.2.2 STEP BY STEP COMPUTATION

Now Chaitra is again interested in identifying the confidence interval surrounding daily bolt production in her 12 plants. But this time, more realistically, she lacks a report from corporate HQ that provides her the population standard deviation. Her best guess to the population standard deviation is the sample standard deviation, which she computes in Excel (or SPSS) as 2198.

For our new confidence interval formula, we must first identify the appropriate t-score to represent the desired level of confidence. As before, we typically default to a 95% interval.

To identify this value, we must refer to a t-table, which appears in Appendix A2 (see p. 426). We'll be using the t-table for the next several chapters, so there's a little more information here than we need at the moment. For confidence intervals, we only need to pay attention to the column labelled, conveniently, 'confidence intervals'.

But along the left column, this table looks a bit different than the z-table. Because the sampling distribution is a different shape for every sample size, we must first identify the appropriate shape. This is determined by degrees of freedom, often abbreviated d.f. Degrees of freedom are calculated differently depending on what test or statistic you are trying to calculate. In this case, to compute degrees of freedom for the confidence interval surrounding a mean, the appropriate degrees of freedom are: $n - 1$.

WHY 'DEGREES OF FREEDOM'?

One of the most confusing terms for those just beginning to learn about statistics is 'degrees of freedom'. What exactly is 'free' and why does it have 'degrees'?

This term refers to the number of independent pieces of information that are available to estimate a value of interest. In the case of confidence intervals, we need to estimate the standard error, so one piece of information has been constrained. However, we have n cases from which to estimate that value. Thus, the degrees of freedom when computing a confidence interval are $n - 1$.

Degrees of freedom will be different for each calculation where standard errors need to be estimated. We'll revisit this concept in several later chapters.

Since Chaitra has 12 plants, d.f. $= 12 - 1 = 11$. So in the t-table, find the 95% confidence interval column, and scan down until you identify the appropriate t-score for 11 degrees of freedom (Figure 6.14).

	Confidence intervals			
	90%	95%	98%	99%
	Two-tailed α			
	.10	.05	.02	.01
d.f.	One-tailed α			
	.05	.025	.01	.005
1	6.314	12.706	31.821	63.657
2	2.920	4.303	6.965	9.925
3	2.353	3.182	4.541	5.841
4	2.132	2.776	3.747	4.604
5	2.015	2.571	3.365	4.032
6	1.943	2.447	3.143	3.707
7	1.895	2.365	2.998	3.499
8	1.860	2.306	2.896	3.355
9	1.833	2.262	2.821	3.250
10	1.812	2.228	2.764	3.169
11	1.796	2.201	2.718	3.106
12	1.782	2.179	2.681	3.055

FIGURE 6.14   Looking up Appendix A2 for the critical t-score in the confidence interval formula

From this, we can conclude that the t-score associated with a 95% confidence interval with 11 degrees of freedom is 2.201. You will need to look up the appropriate t-score every time you need to compute a confidence interval this way.

If the t-score you need is skipped, use the next smaller value provided in the table. For example, if you want the t-score associated with d.f. $= 34$, use the values in the row associated with d.f. $= 30$.

To test yourself, see if you can identify the *t*-score associated with a 99% confidence interval and 11 degrees of freedom. If you do it correctly, you should find that it is 3.106.

Now we have almost everything we need to compute the bounds of the CI. All that's remaining is the standard error. This time, Chaitra computed the sample standard deviation at 2200 from a sample of 12 plants, as shown in Figure 6.15.

$$s_{\bar{x}} = \frac{s}{\sqrt{n}}$$

$$= \frac{2200}{\sqrt{12}}$$

$$= \frac{2200}{3.464102}$$

$$= 635.085226$$

FIGURE 6.15   Step by step computation of the standard error for the case study dataset when the population standard deviation is not provided

Since we'll be using the computed standard error in new formulas, we'll keep it rounded to six digits. Don't ever round early. We'll next compute the actual bounds of the 95% confidence interval separately, using the same mean of 14000 bolts from before – see Figures 6.16 and 6.17.

$$CI_{95LB} = \bar{x} - ts_{\bar{x}}$$

$$= 14000 - 2.201(635.085226)$$

$$= 14000 - 1397.822582$$

$$= 12602.177418$$

$$= 12602.18$$

FIGURE 6.16   Step by step calculations for the lower bound of a 95% confidence interval when σ is unknown

$$CI_{95UB} = \bar{x} + ts_{\bar{x}}$$

$$= 14000 + 2.201(635.085226)$$

$$= 14000 + 1397.822582$$

$$= 15397.822582$$

$$= 15397.82$$

FIGURE 6.17   Step by step calculations for the upper bound of a 95% confidence interval when σ is unknown

From this, we can make a more formal statistical conclusion about the confidence interval:

$$CI_{95} = [12602.18, 15397.82]$$

We can then also interpret this interval just as we did before: if 14000 bolts is truly the population mean, 95% of samples drawn from that population would fall between 12602.18 and 15397.82.

Also just as before, each of these statements – a formal statistical conclusion and an interpretation – is required when reporting a confidence interval.

If you compare these values with those we computed when we did not know the population standard deviation, you'll see the effect of estimating the population standard deviation. Remember that the means and sample sizes are identical:

$$CI_{Z95} = [12868.39, 15131.61]$$

$$CI_{T95} = [12602.18, 15397.82]$$

When we don't know the population standard deviation, we are less confident in our interval estimate. This results in a *wider interval* and less precision. This demonstrates that if the population standard error is known, we should always use it (and the z-distribution) instead of the sample standard error (and the t-distribution) to get the most precise estimate of the bounds that we can. It is only when we don't know the population standard error that we *must* use the t-distribution – because it's the best we have available.

6.3.3 MARGIN OF ERROR

We often hear the term 'margin of error' in news reports. For example, 'the margin of error is 2%', 'the survey results are accurate to within 2%' or 'the result is 5 plus or minus 2%'. On the surface, this certainly seems less confusing to a reader than reporting confidence interval bounds, but what does it really mean?

Margin of error generally refers to half of a confidence interval, converted into a percentage of the value being estimated. As an example, let's assume:

- an estimated mean of 5.

- a 95% confidence interval of [3, 7].

From this, we can conclude that the margin of error is 2 points; 5 is 2 points away from both 3 and 7. Two points is 40% of 5, and therefore the margin of error is 40%.

Let's try this with our case study data. When we computed the confidence interval using the t-distribution to estimate the standard error, we did this:

$$CI_{95} = \bar{x} \pm ts_{\bar{x}} = 14000 \pm 2.201(635.085226) = 14000 \pm 1397.822582$$

The second part of the formula is all we need to compute margin of error: 1397.822582. We just need to figure out what percentage of the mean this value is – see Figure 6.18.

$$ME = \frac{1397.822582}{14000}$$

$$= .099844$$

$$= .10$$

$$= 10\%$$

FIGURE 6.18   Step by step computations for the margin of error for the case study

From this, we can conclude that the margin of error for Chaitra's estimate of bolt production is 10%.

We can summarize all of these efforts with the formulas in Figures 6.19 and 6.20.

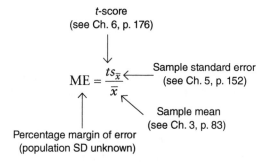

FIGURE 6.19   Annotated formula for the margin of error when σ is unknown

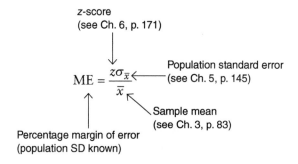

FIGURE 6.20   Annotated formula for the margin of error when σ is known

6.4 APPLYING ESTIMATION AND CONFIDENCE INTERVALS

To apply what you've learned from this chapter, consider the following case study, questions posed about that case study, and discussion of those questions.

6.4.1 APPLICATION CASE STUDY

Eban is the owner of Posies and Pansies, a flower shop. One of the trickiest parts of Eban's responsibilities is to ensure that he orders flowers from his distributor so that they are freshest when they are ordered by customers. Unfortunately, customers are not very consistent. Some weeks, Eban orders too many flowers. Stems are left unsold, wilt, and represent a loss of profit. Other weeks, he orders too few, missing out on sales to customers who would have purchased those orders.

To better forecast his orders and ultimate costs, Eban computed means and standard deviations for each type of flower that he sells each day when he does not run out. While these summarize his data, he is not sure they solve his problem entirely.

Is this a situation where a confidence interval would help? If he computes a confidence interval, will he have the information he needs to predict flower sales in the future better than with a mean?

6.4.2 APPLICATION DISCUSSION

Eban wants to do what statisticians all hope to do: predict the future! Unfortunately, as he has learned, this can be quite difficult. The means that he has computed can be considered point estimates, and those are the best single estimates of flowers needed that he has. However, we know nothing about the precision of those estimates without a confidence interval.

With a confidence interval, a type of interval estimate, Eban can make broader conclusions about how well his sample means represent the population means from which they are drawn. For example, if the confidence intervals for one type of flower are wider than another type of flower, Eban knows that his estimate of daily needs for that flower type is not as precise as his estimates of others. Thus, those flowers represent greater risk and perhaps justify more cautious ordering.

EXPLORING ESTIMATION AND CONFIDENCE INTERVALS IN EXCEL AND SPSS

EXCEL

Download the Excel dataset for the demonstration below as **chapter6.xls**. As you read this section, try to apply the terms you've learned in this chapter to the dataset and follow along with Excel on your own computer.

You can also get a video demonstration of the section below under **Excel Video: Chapter 6**.

In our case study, Chaitra needs to produce an interval estimate of the overall production level of her plants. She has a convenience sample of all of her plants' most recent month of production levels, although it is stratified in that she has sampled each of her plants once (see Chapter 5 for a review of sampling methods).

Instead of reporting a point estimate of her plants' typical production levels alone, she should also provide a confidence interval indicating the precision of those estimates. To do this, she needs to first compute the means of each variable. Do so in Row 14 so that you end up with something like Figure 6.21 (review Chapter 3, p. 96, if you've forgotten how to compute means in Excel).

10	9	11813	14028	10654	18013	6259	5172	4153
11	10	11683	12339	10930	17968	5469	4340	5479
12	11	11660	17033	10805	18083	6427	4269	1333
13	12	10840	13467	10921	18007	5889	1910	1927
14	Mean	11508.92	14000.92	10975.42	18013.83	6076.833	4848.083	3755.083
15								

FIGURE 6.21   Excel case study dataset after computing means

We're next going to consider two situations to illustrate these concepts in Excel. First, we'll consider a scenario where Chaitra has access to population standard deviations (or standard errors). Second, we'll consider a scenario where she doesn't.

COMPUTING STANDARD DEVIATION AND MARGIN OF ERROR WITH A KNOWN POPULATION SD

Let's first explore a scenario where the population standard deviation was provided to Chaitra. Enter the population values in Row 16, as in Figure 6.22.

11	10	11683	12339	10930	17968	5469	4340	5479
12	11	11660	17033	10805	18083	6427	4269	1333
13	12	10840	13467	10921	18007	5889	1910	1927
14	Mean	11508.92	14000.92	10975.42	18013.83	6076.833	4848.083	3755.083
15								
16	Pop SD	900	2000	200	75	300	2000	1900

FIGURE 6.22   Excel case study dataset after entering population standard deviations

Remember that we only use z-score-based formulas for confidence intervals when we know the population standard deviation. The only way you'd know this is if that information was given to you.

Next, add four new row headers (Figure 6.23). The first, ConfZ, will contain the product of the standard error and 95% confidence interval z-score. The second will contain the lower bound of the confidence interval. The third will contain the upper bound of the confidence interval. The fourth will contain the margin of error.

12		11	11660	17033	10805	
13		12	10840	13467	10921	
14	Mean		11508.92	14000.92	10975.42	1
15						
16	Pop SD		900	2000	200	
17	ConfZ					
18	CI Z LB					
19	CI Z UB					
20	ME					

FIGURE 6.23   Excel case study dataset after creating confidence interval template

(Continued)

(Continued)

In B17, we'll enter the formula to produce the product of the standard error and 95% confidence interval z-score, $z\sigma_{\bar{x}}$:

1. **Excel 2010 or later:** in B17, type: =CONFIDENCE.NORM(5%,B16,12).
2. **Excel 2007 or earlier:** in B17, type: =CONFIDENCE (5%,B16,12).

Each of these formulas takes three arguments:

1. The first number needed is the proportion of cases falling in the tails of the confidence interval. Since we want a 95% confidence interval, 5% falls in the tails.
2. The second number is the population standard deviation. Since we typed this manually into B16, we type B16 to reference that cell.
3. The third number is the sample size, n. Since we have 12 cases, we type 12. We could instead here enter a function that counts the number of cells, for example: COUNT(B2:B13). But since we know there are 12 and exactly 12 cases, simply entering the number 12 is a little less complicated.

Once you have entered the correct formula in B17, fill right to H17 (if you've forgotten fills, see Chapter 3, p. 97). If you enter these formulas correctly, you should end up with Figure 6.24.

13	12	10840	13467	10921	18007	5889	1910	1927
14	Mean	11508.92	14000.92	10975.42	18013.83	6076.833	4848.083	3755.083
15								
16	Pop SD	900	2000	200	75	300	2000	1900
17	ConfZ	509.2136	1131.586	113.1586	42.43447	169.7379	1131.586	1075.006
18	CI Z LB							

FIGURE 6.24   Excel case study dataset after computing product of the standard error and z-score

Now that we have the second half of the confidence interval formula, we simply need to add or subtract that value from the mean to determine the bounds.

To compute the lower bound in B18, type: =B14 – B17.

To compute the upper bound in B19, type: =B14+B17.

In these two cells, we are simply realizing the confidence interval formula: B14 contains the mean, while B17 contains the product of the z-score and standard error.

Once you have these two values entered, fill right. You should end up with Figure 6.25.

16	Pop SD	900	2000	200	75	300	2000	1900
17	ConfZ	509.2136	1131.586	113.1586	42.43447	169.7379	1131.586	1075.006
18	CI Z LB	10999.7	12869.33	10862.26	17971.4	5907.095	3716.498	2680.077
19	CI Z UB	12018.13	15132.5	11088.58	18056.27	6246.571	5979.669	4830.09
20	ME							

FIGURE 6.25   Excel case study dataset after computing upper and lower bounds of the CI

From this, we can construct formal statistical conclusions and interpretations of each. For example:

$$CI_{95Pins} = [17971.40, 18056.27]$$

Conclusion: 95% of samples of $n = 12$ drawn from a population with mean pin production of 18013.83 would fall between 17971.40 and 18056.27.

To compute the margin of error, we will follow the formula discussed earlier in this chapter: divide the product of the standard error and z-score (which we have labelled ConfZ) by the mean.

Thus, to compute the margin of error in B20, type: =B17/B14.

Fill right, and you should end up with Figure 6.26.

16	Pop SD	900	2000	200	75	300	2000	1900
17	ConfZ	509.2136	1131.586	113.1586	42.43447	169.7379	1131.586	1075.006
18	CI Z LB	10999.7	12869.33	10862.26	17971.4	5907.095	3716.498	2680.077
19	CI Z UB	12018.13	15132.5	11088.58	18056.27	6246.571	5979.669	4830.09
20	ME	0.044245	0.080822	0.01031	0.002356	0.027932	0.233409	0.28628

FIGURE 6.26 Excel case study dataset after computing CI bounds and margin of error

With this, we can state all margins of error. For example, the margin of error for rivets is 28.63%.

COMPUTING STANDARD DEVIATION AND MARGIN OF ERROR WITH AN UNKNOWN POPULATION SD

Let's now explore a more realistic scenario: the population standard deviation is not known. Instead, Chaitra's best guess as to her population standard deviation is her sample standard deviation. In Row 22, compute the standard deviation of the values contained between B2 and B13. If you don't remember how to compute standard deviations, see Chapter 3 (p. 98). Also create four new row headers, similar to what we did when the population SD was known. It should look like Figure 6.27.

18	CI Z LB	10999.7	12869.33	10862.26	17971.4	5907.095	3716.498	2680.077
19	CI Z UB	12018.13	15132.5	11088.58	18056.27	6246.571	5979.669	4830.09
20	ME	0.044245	0.080822	0.01031	0.002356	0.027932	0.233409	0.28628
21								
22	Samp SD	908.3161	2197.609	201.6389	78.89214	300.9799	1939.095	1854.271
23	ConfT							
24	CI T LB							
25	CI T UB							
26	ME							

FIGURE 6.27 Excel case study dataset after computing sample standard deviations

(Continued)

(Continued)

These headers are similar to what we had before, with a few key differences. ConfZ has become ConfT, as it represents $ts_{\bar{x}}$, instead of $zs_{\bar{x}}$, containing the product of the standard error and 95% confidence interval t-score. CI Z has become CI T, as it is based on the t-distribution instead of the z-distribution.

In B23, we'll enter the formula to produce the product of the standard error and 95% confidence interval t-score, $ts_{\bar{x}}$:

1. **Excel 2010 or later:** To compute this product in B23, type: =CONFIDENCE.T(5%,B22,12).

   The arguments for the formula in Excel 2010 are essentially identical to that of CONFIDENCE. NORM, requiring the proportion of the distribution in the tails, sample standard deviation and sample size.

2. **Excel 2007 or earlier: To compute this product in B23, type: =TINV(5%,11)*B22/SQRT(12).**

   In Excel 2007 and earlier, there is no built-in function to compute a confidence interval for the t-distribution. Instead, we must create this term manually. We first compute the t-value with TINV (the first argument represents the proportion of the distribution in the tails, while the second term represents degrees of freedom). We multiply this by the standard error (standard deviation divided by the square root of n). Note that we could take a similar approach in Excel 2010 to compute this term manually, but the CONFIDENCE.T function makes this much simpler.

Once you have entered the correct formula in B23, fill right to H23. If you enter these formulas correctly, you should end up with Figure 6.28.

18	CI Z LB	10999.7	12869.33	10862.26	17971.4	5907.095	3716.498	2680.077
19	CI Z UB	12018.13	15132.5	11088.58	18056.27	6246.571	5979.669	4830.09
20	ME	0.044245	0.080822	0.01031	0.002356	0.027932	0.233409	0.28628
21								
22	Samp SD	908.3161	2197.609	201.6389	78.89214	300.9799	1939.095	1854.271
23	ConfT	577.1165	1396.294	128.1153	50.12567	191.2335	1232.042	1178.148
24	CI T LB							
25	CI T UB							
26	ME							

FIGURE 6.28   Excel case study dataset after computing product of standard error and t-score

Follow the same pattern as before to compute the bounds and the margin of error:

To compute the lower bound in B24, type: =B14 – B23.
To compute the upper bound in B25, type: =B14+B23.
To compute the margin of error in B26, type: =B23/B14.
Once you have these three values entered, fill right. You should end up with Figure 6.29.

19	CI Z UB	12018.13	15132.5	11088.58	18056.27	6246.571	5979.669	4830.09
20	ME	0.044245	0.080822	0.01031	0.002356	0.027932	0.233409	0.28628
21								
22	Samp SD	908.3161	2197.609	201.6389	78.89214	300.9799	1939.095	1854.271
23	ConfT	577.1165	1396.294	128.1153	50.12567	191.2335	1232.042	1178.148
24	CI T LB	10931.8	12604.62	10847.3	17963.71	5885.6	3616.041	2576.936
25	CI T UB	12086.03	15397.21	11103.53	18063.96	6268.067	6080.126	4933.231
26	ME	0.050145	0.099729	0.011673	0.002783	0.031469	0.25413	0.313747

FIGURE 6.29   Excel case study dataset after computing CI bounds and margin of error

From this, we can again construct formal statistical conclusions and interpretations of each. For example:

$$CI_{95Pins} = [17963.71, 18063.96]$$

Conclusion: 95% of samples of $n = 12$ drawn from a population with mean pin production of 18013.83 would fall between 17963.71 and 18063.96.

You will notice that the confidence intervals without a known population standard deviation are slightly wider than those with a known population standard deviation. The margins of error are also slightly larger. This is the effect of the larger tails in the t-distribution, since the standard deviations are similar and the 'n's identical.

Using her work here, Chaitra can report the confidence intervals, giving her superiors a better sense of how confident she is in each of the estimates. For example, she is quite confident in her estimates of screws, pins and washers (1%, .2% and 3% margins of error, respectively), but much less so in her estimates of anchor and rivet production (25% and 31% margins of error).

SPSS

Download the SPSS dataset for the demonstration below as **chapter6.sav**. As you read this section, try to apply the terms you've learned in this chapter to the dataset and follow along with SPSS on your own computer.

You can also get a video demonstration of the section below under **SPSS Videos: Chapter 6**.

In our case study, Chaitra needs to produce an interval estimate of the overall production level of her plants. She has a convenience sample of all of her plants' most recent month of production levels, although it is stratified in that she has sampled each of her plants once (see Chapter 5 for a review of sampling methods).

Instead of reporting a point estimate of her plants' typical production levels alone, she should also provide a confidence interval indicating the precision of those estimates (or the margin of error).

Because it is so uncommon for the population standard deviation to be known, SPSS only includes functions to compute the confidence interval using the t-distribution.

To identify the confidence interval, in the **Analyze** menu, select **Compare Means**, followed by **One-Sample T Test**. In the following dialogue, move all of your variables to the right. Ensure that the 'Test Value' is 0 – see Figure 6.30.

(Continued)

(Continued)

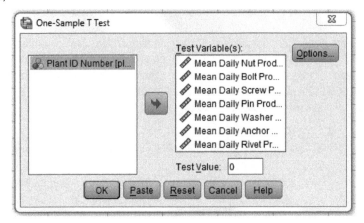

FIGURE 6.30   One-sample t-test SPSS dialogue

If you need something other than a 95% confidence interval, you can change this by clicking on the **Options** button. For now, simply click **OK**.

In the resulting table, shown in Figure 6.31, confidence intervals can be found under the '95% Confidence Interval of the Difference' heading. We'll return to the rest of this table in Chapter 8.

One-Sample Test

	Test Value = 0					
					95% Confidence Interval of the Difference	
	t	df	Sig. (2-tailed)	Mean Difference	Lower	Upper
Mean Daily Nut Production	43.892	11	.000	11508.917	10931.80	12086.03
Mean Daily Bolt Production	22.070	11	.000	14000.917	12604.62	15397.21
Mean Daily Screw Production	188.555	11	.000	10975.417	10847.30	11103.53
Mean Daily Pin Production	790.975	11	.000	18013.833	17963.71	18063.96
Mean Daily Washer Production	69.941	11	.000	6076.833	5885.60	6268.07
Mean Daily Anchor Production	8.661	11	.000	4848.083	3616.04	6080.13
Mean Daily Rivet Production	7.015	11	.000	3755.083	2576.94	4933.23

FIGURE 6.31   Results of one-sample t-test analysis in SPSS for case study dataset

For now, these numbers can be interpreted directly as the *t*-distribution confidence intervals. Remember both your formal test and interpretation. For example:

$$CI_{95Screws} = [10847.30, 11103.53]$$

Conclusion: If we assume the sample mean of screws represents the population mean, 95% of samples drawn from that population would fall between 10847.30 and 11103.53.

To compute the margin of error, your only option is a calculator: subtract the upper confidence interval from the mean to determine $ts_{\bar{x}}$, and divide that value by the mean. For example, for screws:

$$ts_{\bar{x}} = CI_{UB} - \bar{x} = 11103.53 - 10975.42 = 128.11$$

$$ME = \frac{ts_{\bar{x}}}{\bar{x}} = \frac{128.11}{10975.42} = 0.011672 = 1.17\%$$

Using these calculations, Chaitra can report the confidence intervals, giving her superiors a better sense of how confident she is in each of the estimates. For example, she is quite confident in her estimates of screws, pins and washers (1%, .2% and 3% margins of error respectively), but much less so in her estimates of anchor and rivet production (25% and 31% margins of error).

STATISTICS IN THE REAL WORLD

 These web links can be accessed directly from the book's website.

Dan Gilbert, psychologist at Harvard University, describes how our intuitions about estimation are often misleading: www.ted.com/talks/dan_gilbert_researches_happiness.

When are we safe relying on our own judgement for making business decisions, and when do we need to collect data?

In statistics, we must embrace the fact that we can never be completely certain; we must stick to educated guesses, estimates and predictions instead, which is not how most people think about the world. Kathryn Schulz, author of *Being Wrong: Adventures in the Margin of Error*, describes how humans tend to do whatever possible to avoid and reject being wrong: www.ted.com/talks/kathryn_schulz_on_being_wrong.

How can requiring complete certainty for decision-making harm an organization's ability to succeed?

TEST YOURSELF

☑ **After you've completed the questions below, check your answers online.**

1   You identify a 95% confidence interval of [26, 73]. Is it appropriate to conclude that there is a 95% chance that the population mean is between 26 and 73? Why or why not?

2   Determine the critical value for each of the following situations:

a   60% confidence, σ known, $n = 26$.
b   98% confidence, σ unknown, $n = 31$.

3   A co-worker comes to you with a problem: 'I'm preparing a report for upper management about production costs at the plant I'm responsible for. Using Excel, I produced a mean production rate and a confidence interval surrounding that production rate. Which one do you think I should put in the report?' How do you answer this question and why?

(Continued)

(Continued)

4 How do you know to calculate the confidence interval with the *t*-distribution instead of the *z*-distribution?

5 Determine appropriate degrees of freedom for the following sample sizes, assuming σ is unknown:

   a *n* = 246.
   b *n* = 32.
   c *n* = 543.

DATA SKILL CHALLENGES

☑ **After you've completed the questions below, check your answers online.**

1 Your organization has conducted a survey of customer satisfaction, finding these scores: 1, 5, 3, 2, 4, 1, 1, 2, 4, 4, 3, 5, 2, 3, 5, 2, 3, 4, 4, 3, 5, 4. Identify the appropriate confidence interval for the mean.

2 You conduct a study of employee stress levels within your organization, finding these scores: 3.16, 2.12, 5.12, 3.21, 1.11, 4.32, 4.87, 3.79. The test manual you received when ordering the stress survey says that, on average, scores on this test vary by 1.25. Identify the appropriate confidence interval for the mean.

3 When looking through a report in Forbes, you read about a survey of 240 Chief Financial Officers (CFOs) that they conducted, finding that on a five-point scale, on average, CFOs report that their organization's 'financial health' is 4.1, with a standard deviation of .4. What's the margin of error for this mean?

4 In an examination of your sales numbers, you find that mean monthly sales for your store over the past 18 months was £12000. On average, sales each month varied from this mean by £3000. What's the margin of error for your monthly sales estimate?

NEW TERMS

Bayesianism: confidence: confidence interval: degrees of freedom: frequentism: interval estimate: lower bound: point estimate: student's *t*-distribution: *t*-distribution: upper bound

NEW STATISTICAL NOTATION AND FORMULAS

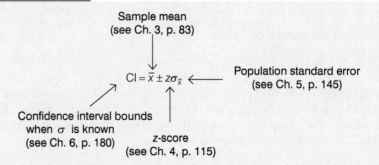

FIGURE 6.32 Annotated confidence interval formula when population standard deviation/error is known

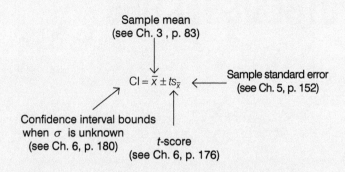

FIGURE 6.33   Annotated confidence interval formula when population standard deviation/error is unknown

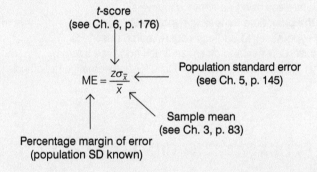

FIGURE 6.34   Margin of error formula when population standard deviation/error is known

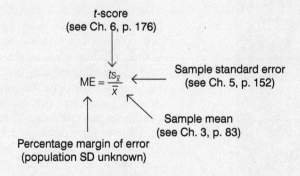

FIGURE 6.35   Margin of error formula when population standard deviation/error is unknown

Visit https://study.sagepub.com/landers2e **for free additional online resources related to this chapter.**

7 HYPOTHESIS TESTING

WHAT YOU WILL LEARN FROM THIS CHAPTER

- How to test hypotheses using confidence intervals
- How to follow the procedure for testing hypotheses
- How to set up hypotheses to address your research questions
- How to distinguish between and minimize Type I and Type II errors
- How to identify the appropriate number of tails for an alternative hypothesis

CASE STUDY   DO MY EXPERTS PREDICT THE FUTURE OR ARE THEY JUST GUESSING?

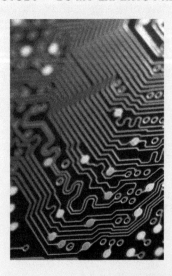

Jesse is the owner of a small non-profit think tank called The Technology Institute. The mission of the Institute is to identify the timing of major upcoming technology shifts among consumers in order to advise standards organizations and the government about these shifts. For example, the Institute predicted the rising importance of smartphones several years ago, allowing it to make regulation and policy recommendations about how to most appropriately react to this change. While this is their primary mission, the think tank also takes consulting projects from individual clients to stay financially solvent.

The company has about two dozen employees, selected from diverse backgrounds in order to have a wide variety of opinions. Any time Jesse lands a new client, he presents the core problem and its context to his employees. After conducting independent research, the employees meet to discuss the issues of interest and must come to a group recommendation, which sometimes takes several weeks. He then passes the conclusions along to the client.

Recently, Jesse has become concerned that his think tank isn't producing useful information. Several of their predictions have turned out to be false. But how many 'bad answers' does the Institute need to push to its clients before he should be worried? If he considers 'the overall performance of his think tank' to be the population, he knows from reading Chapter 5 that looking at any one particular decision is not very helpful; a sample of one won't tell him anything about the population. He also knows from Chapter 6 that confidence intervals can be quite wide, but how wide is too wide? Is there some objective standard with which he can compare his think tank's performance? How does he know if they are producing useful information or just guessing?

This chapter is different from all the other chapters in this textbook. It doesn't have data! There is no dataset to examine in Excel or SPSS. Only the theoretical concept of hypothesis testing and its application to business settings are covered here.

That's because the logic of hypothesis testing is so critical to your success in understanding the rest of this textbook, I didn't want to distract you with calculations just yet. Learning about the logic of hypothesis testing and trying to work through the mathematics simultaneously is unnecessarily difficult! This is one of the most difficult topics for most students to grasp because it can be highly abstract and builds on abstract concepts from several previous chapters, focusing on sampling distributions. Learning the mathematics of it simultaneously just isn't fair, so we won't do it. That'll come in the next chapter.

For now, if you don't have a complete grasp of sampling distributions yet, do yourself a favour and review Chapters 5 and 6 until they make sense. Sampling distributions are at the core of hypothesis testing, and without understanding them first, this chapter and all future chapters will be intensely confusing!

In our case study, Jesse has already faced some of this confusion. He knows that the performance of his think tank is likely to fluctuate widely – no one can predict the future 100% of the time. But given that they make the wrong conclusion fairly often, he is not sure if that means they've been guessing the whole time. The incorrect conclusions may be because his think tank doesn't work as intended, but it might instead be only because of chance. This chapter will provide a framework for Jesse to figure out which.

7.1 'PROVING' SOMETHING WITH STATISTICS

We often hear phrases like 'this study proves' in conjunction with statistics. Someone has conducted an experiment or correlational study, and the news media report that a statistical test they ran 'proves' something. They often throw around terms like 'statistically significant'.

One of the dirty secrets of statistics is that no one can ever 'prove' anything. As you read in Chapter 6, distributions are probabilistic. While something may happen 'most of the time', virtually anything is *possible*. For example, you might flip a coin a dozen times and end up with heads every time. Although this is very unlikely, it doesn't necessarily mean that the coin is necessarily biased to show heads more often than tails. If it were biased, we would call that an 'unfair' coin, but a series of unlikely flips alone doesn't prove this.

Instead, if we want to make a conclusion about that coin being unfair, we must decide, 'at what point are these flips sufficiently unlikely that we'd conclude the coin was unfair?' Five heads in a row? Ten? Twenty?

In terms of samples and populations, we are trying to answer this research question: is it probable that our sample of flips from this coin came from a population of flips from a fair coin?

We can make a formal statement of the hypothesis that our research question describes like this:

$$H_0: \mu = 50\%$$

This is a **null hypothesis**. It is a statement of our assumptions about a population parameter that we want to try to disprove. We call it null because it requires no statistical testing; it represents whatever we assume to be true until proven otherwise. In this case, if the coin is fair, the population of coins should produce 'heads' flips 50% of the time. Thus, we assume the population mean should be equal to 50%.

We would pronounce the null hypothesis above ($H_0: \mu = 50\%$) as, 'the null hypothesis is that mu is equal to fifty per cent' or 'the null hypothesis is that the population mean is equal to fifty per cent'.

Given this hypothesis and a sample to assess it, we can then construct a confidence interval around our population mean and see if our sample mean falls within that interval. Let's try two example coins, given ten coin flips from each. In Figure 7.01, I've created the sampling distribution of a fair coin flipped ten times and also placed two sample means on that distribution: one heads (.1) and seven heads (.7). These represent two different coins, each flipped ten times; the first coin landed heads once, while the second coin landed heads seven times.

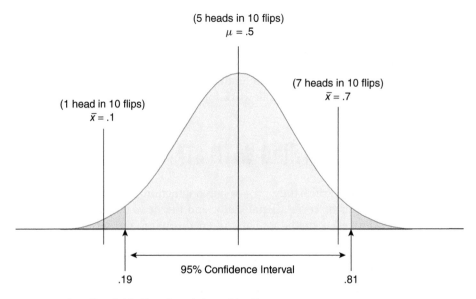

FIGURE 7.01   Sampling distribution of a coin tossed ten times

From the 95% confidence interval surrounding the null hypothesis, we see that with a sample of ten flips and a population mean of 50%, we would expect 95% of samples to fall between 19% and 81%. (If this seems confusing to you, I recommend reviewing the meaning of confidence intervals in Chapter 6, p. 168. Also remember that this is not a figure of a population; instead, it is a figure of a sampling distribution, which we covered in Chapter 5.)

The sample mean from our first coin falls outside our 95% confidence interval. That means it is unlikely for a sample of one head out of ten flips to be drawn from a population where we'd expect 50% heads if the coin was fair. Given this, we would reject the null hypothesis, concluding that it is unlikely that this coin came from a population of fair coins.

The sample mean from our second coin falls inside our 95% confidence interval. That means it is likely for a sample of seven heads out of ten flips to be drawn from a population where we'd expect 50% heads if the coin was fair. Given this, we would retain the null hypothesis, concluding that there is insufficient evidence to say that this coin didn't come from a population of fair coins.

It's important to note the imbalance between these two statements. When we reject the null, we conclude that our sample is unlikely to have come from the population described by the null. When we retain the null, we conclude that we didn't have enough information to reject the null. *This distinction is very important.*

We can *never* statistically conclude that the null is true. Instead, we assume it to be true in order to test it. There is no way to affirmatively conclude that any null hypothesis is true. When we retain the null, we are saying, 'We assumed the null to be true, and we did not find enough evidence to demonstrate otherwise'.

When we reject the null, we can also conclude that we have demonstrated statistical significance – these are synonyms. In this case, the difference between the first coin and a fair coin is statistically significant, while the difference between the second coin and a fair coin is not.

7.2 A FORMAL PROCESS FOR TESTING HYPOTHESES

Having read the previous section, you should now have a basic understanding of what is involved in hypothesis testing – considering whether or not a sample statistic is likely to have occurred given a particular null hypothesis, and then rejecting or retaining that null. But this is a simplified view of the process – there are eight steps involved that you must follow every time you conduct a hypothesis test. At first, this will seem long and complicated, but I promise it will go faster as you become more familiar with it. Here are the steps:

1 State the research question and operationalize variables.

2 State the null and alternative hypotheses.

3 Set the desired significance level and derive a decision rule.

4 Collect a sample to test the null hypothesis.

5 Conduct a statistical test.

6 Formally state the results of the statistical test.

7 Conduct supplemental analyses as appropriate.

8 State all appropriate conclusions.

We'll use our case study to illustrate each of these steps.

7.2.1 STEP 1: STATE THE RESEARCH QUESTION AND OPERATIONALIZE VARIABLES

A research question is a sentence stating whatever problem it is that you want to address using statistics. In forming a research question, you must remember four key elements:

1 A research question must be testable.

2 You can never produce statistical evidence to support 'no difference'.

3 You should state your research question in terms of constructs, not operational definitions, whenever possible.

4 Be specific.

Because we can never prove our assumptions about a population, we can't state research questions like 'Are these groups the same?' or 'Are men and women identical in customer satisfaction?'. These questions are *untestable*. We can only ask research questions that assess differences. These research questions are also very unspecific. Are which groups the same? Are we trying to draw conclusions about people in general, or just those that tend to work for our business? Do we want to know about differences between women and men in the world, in our country, in our town, or in our store?

We can usually convert research questions like these into testable ones by taking a moment to think about what question we are really trying to answer and rephrasing our research question to reflect that. For example, two good research questions derived from the ones above are, 'Do six year olds and seven year olds feel differently in terms of the attractiveness of our product?' or 'Do women have higher customer satisfaction than men among shoppers at our store?'.

In our case study, Jesse wants to know if his think tank is successful at predicting the future of technology. The construct he wants to know about is 'think tank performance'. So this must be part of his research question. He wants to know if his think tank performance is better than would be expected if they were just guessing. This becomes his research question, which we abbreviate RQ:

RQ: Is think tank performance better than would be expected by chance alone?

Jesse believes that if his think tank isn't effective, they would only get the right answer about half of the time. So he operationalizes each of the think tank's past decisions as either 'right' or 'wrong', representing 'right' with a 1 and 'wrong' with a 0. Once he collects his data, he should have a dataset full of 1s and 0s.

7.2.2 STEP 2: STATE THE NULL AND ALTERNATIVE HYPOTHESES

After the research question is set, specific statistical hypotheses must be written to address that research question, and we must set the null hypothesis first. There are three questions we must answer to create a null hypothesis:

1 What is/are the parameter(s) to be tested?

2 What do we wish to test against that parameter?

3 What is the theoretical relationship between the parameter and the test value?

We'll again cover each of these in turn.

7.2.2.1 QUESTION 2A: WHAT IS THE PARAMETER TO BE TESTED?

As of this point in the textbook, we've talked mostly about one parameter: μ, which is a population mean. But any parameter could theoretically be part of a null hypothesis. For example, we could form hypotheses about the standard deviation parameter, σ.

For now, we are only interested in identifying if an observed sample mean is likely to be drawn from a given population. In future chapters there will be more possibilities, depending on the data available.

In our case study, this parameter is at the heart of Jesse's research question. He wants to know if the mean performance of his think tank is better than would be expected by chance if his think tank were only guessing. He wants to compare the likelihood of his against a theoretical μ. The correct parameter is therefore μ.

7.2.2.2 QUESTION 2B: WHAT DO WE WISH TO TEST AGAINST THAT PARAMETER?

Remember that the null hypothesis reflects our assumptions about the population. To identify the test value, we must think about what values we can safely assume.

In Step 1, Jesse determined that his think tank would only get the right answer half of the time if his employees were just guessing. Since our parameter in Step 2a was a mean, our test value must also be a mean: in this case, .5 (or 50%).

It's important to notice here that choosing an unrealistic test value can make the results of the overall hypothesis test meaningless. If 50% isn't a good assumption to test, rejecting the null will not tell us anything useful. We'll discuss realistic assumptions about the null hypothesis in future chapters.

7.2.2.3 QUESTION 2C: WHAT IS THE THEORETICAL RELATIONSHIP BETWEEN THE PARAMETER AND THE TEST VALUE?

We next need to decide how the parameter and test value are related. This is again driven by the research question. Most often, we're interested in determining if our sample mean is likely to have come from a *different* population. If so, we are interested in a two-tailed test. In a two-tailed test, we reject the null if our sample statistic falls in either tail beyond the confidence interval – see Figure 7.02.

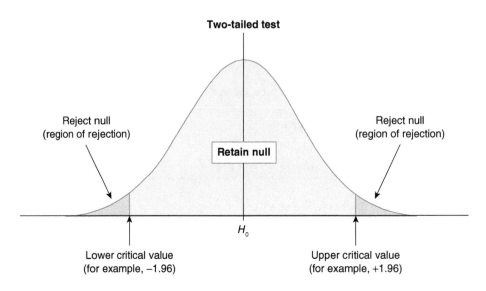

Two-tailed test

Reject null
(region of rejection)

Retain null

Reject null
(region of rejection)

H_0

Lower critical value
(for example, −1.96)

Upper critical value
(for example, +1.96)

FIGURE 7.02   Sampling distribution of a two-tailed test highlighting regions of rejection

With this illustration, we introduce two new concepts. First, the critical value refers to the threshold at which a sample mean is considered sufficiently unlikely that we believe it to have come from a different population than the one described by the null hypothesis.

In a two-tailed test, these are the bounds of the associated confidence interval around H_0. In our example above involving coin flips, the critical values were .19 and .81. We can express critical values in terms of unstandardized values (for example, proportions of .19 and .81) or standardized values (for example, statistics with values −1.96 or +1.96; for a review of standardization, see Chapter 4, p. 117).

We refer to the area of the sampling distribution beyond the critical values as the region of rejection. This is just what it sounds like: if we found the sample statistic in the region of rejection, we would reject the null hypothesis.

Is our case study's Jesse interested in a two-tailed test? His research question reads: 'Is think tank performance better than would be expected by chance alone?' 'Better' doesn't sound like 'different' – it sounds as if Jesse is only concerned with one tail.

Sometimes we are not interested in overall differences between a sample mean and the population described by the null hypothesis. Instead, we want to know if our sample came from a population with a mean greater than the one described by the null hypothesis. This describes our case study; Jesse wants to know if his think tank is *better than* (greater than, >) chance. To test this, he'll need to test the opposite: does his think tank come from a population that is *the same as or worse than* (less than or equal to, ≤) chance?

In Figure 7.03, we have placed the entire region of rejection in the upper tail. If our sample mean is below the upper critical value, we would conclude that that sample came from the population that performs the *same as or worse than* (≤) chance.

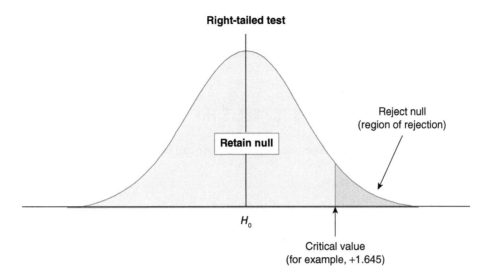

FIGURE 7.03   Sampling distribution of a right-tailed test highlighting region of rejection

Note that when we use a one-tailed test, the critical value is closer to the null than when we used a two-tailed test. In a sense, it is 'easier' to reject the null with a one-tailed test, as your sample mean does not need to be as extreme for it to fall in the region of rejection. We'll get to the reason for this in Step 3.

If we mirror these features, we can construct a left-tailed test, as in Figure 7.04.

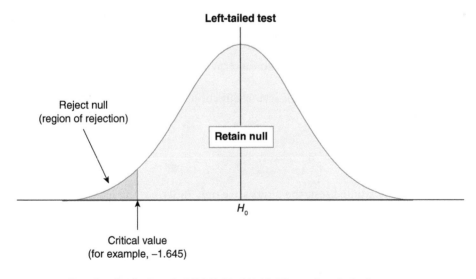

FIGURE 7.04   Sampling distribution of a left-tailed test highlighting region of rejection

Which does Jesse need? Since Jesse wants to know 'Is think tank performance *better*', he wants a right-tailed test. He wants to reject the null when scores are *above* (>) his critical value. If he was interested in knowing 'Is think tank performance *worse*' (<), he would want a left-tailed test.

In practice, many students determine the appropriate sign for the null by taking whatever direction the research question is interested in demonstrating and identifying the opposite of it. For example, if the research question suggests 'less than', the null must contain 'greater than or equal to'.

7.2.2.4 USING THESE ANSWERS TO CREATE THE NULL HYPOTHESIS

Based upon our answers to Questions 2a, 2b and 2c, we can construct the null hypothesis (H_0).

$H_0: \mu \le .5$

From Question 2a, we determined that the appropriate parameter to test was the population mean, μ.

From Question 2b, we determined that the appropriate test value was .5.

From Question 2c, we determined that the appropriate relationship was less than or equal to.

This describes what Jesse will assume to be true until he can prove otherwise. He assumes that his think tank's performance is worse than or as good as chance alone would suggest until he gathers evidence to the contrary.

7.2.2.5 USING THE NULL HYPOTHESIS TO CREATE THE ALTERNATIVE HYPOTHESIS

The alternative hypothesis describes what we assume the value of the parameter must be if the null is not true. It is noted with the symbol H_1 (pronounced 'H-sub-one'). It is set up to contain all possible values for the parameter the sample being tested represents if the null hypothesis is rejected.

Therefore, if set up appropriately, the alternative must be accepted when the null is rejected.

For example, if the null hypothesis is non-directional, the alternative must contain information about both tails:

$H_0: \mu = 45$
$H_1: \mu \ne 45$

If conducting a left-tailed test, the alternative only describes the left tail:

$H_0: \mu \ge 45$
$H_1: \mu < 45$

If conducting a right-tailed test, the alternative only describes the right tail:

$H_0: \mu \le 45$
$H_1: \mu > 45$

Together, the null and alternative hypotheses must contain *every possible outcome*. For example, you could not put > in the null and < in the alternative, because = would be unaccounted for. The reason that we can accept the alternative when we reject the null is because *there is no other option*. When you set up two opposing hypotheses – where 100% of the time, one of them must be true – to reject the null means you must accept the alternative.

For our case study, we must create the opposite of $H_0: \mu \le .5$ – i.e., $H_1: \mu > .5$.

Directionality can be confusing. The easiest way to determine if a research question is directional is to look for words in the research question that indicate directionality. Some common terms appear in Figure 7.05. But remember: for these signal words to be helpful, you need to have created a meaningful research question in the first place!

Common terms	Directionality	Null hypothesis	Alternative hypothesis
'different', 'changed', 'contrast', 'distinct'	Non-directional (two-tailed)	=	≠
'increase', 'augment', 'build', 'grow', 'more', 'larger', 'greater', 'bigger', 'increment'	Directional (one-tailed)	≤	>
'decrease', 'less', 'diminish', 'shrink' 'smaller', 'fewer', 'littler', 'decrement'	Directional (one-tailed)	≥	<

FIGURE 7.05   Common terms indicating a directional hypothesis and associated tests

WHY ISN'T THE NULL HYPOTHESIS WHAT I WANT TO PROVE?

At this point, you may be asking yourself, 'If I want to know about something, why don't I just test that as the null hypothesis?' For example, if you are running five manufacturing plants and want to know if the average job performances among your employees at those five plants are different from one another, why wouldn't your null hypothesis be that they're different? Why test that they're the same instead?

The key to understanding hypothesis testing is that in all hypothesis tests, you must make an assumption about a population and see if your sample reflects that assumption. This setup is because it is logically impossible to prove the absence of something (sometimes called 'proving a negative'). For example, if someone says, 'all of my employees are always late', you can disprove this by finding even one employee who is not late. If someone says, 'none of my employees are ever late', you can only disprove this by examining the tardiness of every employee, individually. If even one of them is ever late, then that person's assertion is false, so you cannot rely on randomly identified employees (i.e., samples) to disprove it; you must look at every individual instead (i.e., the population). And if you had access to the population, you wouldn't need hypothesis testing at all; you could just describe the population using the various descriptive statistics we've already covered, like frequencies, means and medians.

7.2.3 STEP 3: SET THE DESIRED SIGNIFICANCE LEVEL AND DERIVE A DECISION RULE

When comparing to a 95% confidence interval, we reject the null when less than 5% of samples drawn from a particular population would fall in the region of rejection. We call this 5% the significance level, and we label it with the Greek letter alpha (α). Therefore, we might write $\alpha = .05$ to indicate that the significance level is 5%.

$\alpha = .05$ is the default significance level; that is, absent any other information, you should generally assume that α is .05. Other common significance levels are .10 and .01, depending upon your specific field's standards. If you're going to be conducting a lot of tests within a particular field (for example, quality assurance), check a research methods textbook within your field for typical, recommended alphas.

So why do different fields have different standards for alpha? Because there is a trade-off between alpha and the sample size required to reject the null. To explore why this might be the case, let's return to the sampling distribution of H_0, depicted in Figure 7.06. We'll only consider one-tailed tests for now, because two-tailed tests would make this figure much more complicated.

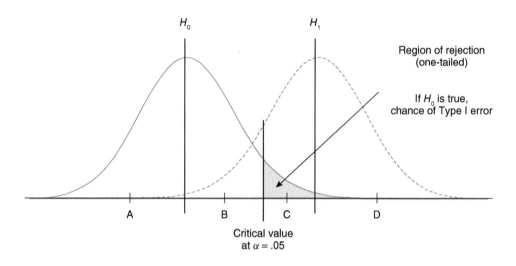

FIGURE 7.06   Four theoretical sample means and their position on H_0 when H_0 is true

Any time you engage in hypothesis testing, one of your two hypotheses is objectively true: either H_0 is true or H_1 is true. Figure 7.06 depicts what might occur if H_0 is true. A, B, C and D represent four different sample means drawn from H_0. If H_0 were true, what would happen if our study produced these means?

1   Samples A and B are not in the region of rejection. We would retain the null in both cases. H_0 is true, so these are correct decisions. We should have retained the null, and we did retain the null.

2   Samples C and D are in the region of rejection. We would reject the null in both cases. H_0 is true, so these are incorrect decisions – we call these Type I errors. We should have retained the null, but we mistakenly rejected it instead.

Thus, a Type I error occurs if we incorrectly reject the null when we should have retained it, because the null was in fact true. The probability that we will commit a Type I error if the null hypothesis were true is alpha; thus, if $\alpha = .05$, we will incorrectly reject the null in 5% of tests. We can minimize Type I errors by setting a lower alpha, reducing the size of the region of rejection. But what's the trade-off?

In Figure 7.07, H_1 is true. The figure again depicts four different sample means, but this time drawn from H_1: A, B, C and D. If H_1 is true, what would happen to our conclusions from these samples?

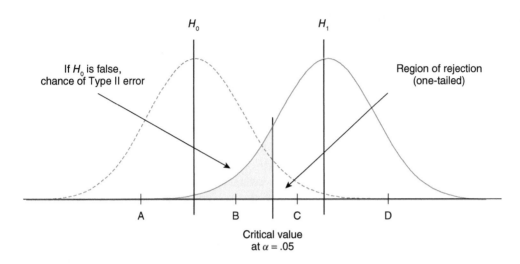

FIGURE 7.07 Four theoretical sample means and their position on H_0 when H_0 is false

1 Samples C and D are in the region of rejection. We would reject the null in both cases. H_0 is false, so these are correct decisions. We should have rejected the null, and we did reject the null.

2 Samples A and B are not in the region of rejection. We would retain the null in both cases. H_0 is false, so these are incorrect decisions – we call these Type II errors. We should have rejected the null, but we mistakenly retained it instead.

Thus, a Type II error occurs if we incorrectly retain the null when we should have rejected it, because the null was in fact false. The probability that we will commit a Type II error if the null hypothesis were true is represented with the Greek letter beta (β). We can only control beta indirectly; increasing the sample size reduces beta and increases its inverse, called power. Power is the probability that we will correctly reject the null when that null should have been rejected.

If we set a more stringent alpha (for example, using $\alpha = .01$ instead of $\alpha = .05$), we shift the critical value to the right in a right-tailed test. This reduces the risk that we'll commit a Type I error if H_0 is true, but it increases the risk that we'll commit a Type II error if H_1 is true.

The goal of good research design is to minimize both Type I errors and Type II errors simultaneously. You have direct control over alpha, so if you want to minimize Type I error, set α low. To minimize Type II error (β) (and maximize power), you'll need a large sample size. There are calculations you can do to determine exactly how large a sample you need to get a desired level of beta (and therefore power), but they differ for each statistical test and are outside the scope of this textbook (this is hard enough already!).

We summarize the results of the researcher's decision to reject or retain a null hypothesis, given what is objectively true, in Figure 7.08.

	The statistical test suggests to…	
	Retain H_0	Reject H_0
If H_0 is objectively true…	Correct decision	Type I error (α)
If H_0 is objectively false…	Type II error (β)	Correct decision (power = $1 - \beta$)

FIGURE 7.08   Outcome when rejecting or retaining the null when the null is or is not true

Let's briefly return to our coin example. Recall we found that the difference between the sample of Coin 1 flips ($\bar{x} = .1$) and flips from a population of fair coins ($\mu = .5$) was statistically significant, while the difference between the sample from Coin 2 ($\bar{x} = .7$) and a population of fair coins ($\mu = .5$) was not statistically significant. Given this, can we definitively conclude that the first coin is unfair while the second coin is fair?

Absolutely not! Remember, we can never 'prove' anything with statistics. We can only conclude if our observations are likely or unlikely given a particular null.

We believe it is likely that the first coin does not come from the H_0 population and this might be true: the coin might in reality be drawn from a population of unfair coins (correct answer). However, it might instead be an unlikely draw from a population of fair coins (Type I error).

We believe it is likely that the second coin does come from the H_0 population and this might also be true: it might in reality be drawn from a population of fair coins (correct answer). However, it might instead be an unlikely draw from a population of unfair coins (Type II error).

In our case study, Jesse faces the same problem. Even if he finds statistical significance – that is, his think tank's performance is unlikely to have been drawn from a population where they were just guessing – it does not necessarily mean that the think tank really does perform better than chance would suggest. We might just be making a statistical error. However, by minimizing α and β, we minimize the chances that we will make such an error.

Once we have a significance level in mind, we identify the specific desired critical values for our statistical test. If we're using Excel or SPSS, we can skip identifying a critical value, because Excel and SPSS will compute these values for us automatically. The process of identifying critical values differs by statistical test, so we'll cover this in each remaining chapter in Part 2.

7.2.4 STEP 4: COLLECT A SAMPLE TO TEST THE NULL HYPOTHESIS

Experimental design and data collection (identifying a sample and collecting data) should generally take place after setting a decision rule. This is because of how probability works. When you identify critical values from an alpha you've set, you are saying, 'I am willing to accept this probability that I will commit a Type I error'. Once you've collected your sample, your alpha and beta no longer matter – you either do or do not have statistically significant results, and you will or will not have committed a Type I or Type II error. As soon as you have finished collecting data, your conclusion has been made.

Sometimes this isn't possible, because the data already exist and you need to analyse them. Most of the cases in this textbook take this form, since there's no way for you to actually collect these data. But when running your own studies, you should set objective standards (alpha and beta) before collecting data and then *stick to them*.

This is as much detail about data collection as this textbook will get into. If you complete a research methods course (or read a research methods textbook), this topic will be covered in much more detail.

7.2.5 STEP 5: CONDUCT A STATISTICAL TEST

Once you've collected your sample, it's time to conduct an appropriate statistical test. There are many possible tests, depending upon your sample and research question. We'll be covering one or two statistical tests per chapter for the remainder of this book and will go into detail about their computation there.

Whichever test you do, you'll be either testing or identifying a p-value. These range from .00 to 1.00 and represent the probability that your sample statistic came from the population represented by the null hypothesis.

Low p-values mean that your sample statistic is unlikely to have come from the population in the null. For example, if $p = .02$, only 2% of sample statistics drawn from the given population would have been as extreme as or more extreme than the sample statistic that was actually calculated. If $p = .07$, there is a 7% chance.

We compare p-values with alpha to determine if a result is statistically significant. For example, if $\alpha = .05$, $p = .02$ describes a significant difference while $p = .07$ does not describe a significant difference. If $\alpha = .10$, both of these results are statistically significant.

There are two ways to test p-values:

1 If you have access to Excel or SPSS, you can compute a precise p-value. You then compare the p-value with alpha to determine if your result is statistically significant. If $p < \alpha$, you've found statistical significance. If $p \geq \alpha$, you have not found statistical significance.

2 If you are computing values by hand, you instead compute a critical value and compare your sample statistic with that value. For example, if your critical value was ± 1.96, and you computed a test statistic of 2.15 (that is, 2.15 is in the tail beyond ± 1.96), you would have found statistical significance. If you computed a test statistic of 1.10 (that is, 1.10 is not in the tail beyond ± 1.96), you would conclude that $p \geq \alpha$.

7.2.6 STEP 6: FORMALLY STATE THE RESULTS OF THE STATISTICAL TEST

Once you have computed your test statistic and determined if it was statistically significant, you must report your findings. There are two ways to do this.

7.2.6.1 STEP 6A: IF YOU KNOW THE PRECISE P-VALUE (EXCEL OR SPSS)

If you know the precise *p*-value (for example, if you were using Excel or SPSS to calculate it):

statistic = result, p = p-value

then when reporting a statistic like this, replace each of the bold words with your findings. For example:

$z = 1.35, p = .18$

In this example, the test statistic is a *z*-statistic, which we'll learn about in the next chapter. The value calculated for the *z*-statistic is 1.35. The *p*-value returned from SPSS (or Excel) is .18.

7.2.6.2 STEP 6B: IF YOU DON'T KNOW THE PRECISE P-VALUE (HAND CALCULATION)

If you don't know the precise *p*-value (for example, if you were calculating the test statistic by hand):

statistic = result, p relationship α

Again, replace each of the bold terms with your findings. Using the same value from the previous example:

$z = 1.35, p > .05$

In this example, the test statistic is again a *z*-statistic. The value calculated for the *z*-statistic is 1.35. The test statistic did not fall outside the critical value, so we concluded that $p > .05$ – that is, we retained the null and did not find statistical significance.

7.2.7 STEP 7: CONDUCT SUPPLEMENTAL ANALYSES AS APPROPRIATE

Depending on the results of your test, you may at this point need to conduct supplemental analyses. These differ by test, so we'll cover this in more detail in subsequent chapters. But as an example, computing a confidence interval might be included in this step.

7.2.8 STEP 8: STATE ALL APPROPRIATE CONCLUSIONS

Remember, the purpose of statistics is to translate data into an understandable message. Statistics without interpretation are useless. As a statistician, it's your job to interpret your findings. Good conclusions have four components:

1   A formal statement about retaining the null or rejecting the null and accepting the alternative.

2   A formal statement about the statistical significance of the finding.

3   A sentence interpreting the results in terms of the research question.

4   Interpretation of any supplemental analyses.

We'll again cover each in turn.

7.2.8.1 STEP 8A: FORMAL STATEMENT ABOUT THE NULL

We first make a formal conclusion about our test statistic. In the example above ($z = 1.35$, $p = .18$), the difference was not statistically significant. Thus our conclusion would be:

Retain the null.

If the difference was statistically significant, we would conclude:

Reject the null and accept the alternative.

These are the only two possible formal statements about the null hypothesis. So, at the least, you've got a 50/50 chance of getting it right!

7.2.8.2 STEP 8B: FORMAL STATEMENT ABOUT STATISTICAL SIGNIFICANCE

The statement about statistical significance is very straightforward:

The concept-being-tested was (not) statistically significant.

For example, to this point in the textbook, we've been looking at mean differences. Thus, if $p < \alpha$ in the test of a mean difference (that is, if we rejected the null and accepted the alternative), we would conclude:

The difference was statistically significant.

If $p > \alpha$ (that is, if we retained the null), we would conclude:

The difference was not statistically significant.

7.2.8.3 STEP 8C: SENTENCE INTERPRETING THE RESULTS IN TERMS OF THE RESEARCH QUESTION

Once you have rejected or retained the null, you must interpret that sentence. This again differs by research question. Say, for example, our research question was this:

RQ: Do male and female customers have different levels of satisfaction with our store?

If we rejected the null and accepted the alternative, we would conclude:

Male and female customers have different levels of satisfaction with our store.

If we retained the null, we would conclude:

There is not sufficient evidence to conclude that male and female customers have different levels of satisfaction with our store.

Again, it's critical to remember that we can never affirmatively endorse the null. We cannot ever conclude 'male and female customers are the same'. Instead, we can only conclude 'there is not enough evidence to conclude male and female customers are different'.

Also note that we can only make conclusions about directionality if we conducted a directional test. If you test for increases, both your RQ and conclusion must be in terms of increases as well. If you test for non-directional differences, both your RQ and conclusion must be in terms of differences only.

7.2.8.4 STEP 8D: INTERPRET SUPPLEMENTAL ANALYSES

The final step in creating a valid statistical conclusion is to interpret any supplemental analyses you may have calculated. For example, if you computed a confidence interval, you need a sentence explaining what that confidence interval means. Since this differs by statistical test, we'll again cover this in more detail in subsequent chapters.

7.3 APPLYING THE HYPOTHESIS TESTING PROCESS

Now that we have the many, many puzzle pieces involved in the formal process of statistical significance testing, let's look back at our case study to examine how these all fit together. If you've forgotten the details of the scenario, here's a summary.

Jesse has become concerned that his think tank isn't producing useful information. Several of their predictions have turned out to be false. But how many 'bad answers' does the Institute need to push to its clients before he should be worried? If he considers 'the overall performance of his think tank' to be the population, he knows from Chapter 5 that looking at any one particular decision is not very helpful; a sample of one won't tell him anything about the population. He also knows from Chapter 6 that confidence intervals can be quite wide, but how wide is too wide? Is there some objective standard to which he can compare his think tank's performance? How does he know if they are producing useful information or just guessing?

7.3.1 STEP BY STEP

STEP 1

As discussed above, Jesse's research questions can be stated like this:

RQ: Is think tank performance better than would be expected by chance alone?

Operationalizations are discussed above.

STEP 2

$H_0: \mu \leq .5$
$H_1: \mu > .5$

STEP 3

Don't worry about the mathematics of determining a decision rule just yet. Just take my word for it (for now) that the critical value is +1.645 (notice that there is only one critical value – just a single positive number – since this is a right-tailed test).

$\alpha = .05$

Critical value: +1.645

STEP 4

Jesse conducts a correlational study and collects a sample of $n = 50$ incidents, identifying for each if his think tank predicted the future correctly. In 33 cases, they predicted the future correctly. In 17 cases, they did not.

STEP 5

Jesse conducts his statistical test and finds the following (again, don't worry about the mathematics just yet):

$z = 1.98$

STEP 6

Since 1.98 is beyond the critical value, p is less than .05 and we have found statistical significance. We state this formally like so:

$z = 1.98, p < .05$

STEP 7

We'll also conduct a confidence interval here, since this is a z-test (more information on this in the next chapter). Confidence intervals are always two-tailed, even if the statistical test is one-tailed.

$CI_{95} = [.50, .78]$

STEP 8

Finally, we must interpret both the test and the confidence interval:

Conclusion: Reject the null. The difference is statistically significant. Think tank performance is better than chance alone. If we assume this sample to represent the population, we would expect 95% of sample means to fall between .50 and .78.

7.3.2 ALL TOGETHER NOW

We can condense this into a single set of statements, as you might see it on a test, or as you might put together for your own research:

RQ: Is think tank performance better than would be expected by chance alone?

$H_0: \mu \le .5$
$H_1: \mu > .5$

$\alpha = .05$
Critical value: $+1.645$

$z = 1.98, p < .05$
$CI_{95} = [.50, .78]$

Conclusion: Reject the null. The difference is statistically significant. Think tank performance is better than chance alone. If we assume this sample to represent the population, we would expect 95% of sample means to fall between .50 and .78.

So that's not so bad, right? Don't worry – as you can see from this condensed version, the amount of information that comes out of hypothesis testing is not very extensive. While there is a lot of thought behind this relatively small set of final results, you'll find that these decisions become much easier with practice.

In the next chapter, we'll put this into practice with our first two statistical tests: the z-test and the t-test.

7.4 APPLYING HYPOTHESIS TESTING

To apply what you've learned from this chapter, consider the following case study, questions posed about that case study, and discussion of those questions.

7.4.1 APPLICATION CASE STUDY

Harold is the lead designer at Dead Pixels Games, a videogame developer. He is responsible for managing the programming and design team to ensure that the product is delivered on time. This primarily involves the management of the people in his team, with special attention paid to scheduling.

At an industry conference, Harold recently heard that videogame developers are overworked. According to a presentation at the conference, the average programmer works 55 hours per week! Harold believes things are probably about the same at Dead Pixels, but he wants to be sure. So what else would he do but design a research study!

To conduct his research, Harold collects the weekly timecards of all of his programmers over the past year. He wants to see if the number of hours worked per week is about the same here as it is across the industry.

1 Is Harold conducting a directional or non-directional test? How do you know?

2 State the hypotheses.

3 Given this description, what should alpha be set to and why?

4 Can Harold actually confirm what he seeks to confirm with a statistical test?

5 If Harold rejects the null, what can he claim?

6 If Harold retains the null, what can he conclude?

7.4.2 APPLICATION DISCUSSION

Harold's research study offers an excellent opportunity to explore the implications of hypothesis testing. We'll cover each question one by one.

1 Harold is conducting a non-directional test. We know this because he wants to see if the number of hours is 'about the same'. That does not imply direction, so it is non-directional.

2 Second, the hypotheses can be stated as such (remember that this is non-directional):

$H_0: \mu = 55$
$H_1: \mu \neq 55$

3 Alpha should be set to .05 because we have no other information to lead us to choose another alpha.

4 Harold cannot confirm what he seeks to confirm. Remember from the description: 'He wants to see if the number of hours worked per week is about the same here as it is across the industry.' We can never statistically confirm that a sample comes from a population because this is a null. *We can never accept a null.* Instead, we assume a null to be true until we find evidence to the contrary. While Harold can find confirmation that his team is different, he cannot confirm that his team is the same.

5 If Harold rejects the null, he can conclude that the weekly work hours of his developers are not the same as those of the industry at large.

6 If Harold retains the null, he can conclude that he does not have sufficient evidence to conclude that his developers are not the same as those of the industry at large. Note that he cannot conclude they are the same; remember, *we can never accept a null.*

STATISTICS IN THE REAL WORLD

 These web links can be accessed directly from the book's website.

Hugh Courtney and colleagues describe how to make decisions in a business world sometimes lacking in stability and predictability: https://hbr.org/2013/11/deciding-how-to-decide.

How do you know when hypothesis testing is the right approach to address a business problem? Entrepreneurship expert Jeff Cornwall explains why hypothesis testing is critical to entrepreneurship: www.businessinsider.com/the-null-hypothesis-the-best-way-to-uncover-your-business-models-weakness-is-to-prove-that-it-cant-work-2010-12.

What sort of questions should you ask yourself when creating a new business? What hypotheses should you test, statistically or otherwise?

TEST YOURSELF

☑ **After you've completed the questions below, check your answers online.**

1 For each of the following, is it a good research question? Why or why not?

  a This year, is customer satisfaction the same as last year?
  b Are sales better now?
  c Is mean employee performance this year worse than last year?

2 Do each of the following describe one-tailed or two-tailed tests? How do you know?

  a Do women have more fun than men in our store?
  b Is employee retention different between branches?
  c Did sales increase after sales training?

3 In each of the following situations, is the test significant?

  a $\alpha = .01$; $p = .02$.
  b $\alpha = .05$; $p = .06$.
  c $\alpha = .10$; $p = .06$.

4 Draw appropriate conclusions for each of the following situations:

   a Do women have more fun than men at our store? α =.01; p =.02.
   b Is employee retention different between branches? α =.10; p =.06.
   c Did sales increase after sales training? α =.05; p =.01.

5 State the alternative hypothesis for the given null:

   a $H_0: \mu = 10$.
   b $H_0: \mu \geq 0$.
   c $H_0: \mu \leq 15$.

6 State the null hypothesis for the given alternative:

   a $H_1: \mu > -10$.
   b $H_1: \mu \neq 60$.
   c $H_1: \mu < 100$.

7 Given the same data, are you more likely to reject the null if α =.05 or if α =.10? Why?

8 If you were computing a ξ statistic, found a value of .02, and determined that it was not statistically significant at α =.05, how would you formally state your results? You do not need to know what a ξ statistic is to answer this question.

NEW TERMS

hypothesis test(ing): null hypothesis: one-tailed test: p-value: power: region of rejection: reject the null: reject the null hypothesis: retain the null: retain the null hypothesis: significance level: statistical significance: two-tailed test: Type I error: Type II error:

NEW STATISTICAL NOTATION AND FORMULAS

H_0: the null hypothesis (can also be pronounced 'H sub zero')
H_1: the alternative hypothesis (can also be pronounced 'H sub one')
α: the significance level chosen for any particular statistical test, and the probability of committing a Type I error
β: the probability of committing a Type II error (power = $1 - \beta$)

Visit https://study.sagepub.com/landers2e for free additional online resources related to this chapter.

8 Z-TESTS AND ONE-SAMPLE T-TESTS

WHAT YOU WILL LEARN FROM THIS CHAPTER

- How to complete the hypothesis testing procedure for one-sample tests
- How to determine when z-tests and one-sample t-tests are appropriate given the data available
- How to identify the critical value(s)
- How to determine degrees of freedom for one-sample t-tests
- How to choose between unstandardized and standardized effect sizes

DATA SKILLS YOU WILL MASTER FROM THIS CHAPTER

- Computing a z-test
- Computing a one-sample t-test
- Computing unstandardized effect sizes
- Computing Cohen's d

CASE STUDY   HOW DO WE COMPARE WITH NATIONAL AVERAGES?

Grace is the manager of a small company that provides tutoring to primary school students called Prescription for Success. She coordinates 27 tutors who each work 25-hour weeks tutoring students one-to-one. They have several hundred clients.

She's very proud of her tutors, and she wants to find ways to prove that her tutors are the best in her area. Her goal is to produce a pamphlet with 'scientific evidence' that her tutors are superior to all others in the area.

Part of her organization's mission is to connect 'kind, compassionate and caring tutors' with students in need. So she decides to assess her employees' kindness, compassion and care for children, with the goal of comparing these scores to those in her area. After consulting with a research psychologist, she identifies three surveys that can be used to assess the three traits she believes to be strong in her tutors: the MacMillen Kindness Inventory, the Cincinnati Index of Compassion and the Child Focus Survey. Each produces a score on a scale of 0 to 100, with 100 indicating maximum kindness, compassion and child focus, respectively.

To get the rights to administer these surveys, Grace purchases 27 copies of each survey plus the manual for each test. The manual for the MacMillen Kindness Inventory contains a national average (mean of 45) and standard deviation (SD of 12) based upon a random stratified sample of 240000 people. The Cincinnati Index and Child Focus Survey both provide national averages (means of 55 and 67, based upon samples of 150000 and 400000, respectively), but Grace can't find any standard deviations in the manuals. Since the sample sizes are so incredibly large for these national averages, Grace decides she can safely consider them to be equivalent to populations, and she wants to know how her employees compare with these populations.

She plans to administer the three surveys to her 27 tutors. She knows from reading Chapter 1 that she is conducting a correlational study, and that she has operationalized kindness, compassion and care with these three surveys.

She also knows from Chapter 5 that she is using convenience sampling, since these are the only 27 tutors available right now from all the tutors she has ever employed. She wants to draw conclusions about the kindness, compassion and care for children of her tutors in general, believing that they are better than those of her competitors. Without random sampling, she can only hope that her current tutors are representative of the tutors she typically employs.

She knows from Chapter 7 that what she has done is formed hypotheses about her tutors that she needs to test. She realizes she has three research questions that need to be answered, and writes them down:

RQ$_1$: Are the tutors at Prescription for Success kinder than the competition?

RQ$_2$: Are the tutors at Prescription for Success more compassionate than the competition?

RQ$_3$: Do the tutors at Prescription for Success care for children more than the competition?

But now she's stuck. She has different information available for the national data from each survey – some have standard deviations and some don't. She knows from Chapter 6 that missing standard deviations are important. But what does she do about it? Can she answer her research questions with the data she has available?

Take a look at Grace's psychological data on her employees for yourself in chapter8.xls (Excel) or chapter8.sav (SPSS) online.

Armed with the toolkit of hypothesis testing introduced in Chapter 7, you should see the problem that Grace faces. While she has a procedure to set up and test her hypotheses, she doesn't yet know how to actually test those hypotheses given real data. She wants data-driven answers to her questions!

In this chapter, we'll explore the first two hypothesis tests in the context of the eight-step hypothesis testing process: z-tests and one-sample t-tests. Each of these tests allows a researcher to compare a given sample with a theoretical population, which precisely describes Grace's problem. She has a sample, national averages, and some national standard deviations. As you read Chapter 8, think about how the formulas covered can turn these numbers into meaningful conclusions.

8.1 REVIEWING THE STEPS OF HYPOTHESIS TESTING FOR ONE-SAMPLE TESTS

In Chapter 7, we discussed the eight steps to hypothesis testing. To review:

1 State the research question and operationalize variables.

2 State the null and alternative hypotheses.

3 Set the desired significance level and derive a decision rule.

4 Collect a sample to test the null hypothesis.

5 Conduct a statistical test.

6 Formally state the results of the statistical test.

7 Conduct supplemental analyses as appropriate.

8 State all appropriate conclusions.

This time, let's follow these steps with our case study and some real data.

8.1.1 ONE-SAMPLE HYPOTHESIS TESTING: STEP 1 (STATE THE RQS)

In our case study, Grace has done the first of these steps already: she has stated her research questions (RQ_1, RQ_2 and RQ_3) and operationalized her variables with the three surveys recommended by the research psychologist. Next she needs to state her hypotheses.

8.1.2 ONE-SAMPLE HYPOTHESIS TESTING: STEP 2 (STATE THE HYPOTHESES)

We've actually already talked about the form that hypotheses take for data that look like Grace's. These are called one-sample tests, because they involve the comparison of a single sample mean to a given population mean. We'll actually learn about two different one-sample tests in this chapter, but both have the same setup for their hypotheses.

Given the data presented in the case study, Grace can create a set of hypotheses for each of her RQs:

RQ_1: Are the tutors at Prescription for Success kinder than the competition?
H_0: $\mu \leq 45$
H_1: $\mu > 45$

RQ_2: Are the tutors at Prescription for Success more compassionate than the competition?
H_0: $\mu \leq 55$
H_1: $\mu > 55$

RQ_3: Do the tutors at Prescription for Success care for children more than the competition?
$H_0: \mu \leq 67$
$H_1: \mu > 67$

So where did I get those three numbers: 45, 55 and 67? They were provided in the test manuals, as described in the case study. One-sample tests *require* a given population mean. You cannot conduct a one-sample test without one. In this case study, these numbers were provided in the test manuals that Grace purchased when she also purchased the surveys themselves.

8.1.3 ONE-SAMPLE HYPOTHESIS TESTING: STEP 3 (SET SIGNIFICANCE LEVEL AND DECISION RULE)

FOUNDATION CONCEPTS

The **region of rejection** is the area of the sampling distribution surrounding the null hypothesis beyond which we would reject that null. See Chapter 7, p. 198.

A **two-tailed test** is a hypothesis test in which the region of rejection falls in both tails. We represent this with a ≠ in the alternative hypothesis and = in the null hypothesis. See Chapter 7, p. 198.

A **one-tailed test** is a hypothesis test in which the region of rejection falls in either the upper or lower tail alone. We represent this with a < or > in the alternative hypothesis and ≤ or ≥ in the null hypothesis. See Chapter 7, p. 199.

Lacking any information to the contrary, we set our significance level to the default: $\alpha = .05$. Remember, as discussed in Chapter 7, that means we are willing to accept a 5% chance of committing a Type I error (see Chapter 7, p. 202). We must remember to formally state this as a part of Step 3:

$\alpha = .05$

But unlike in Chapter 7, this time we have real data! That means we can actually determine which test to use and derive decision rules for that test. There are two major types of one-sample tests: z-tests and one-sample t-tests. How do we determine which to use? It depends entirely on σ, the population standard deviation – see Figure 8.01. Much like when computing confidence intervals, if you know σ, use a z-test. If you don't know σ, use a one-sample t-test.

The names of these statistics should be familiar: we've used both t and z in the creation of confidence intervals. We found the z-score or t-score associated with our desired confidence level and multiplied it by the standard error. This allowed us to identify the range of likely values for a sample mean given a particular population mean.

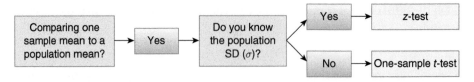

FIGURE 8.01   Decision tree for deciding between *z*-test and one-sample *t*-test

When computing *z*-statistics and *t*-statistics, we are asking the reverse question. We want to know: 'How likely is this particular sample mean given the population mean described by the null hypothesis (H_0)?' When we compute a *z*-statistic or *t*-statistic, we determine how many standard errors away the sample mean is from the population mean. We can then compare this statistic with the *z*-table or *t*-table to see how probable it is. In both *z*-tests and *t*-tests, we conduct the same basic procedure: put an observed difference in standard error units.

Thus, when we identify a critical value, what we are asking is this: 'If the null hypothesis were true, how unusual would my sample mean need to be to reject that null hypothesis as the population from which my sample was drawn?' The process for identifying a critical value is a little different, depending on whether you need *z* or *t*.

8.1.3.1 CRITICAL VALUES IN *Z*-TESTS

In our case study, the population standard deviation is provided for only RQ_1: μ is 45 and σ is 12. That means we'll be using a *z*-test to address RQ_1 only.

It is often helpful at this point to draw the sampling distribution of H_0, to ensure you have the correct tail in mind. Figure 8.02 shows H_0: $\mu \leq 45$.

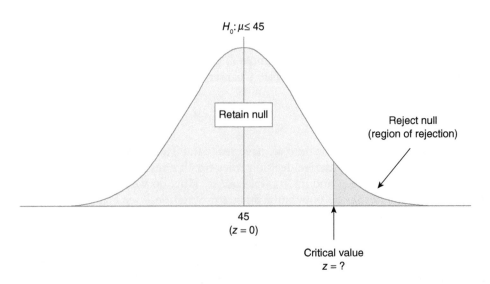

FIGURE 8.02   Sampling distribution of *z* for sample problem

Since the region of rejection is only on one side, we'll only have one critical value. The centre of the sampling distribution is 45 (since that's our population mean). The z-statistic that represents this 45 is zero – this is because a sample mean of 45 would be zero standard errors from the population mean (of 45). We need to know how many standard errors away from the population mean a sample mean needs to be for us to reject H_0.

We compute this value by considering what percentage of the distribution falls in the tails, based upon the significance level. Since $\alpha = .05$, 5% of the sampling distribution should fall in the upper tail.

We can then consult the z-table (see Appendix A1) to identify at what z-score 5% of values fall in the upper tail. We do this the same way that we did when converting z-scores to proportions (if this seems unfamiliar, review Chapter 4).

Since we want to identify the point at which 5% of scores fall in the upper tail, we need to locate .05 in the proportions of the z-table – see Figure 8.03.

z	0	0.01	0.02	0.03	0.04	0.05	0.06	0.07	0.08	0.09
1	0.1587	0.1562	0.1539	0.1515	0.1492	0.1469	0.1446	0.1423	0.1401	0.1379
1.1	0.1357	0.1335	0.1314	0.1292	0.1271	0.1251	0.1230	0.1210	0.1190	0.1170
1.2	0.1151	0.1131	0.1112	0.1093	0.1075	0.1056	0.1038	0.1020	0.1003	0.0985
1.3	0.0968	0.0951	0.0934	0.0918	0.0901	0.0885	0.0869	0.0853	0.0838	0.0823
1.4	0.0808	0.0793	0.0778	0.0764	0.0749	0.0735	0.0721	0.0708	0.0694	0.0681
1.5	0.0668	0.0655	0.0643	0.0630	0.0618	0.0606	0.0594	0.0582	0.0571	0.0559
1.6	0.0548	0.0537	0.0526	0.0516	0.0505	0.0495	0.0485	0.0475	0.0465	0.0455
1.7	0.0446	0.0436	0.0427	0.0418	0.0409	0.0401	0.0392	0.0384	0.0375	0.0367
1.8	0.0359	0.0351	0.0344	0.0336	0.0329	0.0322	0.0314	0.0307	0.0301	0.0294
1.9	0.0287	0.0281	0.0274	0.0268	0.0262	0.0256	0.0250	0.0244	0.0239	0.0233

FIGURE 8.03 Finding the critical value of z for sample problem

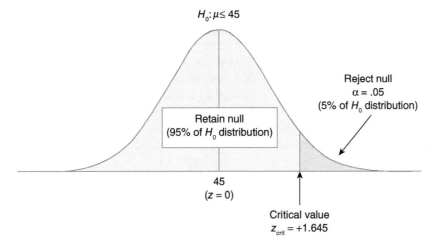

FIGURE 8.04 Sampling distribution of z for sample problem, critical value added

We see that .05 falls directly between two values: 1.64 and 1.65. We'll use the average of these two values: 1.645.

With a one-tailed test, we next need to determine the sign of the critical value. Since this is a right-tailed test, the critical value will be positive: $+1.645$. If this were a left-tailed test, the critical value would be negative: -1.645.

We typically label our critical z-statistic as z_{crit}. Thus: $z_{crit} = +1.645$ (pronounced, 'the critical z is positive 1.645') – see Figure 8.04.

We've now identified the critical value for the one-tailed test. But what if this had been a two-tailed test?

Although alpha is still .05, we would need to split that area into two pieces: .025 would fall in the lower tail and .025 would fall in the upper tail. We would also now have two critical values instead of one – see Figure 8.05.

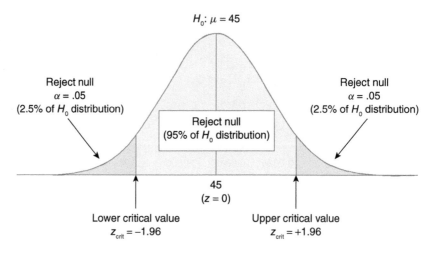

FIGURE 8.05   Sampling distribution of z for sample problem, had it been a two-tailed test

If α had been .01, we would have had .005 in each tail – the amount in the tail is always equal to $\alpha/2$ in a two-tailed test. In the formal process of hypothesis testing, we represent the critical values as a single expression: in this case, $z_{crit} = \pm 1.96$ (pronounced 'the critical z is plus or minus 1.96').

To identify the critical value associated with a two-tailed test, you must look up the value associated with the percentage of the curve falling above the upper critical value. Although $\alpha = .05$ in this example, only 2.5% of the sampling distribution falls beyond the critical value. Look up that value in the z-table (Appendix A1) now – you should find that it is 1.96.

Because there is only one sampling distribution for z, we can summarize common critical values in Figure 8.06. For practice, ensure that you can find where each of these values is found in the z-table.

	$\alpha = .05$	$\alpha = .01$
Two-tailed z-test	±1.96	±2.58
Left-tailed z-test	−1.645	2.33
Right-tailed z-test	+1.645	+2.33

FIGURE 8.06   Common critical values of the z-test

8.1.3.2 CRITICAL VALUES IN ONE-SAMPLE *T*-TESTS

FOUNDATION CONCEPT

Degrees of freedom are the number of independent pieces of information that are available to estimate a value of interest. See Chapter 6, p. 178.

In a one-sample *t*-test, the principle for finding a critical value is similar to what we do for a *z*-test – we still draw the sampling distribution, identify the number of tails, and find critical values appropriate for our desired level of significance. However, because the *t*-distribution has different shapes depending on its degrees of freedom, the process for looking up critical values is a little different (see Chapter 6 if you're fuzzy on degrees of freedom). Let's go through an example.

In our case study's RQ_2 and RQ_3, we are comparing sample means to population means for which the population standard deviation is not provided. That means we'll be using one-sample *t*-tests for both of these research questions. Both are one-tailed tests, so we'll only have one critical value for each.

In the *t*-table (see Appendix A2), we'll need to find the intersection of our desired significance level and the appropriate degrees of freedom. As with confidence intervals (see Chapter 6), when we are conducting a one-sample *t*-test, degrees of freedom equal $n - 1$. Since Grace's dataset contains 27 cases, degrees of freedom are $27 - 1 = 26$.

With that, we have all the pieces of the puzzle to find the appropriate critical value in the *t*-table: a one-tailed test at $\alpha = .05$ with 26 degrees of freedom – see Figure 8.07.

	Confidence intervals			
	90%	95%	98%	99%
	2-tailed α			
	.10	.05	.02	.01
d.f. ↓	One-tailed α			
	.05	.025	.01	.005
21	1.721	2.080	2.518	2.831
22	1.717	2.074	2.508	2.819
23	1.714	2.069	2.500	2.807
24	1.711	2.064	2.492	2.797
25	1.708	2.060	2.485	2.787
26	1.706	2.056	2.479	2.779
27	1.703	2.052	2.473	2.771
28	1.701	2.048	2.467	2.763
29	1.699	2.045	2.462	2.756
30	1.697	2.042	2.457	2.750

FIGURE 8.07   Finding the critical value for the one-sample *t*-test in Appendix A2

Thus, the critical value is 1.706 plus a sign – either negative or positive. If this were a left-tailed test, the sign would be negative: -1.706. But since these are both right-tailed tests, both signs are positive: $+1.706$.

To report this critical value, we also add the degrees of freedom to our statement of t_{crit} by adding parentheses: $t_{crit}(26) = +1.706$ (pronounced, 'the critical t with 26 degrees of freedom is positive 1.706').

Check your understanding by reporting what the critical value for t would have been if Grace had needed a two-tailed test. You should have stated: $t_{crit}(26) = \pm 2.056$.

8.1.4 ONE-SAMPLE HYPOTHESIS TESTING: STEP 4 (COLLECT A SAMPLE)

Let's catch up with where Grace is now. She has stated her research questions, stated the hypotheses, set the significance level and derived decision rules. Since there are three RQs, she has three sets of results so far:

RQ_1: Are the tutors at Prescription for Success kinder than the competition?

$H_0: \mu \leq 45$
$H_1: \mu > 45$

$\alpha = .05$
$z_{crit} = +1.645$

RQ_2: Are the tutors at Prescription for Success more compassionate than the competition?

$H_0: \mu \leq 55$
$H_1: \mu > 55$

$\alpha = .05$
$t_{crit}(26) = +1.706$

RQ_3: Do the tutors at Prescription for Success care for children more than the competition?

$H_0: \mu \leq 67$
$H_1: \mu > 67$

$\alpha = .05$
$t_{crit}(26) = +1.706$

From this, we can conclude that we will eventually conduct three right-tailed tests. The first of these will be a z-test, while the second and third will be one-sample t-tests.

Now that everything is set, Grace can collect her sample. She administers the three surveys to her 27 tutors.

The data from this effort are found in chapter8.xls (Excel) or chapter8.sav (SPSS).

8.1.5 ONE-SAMPLE HYPOTHESIS TESTING: STEP 5 (CONDUCT STATISTICAL TEST)

We next need to conduct our three statistical tests: one z-test and two one-sample t-tests. For each of these tests, the formula is similar: we are comparing the sample mean with the population mean, and stating the result in terms of standard errors. For example, both a z-statistic and a t-statistic of 1.5 indicate that the sample mean and population mean are 1.5 standard errors apart.

Let's step through the computations individually.

8.1.5.1 CONDUCTING A Z-TEST

The formula for a z-statistic is very similar to that of a z-score – see Figure 8.08 – but with two important changes:

1 In the z-score formula, we compare a raw score with a sample mean. In the z-test formula, we compare a sample mean with a population mean.

2 In the z-score formula, we put this difference in standard deviation units. In this context, $z = -1$ means 'the score is one standard deviation below the sample mean'. In the z-test formula, we put this difference in standard error units. In this context, $z = -1$ means 'the sample mean is one standard error below the population mean'.

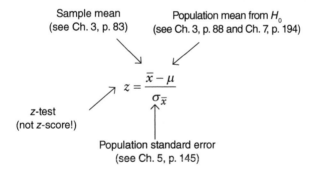

FIGURE 8.08   Formula for a z-test

From this formula, we can conclude that to calculate the value of z for a z-test, we need to know:

1 The sample mean (computed from the dataset).

2 The population mean described by the null hypothesis (determined by H_0).

3 The population standard error, which is calculated with:
   a The population standard deviation (given as part of the problem).
   b The sample size (computed from the dataset).

For our case study data, we're only computing a z-test for RQ_1, which is represented with the 'kindness' variable. You need to determine the mean and the sample size from the given dataset. You could use Excel/SPSS to calculate this or compute it by hand – we covered both in Chapter 3. In doing so, you should find that the mean of the kindness variable is 57.669090.

The rest of the information is provided for us: the null hypothesis states a population value of 45. The problem tells us that the standard deviation of the population is 12. We know we have 27 cases.

We can summarize all of this with a list of our known variables (always a good idea when working out a problem):

- $\bar{x} = 57.669090$

- $\mu = 45$

- $\sigma = 12$

- $n = 27$

Since we need the standard error, we should calculate that first – see Figure 8.09.

$$\sigma_{\bar{x}} = \frac{\sigma}{\sqrt{n}} = \frac{12}{\sqrt{27}} = \frac{12}{5.196152} = 2.309401$$

FIGURE 8.09   Calculating the standard error for our case study z-test ('kindness' variable)

Finally, we plug these values into the z-test formula and solve for z (Figure 8.10).

$$z = \frac{\bar{x} - \mu}{\sigma_{\bar{x}}}$$
$$= \frac{57.669090 - 45}{2.309401}$$
$$= \frac{12.669090}{2.309401}$$
$$= 5.485877$$
$$= 5.49$$

FIGURE 8.10   Calculating the case study z-test

8.1.5.2 CONDUCTING A ONE-SAMPLE T-TEST

The formula for a t-statistic is very similar to that of a z-statistic – but with one important change. Because the population standard deviation is not known, we must replace the population standard error with the sample standard error – see Figure 8.11.

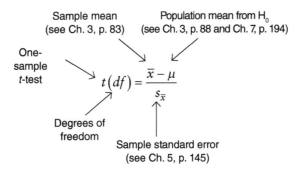

One-sample *t*-test

Sample mean (see Ch. 3, p. 83)

Population mean from H_0 (see Ch. 3, p. 88 and Ch. 7, p. 194)

$$t(df) = \frac{\bar{x} - \mu}{s_{\bar{x}}}$$

Degrees of freedom

Sample standard error (see Ch. 5, p. 145)

FIGURE 8.11   Formula for a one-sample *t*-test

From this formula, we can conclude that to calculate the value of *t* for a *t*-test, we need to know:

1   The sample mean (computed from the dataset).

2   The population mean described by the null hypothesis (determined by H_0).

3   The sample standard error, which is calculated with:

   a   The sample standard deviation (computed from the dataset).

   b   The sample size (computed from the dataset).

For our case study data, we're computing a *t*-test for RQ_2 and RQ_3, which are represented with the 'compassion' and 'childcare' variables, respectively. You need to determine the mean, standard deviation and the sample size from the given dataset. You could use Excel/SPSS to calculate this or compute it by hand – again, we covered both in Chapter 3. In doing so, you should find these values:

■ RQ_2: 'compassion' variable

   ○ Mean   55.103903
   ○ SD   10.867983
   ○ *N*   27

■ RQ_3: 'childcare' variable

   ○ Mean   56.311986
   ○ SD   13.578359
   ○ *N*   27

The only remaining information needed is provided for us: the null hypotheses state population values of 55 and 67.

We can summarize all of this with a list of our known variables (always a good idea when working out a problem):

■ RQ_2: 'compassion' variable

   ○ $\bar{x} = 55.103903$
   ○ $\mu = 55$
   ○ $s = 10.867983$
   ○ $n = 27$

- RQ$_3$: 'childcare' variable
  - $\bar{x}$ = 56.311986
  - μ = 67
  - s = 13.578359
  - n = 27

Since we need the standard errors, we should again calculate them first (Figure 8.12).

$$\text{RQ2: } s_{\bar{x}} = \frac{s}{\sqrt{n}} = \frac{10.867983}{\sqrt{27}} = \frac{10.867983}{5.196152} = 2.091544$$

$$\text{RQ3: } s_{\bar{x}} = \frac{s}{\sqrt{n}} = \frac{13.578359}{\sqrt{27}} = \frac{13.578359}{5.196152} = 2.613157$$

FIGURE 8.12   Step by step calculations of the standard errors for the case study t-tests ('compassion' and 'childcare' variables)

Finally, we plug these values into the t- test formula and solve for t (Figures 8.13 and 8.14).

$$\text{RQ2}: t(26) = \frac{\bar{x} - \mu}{s_{\bar{x}}}$$

$$= \frac{55.103903 - 55}{2.091544}$$

$$= \frac{.103903}{2.091544}$$

$$= .049678$$

$$= .05$$

FIGURE 8.13   Step by step calculations for the case study t-test for the 'compassion' variable

$$\text{RQ3}: t(26) = \frac{x - \mu}{s_{\bar{x}}}$$

$$= \frac{56.311986 - 67}{2.613157}$$

$$= \frac{-10.688014}{2.613157}$$

$$= -4.090077$$

$$= -4.09$$

FIGURE 8.14   Step by step calculations for the case study t-test for the 'childcare' variable

8.1.6 ONE-SAMPLE HYPOTHESIS TESTING: STEP 6 (FORMALLY STATE RESULTS)

Now that we have calculated the results of our three tests, we need to formally state the results of those tests. To do this, we determine if each of our computed test statistics is in the region of rejection.

8.1.6.1 EVALUATING THE RESULTS OF A Z-TEST

The easiest way to evaluate the results of a *z*-test is to refer to the sampling distribution of H_0. Draw a line representing your computed *z*-statistic. If the value falls in the region of rejection, reject the null and accept the alternative (finding statistical significance). If it doesn't, retain the null (not finding statistical significance).

In this case (Figure 8.15), +5.49 is clearly in the region of rejection. We should reject the null and accept the alternative; we have found statistical significance.

Using the rules discussed in Chapter 7 (see p. 206), we formally report the results of this *z*-test as so:

$z = 5.49, p < .05$

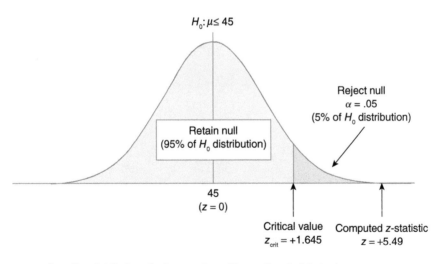

FIGURE 8.15   Sampling distribution of *z* for sample problem, with calculated values

8.1.6.2 EVALUATING THE RESULTS OF A ONE-SAMPLE T-TEST

As with a *z*-test, the easiest way to evaluate the results of a one-sample *t*-test is to refer to the sampling distribution of H_0. Draw a line representing your computed *t*-statistic. If the value falls in the region of rejection, reject the null and accept the alternative (finding statistical significance). If it doesn't, retain the null (not finding statistical significance). Figure 8.16 shows the test of RQ_2.

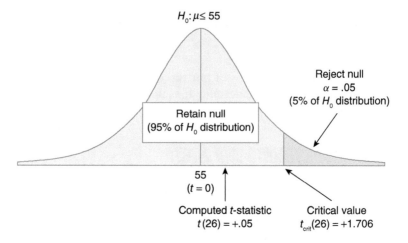

FIGURE 8.16   Sampling distribution of t for RQ$_2$, with calculated values

In this case, $+.05$ is not in the region of rejection. We should retain the null; we have not found statistical significance.

We formally report the results of a t-test as we report a z-test, with the addition of the associated degrees of freedom in parentheses:

$t(26) = .05, p > .05$

Next, we'll look at the test of RQ$_3$ (Figure 8.17).

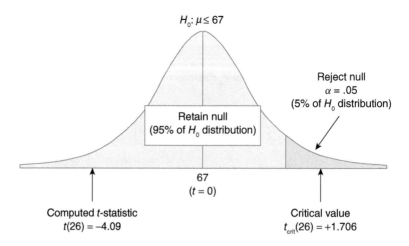

FIGURE 8.17   Sampling distribution of t for RQ$_3$, with calculated values

Once again, the test statistic (-4.09) is not in the region of rejection. It's important to note that, objectively, 4.09 is a very large value. However, it does not have the correct sign, so we do not reject the null. Once again, we retain the null, formally stating:

$t(26) = -4.09, p > .05$

8.1.7 ONE-SAMPLE HYPOTHESIS TESTING: STEP 7 (CONDUCT SUPPLEMENTAL ANALYSES)

When we have computed a one-sample *t*-test or a *z*-test, we compute up to two supplemental analyses, depending upon the results of the formal test:

- If we found statistical significance, compute a confidence interval and an effect size.

- If we did not find statistical significance, compute a confidence interval only.

8.1.7.1 SUPPLEMENTAL ANALYSIS AFTER REJECTING THE NULL

Since we found statistical significance for RQ_1, we need to conduct two supplemental analyses.

First, we compute a confidence interval. If you don't remember confidence intervals, you might want to review Chapter 6. If you used a *z*-test, use the formula for a confidence interval when σ is known. If you used a *t*-test, use the formula for a confidence interval when σ is unknown.

There's one aspect of these formulas that often trips students up – you do not necessarily use the same critical values in hypothesis testing as you do to compute the bounds of confidence intervals. Confidence intervals are always two-tailed. If you conducted a two-tailed test, your critical values will be the same. If you conducted a one-tailed test, they will be different.

As an example of this, remember that RQ_1 was one-tailed. Because of this, we used a critical *z*-value of $+1.645$. However, since confidence intervals are always two-tailed, we'll use 1.96 as the *z*-score in the confidence interval formula – see Figures 8.18 and 8.19.

$$
\begin{aligned}
CI_{95LB} &= \bar{x} - z\sigma_{\bar{x}} \\
&= 57.669090 - 1.96(2.309401) \\
&= 57.669090 - 4.526426 \\
&= 43.142664 \\
&= 43.14
\end{aligned}
$$

FIGURE 8.18   Step by step calculations for the lower bound of the CI for RQ_1

$$
\begin{aligned}
CI_{95UB} &= \bar{x} + z\sigma_{\bar{x}} \\
&= 57.669090 + 1.96(2.309401) \\
&= 57.669090 + 4.526426 \\
&= 62.195516 \\
&= 62.20
\end{aligned}
$$

$$
CI_{95} = [43.14, 62.20]
$$

FIGURE 8.19   Step by step calculations for the upper bound of the CI for RQ_1

Second, because we found statistical significance, we'll compute an effect size. Effect sizes represent the observed difference between two values and represent the practical significance of a finding. They may be standardized or unstandardized.

Practical significance refers to the 'real world' value of a particular finding. Because hypothesis testing relies on sample size to get strong estimates of parameters (that is, it is more likely to find statistical significance with a larger sample than with a smaller sample), large sample sizes sometimes hide effects that are not very practically useful.

For example, imagine that a large retailer conducted a satisfaction survey of all of its employees and wanted to identify if employee satisfaction had changed over the past year. Last year, the mean score on their five-point survey was 3.1. This year, it was 3.0. But because the company survey received responses from 2000 employees, the difference between these two values was statistically significant. If your analysis stopped there, you might think that customer satisfaction had dropped meaningfully and that you needed to step in immediately to see what the problem was. However, if you looked at the *practical significance* of the result, you'd immediately notice that satisfaction dropped only one-tenth of a point. Thus, effect sizes provide perspective for the importance of statistically significant results, regardless of sample size.

You generally want to report unstandardized effect sizes, unless the unstandardized value is not easy to interpret. For example, imagine that we'd conducted a z-test on units sold at our store in comparison to our company's overall average. Our company as a whole averages 500 units per month, while we average 600 units per month. The unstandardized effect size is therefore $600 - 500 = 100$ units per month. We interpret this exactly as it sounds: 'Our store sells 100 units per month more than the company average.' We also call this type of effect size a difference score because it is, simply, the difference between two numbers. We can also express this concept as a formula, which is really just the top half of the z-test and t-test formulas – see Figure 8.20.

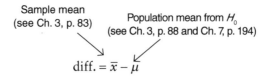

FIGURE 8.20   Annotated formula for an unstandardized effect size (difference score) for z-test and one-sample t-test

In cases like the present case study, the unstandardized effect size is difficult to interpret. For RQ_1, the population mean was 45 and the sample mean was 57.669090. Thus, the unstandardized effect is $57.669090 - 45 = 12.669090 = 12.67$.

But 12.67 what? Points on a 100-point survey? Since 'points on a survey' is not easily interpretable, researchers typically report standardized effect sizes instead. The most common of these is Cohen's *d*, often referred to as simply: *d*.

Cohen's *d* represents the difference between a sample mean and population mean in standard deviation units. It is computed by dividing the difference score by the best estimate of the standard deviation available. For a z-test or one-sample t-test, see Figures 8.21 and 8.22.

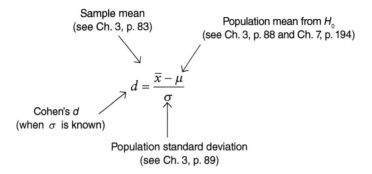

FIGURE 8.21   Annotated formula for a standardized effect size for when σ is known (for example, for a *z*-test)

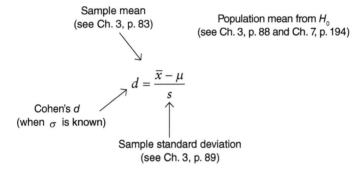

FIGURE 8.22   Formula for a standardized effect size for when σ is known (for example, for a one-sample *t*-test)

For RQ_1, we can plug in the values from the problem to determine d, as shown in Figure 8.23.

$$d = \frac{\bar{x} - \mu}{\sigma} = \frac{57.669090 - 45}{12} = \frac{12.669090}{12} = 1.055758 = 1.06$$

FIGURE 8.23   Step by step calculations for the standardized effect size for the case study's RQ_1

d is a little easier to interpret because it tells us the difference between two means in standard deviation units (this is sort of like a z-score, but comparing means to means instead of scores to means). Different fields have different standards for how to interpret d, but Figure 8.24 gives some general guidelines.

Absolute value of *d*	Size of effect
<0.2	Very small effect
.2 – .5	Small effect
.5 – .8	Medium effect
>0.8	Large effect

FIGURE 8.24   Interpretations of Cohen's *d*

In this case, $d = 1.06$ ($> .8$), so we conclude that this is a large effect, which we report in the next hypothesis testing step.

SO DO I USE AN UNSTANDARDIZED OR STANDARDIZED EFFECT?

There is no consistent answer for this question; it depends on the situation and to whom you are explaining your results. You must evaluate whether or not the difference score would be meaningful if it stood alone. Unstandardized effects *can* give you more information than standardized effects alone do, but they might not be interpretable. You can figure this out for yourself by asking if the unstandardized effect is meaningful to you, personally. For example, an unstandardized effect of £50000 means something very concrete, so you would keep it unstandardized. A difference of two points on a survey is very abstract, so you would probably standardize it. If you are not sure which is best, standardized is typically a safer choice.

8.1.7.2 SUPPLEMENTAL ANALYSIS AFTER RETAINING THE NULL

In RQ_2 and RQ_3, we retained the null. In these cases, we do not compute an effect size; we only compute a confidence interval. Remember that the t-value used in the confidence interval formula will not be the same as your critical t if you conducted a one-tailed test (as we did for these research questions). First, the confidence interval for RQ_2, as shown in Figures 8.25 and 8.26.

$$CI_{95LB} = \bar{x} - ts_{\bar{x}}$$
$$= 55.103903 - 2.056(2.091544)$$
$$= 55.103903 - 4.300214$$
$$= 50.803689$$
$$= 50.80$$

FIGURE 8.25   Step by step calculations for the lower bound of the CI for RQ_2

$$CI_{95UB} = \bar{x} + ts_{\bar{x}}$$
$$= 55.103903 + 2.056(2.091544)$$
$$= 55.103903 + 4.300214$$
$$= 59.404117$$
$$= 59.40$$

$$CI_{95} = [50.80, \ 59.40]$$

FIGURE 8.26   Step by step calculations for the upper bound of the CI for RQ_2

On your own, try computing the confidence interval for RQ$_3$. You should find:

CI$_{95}$ = [50.94, 61.68]

8.1.8 ONE-SAMPLE HYPOTHESIS TESTING: STEP 8 (DRAW ALL CONCLUSIONS)

Now that we've completed all analyses for each research question, all that's left is to put it all together and interpret the results. Use the guidelines in Chapter 7 to help you put together your conclusions, and note the interpretation of effect size for RQ$_1$ (highlighted in bold).

RQ$_1$: Are the tutors at Prescription for Success kinder than the competition?

$H_0: \mu \leq 45$
$H_1: \mu > 45$

$\alpha = .05$
$z_{crit} = +1.645$

$z = 5.49, p<.05$ CI$_{95}$ = [43.14, 62.20]
$d = 1.06$

Conclusion: Reject the null and accept the alternative. The difference is statistically significant. Tutors at Prescription for Success are kinder than the competition. If we assume this sample to represent the population, we would expect 95% of sample means to fall between 43.14 and 62.20. **The difference between Prescription for Success and its competition was large.**

RQ$_2$: Are the tutors at Prescription for Success more compassionate than the competition?

$H_0: \mu \leq 55$
$H_1: \mu > 55$

$\alpha = .05$
$t_{crit}(26) = +1.706$

$t(26) = 0.05, p >.05$
CI$_{95}$ = [50.80, 59.40]

Conclusion: Retain the null. The difference was not statistically significant. Tutors at Prescription for Success are less compassionate than or as compassionate as the competition. If we assume this sample to represent the population, we would expect 95% of sample means to fall between 50.80 and 59.40.

RQ$_3$: Do the tutors at Prescription for Success care for children more than the competition?

$H_0: \mu \leq 67$
$H_1: \mu > 67$

$\alpha = .05$

$t_{crit}(26) = +1.706$

$t(26) = -4.09, p > .05$

$CI_{95} = [50.94, 61.68]$

Conclusion: Retain the null. The difference was not statistically significant. Tutors at Prescription for Success care for children less than or as much as the competition. If we assume this sample to represent the population, we would expect 95% of sample means to fall between 50.94 and 61.68.

8.2 APPLYING Z-TESTS AND ONE-SAMPLE T-TESTS

To apply what you've learned from this chapter, consider the following case study, questions posed about that case study, and discussion of those questions.

8.2.1 APPLICATION CASE STUDY

Isaac is a consultant brought in to assess the performance of the Holby Police Service, which serves the town of Holby. A recent report brought to the attention of the national media indicated that, nationally, only 60% of reported crimes each month were solved. The local government of Holby decided that this rate was far too low to possibly represent their town, so they hired Isaac to conduct an unbiased study of the police force.

To conduct this study, Isaac acquired monthly apprehension rates from Holby police records over the past five years. Using these data, Isaac hopes to provide evidence for or against the position of Holby's councillors.

Given this information:

1 State the research question.

2 State the null and alternative hypotheses.

3 If Isaac rejected the null, what would he conclude?

4 If Isaac calculated a d- statistic, how could he interpret this statistic to add meaning to his report to Holby?

5 If Isaac retained the null, what would he conclude?

8.2.2 APPLICATION DISCUSSION

Once again, we'll cover these questions one at a time.

1 Does the Holby Police Service have an apprehension rate higher than 60%?

2 $H_0: \mu \leq 60\%$. $H_1: \mu > 60\%$.

3 If Isaac rejects the null, he can conclude that the apprehension rate by Holby police is better than the national average.

4   A *d*-statistic would tell Isaac how many standard deviations better than the national average Holby Police Service functioned. Given that value, Isaac could even refer to a *z*-distribution to conclude how unusual that level of performance was in comparison to other departments. For example, if $d = +2$, Isaac could conclude that Holby's police force was in the top 1.5% of departments.

5   If Isaac retains the null, he can only conclude that there is insufficient evidence to say that Holby is better than the national average. He cannot conclude that Holby is definitively worse or the same; instead, his results are inconclusive.

EXPLORING Z-TESTS AND ONE-SAMPLE T-TESTS IN EXCEL AND SPSS

EXCEL

Download the Excel dataset for the demonstration below as **chapter8.xls**. As you read this section, try to apply the terms you've learned in this chapter to the dataset and follow along with Excel on your own computer.

You can also get a video demonstration of the section below under **Excel Video: Chapter 8**.

In Excel, *z*-tests and one-sample *t*-tests are more frustrating than the rest of the tests we'll cover in Part 2 because Excel has no built-in tools to conduct them. Instead, we will need to calculate each test step by step, in a similar fashion to doing so by hand.

When calculating the values for *z*-tests and one-sample *t*-tests in Excel, it's helpful to first record known values somewhere in your spreadsheet while also labelling everything else you'll need to calculate. I'll start by setting up three new columns in F, G and H where I'll put analyses for each variable.

Write in μ and σ from the information provided in Rows 2 and 3. Put 'N/A' (not applicable) in G3 and H3 because σ is not known for those variables. Use the techniques you learned in Chapter 3 (see p. 89) to compute the mean and standard deviation of each set of data to the left and place those in Rows 5 and 6. If you do all of this correctly, you should end up with Figure 8.27.

E	F	G	H
	kindness	compassic	childcare
mu	45	55	67
sigma	12	N/A	N/A
x bar	57.67	55.10	56.31
s	12.10	10.87	13.58
n			
df			
se			
z			
t			
left-tailed p			
right-tailed p			
2-tailed p			

FIGURE 8.27   Setting up Excel to compute *z*-tests and one-sample *t*-tests

(Continued)

(Continued)

In F7, we need to determine *n*. You can do this by either manually counting the number of rows of data or by using this formula:

=COUNT(A:A)

This will count all numeric values in column A and put the result in F7. Since we need degrees of freedom in F8, and d.f. is in this case $n - 1$, enter this formula in F8:

=F7-1

Highlight both F7 and F8, then fill right, and you should end up with Figure 8.28.

E	F	G	H
	kindness	compassic	childcare
mu	45	55	67
sigma	12	N/A	N/A
x bar	57.67	55.10	56.31
s	12.10	10.87	13.58
n	27	27	27
df	26	26	26
se			
z			
t			
left-tailed p			
right-tailed p			
2-tailed p			

FIGURE 8.28   Excel dataset after computing means, standard deviations, sample sizes and degrees of freedom

The new row of interest is the standard error. Remember that this is different depending on what information is available – the formula will be different for Column F (where sigma is known) and Columns G and H (where sigma is not known).

- In F9, type: =F3/SQRT(F7).
- In G9, type: =G6/SQRT(G7).
- In H9, type: =H6/SQRT(H7).

Notice the difference between these values. For Column F, we used σ. That means F9 represents *sx*. For Columns G and H, we used the sample's *s*. That means G9 and H9 represent $s_{\bar{x}}$. We did this because we will be conducting a *z*-test for the kindness variable and one-sample *t*-tests for the compassion and childcare variables.

Next, we need to compute test statistics. Again, I'll use 'N/A' to represent cells where we should not have any values. Placing N/A in appropriate locations in Rows 11 and 12, you should end up with Figure 8.29.

x bar		57.67	55.10	56.31
s		12.10	10.87	13.58
n		27	27	27
df		26	26	26
se		2.31	2.09	2.61
z			N/A	N/A
t		N/A		

FIGURE 8.29   Excel dataset after setting up pattern of desired z-tests and one-sample t-tests

This is because we'll be computing z for the data in Column F and t for the data in Columns G and H. To compute z, we will simply follow the z-test formula. In F11, type:

- = (F5-F2)/F9.

Using this formula, we subtract the population mean from the sample mean and divide it by the standard error we computed earlier. In G12, type:

- = (G5-G2)/G9.

This is the same pattern, but we have calculated a t-statistic instead of a z-statistic. This is because the standard error in this column uses s instead of σ. Fill right from this cell into H12. You should end up with Figure 8.30.

z		5.49	N/A	N/A
t		N/A	0.05	-4.09

FIGURE 8.30   Excel dataset after computing values for z-statistics and t-statistics

These numbers should look familiar – they are the z-statistic and t-statistics that we calculated by hand in this chapter!

At this point, the approach to computing p-values differs a bit between Excel 2007 and 2010, so we're going to split this section in two. If you're using Excel 2010, jump ahead to that section.

(Continued)

(Continued)

COMPUTING *P*-VALUES IN EXCEL 2007

For the z-test, Excel 2007's built-in functions only return left-tailed p-values. Because of this, we have to use a few unusual functions to get other p-values that we might want (for example, right-tailed and two-tailed). The mathematics behind this is a bit more complicated than is needed for this textbook; if you'd like further information about why these functions work the way they do, ask your instructor. If you'd like to use functions that make more sense, upgrade to Excel 2010 (Excel 2010 changed many of its functions from their Excel 2007 counterparts for greater versatility, and also named them more logically).

To get the left-tailed p-value in F14, type:

■ =NORMSDIST(F11).

This function takes the z- statistic in F11 and converts it into a left-tailed p-value.
To get the right-tailed p-value in F15, type:

■ =1-F14.

To get the two-tailed p-value in F16, type:

■ =2*MIN(F14:F15).

It should look like Figure 8.31.

z		5.49	N/A		N/A	
t	N/A			0.05		-4.09
left-tailed p		1.000				
right-tailed p		0.000				
2-tailed p		0.000				

FIGURE 8.31   Calculated p-values in Excel 2007 for the z-test

From this, we can make conclusions as appropriate given our z-test. Since our hypotheses dictated a right-tailed test, we can simply look at the 'right-tailed p' to identify the appropriate p-value. In this case, it is very small – it rounds to .000.

Remember from Chapter 7 (p. 205) that we always report the exact p-value if we know it. That means if you conduct this test in Excel, your formal test of the hypothesis changes just a little:

$z = 5.49, p = .00$

Since $p < \alpha$ – that is, .00 is less than .05 – we would conclude here that the difference is statistically significant.

To compute the *p*-value for the one-sample *t*-tests, the formulas get even stranger. Excel 2007 will only return *p*-values for positive *t*-statistics, even if they should be negative. To compute the left-tailed *p*-value in G14, type:

■ =IF(G12>0,1-TDIST(G12,G8,1),TDIST(-G12,G8,1)).

This code is designed to return the correct left-tailed *p*-value regardless of whether or not your observed *t*-statistic is negative. And lucky for you, that's really all you need to know about it. In G15, type:

■ =1-G14.

And finally, in G16, type:

■ =2*MIN(G14:G15).

Highlight G14 through G16 and fill right. You should end up with Figure 8.32.

z		5.49	N/A		N/A
t	N/A		0.05		-4.09
left-tailed p		1.000	0.520		0.000
right-tailed p		0.000	0.480		1.000
2-tailed p		0.000	0.961		0.000

FIGURE 8.32   Calculated *p*-values in Excel 2007 for *z*-test and one-sample *t*-test

From this, we can draw conclusions just as we did when doing this by hand, except now we can report exact *p*-values from the right-tailed rows:

$t(26) = .05, p = .48$

$t(26) = -4.09, p = 1.00$

Since $p > \alpha$ – that is, both .48 and 1.00 are more than .05 – we would conclude here that neither difference is statistically significant.

If you needed left-tailed values, you would report those rows; if you needed two-tailed values, you would report those rows.

We would normally, at this point, compute confidence intervals for each of these – see Chapter 6 for more details on how to do this.

Also, since we found statistical significance for the kindness variable, we should now compute Cohen's *d*. In F18, type:

■ =(F5-F2)/F3.

(Continued)

(Continued)

You should end up with Figure 8.33.

E	F	G	H
	kindness	compassic	childcare
mu	45	55	67
sigma	12	N/A	N/A
x bar	57.67	55.10	56.31
s	12.10	10.87	13.58
n	27	27	27
df	26	26	26
se	2.31	2.09	2.61
z	5.49	N/A	N/A
t	N/A	0.05	-4.09
left-tailed p	1.000	0.520	0.000
right-tailed p	0.000	0.480	1.000
2-tailed p	0.000	0.961	0.000
Cohen's d	1.0557575	N/A	N/A

FIGURE 8.33   Completed z-tests and one-sample t-tests in Excel 2007

COMPUTING P-VALUES IN EXCEL 2010

Excel 2010's functions for computing p-values are much improved from those in Excel 2007, but they are still not very user-friendly. Functions are available to compute p-values for right-tailed tests directly from data, but you are better off using those values to compute other p-values.

We'll start by computing the right-tailed p-values for the z-test. In F15, type:

■ =Z.TEST(A2:A28,F2,F3).

The first term of this formula (A2:A28) refers to which data you want to test. The second term (F2) refers to μ. The third term (F3) refers to σ.

We'll next compute the right-tailed p-values for the one-sample t-tests. In G15, type:

■ =T.DIST.RT(G12,G8).

The first term of this formula (G12) specifies your t-statistic. The second term (G8) refers to your degrees of freedom. Fill this formula into H15, and you should end up with Figure 8.34.

z		5.49	N/A	N/A
t	N/A		0.05	-4.09
left-tailed p				
right-tailed p		0.000	0.480	1.000
2-tailed p				

FIGURE 8.34   Calculated right-tailed *p*-values in Excel 2010

From this alone, we can already make all the conclusions we need to make from this dataset, because all of our tests were right-tailed. Remember that we want to use exact *p*-values in our formal reports of hypothesis tests whenever we know them. This changes our formal tests a bit:

$z = 5.49, p = .00$
$t(26) = .05, p = .48$
$t(26) = -4.09, p = 1.00$

For the *z*-test, $p < \alpha$ – that is, .00 is less than .05 – so we would conclude that this difference is statistically significant.

For the *t*-tests, $p > \alpha$ – that is, both .48 and 1.00 are more than .05 – so we would conclude that neither of these differences is statistically significant.

For the sake of completeness, we'll now calculate the left-tailed and two-tailed *p*-values. You would refer to these values instead if you were interested in a left-tailed test or two-tailed test. In F14, type:

■ =1-F15.

Fill this formula all the way to the right. In F16, type:

■ =2*MIN(F14:F15).

Also fill this formula all the way to the right. You should end up with the final set of values shown in Figure 8.35.

z		5.49	N/A	N/A
t	N/A		0.05	-4.09
left-tailed p		1.000	0.520	0.000
right-tailed p		0.000	0.480	1.000
2-tailed p		0.000	0.961	0.000

FIGURE 8.35   All calculated *p*-values for *z*-test and one-sample *t*-test in Excel 2010

(Continued)

(Continued)

We would normally, at this point, compute confidence intervals for each of these – see Chapter 6 for more details on how to do this.

Also, since we found statistical significance for the kindness variable, we should now compute Cohen's *d*. In F18, type:

■ =(F5-F2)/F3.

You should end up with Figure 8.36.

E	F	G	H
	kindness	compassic	childcare
mu	45	55	67
sigma	12	N/A	N/A
x bar	57.67	55.10	56.31
s	12.10	10.87	13.58
n	27	27	27
df	26	26	26
se	2.31	2.09	2.61
z	5.49	N/A	N/A
t	N/A	0.05	-4.09
left-tailed p	1.000	0.520	0.000
right-tailed p	0.000	0.480	1.000
2-tailed p	0.000	0.961	0.000
Cohen's d	1.0557575	N/A	N/A

FIGURE 8.36   Completed *z*-test and one-sample *t*-test in Excel 2010

SPSS

Download the SPSS dataset for the demonstration below as **chapter8.sav**. As you read this section, try to apply the terms you've learned in this chapter to the dataset and follow along with SPSS on your own computer.

▷   You can also get a video demonstration of the section below under **SPSS Videos: Chapter 8**.

SPSS does not include functions for conducting *z*-tests, although you can compute means and standard deviations quickly to speed up your hand computations (see Chapter 3, p. 89). You cannot compute the population standard error in SPSS, because there is no way to input σ.

One-sample *t*-tests, however, are included. To conduct a one-sample *t*-test, open **Analyse > Compare Means > One-Sample T Test** (see Figure 8.37).

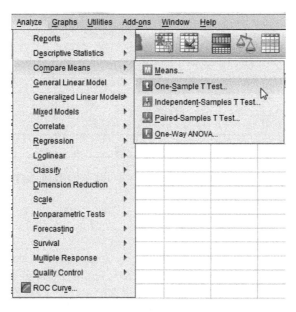

FIGURE 8.37   Finding the one-sample *t*-test in SPSS

Since we have three different values for μ, we must compute the one-sample *t*-test separately for each of our two *t*-tests.

For RQ$_2$, which is represented here as the compassion variable, we must compare with $\mu \leq 55$. Move the Cincinnati Compassion Index to the right and type '55' for the test value (Figure 8.38).

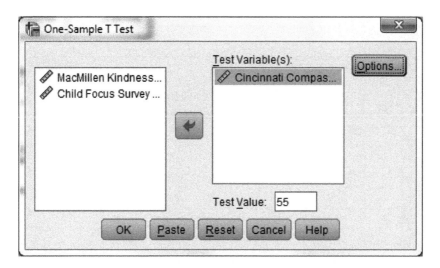

FIGURE 8.38   One-sample *t*-test dialogue in SPSS, testing the case study's RQ$_2$

(Continued)

(Continued)

Click **OK**, and the output pane should pop up with the results, as shown in Figure 8.39.

One-Sample Test

	Test Value = 55					
	t	df	Sig. (2-tailed)	Mean Difference	95% Confidence Interval of the Difference	
					Lower	Upper
Cincinnati Compassion Index	.050	26	.961	.10390	-4.1953	4.4031

FIGURE 8.39   Output of a one-sample *t*-test conducted for RQ$_2$ in the case study dataset in SPSS

Here, we can see almost all of the pieces needed for the formal test of the hypothesis. We see the *t*-statistic under 't', we can see degrees of freedom under 'df' and we can see a *p*-value under 'Sig. (2-tailed)'.

However, this *p*-value is, as the heading implies, for a two-tailed test. You need to divide this value in half to get the one-tailed *p*-value. In this case, $p = .961/2 = .4805 = .48$.

An important warning: Dividing the *p*-value in half is only accurate if the computed *t*-statistic is consistent with the direction of the region of rejection. For this variable, the region of rejection is in the right tail and the *t*-statistic is positive, so this is fine. If they are mismatched (that is, if the region of rejection is opposite the *t*-statistic), you should always retain the null.

Remember from Chapter 7 that we report exact *p*-values whenever possible. We would therefore report this test as:

$t(26) = .05, p = .48$

Because $p > \alpha$ – that is, .48 is greater than .05 – we would conclude that this difference is not statistically significant.

Now, let's try the second test. Reopen the one-sample *t*-test dialogue, change the test value to 67, and move the childcare variable to the right (Figure 8.40).

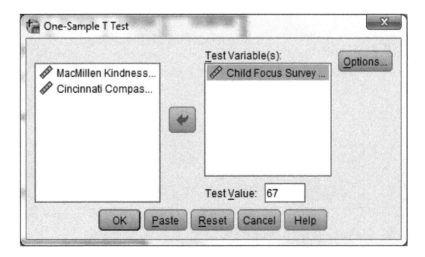

FIGURE 8.40   One-sample *t*-test dialogue in SPSS, testing the case study's RQ$_3$

Click OK, and you should see the results shown in Figure 8.41.

One-Sample Test

| | Test Value = 67 | | | | | |
| | | | | | 95% Confidence Interval of the Difference | |
	t	df	Sig. (2-tailed)	Mean Difference	Lower	Upper
Child Focus Survey Result	-4.090	26	.000	-10.68801	-16.0594	-5.3166

FIGURE 8.41   Output of a one-sample *t*-test conducted for RQ$_3$ in the case study dataset in SPSS

Because the *p*-value is less than , you might be inclined to conclude that this difference is statistically significant. However, it is not. The *t*-statistic is in *the wrong direction*. Since we are interpreting this as a one-tailed test, we must ensure that the *t*-statistic is consistent with the region of rejection. Since the region of rejection and therefore the critical value are on the positive side of the distribution, whereas this test statistic is negative, we must retain the null. When this is true, SPSS cannot compute an exact *p*-value. You must instead rely on the old format:

$$t(26) = -4.09, p > .05$$

This result is not statistically significant.

To compute the confidence intervals surrounding these two estimates, we must conduct new analyses. The confidence intervals that you see in these images are adjusted for the population test value. To get the unadjusted values, reopen the one-sample *t*-test dialogue and change the 'test value' to 0 (Figure 8.42).

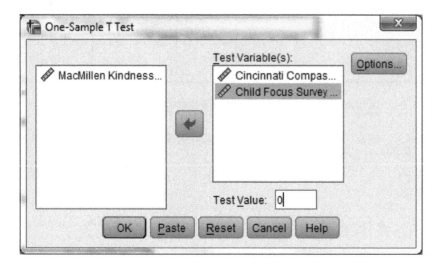

FIGURE 8.42   One-sample *t*-test dialogue in SPSS, specified to compute confidence interval bounds for both RQ$_2$ and RQ$_3$

Click OK and you should see the results shown in Figure 8.43.

(Continued)

(Continued)

One-Sample Test

				Test Value = 0		
					95% Confidence Interval of the Difference	
	t	df	Sig. (2-tailed)	Mean Difference	Lower	Upper
Cincinnati Compassion Index	26.346	26	.000	55.10390	50.8047	59.4031
Child Focus Survey Result	21.549	26	.000	56.31199	50.9406	61.6834

FIGURE 8.43   Output of one-sample t-tests conducted to determine the confidence intervals for RQ_2 and RQ_3 in the case study dataset in SPSS

Thus, we can report the two confidence intervals as:

RQ_2: $CI_{95} = [50.80, 59.40]$
RQ_3: $CI_{95} = [50.94, 61.68]$

SPSS does not include automatic effect size calculations for one-sample t. However, you can use the other output provided when conducting the one-sample t-test to make it easier to calculate Cohen's d by hand – see Figure 8.44.

One-Sample Statistics

	N	Mean	Std. Deviation	Std. Error Mean
Cincinnati Compassion Index	27	55.1039	10.86798	2.09154
Child Focus Survey Result	27	56.3120	13.57836	2.61316

FIGURE 8.44   Summary statistics reported by SPSS when computing a one-sample t-test

From each of these, we could subtract the displayed mean from the population mean and divide by the given standard deviation to determine the value of Cohen's d. However, since we did not find statistical significance for either of these analyses, we will not compute any effect sizes at this time.

STATISTICS IN THE REAL WORLD

These web links can be accessed directly from the book's website.

Pete Slease, Principal Executive Advisor at Gartner, along with Rick DeLisi and Matthew Dixon, explain why call length in service organizations is a poor way to measure customer service: https://hbr.org/2017/02/call-length-is-the-worst-way-to-measure-customer-service.

If you conducted a z-test comparing a call centre's average call length to a desirable 'average call length', what would you conclude from that? What else should you consider?

Stacy Jones and Jaclyn Trop collected data for Fortune Magazine on the diversity of 14 technology companies: http://fortune.com/2015/07/30/tech-companies-diveristy.

Is this enough information to check to see if these companies come from populations with equal gender representation? Which companies make the cut?

TEST YOURSELF

 After you've completed the questions below, check your answers online.

1. How are z-scores and z-statistics similar? How are they different?

2. Given the following information, can the sample size be identified? If so, what is it?
   a $t(25) = 4.5, p < .05$.
   b $z = 2.3, p < .05$.
   c $z = 1.2, p > .01$.

3. Given this result from a one-sample *t*-test: $t(17) = .90, p > .01$
   a What was the sample size?
   b What were the degrees of freedom?
   c What was alpha?
   d Did the research conclude the difference was statistically significant?
   e Interpret the meaning of '.90' in words.

4. We conduct a z-test on each of the following. Is a standardized or unstandardized effect size more appropriate?
   a Difference between our employees and national averages on employee engagement.
   b Difference between national average yearly accidents and our company's accidents.
   c Difference between our customers' satisfaction and the level required by corporate.

5. What would the critical value(s) be for each of the following situations, assuming you were conducting a one-sample test? Assume $= .05$.
   a $n = 15, \sigma = 12$; one-tailed (left).
   b $s = 5.4$, d.f. $= 14$; two-tailed.
   c $\sigma = 92, n = 48$; two-tailed.

DATA SKILL CHALLENGES

 After you've completed the questions below, check your answers online.

1 Jill from Jill's Used Cars in the case study from Chapter 4 has decided to compare her employees' December sales with mean sales per employee for her region of the country, which she read from an online newspaper was 14. Conduct the complete hypothesis testing process with this dataset (see the textbook's website for chapter4.xls or chapter4.sav).

2 Sue from Tastetastic in the case study from Chapter 3 has become worried that the taste testers she employs may not be representative of typical customer tastes – she thinks they may be too harsh in their ratings! She discovers that one of the dishes in her dataset, Dish #6, won a national award and, as a result, has been tasted and rated by thousands of people on the same scale that she used! She's been told that, on average, people rate the dish a 3.5, with a standard deviation of 1.2. Conduct the complete hypothesis testing process with this dataset (see the textbook's website for chapter3.xls or chapter3.sav).

(Continued)

(Continued)

3 Larry runs a plastics manufacturing company. The most recent issue of a manufacturing trade magazine published an article saying that the average number of industrial accidents for plastics manufacturers is 15.6 per year. Larry wants to know whether his company has fewer accidents than the average for his industry. The data for Larry's company for the past nine years are presented in Figure 8.45. Conduct the complete hypothesis testing process with this dataset.

4 Petra is an employee at a call centre. Her manager has asked her to determine whether the average number of complaints received by the workers at their branch is different from the average number of complaints for the company overall. The company receives an average of 24 complaints per day with a standard deviation of 5.25. The data for Petra's branch over the past five days is provided in Figure 8.46. Conduct the complete hypothesis testing process with this dataset.

Year	Number of accidents
1	13.25
2	11.30
3	9.40
4	12.80
5	11.00
6	10.00
7	10.50
8	12.75
9	11.50

FIGURE 8.45   Plastics manufacturing dataset

Day	Number of complaints
1	23
2	28
3	34
4	26
5	32

FIGURE 8.46   Employee call centre dataset

NEW TERMS

difference score: effect size: one-sample t-test: one-sample test: t-statistic: z-statistic: z-test:

NEW STATISTICAL NOTATION AND FORMULAS

z_{crit}: the critical value(s) of a z-test
t_{crit}: the critical value(s) of a t-test

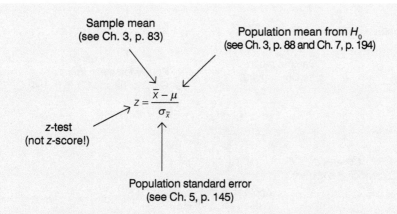

FIGURE 8.47   Annotated formula for a *z*-test

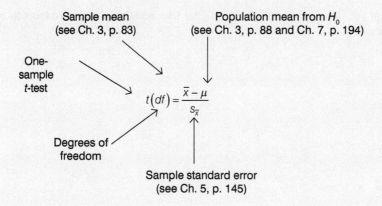

FIGURE 8.48   Annotated formula for a one-sample *t*-test

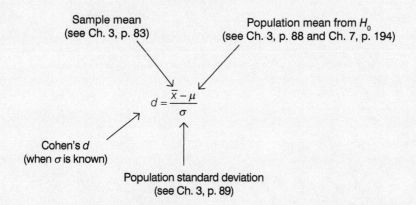

FIGURE 8.49   Annotated formula for Cohen's *d* for a one-sample test when σ is known

(Continued)

(Continued)

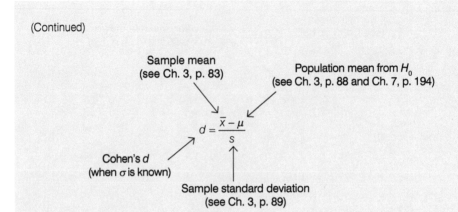

FIGURE 8.50   Annotated formula for Cohen's *d* for a one-sample test when σ is unknown

Visit https://study.sagepub.com/landers2e **for free additional online resources related to this chapter.**

9 PAIRED- AND INDEPENDENT-SAMPLES *T*-TESTS

WHAT YOU WILL LEARN FROM THIS CHAPTER

- How to complete the hypothesis testing procedure for two-sample tests
- How to determine when paired-samples *t*-tests and independent-samples *t*-tests are appropriate given the data available
- How to identify the critical value(s) for these tests
- How to determine degrees of freedom for two-sample *t*-tests

DATA SKILLS YOU WILL MASTER FROM THIS CHAPTER

- Computing a paired-samples *t*-test
- Computing an independent-samples *t*-test

CASE STUDY   ARE WE HIRING THE RIGHT PEOPLE?

Diego is a placement manager at We Work Now, an employment agency specializing in providing temporary workers in minor office roles, especially filing and typing. He is responsible for matching temporary agency workers to institutions interested in hiring them, based upon their skills and experience. With his new-found skill in hypothesis testing learned from Chapter 7, Diego decides that statistics can help him answer some questions he's had lately about his job.

(Continued)

(Continued)

First, he is interested in finding new ways to recruit highly qualified employees. He believes that typists leave his organization as better typists than when they were employed, and that this could be a valuable point during recruitment for being an employee at We Work Now – leave with more skills than when you started.

Second, since he wants to assess typing performance at two different times, he is also curious if satisfaction with office work changes over that same time period. But he is not sure of the direction – while he hopes people become more satisfied after working at We Work Now, they might instead become less satisfied.

Third, when We Work Now was established decades ago, it exclusively employed women for typist roles. But due to changing government regulations, We Work Now updated its human resources policies long ago to stress no preferential employment by gender. Diego is curious if this made a difference in the performance of his typists, but he's not sure who he'd expect to perform better – men or women?

Fourth and finally, for many years We Work Now required its typists to have previous work experience as a typist. As access to the Internet became more common (and more people grew up with keyboards),

his superiors decided that this requirement was unnecessary, because most people would have typing experience in their everyday lives. Diego doesn't think was a good idea. In particular, he doesn't think that those without prior experience as a typist are performing as strongly when employed as those who do have that experience.

With these questions, Diego turns to this textbook. Since he can't randomly assign his employees to be 'new' and 'old', 'experienced' and 'not experienced, or 'male' and 'female', he decides to take a correlational approach, measuring satisfaction and typing performance immediately after employment and also six months later. He collects information on gender and prior experience immediately after employment. From Chapter 8, he learned how to compare a single sample mean with a population mean. But he's not sure how this applies to his current set of problems. From Chapter 7, he recognizes that some of his questions are one-tailed while others are two-tailed. But he doesn't have a population for comparison, does he? What is greater than what? What is equal to what? How can he analyse the data he will collect from this research design to answer his questions?

While we learned about the overall hypothesis testing process in Chapter 7 and the process to compare a sample mean with a given population mean in Chapter 8, statisticians-in-training (that's you!) soon realize that different tests are needed for any particular combination of variables available. In Diego's case, he has two major designs.

First, he is measuring some information – typing performance and satisfaction – at two different points in time. Second, he wants to compare the scores of two groups with each other. In either case, there is no population information provided in the research question, so the techniques we learned before won't work in quite the same way.

As you read Chapter 9, think about how the logic of hypothesis testing discussed in the previous two chapters must change to construct tests for each of Diego's research questions.

9.1 PAIRED DATA

The first two of Diego's research questions involve paired data. Paired data always involve a pair of observations (two variables) that are linked together by the research study's design.

There is nothing special about paired data themselves; you generally can't look at a dataset and say 'those are paired!'. Instead, we identify paired data by their relationship at the construct level (see Chapter 1, p. 13, if you don't remember constructs).

In business, you're most likely to encounter paired data that come from repeated measures research designs. These research designs involve measuring something at two or more time points. For example, we might want to compare employee performance right now with employee performance six months from now after we implement a policy change. We measure the *same employees* twice, collecting performance in exactly the same way each time. While repeated measures can include any number of measurements (for example, semi-annual follow-up measurements taken for five years), paired data always involve two and only two measurements.

Paired data are not necessarily from repeated measures. Another common type of paired data comes from interpersonal relationships. For example, if we ran a toy retailer, we might want to know if there were differences in attitudes to our toys between parents and their children in order to better target our marketing efforts. If we bring pairs of a parent and their child to interact with a toy and rate it, we have created paired data. However, it's important to note that the relationship itself is not what makes this a paired design; instead, it is the way we collected the data. If, instead, we had randomly sampled parents and randomly sampled children separately, this would not produce paired data (since there would be no pairs).

9.2 HYPOTHESIS TESTING WITH PAIRED DATA

Hypothesis testing with paired data is not altogether different from hypothesis testing in one-sample *t*-tests. There are only a few key differences, which I'll highlight as we step through the process. We explore this chapter's case study dataset to examine these issues. Here's a summary of that dataset as it relates to paired data:

Variable 1: type@hire – Typing speed at employment (in words per minute).

Variable 2: type@6mos – Typing speed after six months (in words per minute).

Variable 3: satis@hire – Office work satisfaction at employment.

Variable 4: satis@6mos – Office work satisfaction after six months.

$n = 151$.

9.2.1 PAIRED DATA HYPOTHESIS TESTING: STEP 1 (STATE THE RESEARCH QUESTION)

With Chapter 8 behind you, this first step should be straightforward. Remember to stress the paired nature of the data in the research question and to include directionality if appropriate.

RQ$_1$: Do employees have greater typing skills six months after employment than when they were employed?

RQ$_2$: Do employees have a different level of satisfaction with office work six months after employment than when they were employed?

9.2.2 PAIRED DATA HYPOTHESIS TESTING: STEP 2 (STATE THE HYPOTHESES)

Hypotheses for paired data are very similar to hypotheses from one-sample tests. That's because they essentially *are* one-sample tests. We subtract the mean of one group from the mean of the other group to create a mean difference score, much like the difference scores we calculate as unstandardized effect sizes (see Chapter 8, p. 230). We then compare that mean difference score with a population mean difference score of zero. If we reject the null, we can conclude that the observed difference score is unlikely to have been drawn from a population where there was no difference – and that answers our research questions.

RQ$_1$: Do employees have greater typing skills six months after employment than when they were employed?

$H_0: \mu_d \leq 0$
$H_1: \mu_d > 0$

where $\mu_d = \mu_{T2} - \mu_{T1}$.

The hypotheses themselves are identical to those of a one-sample test except for the addition of the subscript 'd' – whereas μ is a population mean, μ_d is a population mean *difference*. It represents the subtracted difference between two population means.

We represent directionality the same way that we represent it in one-sample tests. Since we are interested in identifying an increase in typing skills, our alternative hypothesis uses a greater than symbol (>).

The biggest change to these hypotheses is the addition of the 'where' clause that defines to what μ_d refers. In this case, we want our population mean difference to represent the result if we subtract the 'Time 1' score (value when employed) from the 'Time 2' score (value six months later). I've represented these as 'T1' and 'T2' respectively in the formula.

WHY T2 – T1 AND NOT T1 – T2?

Why subtract 'Time 1' from 'Time 2' and not the other way round? The key here is for our μ_d to represent a meaningful value. When we calculate (as an estimate of μ_d) we want that value to mean something. By subtracting T2 – T1, positive values indicate increases over time, and negative values indicate decreases over time.

For example, if:

T1 = 5
and T2 = 4
then T2 – T1 = −1

That means that scores decreased one point from Time 1 to Time 2. If we subtracted in the opposite direction, the scores would be flipped – negative would indicate increases and positive would indicate decreases. As a result, we should always calculate T2 – T1 when computing differences for repeated measures data. Computing it the other way isn't wrong as long as you also flip the sign of your critical *t*-statistic – it's just unnecessarily confusing.

If you aren't looking at repeated measures data – for example, if you're comparing spouses – the subtraction order is less important. However, you still need to match the direction of your critical value to reflect the answer to your research question that you want. We'll discuss this more further into this chapter.

Given this, try to produce the hypotheses for RQ_2 on your own. You should come up with this:

RQ_2: Do employees have a different level of satisfaction with office work six months after employment than when they were employed?

$H_0: \mu_d = 0$
$H_1: \mu_d \neq 0$

where $\mu_d = \mu_{T2} - \mu_{T1}$.

The only difference here is the use of the two-tailed equals and not-equals symbols instead of the one-tailed symbols. In tests on paired data, the comparison population value is always zero.

9.2.3 PAIRED DATA HYPOTHESIS TESTING: STEP 3 (SET SIGNIFICANCE LEVEL AND DECISION RULE)

As before, lacking any information leading us to another alpha, we will set our significance level for both tests at $\alpha = .05$.

We'll next derive our decision rule, the process for which is identical to the process we used for one-sample tests. Since we don't know the population standard deviation (and we probably never will, in a paired data context), the most appropriate test for these research questions is the paired-samples *t*-test (also called a matched-samples *t*-test or related-samples *t*-test). We can identify the appropriate t_{crit} the same way that we did in Chapter 8 – look up the desired number of tails and degrees of freedom in the *t*-table (see Appendix A2) and adopt the appropriate sign for it (–, + or ±).

Being so similar to one-sample tests, paired-samples tests have identical degrees of freedom: $n - 1$. Since the dataset is $n = 151$, d.f. $= 151 - 1 = 150$. RQ_1 is a one-tailed test with > in the alternative hypothesis. Given all of this, using the technique we've practised in Chapters 6 and 8, we need to find the critical *t* for: right-tailed $\alpha = .05$ with d.f. $= 150$. Find this value now in Appendix A2.

Once you've identified the correct value, you need to identify its sign. Since this is a right-tailed test, we need a single positive critical value: $t_{crit}(150) = +1.655$.

For RQ_2, everything is the same except for the tails. Find the critical *t* for: two-tailed $\alpha = .05$ with d.f. $= 150$. Since this is a two-tailed test, we need two critical values, one positive and one negative: $t_{crit}(150) = \pm 1.976$.

9.2.4 PAIRED DATA HYPOTHESIS TESTING: STEP 4 (COLLECT A SAMPLE)

At this point, Diego should conduct the study. As before, let's use this time to consolidate everything we know so far:

RQ$_1$: Do employees have greater typing skills six months after employment than when they were employed?

$H_0: \mu_d \leq 0$
$H_1: \mu_d > 0$

where $\mu_d = \mu_{T2} - \mu_{T1}$

$\mu_{d} = .05$
$t_{crit}(150) = \pm 1.655$

RQ$_2$: Do employees have a different level of satisfaction with office work six months after employment than when they were employed?

$H_0: \mu_d = 0$
$H_1: \mu_d \neq 0$

where $\mu_d = \mu_{T2} - \mu_{T1}$

$\alpha = .05$

$t_{crit}(150) = \pm 1.976$

9.2.5 PAIRED DATA HYPOTHESIS TESTING: STEP 5 (CONDUCT STATISTICAL TEST)

Now we will actually compute the value for the paired-samples t-test. As before, the formula for a paired-samples t-test is very similar to that of a one-sample t-test, with a few key differences – see Figure 9.01.

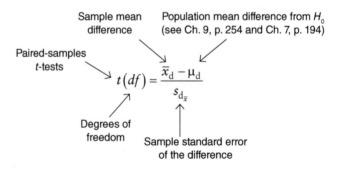

FIGURE 9.01   Annotated formula for paired-samples t-test

In this formula, we replace (1) the sample mean with the sample mean difference, (2) the population mean with the population mean difference and (3) the population standard error with the population standard error of the difference. The formula's structure is identical; the overall change is that instead of comparing sample means directly to population means, we're comparing sample difference scores to population difference scores.

The standard error formula is also similar, but slightly different – see Figure 9.02.

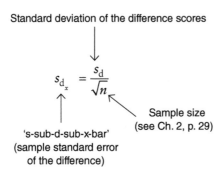

FIGURE 9.02   Annotated formula for sample standard error of the difference

Once again, we replace sample statistics with statistics referring to the difference scores. Here, the standard deviation is replaced with the standard deviation of the difference scores.

Because the computations for this test involve a bit more legwork, we'll look at a smaller-scale example for hand computations. Let's imagine that Diego, as an early pilot test, also collected satisfaction data from nine people three months after employment. Those data are shown in Figure 9.03.

When hired	3 months after hiring
4	2
2	4
1	3
4	4
3	5
4	5
4	5
1	4
4	2

FIGURE 9.03   Subset of case study data to be used in sample problem

Now let's conduct a *t*-test to determine if this subset of Diego's employees had different satisfaction three months after employment than immediately after.

The new step in a paired-samples *t*-test is that you must calculate difference scores, and then you must calculate the mean, standard deviation and standard error based upon those difference scores. The first step is shown in Figure 9.04.

When hired	6 months after hiring	d
2	2	2–2=0
2	4	4–2=0
1	3	3–1=0
4	4	4–4=0
3	5	5–3=2
4	5	5–4=1
4	5	5–4=1
1	4	4–1=3
4	2	2–4=2

FIGURE 9.04   Difference scores calculated for sample problem data

For each pair of data, I have done exactly what the 'where' clause in our hypotheses says to do: I have subtracted one value from the other. In this case, I have subtracted the Time 1 data (when employed) from the Time 2 data (after employment), exactly as our hypotheses suggested. I now have a list of difference scores (labelled 'd' in Figure 9.04).

Next, we need to compute the required parts of the t-test, as specified by our formula. We'll need $\bar{x}_d$, μ_d and $s_d x$.

$\bar{x}_d$ is the sample mean of the difference scores. To compute this, simply take the mean of the values in the 'd' column in Figure 9.04 – see Figure 9.05.

$$\bar{x}_d = \frac{\sum x}{n} = \frac{0+2+2+0+2+1+1+3+(-2)}{9} = \frac{9}{9} = 1$$

FIGURE 9.05   Step by step calculations for the mean difference from the sample data in Figure 9.04

μ_d is the population mean of the difference scores. Much like the one-sample t-test, this is derived from the hypotheses – not the dataset. In our hypotheses, we compare μ_d with 0, so this will be the value of μ_d here as well.

To calculate , we'll need n and s_d. This is easier than it sounds. Just as $\bar{x}_d$ is the mean of the 'd' column, s_d is the standard deviation of the 'd' column. Using the techniques we learned in Chapter 3, you should find $s_d = 1.5$.

Next, compute the sample standard error of the difference, as shown in Figure 9.06.

$$s_{d\bar{x}} = \frac{s_d}{\sqrt{n}} = \frac{1.5}{\sqrt{9}} = \frac{1.5}{3} = 0.5$$

FIGURE 9.06   Step by step calculations for the sample standard error of the difference from data in Figure 9.04

Finally, plug all of these values into the formula for t – see Figure 9.07.

$$t\left(df\right) = \frac{\bar{x}_d - \mu_d}{s_{d_{\bar{x}}}} = \frac{1-0}{.5} = \frac{1}{.5} = 2$$

FIGURE 9.07   Step by step calculations for the *t*-statistic from data in Figure 9.04

Thus, for the mini-dataset above, $t(8) = 2$.

In our 151-row case study dataset, this calculation takes a bit longer. So to speed this up, I've computed all the key values you would need here. Try using this information to produce the correct *t*-statistic for each test. If you don't remember what these labels mean, check the beginning of this chapter (p. 253):

Mean of type@hire difference scores: 2.389602.

Mean of satis@hire difference scores:.032106.

SD of type@hire difference scores: 10.079477.

SD of satis@hire difference scores: 1.819459.

This is all the information you need to compute each *t*-statistic for the full case study data. If you do so correctly, you should find:

RQ_1: $t(150) = 2.91$

RQ_2: $t(150) = 0.22$

9.2.6 PAIRED DATA HYPOTHESIS TESTING: STEP 6 (FORMALLY STATE RESULTS)

This step remains consistent with all *t*-tests; if your test statistic is beyond the critical value (in the region of rejection), reject the null. If not, retain the null. Review Chapters 7 and 8 if you have trouble linking the results of Step 5 with the following:

RQ_1: $t(150) = 2.91, p < .05$

RQ_2: $t(150) = 0.22, p > .05$

9.2.7 PAIRED DATA HYPOTHESIS TESTING: STEP 7 (CONDUCT SUPPLEMENTAL ANALYSES)

The supplemental analyses conducted in Chapter 8 are the same here. With all *t*-tests, you should compute confidence intervals regardless of whether or not you found statistical significance in the previous step (see Chapter 6 for details on computing confidence intervals).

For RQ$_1$, our confidence interval is: CI$_{95}$ = [.77, 4.01].

For RQ$_2$, our confidence interval is: CI$_{95}$ = [−.26, .32].

The interpretation is a bit different here. Our confidence interval now surrounds a difference score rather than a mean, so we should interpret it that way. For example, the first confidence interval would be interpreted: 'If we assume this sample mean difference to represent the population mean difference, we would expect 95% of sample mean differences to fall between .77 and 4.01.'

Also as with all t-tests, if you do find statistical significance, you should compute an effect size (see Chapter 8 for details on effect sizes). Since we found statistical significance for RQ$_1$, we need an effect size for this question. We could compute a Cohen's d by dividing the sample mean difference by the standard deviation of the mean difference. However, the variable analysed for RQ$_1$ is interpretable: it is typing speed in words per minute. An unstandardized effect size means something here, so is informative as a measure of effect: 2.389602 − .032106 = 2.357496 = 2.36 words per minute. After six months, employees, on average, type 2.36 words per minute faster than when they started.

9.2.8 PAIRED DATA HYPOTHESIS TESTING: STEP 8 (DRAW ALL CONCLUSIONS)

Now that we've completed all analyses, we should put everything together in one place and interpret the results. Once again, using the guidelines in Chapter 7, construct your conclusions.

RQ$_1$: Do employees have greater typing skills six months after employment than when they were employed?

$H_0: \mu_d \leq 0$
$H_1: \mu_d > 0$

where $\mu_d = \mu_{T2} - \mu_{T1}$

$\alpha = .05$
$t_{crit}(150) = \pm 1.655$

$t(150) = 2.91, p < .05$
CI$_{95}$ = [.77, 4.01]
diff. = 2.36

Conclusion: Reject the null and accept the alternative. The difference is statistically significant. Employees have greater typing skills six months after hiring than when they were hired. If we assume this sample mean difference to represent the population mean difference, we would expect 95% of sample means to fall between .77 and 4.01. On average, employees type 2.36 words per minute faster after six months than when they were first employed.

RQ$_2$: Do employees have a different level of satisfaction with office work six months after employment than when they were employed?

$H_0: \mu_d = 0$
$H_1: \mu_d \neq 0$

where $\mu_d = \mu_{T2} - \mu_{T1}$

$\alpha = .05$
$t_{crit}(150) = \pm 1.976$

$t(150) = 0.22, p > .05$
$CI_{95} = [-.26, .32]$

Conclusion: Retain the null. The difference was not statistically significant. There is insufficient evidence to conclude that employees have a different level of satisfaction six months after employment than when they were first employed. If we assume this sample mean difference to represent the population mean difference, we would expect 95% of sample means to fall between $-.26$ and $.32$.

9.3 INDEPENDENT VS DEPENDENT SAMPLES

Paired data are also referred to as coming from dependent samples, because the data conceptually come from the same source, even if they are sampled separately. For example, when we collect 'Time 1' and 'Time 2' data, regardless of the amount of time that has passed, the source remains the same. In meaningfully paired data, like parent and child, each pair comes from the same source: 'one family'.

We can contrast this with independent samples, where data come from two or more independent sources. For example, if we wanted to compare customer reactions to a new product we developed in relation to a competing product, we could randomly assign a group of customers to use one or the other and respond to a survey about their reactions. These data come from two different independent sources (those assigned to use the new product and those assigned to use the competing product).

One of the big differences between independent and dependent data is how we represent them in a dataset. Since each row in a dataset represents a unique and independent case, dependent data are represented as new variables (columns) in a dataset. This way, we can keep all of the dependent samples associated with a single case together on one row. Independent data, on the other hand, are represented with additional cases (rows).

The first nine cases of the case study dataset are presented in Figure 9.08 to illustrate this concept.

In this dataset, each case has three dependent pieces of information: one ratio variable (*type@hire*: typing speed at employment in words per minute) and two nominal variables (*gender*: 2 = female, 1 = male; *priorexp*: 1 = prior experience as a typist, 0 = no prior experience as a typist). That means those three numbers are from the same source: the first case had a typing speed of 46.07 words per minute, is male and had no prior typing experience. The second case (74.07, 2 and 0), like all other cases, is independent of the first case.

The *gender* and *priorexp* variables can also be called indicator variables because they indicate from which sample that case came. For example, the first case comes from a sample

Additional variables (dependent)

type@hire	gender	priorexp
46.07	1	0
74.07	2	0
69.97	1	1
57.36	2	1
68.19	1	0
70.40	2	0
78.43	1	1
48.74	2	0
61.20	2	1

Additional cases (independent)

FIGURE 9.08   Illustration of dependent versus independent samples

of males, while the second case comes from a sample of females. Both cases come from a sample of those with no prior experience as a typist.

Sometimes, you won't see the data presented this way. The two datasets in Figure 9.09 contain the same nine cases that you see above, but presented a little differently.

Males		Females	
type@hire	priorexp	type@hire	priorexp
74.07	0	46.07	0
57.36	1	69.97	1
70.40	0	68.19	0
48.74	0	78.43	1
61.20	1		

FIGURE 9.09   Alternate presentation style for same sample data.

If you see data presented this way, it's up to you to determine if they are independent or dependent. For example, if these two tables were titled 'Time 1' and 'Time 2', and had an identical number of cases, they might be dependent! This is why it's so critical to *understand your dataset* before you run any statistics based upon it. You must determine the conceptual relationship between all of your variables first in order to know which statistics are appropriate to calculate from those data.

9.4 HYPOTHESIS TESTING WITH TWO INDEPENDENT SAMPLES OF DATA

The last two of Diego's research questions involve a comparison of two independent samples of data; Diego wants to know if mean typing speeds are different based upon gender and prior experience as a typist. We'll use these last two research questions to explore this type of hypothesis testing.

Fortunately, hypothesis testing with two independent samples is still based on the logic of the *t*-test which we've covered in Chapters 6, 8 and earlier in this chapter. However, since there are now two independent sources of information, there is no way to produce a difference score for each case. So what do we do? We will again explore this chapter's case study dataset to examine this problem and solve it. Here's a summary of the dataset as it relates to the second half of Chapter 9:

Variable 1: type@hire – Typing speed at employment (in words per minute).

Variable 2: gender – Self-reported gender (1 = male; 2 = female).

Variable 3: priorexp – Prior experience as a typist (0 = no; 1 = yes).

$n = 151$.

9.4.1 TWO INDEPENDENT SAMPLES HYPOTHESIS TESTING: STEP 1 (STATE THE RESEARCH QUESTION)

The goal of this type of analysis is to identify if it is probable that two independent samples come from two different populations. Research questions should emphasize the two groups being compared and the directionality of the relationship between them. Remember: *be specific*.

RQ_3: Do male and female employees type at different speeds when employed?

RQ_4: Do employees hired with no prior typing experience type more slowly than employees hired with prior typing experience?

DISTINGUISHING BETWEEN INDEPENDENT AND PAIRED VARIABLES

Because the difference between paired and independent often depends upon research design (and the research question), it is not always obvious to the statistician (you!) which design the researcher intended. Remember that each case within the dataset must be a unique pair; there can be one and only one match in the second variable for any particular value in the first variable. Here are a few examples of both research designs, using the same sets of variables:

Paired variables RQ_A: Do parents and their children have different attitudes?
This is paired because it asks if there is a direct link between each parent and the child of that parent.

Independent variables RQ$_A$: Do parents and children have different attitudes?
This is independent because it asks if parents *in general* and children *in general* are different.

Paired variables RQ$_B$: Does employee productivity increase after we turn up the air conditioning?
This is paired because it implies we're measuring the same employees twice – first without air conditioning, and later with air conditioning.

Independent variables RQ$_B$: Are employees with air conditioning more productive than employees without air conditioning?
This is independent because it implies that we're collecting two distinct samples – one with air conditioning and another without air conditioning.

Paired variables RQ$_C$: Do leadership skills improve as a result of training?
This is paired because we are interested in changes within each person from pre-training to post-training.

Independent variables RQ$_C$: Are leadership skills higher for those who have completed leadership training?
This is independent because we are comparing two different sets of people: those that have completed leadership training versus those that have not.

If there is any overlap between cases (for example, if you have five to ten employees matched to each supervisor, with 15 supervisors in your dataset), this is neither independent nor paired data. This type of data is called 'hierarchical' or 'nested'. This textbook does not cover any analyses appropriate to this type of data.

9.4.2 TWO INDEPENDENT SAMPLES HYPOTHESIS TESTING: STEP 2 (STATE THE HYPOTHESES)

In a paired-samples test, we combine two pieces of information about each member of one population. We then compare our sample difference ($\bar{x}_d$) with the sampling distribution of the population difference (μ_d). In an independent-samples test, we potentially have two populations. We want to determine if the populations our samples come from have the same mean. This results in a slight change to the hypotheses: we now have two μ.

When the test is non-directional, crafting hypotheses for independent-samples tests is quite straightforward. In our case study, RQ$_3$ is a non-directional test, so we'll start with that:

$$\text{RQ}_3\ H_0: \mu_1 - \mu_2 = 0$$
$$\text{RQ}_3\ H_1: \mu_1 - \mu_2 \neq 0$$

By stating these hypotheses, we say that we are collecting two independent samples and subtracting their means, comparing this difference against a hypothetical difference between two populations of zero.

If we reject H_0, we conclude that the difference between our two independent samples is unlikely to have occurred if they came from populations with identical means. Or, in other words, we would conclude that the populations representing our two samples are different from one another.

If we retain H_0, we conclude that the difference between our two independent samples is likely to have occurred if they came from populations with identical means. Or, in other words, we would conclude that our two samples are likely to come from the same population (statistically speaking).

Things get complicated when you add directionality, because the direction that you subtract is important – it changes which critical value represents statistical significance. As stated earlier, this is true of paired tests as well, but there is often a 'natural' order in that context that makes this more obvious. For example, because Time 2 comes after Time 1, it makes sense to calculate Time 2 minus Time 1 (see this chapter, p.254).

With independent samples, there is rarely a logical order. For example, which way do you subtract with 'males' and 'females'? Either direction can be correct, but the decision will have implications for which sign you should use in your hypothesis, as well as the sign of the critical value.

In our research question, we are comparing those with experience as a typist with those having no experience as a typist. Since the decision of subtraction order is essentially arbitrary, let's subtract those without experience from those with experience. To represent this subtraction order, I'll use subscripts to represent the means from the experienced and non-experienced populations: $\mu_{Exp} - \mu_{NoExp}$.

From here, we need to examine our RQ to ensure that the test statistic we calculate represents the direction we want. Here's that RQ again:

RQ_4: Do employees hired with no prior typing experience type more slowly than employees hired with prior typing experience?

The easiest way to match the directions is to write out the relationships with some fake data.

For example, let's use '1' and '2':

If $\mu_{Exp} = 1$ and $\mu_{NoExp} = 2$, then $\mu_{Exp} - \mu_{NoExp} = 1 - 2 = -1$ (negative)
If $\mu_{Exp} = 2$ and $\mu_{NoExp} = 1$, then $\mu_{Exp} - \mu_{NoExp} = 2 - 1 = 1$ (positive)

We want to find statistical significance when μ_{NoExp} is smaller than μ_{Exp}. That describes the second line above, where we found a positive result of subtraction. Since the result we are looking for would be positive with this subtraction order, we should use '>' in H_1. If that result had been negative, we would have used '<' in H_1. You can use this same technique when determining directionality for hypotheses in paired tests.

There are two possible ways to write this formally. Here is the first:

$RQ_4\ H_0: \mu_{Exp} - \mu_{NoExp} \leq 0$
$RQ_4\ H_1: \mu_{Exp} - \mu_{NoExp} > 0$

Using this type of shorthand is fine as long as your subscripts are clear. Try to avoid very short abbreviations (like 'N' and 'E'), but also try to avoid using excessively long subscripts (for example: $\mu_{NoExperience}$ is awkward).

If the subscripts you need are too long, here is the safer option:

$RQ_4\ H_0: \mu_1 - \mu_2 \leq 0$
$RQ_4\ H_1: \mu_1 - \mu_2 > 0$

where μ_1 represents those with experience as a typist and μ_2 represents those without experience as a typist.

As with a paired test, adding a 'where' clause makes it exceptionally clear exactly what you mean and which way you subtracted. Remember, the key is to make it evident to any random reader (or your instructor!) exactly what you did. If there is any potential ambiguity as to your meaning, change it.

9.4.3 TWO INDEPENDENT SAMPLES HYPOTHESIS TESTING: STEP 3 (SET SIGNIFICANCE LEVEL AND DECISION RULE)

As before, lacking any information leading us to another alpha, we will set our significance level for both tests at $\alpha = .05$. We must also remember to state this as part of our conclusions.

The process for setting the decision rule is similar to other t-tests, but with one change: degrees of freedom are now $n - 2$. This is because we are trying to estimate two independent pieces of information instead of one (see Chapter 6, p. 178 for a review of this concept). Otherwise, the process is identical to the one we've now practised several times – look up the appropriate α and d.f. in the t-table (see Appendix A2) to determine the critical value(s). Since $n = 151$, d.f. $= 151 - 2 = 149$.

The value d.f. $= 149$ is not in the t-table. Because of this, we will choose another critical value from the table that will make it *more* difficult to attain statistical significance. Since it is more difficult to attain statistical significance with a smaller sample size (fewer degrees of freedom), we will use the critical value one row up, for d.f. $= 100$. If we were using Excel or SPSS, which compute the t-distribution for us precisely, we would not need to do this.

Thus, for RQ_3, which is non-directional, the relevant critical value is ± 1.984 (d.f. $= 100$, two-tailed, $\alpha = .05$). We can formally state this as:

$$t_{crit}(100) = \pm 1.984$$

For RQ_4, which is directional, the relevant critical value is $+1.660$ (d.f. $= 100$, one-tailed, $\alpha = .05$). As with other t-tests, it is positive because our alternative hypothesis contains '>'. Formally stated:

$$t_{crit}(100) = +1.660$$

9.4.4 TWO INDEPENDENT SAMPLES HYPOTHESIS TESTING: STEP 4 (COLLECT A SAMPLE)

At this point, Diego should conduct the study. As before, let's use this time to consolidate everything we know so far:

RQ_3: Do male and female employees type at different speeds when hired?

$H_0: \mu_1 - \mu_2 = 0$
$H_1: \mu_1 - \mu_2 \neq 0$

where μ_1 represents female employees as a typist and μ_2 represents those without experience as a typist$\alpha = .05$

$t_{crit}(100) = \pm 1.984$

RQ₄: Do employees hired with no prior typing experience type more slowly than employees hired with prior typing experience?

$H_0: \mu_1 - \mu_2 \leq 0$
$H_1: \mu_1 - \mu_2 > 0$

where μ_1 represents those with experience as a typist and μ_2 represents those without experience as a typist

$\alpha = .05$
$t_{crit}(100) = +1.660$

9.4.5 TWO INDEPENDENT SAMPLES HYPOTHESIS TESTING: STEP 5 (CONDUCT STATISTICAL TEST)

We can compare two independent samples with the aptly named independent-samples *t*-test. Like all other *t*-tests, it involves subtracting the population parameter from a sample statistic (in this case, the difference between the sample means) and dividing by the standard error. However, because we're now working with two samples, the nuts and bolts of the formula are a little more complicated, as can be seen in Figure 9.10.

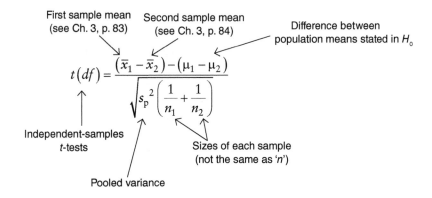

$$t(df) = \frac{(\bar{x}_1 - \bar{x}_2) - (\mu_1 - \mu_2)}{\sqrt{s_p^2 \left(\frac{1}{n_1} + \frac{1}{n_2} \right)}}$$

FIGURE 9.10 Annotated formula for independent-samples *t*-test

To calculate the value on the bottom of this formula, we'll need a new statistic called the pooled variance – see Figure 9.11.

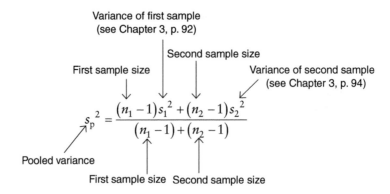

First sample size

Variance of first sample
(see Chapter 3, p. 92)

Second sample size

Variance of second sample
(see Chapter 3, p. 94)

$$s_p^{\ 2} = \frac{(n_1 - 1)s_1^{\ 2} + (n_2 - 1)s_2^{\ 2}}{(n_1 - 1) + (n_2 - 1)}$$

Pooled variance

First sample size   Second sample size

FIGURE 9.11   Annotated formula for pooled variance as used in independent-samples *t*-test

WHY POOL THE VARIANCE?

Because the independent-samples *t*-test is still a type of *t*-test, we need a *single number* to estimate the standard error on the bottom of the formula. However, because we have two samples, we need to combine the variance of both samples into a single estimate.

Theoretically, both populations have the same variance – we must assume this in order to conduct an independent-samples *t*-test. But because both are samples, both sample variances will contain sampling error – neither will perfectly represent the population variance. To account for this, the pooled variance formula does something called 'weighting' in which each variance is multiplied by the sample size. It does this because we'd expect a larger sample size to have a better estimate of the variance. For example, if one group had $n = 10$ while the other group had $n = 5$, both provide useful information about the population, but we'd expect the $n = 10$ group to be more accurate than the $n = 5$ group.

As an example, consider this scenario:
$s_1^2 = 5, n_1 = 10; s_2^2 = 7, n_2 = 20$

If both of these samples had the same population variance, we would expect 7 to be closer to that population variance than 5.

If we took the mean of these two variances, we'd end up with 6. But that's not what we want, because it assumes both estimates are equally accurate. The pooled variance will lean toward whichever variance is associated with a larger sample size because of the way it is calculated; in this case, the pooled variance is 6.35.

The larger the difference between the two sample sizes, the more the pooled variance will be pulled toward the larger sample's variance.

To compute the independent-sample *t*-test, we need a lot more information than we have needed in the past, largely because we need separate information for each sample. This is signified in these formulas with subscripts: subscript 1 indicates the first sample, while subscript 2 indicates the second sample. To compute the value of the *t*-statistic, we'll need to:

Step (1):   Split the dataset by group members and assign group numbers.

Step (2):   Calculate the means of each sample, the variances of each sample and the size of each sample.

Step (3):   Calculate the pooled variance.

Step (4):   Calculate *t*.

Because this requires quite a bit of maths, we'll again use a smaller-scale dataset than our full case study dataset to demonstrate. Again, let's assume that Diego included a three-month pilot study; his data are shown in Figure 9.12.

type @ hire	gender	priorexp
46	1	0
74	2	0
69	1	1
57	2	1
68	1	0
70	2	0
78	1	1
48	2	0
61	2	1

FIGURE 9.12   Subset of case study dataset for independent-samples *t*-sample problem

RQ_3 Step (1): For RQ_3 (non-directional), we'll first need to split the dataset by gender. This usually just involves rewriting the table or the data:

Males (Group 1): 46, 69, 68, 78
Females (Group 2): 74, 57, 70, 48, 61

We've arbitrarily decided to make males 'Group 1' and females 'Group 2'. However, this is completely arbitrary, because we are conducting a non-directional test. If we were conducting a directional test, we'd need to assign the correct numbers to represent the null hypothesis accurately (more on this when we get to RQ_4).

RQ_3 Step (2): Next, we'll calculate the mean and variance of each of these groups and determine their sizes. If you need to review mean and variance calculations, see Chapter 3, pp. 92 and 94.

Males: $\bar{x}_1 = 65.25$; $s_1^2 = 13.598407$; $n_1 = 4$
Females: $\bar{x}_2 = 62$; $s_1^2 = 10.368221$; $n_2 = 5$

RQ_3 Step (3): Now we calculate the pooled variance. It's not as bad as it looks – see Figure 9.13.

$$s_p^2 = \frac{(n_1 - 1)s_1^2 + (n_2 - 1)s_2^2}{(n_1 - 1) + (n_2 - 1)}$$

$$= \frac{(4-1)13.598407 + (5-1)10.368221}{(4-1) + (5-1)}$$

$$= \frac{(3)13.598407 + (4)10.368221}{(3) + (4)}$$

$$= \frac{40.795221 + 41.472884}{7}$$

$$= \frac{82.268105}{7}$$

$$= 11.752586$$

FIGURE 9.13   Step by step calculations of the pooled variance for the data in Figure 9.12

This is an excellent point to check if your pooled variance 'makes sense'. If you calculated it correctly, it should be somewhere between your two sample variances, and it should be a little bit closer to whichever one has the larger n (see 'Why Pool the Variance?' earlier in this chapter for the reason why). In this case, our two sample variances were 13.60 and 10.37. The calculated value 11.75 is indeed between them, and a little closer to 10.37 than to 13.60.

RQ$_3$ Step (4): Finally, we compute the value of t as shown in Figure 9.14. As in all other t-tests, we are dividing the difference between a sample statistic (in this case, the difference between two sample means) and a hypothesized population parameter (in this case, the difference between two population means) by the standard error, which describes the sampling distribution of H_0. Just as with the pooled variance, the standard error looks a little more complicated because we are combining information about two samples into one estimate.

On the top of the formula, you'll notice the term $\mu_1 - \mu_2$. This should be replaced with the hypothesized difference between the population means. In both of our research questions, and in most applications of independent-samples t, this is always the same: zero. It's zero because we want to know, 'Is the difference between these two sample means likely to occur if they came from populations with equal means?'

From Figure 9.14, with seven degrees of freedom $(n - 2)$, for RQ$_3$ in our mini-dataset, $t(7) = 1.41$.

For RQ$_4$ (directional), the process is mostly the same, but we need to pay closer attention to subtraction order.

RQ$_4$ Step (1): Split the dataset by prior experience, as before. We'll need to refer to our RQ$_4$ hypotheses to determine the subtraction order:

$H_0: \mu_1 - \mu_2 \leq 0$
$H_1: \mu_1 - \mu_2 > 0$

where μ_1 represents those with experience as a typist and μ_2 represents those without experience as a typist.

$$t(df) = \frac{\left(\bar{x}_1 - \bar{x}_2\right) - \left(\mu_1 - \mu_2\right)}{\sqrt{s_p^2\left(\dfrac{1}{n_1} + \dfrac{1}{n_2}\right)}}$$

$$= \frac{(65.25 - 62) - (0)}{\sqrt{11.752586\left(\dfrac{1}{4} + \dfrac{1}{5}\right)}}$$

$$= \frac{3.25}{\sqrt{11.752586(0.45)}}$$

$$= \frac{3.25}{\sqrt{11.752586(0.45)}}$$

$$= \frac{3.25}{\sqrt{5.288664}}$$

$$= \frac{3.25}{\sqrt{5.288664}}$$

$$= \frac{3.25}{2.299710}$$

$$= 1.413222$$

$$= 1.41$$

FIGURE 9.14 Step by step calculation of the *t*-statistic for independent-samples *t*-test

Here, those with prior experience are '1' in the formulas, while those without prior experience are '2' in the formulas.

In the dataset, those with prior experience are '1' while those without prior experience are '0'. *Don't confuse these coding schemes.* Even if '1's or '2's are used in the dataset, it does not necessarily mean they match the '1's and '2's in the formulas. The only way to deal with this is to *think about what those variables really represent.*

In this RQ, prior experience is μ_1, while no prior experience is μ_2. That means:

With prior experience (Group 1): 69, 57, 78, 61
Without prior experience (Group 2): 46, 74, 68, 70, 48

RQ_4 Step (2): Once again, we'll calculate the mean and variance of each of these groups and determine their sizes. If you need to review mean and variance calculations, see Chapter 3.

Males: $\bar{x}_1 = 66.25$; $s_1^2 = 9.287088$; $n_1 = 4$
Females: $\bar{x}_2 = 61.2$; $s_2^2 = 13.160547$; $n_2 = 5$

RQ_4 Step (3): Calculation of the pooled variance follows the same process as before. Try this on your own, and you should find $s_p^2 = 11.500493$.

RQ_4 Step (4): Calculation of the final test statistic also follows the same process as before. On your own, you should find $t(7) = 2.20$.

Now, try these computations on the complete dataset. I'll even give you most of Step 2 (notice that this list includes s, not s^2!):

$$\bar{x}_{Male} = 68.358641$$
$$\bar{x}_{Female} = 69.019917$$
$$\bar{x}_{NoExp} = 66.005206$$
$$\bar{x}_{Exp} = 71.648080$$

$$s_{Male} = 10.640561$$
$$s_{Female} = 9.688166$$
$$s_{NoExp} = 10.108240$$
$$s_{Exp} = 9.379220$$

$$n_{Male} = 74$$
$$n_{Female} = 77$$
$$n_{NoExp} = 79$$
$$n_{Exp} = 72$$

You should find:

RQ_3: $t(149) = -.40$ or $t(149) = .40$
RQ_4: $t(149) = 3.55$

9.4.6 TWO INDEPENDENT SAMPLES HYPOTHESIS TESTING: STEP 6 (FORMALLY STATE RESULTS)

Again, this step remains consistent with all t-tests; if your test statistic is beyond the critical value (in the region of rejection), reject the null. If not, retain the null. Review Chapters 7 and 8 if you have trouble linking the results of Step 5 with the following:

RQ_3: $t(149) = .40, p > .05$
RQ_4: $t(149) = 3.55, p < .05$

9.4.7 TWO INDEPENDENT SAMPLES HYPOTHESIS TESTING: STEP 7 (CONDUCT SUPPLEMENTAL ANALYSES)

While a confidence interval surrounding the observed differences between means is appropriate for independent-samples t, the calculation is a bit tedious, so we're going to skip it. However, you should still compute an effect size if you reject the null. We'll go through two examples for RQ_4.

For an unstandardized effect, simply subtract one mean from the other. Since and , we can simply compute diff. $= 71.648080 - 66.005206 = 5.642874 = 5.64$. Thus, those with prior experience as a typist on average type 5.64 words per minute faster than those without experience.

For a standardized effect, divide the difference between the sample means by the pooled standard deviation. Note that the pooled standard deviation is computed by calculating the square root of the pooled variance, as shown in Figure 9.15.

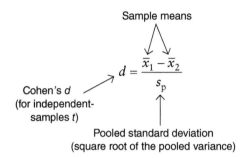

FIGURE 9.15   Annotated formula for Cohen's *d* for an independent-samples *t*-test

In this case, $d = 5.642874 / \sqrt{94.14319} = 0.581575$.

9.4.8 TWO INDEPENDENT SAMPLES HYPOTHESIS TESTING: STEP 8 (DRAW ALL CONCLUSIONS)

Finally, we combine all of our findings and interpret the results.

RQ_3: Do male and female employees type at different speeds when hired?

$H_0: \mu_1 - \mu_2 = 0$
$H_1: \mu_1 - \mu_2 \neq 0$
$\alpha = .05$

$t_{crit}(100) = \pm 1.984$
$t(149) = .40, p > .05$

Conclusion: Retain the null. The difference is not statistically significant. There is insufficient evidence to conclude that male and female employees type at different speeds when hired.

RQ_4: Do employees hired with no prior typing experience type more slowly than employees hired with prior typing experience?

$H_0: \mu_1 - \mu_2 \leq 0$
$H_1: \mu_1 - \mu_2 > 0$

where μ_1 represents those with experience as a typist and μ_2 represents those without experience as a typist.

$\alpha = .05$

$t_{crit}(100) = +1.660$

$t(149) = 3.55, p < .05$

$d = .58$

Conclusion: Reject the null and accept the alternative. The difference is statistically significant. Employees hired with no prior typing experience type more slowly than employees hired with prior typing experience. The difference between experienced and non-experienced typists is a medium effect.

9.5 APPLYING PAIRED-SAMPLES AND INDEPENDENT-SAMPLES *T*-TESTS

To apply what you've learned from this chapter, consider the following case study, questions posed about that case study, and discussion of those questions.

9.5.1 APPLICATION CASE STUDY

Vika is the class and events manager for World Class Fitness, a health club. World Class Fitness provides a wide variety of exercise equipment for use for a modest monthly fee. Vika's responsibilities, however, lie with class and event planning. World Class Fitness runs several weekly and daily classes in specific fitness areas, like Pilates, tai chi and yoga. These classes represent the bulk of revenue for World Class Fitness, so Vika has one of the most critical jobs in the club for its financial stability.

As a result, Vika is interested in identifying the most desirable class types not currently offered by World Class as a direction for expansion. From a set of focus groups he conducted last month, Vika identified two new classes as desirable to members of World Class Fitness: step aerobics or kick-boxing.

Now Vika wants to determine which of these is more desirable. To examine this, he posts a survey at the entrance to the health club, inviting members to complete it on their way in. The survey asks members to answer two questions, one about step aerobics and one about kick-boxing. Each question asks to what extent members agree that a step aerobics/kick-boxing programme is needed at World Class on a five-point Likert-type scale.

1   After the survey is complete, what type of analysis should Vika conduct?

2   What is Vika's research question?

3   What are the hypotheses?

4   If Vika rejects the null, what can he conclude? What else would Vika need to do to meaningfully interpret and act upon his results?

5   If Vika retains the null, what can he conclude? What else would Vika need to do to meaningfully interpret and act upon his results?

9.5.2 APPLICATION DISCUSSION

We will again cover these questions one by one.

1 Because Vika asked both questions to every member and wants to compare member responses between them (step aerobics versus kick-boxing), he has paired data. He should therefore conduct a paired-sample t-test.

2 Vika's research question is: Would members prefer step aerobics or kick-boxing as the new class at World Class Fitness?

3 The hypotheses are:

$H_0: \mu_d = 0$
$H_1: \mu_d \neq 0$

where $\mu_d = \mu_{StepAerobics} - \mu_{KickBoxing}$.

4 If Vika rejects the null, he can conclude that there is a preference between the two programmes. Next, he should compute an effect size to identify which is higher and by how much. He should then adopt whichever class is preferred. However, there may be other concerns worth considering, like cost. If the effect size is relatively small, but the preferred programme is much less profitable, it may still be desirable for Vika to choose the less popular programme.

5 If Vika retains the null, he can conclude that there is not enough evidence to demonstrate a preference between programmes. At this point, he might look at the means and standard deviations of the two programmes to determine how closely they were related. Do members find them both to be a good idea or both to be a bad idea? If they are both a good idea, Vika would be wise to select the more cost effective of the two.

EXPLORING TWO-SAMPLE TESTS IN EXCEL AND SPSS

EXCEL

Download the Excel dataset for the demonstration below as **chapter9.xls**. As you read this section, try to apply the terms you've learned in this chapter to the dataset and follow along with Excel on your own computer.

You can also get a video demonstration of the section below under **Excel Video: Chapter 9**.

PAIRED-SAMPLES T-TEST

Fortunately, Excel's **Data Analysis** tool has built-in functions for solving paired-samples and independent-samples t-tests, making this Excel exercise much simpler than the one in Chapter 8. Ensure you have the Data Analysis tool installed (see Appendix E) before proceeding.

(Continued)

(Continued)

First, we'll recreate the paired-samples tests in Excel for RQ$_1$ and RQ$_2$. Open your **Data Analysis** tool and select 't-Test: Paired Two Samples for Means' (Figure 9.16).

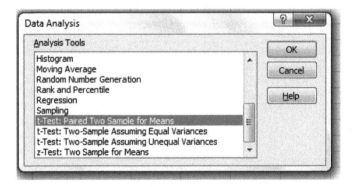

FIGURE 9.16   Excel data analysis tool with paired-samples t-test option highlighted

Next, we'll analyse RQ$_1$, which hypothesizes that typing skill will be higher six months after employment than it is at the start. These variables are in the first two columns of your dataset: A is 'type@hire' and B is 'type@6mos'. Once the dialogue comes up, put the data in Column B into 'Variable 1 Range' and the data in Column A into 'Variable 2 Range'.

The order is important. Excel always calculates the top of the t-formula as: *Variable 1 – Variable 2*. So to ensure that your *t*-statistic has the correct sign (+ or –), enter them in this order. Since we want to calculate *Time 2 – Time 1*, we'll put the *Time 2* variable as *Variable 1* and the *Time 1* variable as *Variable 2*.

We'll put this on a new worksheet called 'RQ1', since this addresses RQ1 – see Figure 9.17.

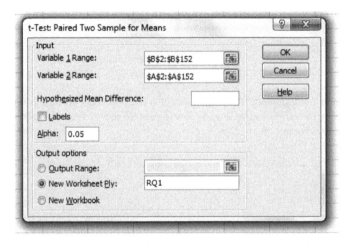

FIGURE 9.17   Dialogue for conducting paired-samples t-test in Excel, with entry for RQ$_1$

Now we'll take a look at the output (Figure 9.18).

⬚	A	B	C
1	t-Test: Paired Two Sample for Means		
2			
3		*Variable 1*	*Variable 2*
4	Mean	71.08545	68.69585
5	Variance	206.0794	102.7672
6	Observations	151	151
7	Pearson Correlation	0.712068	
8	Hypothesized Mean Difference	0	
9	df	150	
10	t Stat	2.913238	
11	P(T<=t) one-tail	0.002062	
12	t Critical one-tail	1.655076	
13	P(T<=t) two-tail	0.004124	
14	t Critical two-tail	1.975905	

FIGURE 9.18 Excel output for paired-samples t-test in RQ$_1$

In the output, we can find all of the vital information we need to state our formal test of the hypothesis – *t*-statistic, degrees of freedom and *p*-value are all there. However, before we can trust that information, we must take a moment to look at the *p*-value.

Excel assumes that whichever direction the data falls is the direction that you are testing. In other words, if the left tail is statistically significant, it will report the *p*-value for the *left-tailed test*. If the right tail is statistically significant, it will report the *p*- value for the *right-tailed test*. You must be vigilant to ensure the *p*-value reflects the tail in which you are actually interested. This is why we still write out our hypotheses even when conducting analyses in Excel.

In the case of RQ$_1$, our alternative hypothesis contains >, so we are looking for a positive *t*-statistic. The *t*-statistic reported by Excel is positive, so we're safe: the *p*-value reported reflects the real *p*-value. If it was in the wrong direction, we would need to report $p > .05$.

From this, we can combine the *t*-statistic, one-tailed *p*-value and degrees of freedom into our formal test of the hypothesis (remember to report an exact *p*-value when it is available):

$$t(150) = 2.91, p = .002$$

Remember that we report three decimal places for *p*-values when we know them exactly.

Next, since this result is statistically significant, we need to compute an effect size. The easiest way to do this is to work within our new RQ$_1$ worksheet. To do this, we'll first add a label in A16 for 'Supplemental Analyses'. In the next two cells, we'll add labels for difference scores and Cohen's *d* – see Figure 9.19.

(Continued)

(Continued)

11	P(T<=t) one-tail	0.002062
12	t Critical one-tail	1.655076
13	P(T<=t) two-tail	0.004124
14	t Critical two-tail	1.975905
15		
16	Supplemental Analyses	
17	Difference Score	
18	Cohen's d	

FIGURE 9.19   Excel output for case study RQ_1 with template for supplemental analyses

For the difference score, use simple subtraction. Remember that Excel calculates *Variable 1 − Variable 2*, so you should do the same thing.

In B17, type: =B4-C4.

If you wanted an unstandardized effect size, you could report this value. For a standardized effect size (Cohen's *d*), we'll need the standard deviation of the difference scores, and Excel does not provide these values automatically. As a result, we'll need to go back to the dataset and compute them manually.

To do this, go back to the **dataset** tab and add a new column, labelled 'd'. To do this, right-click on the letter 'C' above 'satis@hired' and then click on **Insert** (Figure 9.20). This will insert a new column before the current Column C.

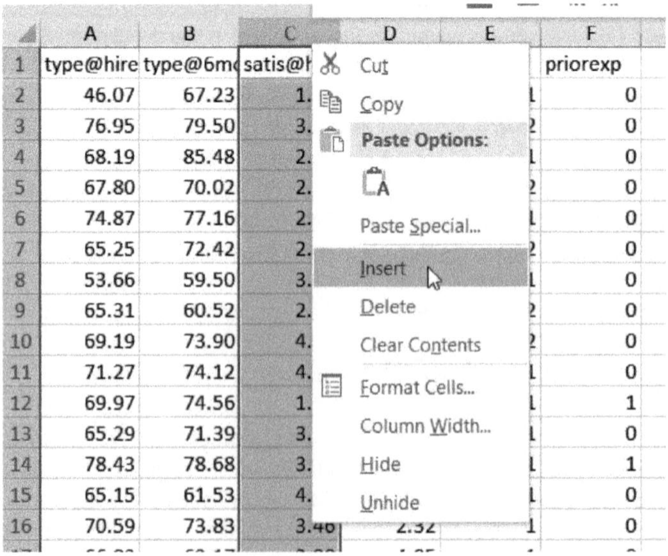

FIGURE 9.20   Inserting a new column in Excel, after right-clicking on the column head

Label this column 'd' in C1. In C2, type: =B2-A2 (see Figure 9.21).

	A	B	C	D
1	type@hire	type@6mos		satis@hire :
2	46.07	67.23	=B2-A2	1.94
3	76.95	79.50		3.03
4	ᴄ8 1ᴏ	8ᴄ 48		ᴣ ᴣᴏ

FIGURE 9.21   Typing formula for difference score in Excel

Fill down to the end of the dataset, and you now have a new column of difference scores. In I1, type 'sd(d)' to indicate that you will be computing the standard deviation of the difference scores. In J1, compute the standard deviation of this new column, using the technique you learned in Chapter 3. You should end up with Figure 9.22.

	C	D	E	F	G	H	I	J
nc d		satis@hire	satis@6mc	gender	priorexp		sd(d)	10.07948
:3	21.15	1.94	1.45	1	0			
·0	2.55	3.03	4.86	2	0			
·8	17.29	2.20	1.83	1	0			
.ᴣ	ᴣ ᴣ1	ᴣ 7ᴄ	ᴄ ᴏᴏ	ᴣ	ᴏ			

FIGURE 9.22   Excel data worksheet after computing standard deviation of the difference scores

Now go back to the **RQ1** worksheet. Click on B18 and type: =B17/.

Do not press Enter – just leave the cursor at the end of the formula. What we just did was set up the top half of the Cohen's *d* formula. We now need to divide that mean difference score by the difference score. Click on the **dataset** tab, and then the J1 cell we just created. If you did so correctly, the formula bar should now look like Figure 9.23.

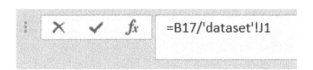

FIGURE 9.23   Dividing a cell on the present worksheet by a cell in the **dataset** worksheet

That tells Excel to divide B17 in the current worksheet by J1 in the **dataset** worksheet. Press **Enter**, and you should see Figure 9.24.

(Continued)

(Continued)

11	P(T<=t) one-tail	0.002062
12	t Critical one-tail	1.655076
13	P(T<=t) two-tail	0.004124
14	t Critical two-tail	1.975905
15		
16	Supplemental Analyses	
17	Difference Score	2.389602
18	Cohen's d	0.237076

FIGURE 9.24   Computed effect sizes for case study dataset RQ$_1$

In A20, A21 and A22, we'll next determine the bounds of the confidence interval. Do this the same way that we did in Chapter 6 (see p. 168), but using the new difference score column. Remember that you'll need to reference your newly computed standard deviation in the formula. If you do everything correctly, it should look like Figure 9.25.

16	Supplemental Analyses	
17	Difference Score	2.3896016
18	Cohen's d	0.237076
19		
20	Confidence	1.6207485
21	Lower Bound	0.7688531
22	Upper Bound	4.0103501

FIGURE 9.25   Computed confidence interval bounds for case study dataset RQ$_1$ in Excel output

That's it! Computation for RQ$_1$ is complete.

Try RQ$_2$ on your own, using the same process. You should get the output shown in Figure 9.26.

	A	B	C
1	t-Test: Paired Two Sample for Means		
2			
3		Variable 1	Variable 2
4	Mean	3.138949	3.106843
5	Variance	4.084355	0.946031
6	Observations	151	151
7	Pearson Correlation	0.437494	
8	Hypothesized Mean Difference	0	
9	df	150	
10	t Stat	0.216836	
11	P(T<=t) one-tail	0.414315	
12	t Critical one-tail	1.655076	
13	P(T<=t) two-tail	0.828631	
14	t Critical two-tail	1.975905	

FIGURE 9.26   Excel output for paired-samples t-test in RQ$_2$

From here, we can once again compute the exact *p*-value. Since the test is non-directional, use the two-tailed *p*- value:

$$t(150) = 0.22, p = .829$$

Since it is not statistically significant, we do not need to compute an effect size, but we do need to compute a confidence interval. This still requires computing the mean difference. Using the techniques discussed above and in Chapter 6 (p. 168), determine the boundaries of the confidence interval. You should end up with Figure 9.27 (note that I just typed the abbreviation for 'not applicable' for Cohen's *d*, since we don't need it when the results are not statistically significant).

16	Supplemental Analyses	
17	Difference Score	0.03210596
18	Cohen's d	N/A
19		
20	Confidence	0.292563389
21	Lower Bound	-0.260457429
22	Upper Bound	0.324669349

FIGURE 9.27   Final supplemental analysis computed for RQ$_2$

INDEPENDENT-SAMPLES T-TEST

We'll now recreate the independent-samples tests in Excel for RQ$_3$ and RQ$_4$. These involve a little bit more work than paired samples – we'll need to sort the data for each analysis.

For RQ$_3$, we are testing for differences between genders. First, click on a cell anywhere in the gender column (Column E). Then open the **Data** tab and click **Sort Smallest to Largest** (Figure 9.28).

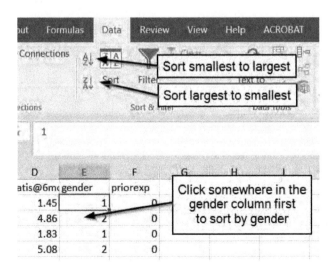

FIGURE 9.28   Portions of Excel relevant to sorting

(Continued)

(Continued)

This will sort the entire dataset in alphanumeric order: 0 to 9, then A to Z. We do this because we'll need to highlight all the values for Males and Females separately.

As with paired-samples *t*-tests, Excel subtracts *Variable 1* − *Variable 2* to compute the top of the *t*-test formula in independent-samples *t*-tests. Ensure that the order you select is consistent with your hypotheses.

Because RQ$_3$ is non-directional, the subtraction order doesn't ultimately matter. We'll use Males for *Variable 1* and Females for *Variable 2* in this analysis.

Here is where Excel is not very user-friendly. We next need to highlight all cases of the variable we're interested in, within each level of indicator variable. That means we need to highlight all cases of type@hire where gender = 1, and put that range in *Variable 1*. We need to highlight all cases of type@hire where gender = 2, and put that range in *Variable 2*.

So where does the break occur? Look at the gender column and scroll down until you see '1' change to '2' (Figure 9.29).

4.65	7.21	1	1
3.26	5.73	1	1
3.01	1.70	1	1
4.53	2.31	1	1
3.31	0.01	1	1
3.03	4.86	2	0
2.75	5.08	2	0
2.15	4.08	2	0
2.90	2.19	2	0

FIGURE 9.29   Identifying the breakpoint between group data after sorting for RQ$_3$

In our dataset, this occurs in Row 76. That means Rows 2 through 75 should be highlighted for *Variable 1*, while Rows 76 through 152 should be highlighted for *Variable 2*. Because we're interested in detecting differences in type@hire, we should do all of this in Column A.

So, to actually conduct the test on your sorted data, open your **Data Analysis** tool (see p. 275) and select 't-Test: Two-Sample Assuming Equal Variances' – see Figure 9.30.

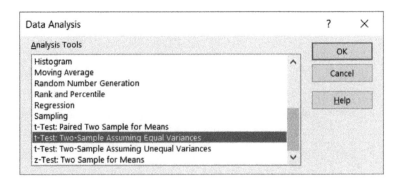

FIGURE 9.30   Data analysis tool, with option for independent-samples t-test highlighted

On the next panel, either highlight your desired cases to compare, or type in the ranges directly (the $ symbol is optional). Remember to title your target worksheet; since we are solving for RQ_3, title it 'RQ$_3$' – see Figure 9.31.

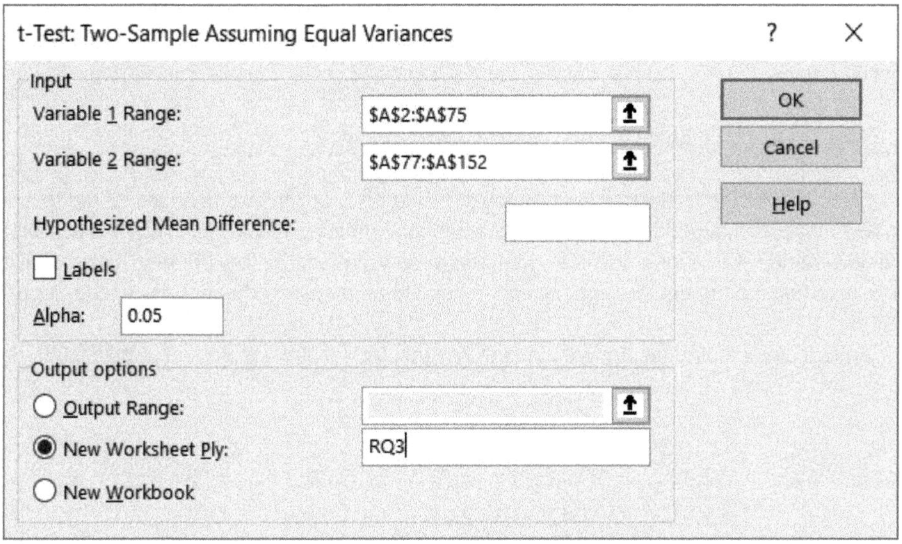

t-Test: Two-Sample Assuming Equal Variances   ?   ✕

Input

Variable 1 Range: $A$2:$A$75   ⬆   OK

Variable 2 Range: $A$77:$A$152   ⬆   Cancel

Hypothesized Mean Difference: Help

☐ Labels

Alpha: 0.05

Output options

◯ Output Range: ⬆

◉ New Worksheet Ply: RQ3

◯ New Workbook

FIGURE 9.31   Data analysis dialogue for independent-samples t-test, set up for RQ$_3$

Click over to the RQ$_3$ worksheet, and you should see the output shown in Figure 9.32.

	A	B	C
1	t-Test: Two-Sample Assuming Equal Variances		
2			
3		Variable 1	Variable 2
4	Mean	68.35864	69.01992
5	Variance	113.2215	93.86057
6	Observations	74	77
7	Pooled Variance	103.3461	
8	Hypothesized Mean Difference	0	
9	df	149	
10	t Stat	-0.39958	
11	P(T<=t) one-tail	0.345018	
12	t Critical one-tail	1.655145	
13	P(T<=t) two-tail	0.690035	
14	t Critical two-tail	1.976013	

FIGURE 9.32   Output from independent-samples t-test conducted on RQ$_3$ in Excel

(Continued)

(Continued)

Once again, we have all the values we need to state our formal test of the hypothesis. Remember to look at the two-tailed *p- value*, since this is a non-directional test:

$t(149) = -.40, p = .690$

Since this is a non-directional test, flipping *Variable 1* and *Variable 2* would also give you a correct answer:

$t(149) = .40, p = .690.$

Since this was not statistically significant, there are no supplemental analyses for this test.

RQ$_4$ calls for a directional test of those with prior experience as a typist versus those without that experience. To conduct this test, we must re-sort the data by the 'priorexp' variable. Do so now. If you do it correctly, you will see all the '0's at the top of the dataset and all the '1's at the bottom.

Again look for the barrier between 0s and 1s – you should find it at Row 81 (Figure 9.33).

77	67.80	70.02	2.75	5.08	2	0
78	65.25	72.42	2.15	4.08	2	0
79	65.31	60.52	2.90	2.19	2	0
80	69.19	73.90	4.62	3.01	2	0
81	69.97	74.56	1.67	1.48	1	1
82	78.43	78.68	3.72	5.26	1	1
83	64.40	74.51	4.83	6.70	1	1
84	81.38	83.50	1.79	2.65	1	1
85	72.37	74.54	2.37	0.00	1	1

FIGURE 9.33   Identifying the breakpoint between group data after sorting for RQ$_4$

That means Rows 2 through 80 represent 'no prior experience', while Rows 81 through 151 represent 'prior experience'. We now need to match this to the subtraction direction of our hypotheses. Recall that we subtracted in this order:

$H_0: \mu_1 - \mu_2 \leq 0$
$H_1: \mu_1 - \mu_2 > 0$

where μ_1 represents those with experience as a typist and μ_2 represents those without experience as a typist.

Since Excel subtracts *Variable 1 – Variable 2*, we need 'with experience' to be *Variable 1* and 'without experience' to be *Variable 2*. Match these up to your dataset, reopen the independent-samples *t*-test dialogue, and you should end up with Figure 9.34.

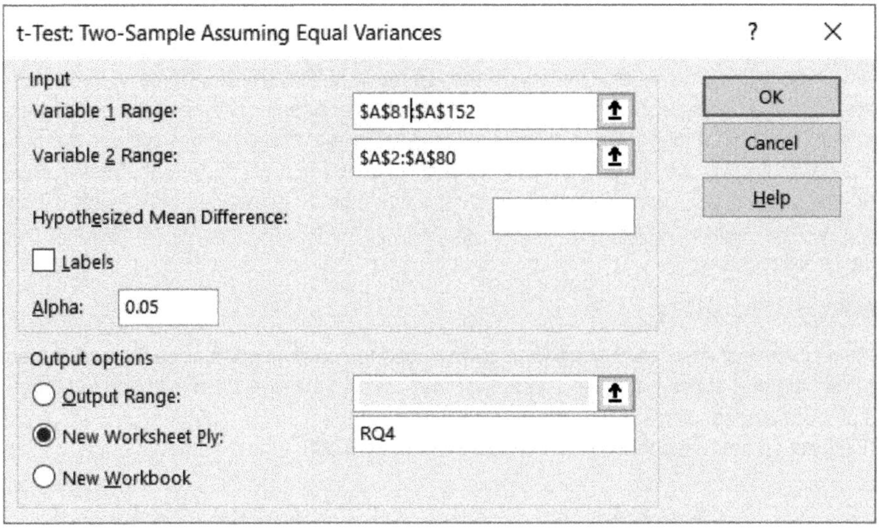

FIGURE 9.34   Data analysis dialogue for independent-samples t-test, set up for RQ$_4$

Run this, to find the output shown in Figure 9.35.

	A	B	C
1	t-Test: Two-Sample Assuming Equal Variances		
2			
3		Variable 1	Variable 2
4	Mean	71.64808	66.00521
5	Variance	87.96977	102.1765
6	Observations	72	79
7	Pooled Variance	95.40686	
8	Hypothesized Mean Difference	0	
9	df	149	
10	t Stat	3.545699	
11	P(T<=t) one-tail	0.000262	
12	t Critical one-tail	1.655145	
13	P(T<=t) two-tail	0.000524	
14	t Critical two-tail	1.976013	

FIGURE 9.35   Output from independent-samples t-test conducted on RQ$_4$ in Excel

(Continued)

(Continued)

As with paired-samples *t*-tests, Excel assumes that whichever direction the data fall is the direction that you are testing. In other words, if the left tail is statistically significant, it will report the *p*-value for the *left-tailed test*. If the right tail is statistically significant, it will report the *p*- value for the *right-tailed test*. You must be vigilant to ensure the *p*-value reflects the tail in which you are actually interested. This is why we still write out our hypotheses even when conducting analyses in Excel.

In the case of RQ$_4$, our alternative hypothesis contains >, so we are looking for a positive *t*-statistic. The *t*-statistic reported by Excel is positive, so we're safe: the *p*-value reported reflects the real *p*-value:

$t(149) = 3.55, p = .000$

Since this result is statistically significant, we'll need to compute effect sizes. This will be similar to the technique we used with paired-samples *t*-tests, except this time we don't need to compute a column of difference scores.

First, set up the labels that you will be filling in (Figure 9.36).

11	P(T<=t) one-tail	0.0002618
12	t Critical one-tail	1.6551445
13	P(T<=t) two-tail	0.0005237
14	t Critical two-tail	1.9760132
15		
16	Supplemental Analyses	
17	Difference Score	
18	Cohen's d	

FIGURE 9.36   Output for RQ$_4$ augmented with template for supplemental analyses in Excel

For the difference score, in B17, type: =B4-B4.
For Cohen's *d*, in B18, type: =B17/SQRT(B7).

This divides the difference score by the square root of the pooled variance. Since the square root of the pooled variance is the pooled standard deviation, this effectively recreates the Cohen's *d* formula. You should end up with the final answers shown in Figure 9.37.

16	Supplemental Analyses	
17	Difference Score	5.6428744
18	Cohen's d	0.5777109

FIGURE 9.37   Final supplemental analyses conducted for RQ$_4$ in Excel

SPSS

Download the SPSS dataset for the demonstration below as **chapter9.sav**. As you read this section, try to apply the terms you've learned in this chapter to the dataset and follow along with SPSS on your own computer.

You can also get a video demonstration of the section below under **SPSS Videos: Chapter 9.**

PAIRED-SAMPLES *T*-TEST

We'll now recreate the paired-samples tests in SPSS for RQ$_1$ and RQ$_2$. First, open the **Analyse** menu, select **Compare Means**, and click on **Paired-Samples T Test...** – see Figure 9.38.

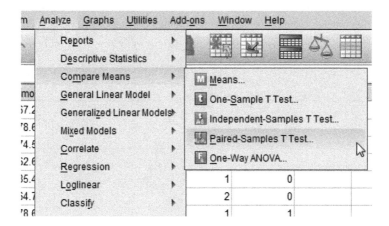

FIGURE 9.38   Menu option to select paired-samples t-test in SPSS

On the right side of the resulting dialogue, SPSS wants you to identify each pair of variables you are interested in analysing. The order you enter them is important. SPSS always subtracts *Variable 1 – Variable 2*, so you want to match the direction of your hypotheses with the order you enter them here. In our hypotheses, we always calculated *Time 2 – Time 1*, so we should replicate that order here too – put each *Time 2* variable as *Variable 1* in the pair and each *Time 1* variable as *Variable 2* in the pair. It is easiest to do this by clicking-and-dragging the names of the variables from the left list to the right. If you do this correctly, you should end up with Figure 9.39.

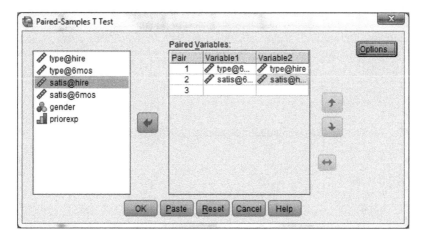

FIGURE 9.39   Paired-sample t-test dialogue set up to run RQ$_1$ and RQ$_2$

(Continued)

(Continued)

When we click OK, this will conduct two paired-samples t-tests. In the first, we will examine type@6mos − type@hire. In the second, we will examine satis@6mos − satis@hire. Click OK, and the output pane will update.

The last table is the most interesting to us for the purposes of evaluating the results of the paired-samples t-test – see Figure 9.40.

Paired Samples Test

| | | Paired Differences | | | | | | | |
| | | | | | 95% Confidence Interval of the Difference | | | | |
		Mean	Std. Deviation	Std. Error Mean	Lower	Upper	t	df	Sig. (2-tailed)
Pair 1	Typing speed after 6 months (wpm) - Typing speed at hiring (wpm)	2.38960	10.07948	.82026	.76885	4.01035	2.913	150	.004
Pair 2	Office work satisfaction after 6 months - Office work satisfaction at hiring	.03211	1.81946	.14807	-.26046	.32467	.217	150	.829

Unstandardized effect size $(\bar{x}_d)$ s_d $s_{d_{\bar{x}}}$ CI_{LB} CI_{UB}

FIGURE 9.40 Annotated output for paired-samples t-test

The best thing you can do, before jumping into the meaning of this table, is double-check that you subtracted in the direction you intended. In the first column, ensure that the order is correct. In this case, we have variables after six months minus variables at hiring. This is correct, so we can proceed.

From this table alone we can make all the necessary formal statements, but the process is a little different depending on the directionality of the test. SPSS does not report one-tailed p-values, so we must infer what one-tailed tests would be, based upon the output available.

For RQ$_1$, the test is directional. When this is true, we must first determine if the direction of the t-statistic is consistent with the alternative hypothesis. If it isn't, we can automatically conclude $p > .05$. In this case, our alternative contains $>$, so we are looking for a positive t-statistic. This t-statistic is positive (+2.913), so we are okay to proceed.

To identify the appropriate p- value for a one-tailed test, we must divide the two-tailed p-value in half. In this case, the two-tailed p is .004, so the one-tailed p is .002. We can report the results of our test as so:

$t(150) = 2.91, p = .002$

For RQ$_2$, we don't need to worry about directionality. We can just report the values as we see them:

$t(150) = 0.217, p = .829$

Confidence interval bounds are reported in the output, so we can simply reproduce these directly:

RQ$_1$ CI$_{95}$ = [.77, 4.01]
RQ$_2$ CI$_{95}$ = [−.26, .32]

In the case of RQ_3, we found statistical significance, so we also need to report an effect size. We can either report the unstandardized effect size provided (2.39) or compute Cohen's *d* by dividing that value by the standard deviation of the difference: $2.38960/10.07948 = .237076 = .24$.

INDEPENDENT-SAMPLES T-TEST

We'll now recreate the independent-samples tests in SPSS for RQ_3 and RQ_4. First, open the **Analyze** menu, select **Compare Means**, and click on **Independent-Samples T Test...** – see Figure 9.41.

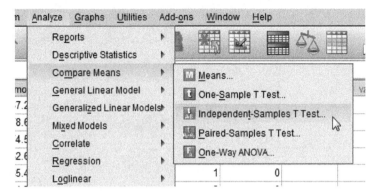

FIGURE 9.41   SPSS menu option to conduct independent-samples t-test

We can run multiple independent-samples *t*-tests simultaneously, but only if they use the same indicator variable. Since RQ_3 and RQ_4 use different indicators (gender and prior experience), we'll need to run this test twice. Let's try RQ_3 first.

Place **type@hire** in the **Test Variable** list, since it contains the data we want to test. Place **gender** in the **Grouping Variable** box (Figure 9.42).

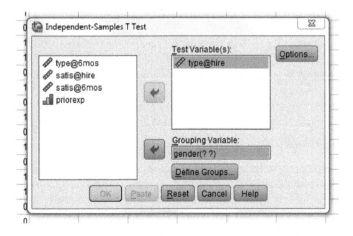

FIGURE 9.42   SPSS dialogue to conduct independent-samples t-test, set up for RQ_3

(Continued)

(Continued)

You should notice the question marks next to gender – that's because SPSS doesn't know which values contained within **gender** you want to compare. Gender is coded in SPSS as '1' and '2', so click on **Define Groups** and enter these values – see Figure 9.43.

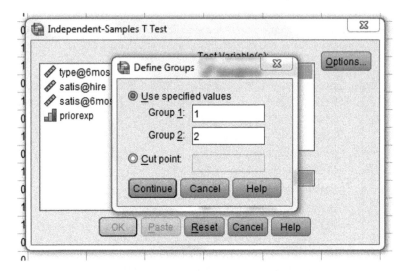

FIGURE 9.43   SPSS subdialogue to specify group indicators for independent-samples t-test, set up for RQ$_3$

Click **Continue** and then **OK** to bring up the output (Figure 9.44).

Independent Samples Test

		Levene's Test for Equality of Variances		t-test for Equality of Means						
									95% Confidence Interval of the Difference	
		F	Sig.	t	df	Sig. (2-tailed)	Mean Difference	Std. Error Difference	Lower	Upper
Typing speed at hiring (wpm)	Equal variances assumed	.001	.980	-.400	149	.690	-.66128	1.65491	-3.93140	2.60885
	Equal variances not assumed			-.399	146.398	.691	-.66128	1.65601	-3.93800	2.61545

FIGURE 9.44   Output for independent-samples t-test, containing data for RQ$_3$Independent Samples Test

From this output we can extract everything we need for our formal test of the hypothesis. Only take values from the top line of the output (the row reading 'Equal variances assumed'):

$t(149) = -.40, p = .690$

Since SPSS reports confidence interval information, you can also report the confidence interval if you wish. Because we did not find statistical significance, we are done analysing RQ$_3$.

The process for RQ$_4$ is mostly the same. Open the independent-samples *t*-test dialogue, change the **Grouping Variable** to **priorexp**, and click **Define Groups**.

Because RQ$_4$ is directional, this step takes a little more thought. SPSS always subtracts *Group 1 – Group 2*, so you need to ensure the subtraction order of your hypotheses is consistent with what SPSS will do. What did our hypothesis say?

$$H_0: \mu_1 - \mu_2 \leq 0$$
$$H_1: \mu_1 - \mu_2 > 0$$

where μ_1 represents those with experience as a typist and μ_2 represents those without experience as a typist.

Since SPSS subtracts *Group 1 − Group 2*, we need 'with experience' to be *Group 1* and 'without experience' to be *Group 2*. Match these up to your dataset and you should end up with Figure 9.45.

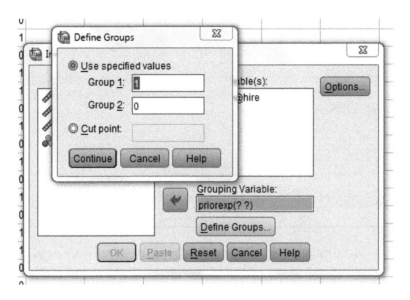

FIGURE 9.45   SPSS subdialogue to specify group indicators for independent-samples t-test, set up for RQ$_4$

Click **Continue** and then **OK**, and you should see the output in Figure 9.46.

		Levene's Test for Equality of Variances		t-test for Equality of Means						
									95% Confidence Interval of the Difference	
		F	Sig.	t	df	Sig. (2-tailed)	Mean Difference	Std. Error Difference	Lower	Upper
Typing speed at hiring (wpm)	Equal variances assumed	.177	.675	3.546	149	.001	5.64287	1.59147	2.49811	8.76764
	Equal variances not assumed			3.558	148.949	.001	5.64287	1.58593	2.50905	8.77670

FIGURE 9.46   Output for independent-samples t-test, containing data for RQ$_4$

As with paired-samples *t*-tests, we can make all the necessary formal statements from this table alone, but SPSS does not report one-tailed *p*-values. As a result, we must infer what one-tailed tests would be, based upon the output available.

For RQ$_4$, the test is directional. When this is true, we must first determine if the direction of the *t*-statistic is consistent with the alternative hypothesis. If it isn't, we can automatically conclude

(Continued)

(Continued)

$p > .05$. In this case, our alternative contains $>$, so we are looking for a positive t-statistic. This t-statistic is positive ($+3.546$), so we are okay to proceed.

To identify the appropriate p value for a one-tailed test, we must divide the two-tailed p-value in half. In this case, the two-tailed p is .001, so the one-tailed p is .0005, which rounds to .000. We can report the results of our test as so:

$t(150) = 3.55, p = .000$

Since SPSS reports confidence interval information, you can also report the confidence if you wish. Because we found statistical significance, we must also compute an effect size. The unstandardized effect size (reported here as 'mean difference') is the only effect size available automatically in this test in SPSS.

If you want to compute a Cohen's d, you'll need to compute a pooled standard deviation. You can do this by scrolling back up in the output to the table shown in Figure 9.47, which reports the group standard deviations.

Group Statistics

	Prior Experience as Typist	N	Mean	Std. Deviation	Std. Error Mean
Typing speed at hiring (wpm)	Yes	72	71.6481	9.37922	1.10535
	No	79	66.0052	10.10824	1.13727

FIGURE 9.47   Group statistics output for independent-samples t-test, used to compute Cohen's d

Next, plug those standard deviations into the pooled variance formula (Figure 9.48).

$$s_p^2 = \frac{(n_1-1)s_1^2 + (n_2-1)s_2^2}{(n_1-1)+(n_2-1)} = \frac{(72-1)9.37922^2 + (79-1)10.10824^2}{(72-1)+(79-1)} = 95.40686$$

FIGURE 9.48   Pooled variance calculated from SPSS output data for RQ$_4$

Finally, plug this value into the Cohen's d formula, using the mean difference score from the first table we looked at – see Figure 9.49.

$$d = \frac{\bar{x}1 - \bar{x}2}{s_p} = \frac{5.64287}{\sqrt{95.40686}} = .57771 = .58$$

FIGURE 9.49   Cohen's d calculated from SPSS output data for RQ$_4$

STATISTICS IN THE REAL WORLD

 These web links can be accessed directly from the book's website.

Elvis Dieguez, head of Analytics at Amazon, describes how *t*-tests are one of the three most fundamental tests needed for business analytics: www.linkedin.com/pulse/three-most-important-statistical-tests-business-elvis-di%C3%A9guez.

What sort of comparisons can you make using *t*-tests to predict future sales?

Angela Stringfellow, Chief Ideation Officer at CODA Concepts, describes how A/B testing can be used to improve a wide variety of small business practices: www.americanexpress.com/us/small-business/openforum/articles/how-to-use-ab-testing-in-small-business.

How can you design studies that utilize *t*-tests to improve your business or the business you want to own?

TEST YOURSELF

 After you've completed the questions below, check your answers online.

1 For each of the following, would you be more likely to use a paired-samples or independent-samples *t*-test? Also, would it be one-tailed or two-tailed?

  a Are employees more satisfied after our policy on smartphone use at work was changed?
  b Are customers who use coupons more satisfied with their purchase than those who don't?
  c Do customers purchase different amounts when they shop in the mornings or in the evenings?
  d Are organizations on 2nd Street more profitable than those on 1st Street?

2 What are degrees of freedom for each of the following situations?

  a Comparing Time 1 to Time 2; 50 people at Time 1, 50 people at Time 2.
  b Comparing males to females; 50 males, 50 females.
  c Comparing stores in the West region to stores in the East region; 60 West, 70 East.
  d Comparing spouses to each other; 30 wives, 30 husbands.

3 Draw all formal conclusions given the data provided.

  a $t(45) = 3.41, p < .05$.
  b $d = 1.10$.
  c $CI_{90} = [4.51, 8.12]$.

4 What is the critical value given each of these tests? Assume $= .05$.

  a Paired, right-tailed, $n = 29$.
  b Independent, two-tailed, $n_1 = 15, n_2 = 17$.
  c Independent, left-tailed, $n = 25$.
  d Paired, two-tailed, $n_1 = 12, n_2 = 12$.

(Continued)

(Continued)

DATA SKILL CHALLENGES

 After you've completed the questions below, check your answers online.

For each of the following scenarios, conduct the complete hypothesis testing process as appropriate given that scenario.

1   A store manager decides to compare the number of purchases customers make before and after implementing a policy change requiring employees to greet customers whenever they are standing within a 3 metre distance in the store. He compares daily purchase numbers from pre-change to post-change, expecting an increase.

Daily purchases for 10 days before policy: 66, 75, 72, 71, 56, 57, 72, 91, 73, 72.
Daily purchases for 11 days after policy: 77, 70, 94, 71, 76, 64, 65, 90, 87, 87, 80.

2   A regional manager implements a policy change for stores in his region to begin greeting customers whenever they are standing within a 3 metre distance in the store. He compares mean daily purchase numbers over one month from pre-change to post-change for each store to see if the change makes a difference in sales.

Mean daily purchases for Store 1 through Store 10 before policy: 82, 103, 91, 91, 83, 76, 90, 114, 88, 92.
Mean daily purchases for Store 1 through Store 10 after policy: 102, 83, 113, 87, 94, 78, 91, 117, 101, 107.

3   A regional manager implements a policy change for stores in his region to begin greeting customers whenever they are standing within a 3 metre distance in the store. After the policy has been in place for one month, he compares average customer satisfaction for his ten stores (Region A) with the average customer satisfaction rating for the ten stores in the next region (Region B). Customer satisfaction is measured on a 1–5 scale with 1 being 'very unsatisfied' and 5 being 'very satisfied'. He expects that his stores will have higher customer satisfaction ratings compared with stores in Region B.

Mean customer satisfaction rating for Stores 1–10 in Region A: 4, 4, 3, 5, 3, 4, 4, 5, 3, 2.
Mean customer satisfaction rating for Stores 1–10 in Region B: 3, 2, 1, 4, 3, 3, 4, 5, 2, 3.

4   A regional manager implements a policy change for stores in his region to begin greeting customers whenever they are standing within a 3 metre distance in the store. He compares employee satisfaction for five employees from pre-change to post-change. Employee satisfaction is measured on a 1–5 scale with 1 being 'very unsatisfied' and 5 being 'very satisfied'. He expects that his stores will have different employee satisfaction ratings before and after the change.

Mean employee satisfaction rating pre-change for Employees 1–5: 4, 4, 3, 5, 4.
Mean employee satisfaction rating post-change for Employees 1–5: 3, 2, 1, 2, 2.

NEW TERMS

dependent samples: independent samples: independent-samples *t*-test: indicator variable: matched-samples *t*-test: paired data: paired-samples *t*-test: related-samples *t*-test: repeated measures:

NEW STATISTICAL NOTATION AND FORMULAS

μ_{d}: population mean difference (for use in paired-samples *t*-tests)

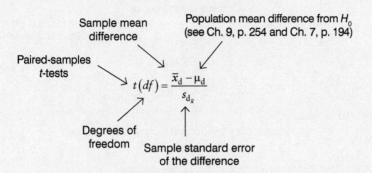

FIGURE 9.50   Annotated formula for the paired samples t-test

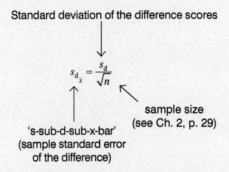

FIGURE 9.51   Annotated formula for the sample standard error of the difference

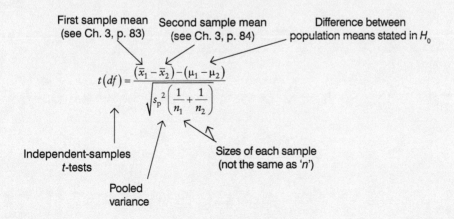

FIGURE 9.52   Annotated formula for the independent samples t-test

(Continued)

(Continued)

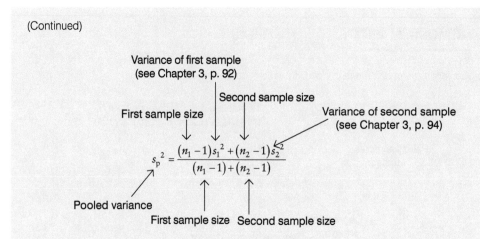

FIGURE 9.53   Annotated formula for the pooled sample variance

Visit https://study.sagepub.com/landers2e **for free additional online resources related to this chapter.**

10 ANALYSIS OF VARIANCE (ANOVA)

WHAT YOU WILL LEARN FROM THIS CHAPTER

- How to complete the hypothesis testing procedure for one-way ANOVA
- How to identify when one-way ANOVA is appropriate given the data available
- How to determine between-groups and within-groups degrees of freedom
- How to identify critical values in an F-distribution
- How to create an ANOVA summary table and interpret it
- How to interpret effect sizes for ANOVA
- How to interpret post-hoc tests

DATA SKILLS YOU WILL MASTER FROM THIS CHAPTER

- Computing sum of squares
- Computing an F-statistic for one-way ANOVA
- Computing an η^2 effect size
- Computing post-hoc tests

CASE STUDY   WHICH OF THESE WEBSITES IS THE BEST CHOICE?

Colleen is the marketing manager for Virtually Viral, an entertainment company that collects viral videos from around the Internet and aggregates them on their website. Whether it's videos of cats or unusual marriage proposals, Virtually Viral collects them all.

Almost all of Virtually Viral's revenue comes from clicks on advertisements surrounding the videos. To maximize profits, Colleen tries to

(Continued)

(Continued)

match ad content to video content. For example, for the 'Wacky Weddings' section of the website, most advertisements link to wedding planners and invitation/paper product suppliers.

As part of this effort, Colleen contracted a web design firm to put together a new look for the website, with the goal of improving the amount of time visitors spend on the website. They produced four different versions, each arranging the videos and advertisements differently. Colleen is unsure which of these designs would result in the greatest amount of time spent on the site.

To solve this problem, Colleen designs an experiment. She sets up a system to randomly assign visitors to the website to experience one of the four designs, recording the number of seconds that they spend on the site.

She wants to compare the groups with each other and see if the different designs result in different lengths of time viewing the website. Whichever results in the longest visits will become the new design for the site in general.

She knows from Chapter 7 that she has a research question and that this calls for some type of hypothesis testing. From Chapter 9, she learned that treating groups differently and comparing them means that she has independent data. But the independent-samples t-test only compares two groups with each other and she has four. Should she run multiple independent-samples t-tests? Or is there a better way?

Take a look at Colleen's psychological data on her employees for yourself in chapter10.xls (Excel) or chapter10.sav (SPSS) online.

As we learned in Chapter 9, different statistical tests are needed for hypothesis testing on different types of data. Up to this point, we've learned several: one-sample z-tests and t-tests for comparing a sample to a known population, paired-samples t-tests for comparing pairs of linked data to each other, and independent-samples t-tests for comparing two independent group means. Colleen's data do not match any of these setups; instead, she has four independent group means.

Colleen's problem can be solved with a type of statistical test we have not yet covered called analysis of variance (ANOVA). ANOVA is one of the most common frameworks for assessing mean differences between groups because it is quite versatile. ANOVA can be adapted to address many different types of research question, and there are many variants of ANOVA to address these questions. The trade-off for this flexibility is that ANOVA is more complex than z or t: instead of comparing two means to each other in standard error units, ANOVA examines a ratio of variances.

In this chapter, we'll be learning about the simplest type of ANOVA: the one-way ANOVA. As you read, think about the similarities and differences between ANOVA, its hypothesis testing process and the hypothesis tests that you have already learned.

10.1 WHY WE ANALYSE VARIANCE

In Chapters 8 and 9, we covered several variants of the t-test. All of these tests used the same basic procedure: subtract a hypothetical population value from a sample statistic, and divide this difference by an appropriate estimate of the standard error.

In the logic of a t-test, we must compare a sample-derived statistic with a given population statistic. In one-sample t-tests, we compare the mean of the sample with the given population mean. In a paired-sample t-test, we compare the difference between paired values with a population difference of zero. In an independent-samples t-test, we compare the difference between two independent sample means with the difference between two population means that are equal.

When we have more than two groups, it is not immediately apparent what we would subtract, and which units would be useful for division. If we compare each pair of sample means with each other in multiple independent-samples t-tests, we must ignore the information about the standard error provided by the samples we are not analysing. Our standard error could be very different for each test, changing the standard of statistical significance for each pair and leading to an overall increased Type I error rate. And if there's one thing that statisticians hate, it's a Type I error.

So instead of comparing means directly, an analysis of variance (ANOVA) does exactly what its name implies – it analyses the variance of those means. Instead of comparing means one pair at a time, it requires calculating a single number to tell how much all of those means vary from each other. This is called the between-groups variability (but might be easier to think of as the 'variability among group means').

For example, in our case study's experiment, we have four groups of people: those randomly assigned to website designs A, B, C and D. If the mean number of seconds that customers spent on the website for those four groups was 91, 87, 90 and 92, there would not be much variance between means because the means cluster together. On the other hand, if the mean number of seconds that customers spent on the website for those four groups was 91, 40, 160 and 110, there is a great deal of variance between means because the means are further apart. The greater the variance of the means, the more likely they are drawn from different populations, and the more likely we would find statistical significance in ANOVA.

We cannot easily put this variance in standard error units. But we can compare it with another variance: how much members of each group vary from one another. We call this the within-groups variability.

At the core of ANOVA is the comparison of between-groups variability to within-groups variability. When we divide these values by one another, we can produce an F-ratio, named for English statistician Sir Ronald Fisher. Figure 10.01 depicts the conceptual formula for F.

$$F = \frac{\text{between-groups variability}}{\text{within-groups variability}}$$

FIGURE 10.01 Conceptual formula for the F-ratio

The larger the F-ratio, the more between-groups variability there is relative to within-groups variability, and the more likely it is that the difference between the means is statistically significant. In most null hypotheses involving F, we assume these values to be equal ($F = 1$).

10.2 BETWEEN-GROUPS VS WITHIN-GROUPS VARIABILITY

An easy way to remember the difference between these two concepts is as follows:

- Between-groups variability: How big is the difference between means?

- Within-groups variability: How closely do members of groups cluster around their group's mean?

Let's look at a few examples, in the context of this chapter's research question.

In Figure 10.02, we can see histograms for four theoretical combinations of between-groups and within-groups variability that might come from our case study dataset. Within each quadrant of the figure, each bell-shaped curve represents one group of people randomly assigned to view a unique website design. Since there are four website designs being tested, each quadrant contains four histograms. We'll look at each part of the figure in turn.

- At the top left, we see low between-groups variability (group means are close together) and low within-groups variability (each group histogram is narrow). It would be difficult to conclude that the groups are different, because there is so much overlap.

- At the bottom left, we see low between-groups variability (group means are close together) and high within-groups variability (each group histogram is wide). This is even worse; because the distributions are so wide, it is even more difficult to conclude that the groups are different.

- At the bottom right, we see high between-groups variability (group means are far apart) and high within-groups variability (each group histogram is wide). This is a little better; now the group means are far apart, so it seems like the two groups in the middle are different from the group to the left and the group to the right, but the distributions are fairly wide, so it is difficult to be sure.

- At the top right, we see high between-groups variability (group means are far apart) and low within-groups variability (each group histogram is narrow). This is the best of the four, if you're looking for differences: the left group and the right group are each clearly different from the middle two. This is because everyone within the left group is low and everyone within the right group is high – there is very little overlap.

Thus, if we want to conclude 'these groups are different', that is most likely to occur when between-groups variability (the top of the F formula) is high and within-groups variability (the bottom of the F formula) is low. In our case study, this would occur if each website design produced very different viewing times from each other design and if customers viewing each design tended to spend roughly the same amount of time as others viewing that design. If the means are close together, or if the designs don't produce consistent viewing times, F will be lower, and we'll be less likely to find statistical significance.

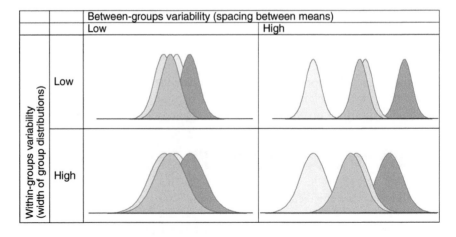

FIGURE 10.02   Histograms comparing high and low between- and within-groups variability

When conducting hypothesis testing with ANOVA, we calculate the between- and within-groups variability, calculate an F-ratio and then examine the sampling distribution of F. The technique to do this is still the familiar eight-step hypothesis testing process, which we've used previously for z- and t-tests, so you should find most of this familiar. We'll highlight the differences as we progress through the steps of the simplest type of ANOVA.

10.2.1　ONE-WAY ANOVA: STEP 1 (STATE THE RESEARCH QUESTION)

The simplest type of ANOVA, and the only type that we'll calculate by hand in this textbook, is called the one-way ANOVA. One-way ANOVA is very similar to an independent-samples t-test in that it involves the comparison of independent group means. However, ANOVA is more flexible than independent-samples t in that it can handle any number of groups. While independent-samples t compares two groups with each other, ANOVA can compare any number.

Because of that, research questions are worded a bit differently than with the other tests we've covered so far. Instead of saying 'is the Group A mean greater than the Group B mean?', we're concerned with *any* differences between *any* of the available means. The research question must reflect this.

There are also no directional tests in one-way ANOVA. We never make specific hypotheses as to which groups are greater or less than other groups. Instead, we look for any differences among all means. In the case study:

RQ: Do any of the website designs produce different viewing times from the other website designs?

10.2.2　ONE-WAY ANOVA: STEP 2 (STATE THE HYPOTHESES)

Because there are no directional tests for one-way ANOVA, hypotheses are also simplified: there is only one kind of null, and it involves a comparison of all possible means. In our case study:

$$H_0: \mu_1 = \mu_2 = \mu_3 = \mu_4$$

For your null hypotheses, you should have as many terms as there are groups to be compared. For example, if you had six groups, your null would be: $H_0: \mu_1 = \mu_2 = \mu_3 = \mu_4 = \mu_5 = \mu_6$.

The alternative hypothesis for one-way ANOVA can be written statistically, but involves a lot of writing. That's because the H_0 is not true if *any* of the following are true:

$\mu_1 \neq \mu_2$	$\mu_1 \neq \mu_4$	$\mu_2 \neq \mu_4$
$\mu_1 \neq \mu_3$	$\mu_2 \neq \mu_3$	$\mu_3 \neq \mu_4$

That means H_1 is technically this:

$$H_1: \mu_1 \neq \mu_2 \;||\; \mu_1 \neq \mu_3 \;||\; \mu_1 \neq \mu_4 \;||\; \mu_2 \neq \mu_3 \;||\; \mu_2 \neq \mu_4 \;||\; \mu_3 \neq \mu_4$$

Each set of pipes ($||$) can be read 'or' – thus, we'd pronounce this as 'the alternative hypothesis is that mu-sub-1 is not equal to mu-sub-2, or mu-sub-1 is not equal to mu-sub-3, or mu-sub-1 is not equal to mu-sub-4, or mu-sub-2 is not equal to mu-sub-3, or mu-sub-2 is not equal to mu-sub-4 or mu-sub-3 is not equal to mu-sub-4'. If any one part of this statement is true, H_1 is true. As a result of this wordiness, we usually simplify the alternative hypothesis to this, which is the same for all one-way ANOVAs:

H_1: At least two means differ

Thus, for this case study, the final hypotheses can be best stated as:

$H_0: \mu_1 = \mu_2 = \mu_3 = \mu_4$
H_1: At least two means differ

10.2.3 ONE-WAY ANOVA: STEP 3 (SET SIGNIFICANCE LEVEL AND DECISION RULE)

As with all hypothesis testing, we must first set our acceptable Type I error rate (α). In this text, two F-tables are provided: $\alpha = .05$ (Appendix A3) and $\alpha = .01$ (Appendix A4). But again, lacking any information to the contrary, we will set $\alpha = .05$.

Because ANOVA results in an F-ratio, we must set a decision rule relative to the sampling distribution of F. F is shaped a bit differently from z or t because it only has one tail. This one tail always contains the only region of rejection, and the peak of the F-distribution is close to 1 – see Figure 10.03.

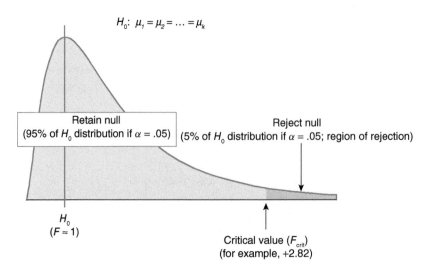

FIGURE 10.03   Sampling distribution of F

Notice the title of this figure uses the term 'k' – this refers to the number of groups being compared. For example, if $k = 6$, we are comparing six groups. If $k = 12$, we are comparing 12 groups. We use the ellipses (...) to indicate that as many means as are needed given k should be included in the null.

We can restate our null hypothesis statistically as '$F = 1$' – that is, the between-groups variability will be equal to the within-groups variability. We're not interested in situations where the between-groups variability is smaller than the within-groups variability (the space to the left of H_0), so F-tests are always one-tailed and positive. When determining that single positive critical value, we are really asking, 'how much bigger must the between-groups variability be than the within-groups variability for us to conclude that the null hypothesis is unlikely to be true?' If $F = 2$, the between-groups variability is twice the within-groups variability. If $F = 3$, the between-groups variability is three times the within-groups variability. So how big is big enough to conclude that the group means really are different?

To determine this value (which we call F_{crit}), we must refer to an F-table. But things have become a little more complicated than they were with t. Because we are now considering two entire categories of information (1. number of groups and 2. number of cases), each contributes its own degrees of freedom, which must be calculated separately.

Between-groups degrees of freedom is the first value we must calculate, which we can symbolize as df_B. To determine df_B, calculate $k - 1$.

In our case study, we are comparing four groups, so $k = 4$. Hence, $df_B = 4 - 1 = 3$.

Within-groups degrees of freedom is the second value we must calculate, which we can symbolize as df_W. To determine df_W, calculate $n - k$.

Although Colleen doesn't know it yet, our case study has 22 cases, so $df_W = n - k = 22 - 4 = 18$.

Critical F-values are written like this: $F_{crit}(df_B, df_W)$.

That means we need to look up $F_{crit}(3, 18)$ in the F-table. Since $\alpha = .05$, we'll use Appendix A3. If α were .01, we would use Appendix A4. Find the intersection of '3' for between-groups degrees of freedom and '18' for within-groups degrees of freedom – see Figure 10.04.

		Between-groups degrees of freedom			
	1	**2**	**3**	**4**	**5**
15	4.54	3.68	3.29	3.06	2.90
16	4.49	3.63	3.24	3.01	2.85
17	4.45	3.59	3.20	2.96	2.81
18	4.41	3.55	3.16	2.93	2.77
19	4.38	3.52	3.13	2.90	2.74
20	4.35	3.49	3.10	2.87	2.71
21	4.32	3.47	3.07	2.84	2.68

(Within-groups degrees of freedom)

FIGURE 10.04 Locating F_{crit} in Appendix A3

Since F_{crit} is always positive, from the chart we can conclude that $F_{crit}(3, 18) = +3.16$.

HOW MANY GROUPS CAN ANOVA REALLY HANDLE?

The maximum number of groups ANOVA can handle really is infinite; if you want to compare 500 group means, you can. However, you are limited in that you must always have available degrees of freedom.

For example, in our case study we have $n = 22$ and $k = 4$. Thus, $df_B = 4 - 1 = 3$ and $df_W = 22 - 4 = 18$. Both numbers are positive, so no problem there.

But what if we wanted to compare 12 people divided into 12 groups? Can we do that? $df_B = 12 - 1 = 11$ and $df_W = 12 - 12 = 0$. We cannot produce a sampling distribution without available degrees of freedom (when $df < 1$), so it is impossible to calculate a p-value under these circumstances.

We must always have a sufficient number of df_W given the number of groups we want to compare – degrees of freedom must always be positive. But it's also important to note that even if we technically have sufficient degrees of freedom to run an ANOVA, too small a sample size given too many groups may still produce results that could mislead us. In such cases, β will be higher than is desirable (see Chapter 7).

10.2.4 ONE-WAY ANOVA: STEP 4 (COLLECT A SAMPLE)

As with t-tests, Step 4 is a good time to collect all the information we have determined so far in one place before actually collecting data. Here's the recap:

RQ: Do any of the website designs produce different viewing times from the other website designs?
$H_0: \mu_1 = \mu_2 = \mu_3 = \mu_4$
H_1: At least two means differ

$\alpha = .05$
$F_{crit}(3, 18) = +3.16$

For our case study, Colleen runs her experiment for 30 minutes one day, ultimately collecting data on 22 visitors.

10.2.5 ONE-WAY ANOVA: STEP 5 (CONDUCT STATISTICAL TEST)

With our data collected, it's time to compute the value for F. ANOVA is unique among the statistical tests that we cover in this textbook in that we must calculate several distinct pieces of information and compile them into a unique table. In fact, there are nine (9) required calculations to end up with an F – Figure 10.05 gives the ANOVA table, highlighting each.

	SS	df	MS	F
Between-groups	SS_B	df_B	MS_B	F
Within-groups	SS_W	df_W	MS_W	
Total	SS_T	df_T		

FIGURE 10.05   Prototype ANOVA summary table

We'll step through each piece, one at a time, using the case study dataset, which you can see reproduced in Figure 10.06.

Design A	Design B	Design C	Design D
55	115	86	71
71	86	108	62
72	98	66	48
62	120	37	69
67	115	90	55
	103		57

FIGURE 10.06   Reorganized case study dataset

10.2.5.1 SUM OF SQUARES, CONCEPTUAL FORMULAS

In the first column, we will calculate the between-group, within-group and total sum of squares. Sum of squares is really shorthand for 'sum of the squared deviations', which we actually saw before in our original discussion of variability in Chapter 3.

Hopefully you recognize Figure 10.07 as the conceptual formula for variance (if not, review Chapter 3!). On the top of this formula, circled in red, you can find a sum of squares calculation – the sum of the squared deviations between each score and the mean.

$$s^2 = \frac{\sum(x - \bar{x})^2}{n - 1}$$

FIGURE 10.07   Variance formula highlighting sum of squares in red

A sum of squares gives us an estimate of the overall variability in a sample. In the variance calculation, we divide this by $n - 1$ (which hopefully you now recognize as degrees of freedom) in order to determine the 'mean variability per degree of freedom', which serves as a bias correction (see Chapter 3, p. 91).

We do the same thing in ANOVA, but with different pairs of values and means depending upon which information we want. Since we don't divide by anything in the sum of squares formula, the sum of squares just gets bigger and bigger as we add cases or groups.

Let's step through the conceptual formulas for each sum of squares calculation.

$$SS_B = \sum\left(\bar{x}_j - \bar{x}\right)^2$$

FIGURE 10.08   Conceptual formula for sum of squares between

For sum of squares between (Figure 10.08), we want to determine the total variability between group means and the overall mean, per case in our dataset. We represent 'group mean' as $\bar{x}_j$ in this formula. We need to calculate this value for every case in our dataset.

First, we need to know the group means and overall mean (from Chapter 3):

$$\bar{x}_A = 65.400000$$

$$\bar{x}_B = 106.166667$$

$$\bar{x}_C = 77.400000$$

$$\bar{x}_D = 60.333333$$

$$\bar{x} = 77.863636$$

From these, we can calculate the distance each group mean is from the overall mean and square the resulting value. In each cell, we subtract the overall mean (for the entire dataset) from that case's group's mean and square the result – see Figure 10.09.

Des.A	$(\bar{x}_A-\bar{x})^2$	Des.B	$(\bar{x}_B-\bar{x})^2$	Des.C	$(\bar{x}_C-\bar{x})^2$	Des.D	$(\bar{x}_D-\bar{x})^2$
55	155.342222	115	801.061564	86	.214958	71	307.311523
71	155.342222	86	801.061564	108	.214958	62	307.311523
72	155.342222	98	801.061564	66	.214958	48	307.311523
62	155.342222	120	801.061564	37	.214958	69	307.311523
67	155.342222	115	801.061564	90	0.214958	55	307.311523
		103	801.061564			57	307.311523

FIGURE 10.09   Case study dataset, conceptually solving for sum of squares between

Next, add up all 22 of those squared deviations to get the sum of the squared deviations: 7428.024422.

Thus, $SS_B = 7428.024422$. Next up is sum of squares within.

$$SS_W = \Sigma\left(x - \bar{x}_j\right)^2$$

FIGURE 10.10   Conceptual formula for sum of squares within

For sum of squares within (Figure 10.10), we want to determine the total variability between each score in our dataset and the mean of the group to which it belongs. We again need to calculate this value for every case in our dataset. We can use the group means we calculated earlier. In each cell, we subtract that case's group's mean from the value of that case and square the result – see Figure 10.11.

Des.A	$(x-\bar{x}_A)^2$	Des.B	$x-\bar{x}_B)^2$	Des.C	$x-\bar{x}_C)^2$	Des.D	$(x-\bar{x}_D)^2$
55	108.160000	115	78.027778	86	73.960000	71	113.777778
71	31.360000	86	406.694444	108	936.360000	62	2.777778
72	43.560000	98	66.694444	66	129.960000	48	152.111111
62	11.560000	120	191.361111	37	1632.160000	69	75.111111
67	2.560000	115	78.027778	90	158.760000	55	28.444444
		103	10.027778			57	11.111111

FIGURE 10.11   Case study dataset, conceptually solving for sum of squares within

Like last time, we next need to add all 22 squared deviations to get their sum: 4342.566666.

Thus, $SS_W = 4342.566666$.

$$SS_T = \Sigma \left(x - \bar{x} \right)^2$$

FIGURE 10.12   Conceptual formula for sum of squares total

Finally, for sum of squares total (Figure 10.12), we want to determine the total variability between each score in our dataset and the overall mean. You should recognize this as the top half of the variance formula, for our entire dataset. In each cell, we subtract the overall mean from that case's value – see Figure 10.13.

Des.A	$(x-\bar{x})^2$	Des.B	$(x-\bar{x})^2$	Des.C	$(x-\bar{x})^2$	Des.D	$(x-\bar{x})^2$
55	522.745868	115	1379.109504	86	66.200413	71	47.109504
71	47.109504	86	66.200413	108	908.200413	62	251.654959
72	34.382231	98	405.473140	66	140.745868	48	891.836777
62	251.654959	120	1775.473140	37	1669.836777	69	78.564050
67	118.018595	115	1379.109504	90	147.291322	55	522.745868
		103	631.836777			57	435.291322

FIGURE 10.13   Case study dataset, conceptually solving for sum of squares total

Again, we next need to add all 22 squared deviations to get their sum: 11770.590908.

Thus, $SS_T = 11770.590908$.

You might have noticed that there was an incredible amount of subtraction involved when following the conceptual formulas. Just like in Chapter 3, we want to avoid gratuitous subtraction whenever possible. Fortunately, the computational formulas allow us to do just that.

10.2.5.2 SUM OF SQUARES, COMPUTATIONAL FORMULAS

Remember that we cover both conceptual and computational formulas because both are important, but in different ways. The conceptual formulas illustrate exactly where variance is going – you can literally see how each sum of squares is the sum of different squared deviations. In the conceptual formulas, this becomes a bit more abstract. Once again, we'll step through each.

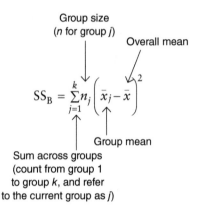

FIGURE 10.14   Annotated computational formula for sum of squares between

While the formula in Figure 10.14 looks more complicated than the conceptual formula for SS_B, it actually involves fewer calculations. Instead of calculating the squared deviation for every score, we calculate it once per group and multiply that value by n. That means we still need the group means and total mean:

$$\bar{x}_A = 65.400000$$

$$\bar{x}_B = 106.166667$$

$$\bar{x}_C = 77.400000$$

$$\bar{x}_D = 60.333333$$

$$\bar{x} = 77.863636$$

But we only calculate each squared deviation once:

$$(\bar{x}_A - \bar{x})^2 = 155.342222$$

$$(\bar{x}_B - \bar{x})^2 = 801.061564$$

$$(\bar{x}_C - \bar{x})^2 = 0.214958$$

$$(\bar{x}_D - \bar{x})^2 = 307.311523$$

Next, we need to expand the 'sum of' symbol to represent the appropriate number of groups. The notation here can be intimidating, so let's step through it piece by piece – see Figure 10.15.

$$SS_B = \sum_{j=1}^{k} n_j \left(\bar{x}_j - \bar{x} \right)^2$$

FIGURE 10.15   Computational formula for sum of squares between

The capital sigma ('sum of') is this time surrounded by additional notation: $j = 1$ and k. The $j = 1$ means 'start with group #1, and we'll refer to each group we look at as j in the formula to the right'. The k means 'we'll keep going through groups until we end with group k'. Thus, if you had four groups (as we do), you'd start with group 1 and repeat $n_j (\bar{x}_j - \bar{x})^2$ four times, replacing j each time with the next group number. When expanded, this looks like Figure 10.16.

$$SS_B = \sum_{j=1}^{k} n_j (\bar{x}_j - \bar{x})^2$$

$$= n_1 (\bar{x}_1 - \bar{x})^2 + n_2 (\bar{x}_2 - \bar{x})^2 + n_3 (\bar{x}_3 - \bar{x})^2 + n_4 (\bar{x}_4 - \bar{x})^2$$

FIGURE 10.16   Expanding the computational sum of squares between formula when k = 4

We've already calculated the squared deviations, so let's plug those in next:

$= n_1$ * 155.342222 + n_2 * 801.061564 + n_3 * .214958 + n_4 * 307.311523

Each n_j represents the group size. To determine those, just count, like we do with sample size: you should find that the groups have 5, 6, 5 and 6 cases, respectively. Plug those in next:

$= 5$ * 155.342222 + 6 * 801.061564 + 5 * .214958 + 6 * 307.311523

Solve this equation to determine SS_B, with much less subtraction than last time.

$= 776.711110 + 4806.369384 + 1.07479 + 1843.869138 = 7428.024422$

Once again, we have found $SS_B = 7428.024422$.

We'll skip the formula for SS_W and come back to it in a moment. Instead, we'll calculate SS_T next. It should look familiar too – it's the top half of the computational variance formula – see Figure 10.17.

$$SS_T = \sum x^2 - \frac{(\sum x)^2}{n}$$

FIGURE 10.17   Computational formula for sum of squares total

Do this the same way that we did in Chapter 3 – calculate a column of 'x' and a column of 'x^2' separately, containing all cases in the entire dataset, and then compute the sum of each column.

You should end up with Figure 10.18.

$$SS_T = \sum x^2 - \frac{(\sum x)^2}{n}$$
$$= 145151 - \frac{(1713)^2}{22}$$
$$= 145151 - \frac{2934369}{22}$$
$$= 145151 - 133380.4091$$
$$= 11770.590909$$

FIGURE 10.18   Step by step computational formula for sum of squares total solved for case study dataset

Once again, we have the same value as with the conceptual formula – it just took much less time.

Finally, we have the astoundingly simple formula for SS_W, once you know the other two – see Figure 10.19.

$$SS_W = SS_T - SS_B$$

FIGURE 10.19   Computational formula for sum of squares within

In this case: $SS_W = 11770.590909 - 7428.024422 = 4342.566487$.

So why does this work? Remember that the purpose of ANOVA is to divide the total variability between between-group and within-group sources. Since SS_T contains *all of the variability in the dataset*, SS_B and SS_W must always add up to SS_T.

10.2.5.3 FILLING IN THE ANOVA TABLE

Let's add these three values to the ANOVA table and see what's left (Figure 10.20).

	SS	df	MS	F
Between-groups	7428.024422	df_B	MS_B	F
Within-groups	4342.566487	df_W	MS_W	
Total	11770.590909	df_T		

FIGURE 10.20   Solving for sample problem, sum of squares added

We calculated the degrees of freedom in Step 3, so we can plug those in too. Only one is missing: df_T. Fortunately, this one's easy: $n - 1$ (Figure 10.21).

	SS	df	MS	F
Between-groups	7428.024422	3	MS_B	F
Within-groups	4342.566487	18	MS_W	
Total	11770.590909	21		

FIGURE 10.21   Solving for the sample problem, degrees of freedom added

An easy way to check if your degrees of freedom are correct is to add them together: if you did it right, $df_B + df_W = df_T$. In this case, $3 + 18 = 21$, so the signs are good.

	SS	df	MS	F
Between-groups	7428.024422	3	2476.008141	F
Within-groups	4342.566487	18	241.253694	
Total	11770.590909	21		

FIGURE 10.22   Solving for sample problem, mean squares added

Next, we need to compute each mean square. The between-groups mean square is the average between-groups variability per degree of freedom, while the within-groups mean square is the average within-groups variability per degree of freedom. To calculate each, divide sum of squares by degrees of freedom.

In this case (Figure 10.22):

$$MS_B = 7428.024422/3 = 2476.008141$$

$$MS_W = 4342.566487/18 = 241.253694$$

Finally, remember that F is the ratio of between-groups variability to within-groups variability. To calculate it, simply divide MS_B by MS_W. In this case, $F = 2476.008141/241.253694 = 10.263089$.

Now that all of our calculations are complete, we can round each value in our table to two decimal places for our completed ANOVA summary table – see Figure 10.23.

	SS	df	MS	F
Between-groups	7428.02	3	2476.01	10.26
Within-groups	4342.57	18	241.25	
Total	11770.59	21		

FIGURE 10.23   Solving for sample problem, table complete

We can therefore summarize most of the formulas in the ANOVA table as in Figure 10.24.

	SS	df	MS	F
Between-groups	SS_B	$k - 1$	SS_B/df_B	MS_B/MS_W
Within-groups	SS_W	$n - k$	SS_W/df_W	
Total	SS_T	$n - 1$		

FIGURE 10.24   Shortcut formulas for ANOVA summary table

10.2.6 ONE-WAY ANOVA: STEP 6 (FORMALLY STATE RESULTS)

This step is similar to what we did with *t*-tests; however, this time, remember that we have two numbers to report for degrees of freedom. But still, as before, if your test statistic is beyond the critical value (in the region of rejection), reject the null. If not, retain the null. Since *F* can only have positive critical values, this is a little easier (see Figure 10.25):

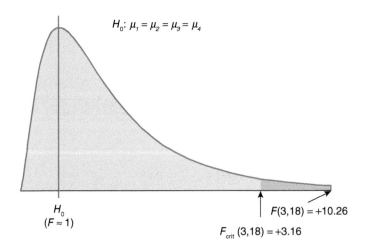

FIGURE 10.25   Sampling distribution of *F* for sample problem

$F(3,18) = 10.26, p < .05$

10.2.7 ONE-WAY ANOVA: STEP 7 (CONDUCT SUPPLEMENTAL ANALYSES)

If we do not find statistical significance for *F*, there are no supplemental analyses, because we have not found any evidence of an effect. However, if we do find statistical significance, there are two: an overall effect size calculation and post-hoc tests. Each provides very different information about the size of the effect found.

10.2.7.1 OVERALL EFFECT SIZE FOR ONE-WAY ANOVA

First, we must compute the overall effect of group membership. For this analysis, we use a new standardized effect size: η^2 (pronounced 'eta-squared'). The calculation for eta-squared is very straightforward – see Figure 10.26.

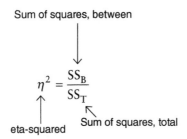

FIGURE 10.26   Annotated formula for eta-squared

You should just grab these values from your ANOVA summary table. This statistic tells us what percentage of the total variance is explained by group membership:

$\eta^2 = SS_B/SS_T = 7428.024422/11770.590909 = .631066 = .63.$

We can therefore interpret this as so: '63% of the total variance is explained by website design'.

10.2.7.2 POST-HOC TESTS

Second, although we have identified that there is an overall effect ('at least two means differ') and its overall size ('63% of variance explained'), that doesn't really answer the practical question we want ANOVA to answer in our case study: which website design should Colleen use? The F-test only tells us that there are differences somewhere – to determine which specific groups are different from one another, we must use post-hoc tests.

Post hoc means 'after the fact', and that's just what we're doing: only after finding a statistically significant F do we look for differences among the means. We do this to reduce the effects of Type I error.

That has an important implication: if you were to compute post-hoc tests when F was not statistically significant, those post-hoc tests might still be statistically significant. However, they are not interpretable: without a statistically significant F, post-hoc tests are meaningless, regardless of the outcome.

There are actually many types of post-hoc test: some of the most common are least significant differences (LSD), Tukey's honestly significant differences (HSD) and Scheffe's test. Each type of post-hoc test has its own advantages and disadvantages in comparison to others. In this textbook, we'll only cover Scheffe's test.

Scheffe's test is one of the most conservative post-hoc tests – in other words, you are less likely to find statistical significance with Scheffe's tests than most others. However, it is very flexible and easier to calculate than most post-hoc tests.

The procedure for all post-hoc tests is the same:

1 Compute the difference between each pair of means.

2 Compute critical mean differences for each of those pairs.

3 Compare each mean difference with the critical mean difference.
   a If the mean difference is larger, the difference is statistically significant.
   b If the mean difference is smaller, the difference is not statistically significant.

To do this, we will complete the table shown in Figure 10.27 step by step. This is not a standard table design, like the ANOVA summary table, but it is still a convenient way to organize the information needed.

Group 1	n_1	Group 2	n_2	Mean difference	Critical mean difference	Significant?

FIGURE 10.27   Prototype post-hoc computation table

For Step 1, we must list and then calculate each mean difference. For the four groups in our case study there are six comparisons, which will make six lines in our table. We'll also write down the number of cases in each group, as shown in Figure 10.28.

Group 1	n_1	Group 2	n_2	Mean difference	Critical mean difference	Significant?
A	5	B	6			
A	5	C	5			
A	5	D	6			
B	6	C	5			
B	6	D	6			
C	5	D	6			

FIGURE 10.28   Post-hoc computation table with given information added

If we had three groups, there would be only three comparisons. If we had five groups, there would be ten.

Next, we need to calculate each mean difference. Remember that we calculated each group mean for the SS_B formula, so just refer to your previous work to get these values:

$A - B = 65.400000 - 106.166667 = -40.766667$

$A - C = 65.400000 - 77.400000 = -12.000000$

$A - D = 65.400000 - 60.333333 = 5.066667$

$B - C = 106.166667 - 77.400000 = 28.766667$

$B - D = 106.166667 - 60.333333 = 45.833334$

$C - D = 77.400000 - 60.333333 = 17.066667$

We place these in the table, as well, removing any negative signs as we do so (Figure 10.29).

Group 1	n_1	Group 2	n_2	Mean difference	Critical mean difference	Significant?
A	5	B	6	40.766667		
A	5	C	5	12.000000		
A	5	D	6	5.066667		
B	6	C	5	28.766667		
B	6	D	6	45.833334		
C	5	D	6	17.066667		

FIGURE 10.29   Post-hoc computation table with mean differences calculated

To compute the critical mean differences for Scheffe's test, we must run through the formula shown in Figure 10.30.

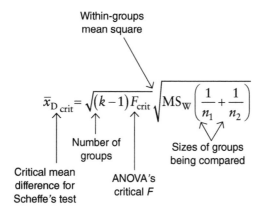

FIGURE 10.30   Annotated formula for Scheffe's test

Since the formula requires the sizes of the two groups being compared (n_1 and n_2), we'll need to compute a critical mean difference for each unique combination of group sizes. In Figure 10.29, there are three unique combinations: 5 & 5, 5 & 6 and 6 & 6. That means we'll need to compute three critical mean differences:

For 5 & 5, see Figure 10.31.

$$\bar{x}_{D_{crit}} = \sqrt{(4-1)3.16}\sqrt{241.253694\left(\frac{1}{5}+\frac{1}{5}\right)} = \sqrt{9.48}\sqrt{241.253694(0.4)}$$

$$= 3.078961\sqrt{96.501478}$$

$$= 3.078961 * 9.823517 = 30.246226$$

FIGURE 10.31   Solving the Scheffe's test formula for combination #1: 5 & 5

For 5 & 6, see Figure 10.32.

$$\bar{x}_{D_{crit}} = \sqrt{(4-1)3.16}\sqrt{241.253694\left(\frac{1}{5}+\frac{1}{6}\right)} = \sqrt{9.48}\sqrt{241.253694(0.366667)}$$

$$= 3.078961\sqrt{88.459768} = 3.078961 * 9.405305 = 28.958567$$

FIGURE 10.32   Solving the Scheffe's test formula for combination #2: 5 & 6

For 6 & 6, see Figure 10.33.

$$\bar{x}_{D_{crit}} = \sqrt{(4-1)3.16}\sqrt{241.253694\left(\frac{1}{6}+\frac{1}{6}\right)} = \sqrt{9.48}\sqrt{241.253694(0.333333)}$$

$$= 3.078961\sqrt{80.417818} = 3.078961 * 8.967598 = 27.610885$$

FIGURE 10.33   Solving the Scheffe's test formula for combination #3: 6 & 6

Finally, plug these values into the table (Figure 10.34). If the mean difference is greater than the critical mean differences, the result is statistically significant. If it's smaller, the result is not statistically significant.

Group 1	n_1	Group 2	n_2	Mean difference	Critical mean difference	Significant?
A	5	B	6	40.766667	28.958567	Yes
A	5	C	5	12.000000	30.246226	No
A	5	D	6	5.066667	28.958567	No
B	6	C	5	28.766667	28.958567	No
B	6	D	6	45.833334	27.610885	Yes
C	5	D	6	17.066667	28.958567	No

FIGURE 10.34   Post-hoc computation table, complete

Interpretation of this table is the final step needed to complete the post-hoc test. The easiest way to make sense of this is to first draw a vertical line containing all of your means (the distance between them doesn't need to be to scale). Start with the highest mean at the top of the line and work your way down to the smallest mean – see Figure 10.35.

←———Design B: 106.17

←———Design C: 77.40

←———Design A: 65.40

←———Design D: 60.33

FIGURE 10.35   Identifying homogeneous subsets, step 1

Start with the top group, and draw a new line connecting that group to any other groups from which it is *not* statistically significant. Since Design B is not significantly different from Design C (but is significantly different from both Designs A and D), we'll only draw a short line (Figure 10.36).

FIGURE 10.36   Identifying homogeneous subsets, step 2

Next, move down one group and repeat. In this case, check Design C against all lower means. Since C is significantly different from no other means, draw the line to the bottom (Figure 10.37).

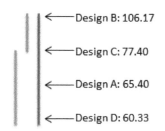

FIGURE 10.37   Identifying homogeneous subsets, complete

Thus, we have identified two homogeneous subgroups within the data: one containing Designs B and C, another containing Designs C, A and D. Groups within each subgroup are not statistically significant from one another.

Interpretation involves a description of these differences. In this case, the first subgroup, containing Designs B and C, results in longer viewing times than the second subgroup, containing Designs C, A and D.

WHY IS DESIGN C IN TWO SUBGROUPS?

When students notice a group belonging to two subgroups, they often wonder how that's possible. Isn't each group distinct? Remember that in statistics, nothing is definite – everything is probabilistic. So while Design B is unlikely to come from the same population as Designs A and D, Design C could have come from either. However, there is no way to know given the collected data.

At this point, if Colleen really needed help, there are two practical interpretations she might use: (1) Design B and Design C are essentially the same, so use either; or (2) Design B has a much higher mean than the other groups, so we should collect additional data to be sure that B and C are really equivalent.

Of the two, I'd recommend Approach #2 – just to be safe.

10.2.8 ONE-WAY ANOVA: STEP 8 (DRAW ALL CONCLUSIONS)

Finally, we must collect all of our results and interpretations in one place. Procedurally, it's very similar to the final set of conclusions we draw with *t*-tests, with the addition of post-hoc analyses and their interpretation.

RQ: Do any of the website designs produce different viewing times from the other website designs?

H_0: $\mu_1 = \mu_2 = \mu_3 = \mu_4$
H_1: At least two means differ

$\alpha = .05$
$F_{crit}(3, 18) = +3.16$
$F(3, 18) = 10.26, p < .05$
$\eta^2 = .63$

Conclusion: Reject the null and accept the alternative. The ratio is statistically significant. One or more website designs produce different viewing times from other designs. Website design accounts for 63% of the total variance in viewing times. In post-hoc analyses, two homogeneous subgroups were identified. The first subgroup, containing Designs B and C, resulted in longer viewing times than the second subgroup, containing Designs C, A and D.

Given this analysis, Colleen would do best to adopt Design B or Design C.

10.3 BEYOND ONE-WAY ANOVA

As mentioned before, ANOVA is a very powerful test because *F*-ratios can be used to compare variances in many different contexts. One-way ANOVA is the simplest form of ANOVA. Although we won't cover more complex forms of ANOVA in depth in this text, you should be aware of them, in case you do need them.

One-way ANOVAs are in fact the simplest type of *n*-way ANOVA, where *n* refers to the number of grouping variables. For example, a two-way ANOVA incorporates two grouping variables, whereas a three-way ANOVA incorporates three grouping variables. All *n*-way ANOVAs involve just one outcome variable.

If we're interested in more than one grouping variable, you might think to yourself, 'why not compute multiple one-way ANOVAs?' The key advantage to an *n*-way ANOVA over a one-way ANOVA is that it can detect an interaction. An interaction occurs when the unique combination of one or more categories on the first variable with one or more categories on the second variable creates a joint effect that we would not expect given either one of the variables alone.

This is a very powerful analytic technique, but it is only valuable in particular circumstances. That is, it is only valuable when you believe the *unique* combination of two or more variables leads to outcomes you wouldn't expect from the effect of each of those variables alone. For example, in our case study, Colleen might have reason to believe that men and women have different patterns of preferences between the various website designs. With a one-way ANOVA, we could conclude that people have different preferences among the website designs (for example, 'visitors spend more time with these designs versus those

designs'). With a one-way ANOVA, we could conclude that men and women have different overall levels of preference (for example, 'men spend more time on our website than
women'). But only with a two-way ANOVA could we conclude that men and women have
differences in their preferences (for example, 'men spend more time with these designs,
while women spend more time with those designs'). You can see an example of a line graph
produced by a two-way ANOVA in Figure 10.38.

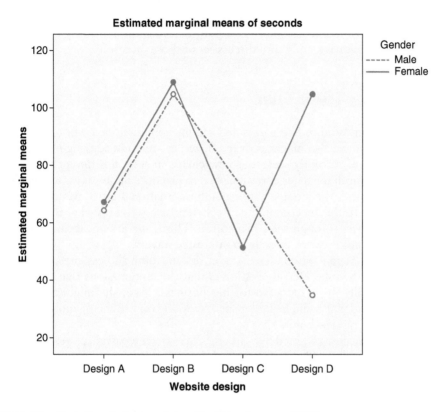

FIGURE 10.38   Illustration of a two-way interaction from a two-way ANOVA

In this graph, we see evidence of a two-way interaction: whereas women spend approximately 105 seconds when viewing Design D, men only spend 35. The results of a two-way
ANOVA would tell us if this interaction was statistically significant.

Although we won't cover ANOVA interactions in this text, we will cover chi-squared
interactions in detail in Chapter 11.

HOW RELATED ARE ANOVA AND *T*-TESTS?

ANOVA and *t*-tests are actually part of a family of statistical analyses that examine sample means
in similar ways. Like ANOVA, *t*-tests examine ratios of variances; you just don't normally calculate it that way. But it can be converted, if you wanted to. The *F*-ratio from a two-group one-way
ANOVA can be converted to its value as an independent-sample *t*-test by calculating its square root
($t = \sqrt{F}$). Similarly, the *t*-statistic from an independent-sample *t*-test can be converted into an *F*-ratio

by squaring it ($F = t^2$). However, it's important to remember that this only works with a two-group one-way ANOVA. If you have more than two groups, or a more complicated ANOVA, you cannot convert its F into t because you lose important information about group membership that changes the shape of the sampling distribution.

10.4 APPLYING ANALYSIS OF VARIANCE

To apply what you've learned from this chapter, consider the following case study, questions posed about that case study, and discussion of those questions.

10.4.1 APPLICATION CASE STUDY

Janna manages an art studio. She paints and sculpts commissioned work based upon the orders of clients, but she also manages over a dozen apprentices copying her work for sale as reproductions. She currently seeks out new clients in several different ways. First, she relies on word-of-mouth from her current clients to promote her business to friends, family and colleagues. Second, she attends national and international art conventions, where she promotes her work to the art community. Reporters also write up what they see, and she attracts new customers through their promotion. Third, she attends local art fairs, where she promotes her studio's work directly to interested buyers.

Recently, she has begun to wonder if the effort and time she expends on conventions and art fairs is worthwhile. Her impression is that the commissions that come by word-of-mouth are typically more lucrative for her business. If so, she might be wasting time attending such events that could be better spent working on producing more saleable art or experimenting with new techniques.

To investigate this, she examined her sales records over the past three years and recorded the source of the sale alongside the commission fee. She wants to see if there are differences in profit among the three but is not sure how to proceed from here.

1 Is independent-samples t-test or ANOVA more appropriate for Janna's data? Why?

2 What is Janna's research question?

3 What are the hypotheses?

4 If Janna rejects the null, what should she do next? What else would Janna need to do to meaningfully interpret and act upon her results?

5 If Janna retains the null, what can she conclude?

10.4.2 APPLICATION DISCUSSION

We will again cover these questions one by one.

1 Because Janna wants to compare three groups, she should use one-way ANOVA. If she had two groups (for example, if she was just comparing fairs to conventions), she would use independent-samples t.

2 Janna's research question is: Do commissions that come from the three different sources have different values?

3 The hypotheses are:

H_0: $\mu_1 = \mu_2 = \mu_3$
H_1: At least two means differ

4 If Janna rejects the null, she should next conduct post-hoc tests. These will tell her precisely which means differed. Without this information, she can only conclude that at least one mean differs from one of the other means. This is not enough information to make a practical decision. Once she has conducted post-hoc tests, she might be able to conclude that commissions from one approach are typically less than from other approaches. She should next examine the effect sizes to see if they are *sufficiently* less (that is, the effect is large enough) to justify dropping the approach.

5 If Janna retains the null, she can conclude that there is not enough evidence to demonstrate a difference in commissions between promotion approaches. At this point, she might look at the means and standard deviations of the three groups to determine how closely they were related. Are the effect sizes large? If so, it might be worthwhile to collect more data over a longer time period and test again later. If not, her question has likely been resolved.

EXPLORING ANOVA IN EXCEL AND SPSS

EXCEL

	A	B	C	D	E	F	G
1	webdesig	seconds		Design A	Design B	Design C	Design D
2	1	55					
3	1	71					
4	1	72					
5	1	62					
6	1	67					
7	2	115					
8	2	86					
9	2	98					
10	2	120					
11	2	115					
12	2	103					
13	3	86					
14	3	109					

Download the Excel dataset for the demonstration below as **chapter10.xls**. As you read this section, try to apply the terms you've learned in this chapter to the dataset and follow along with Excel on your own computer.

You can also get a video demonstration of the section below under **Excel Video: Chapter 10**.

(Continued)

(Continued)

ANOVA in Excel is not very effectively presented. We must manually restructure the data to an atypical format to conduct the ANOVA itself, and then we must calculate post-hoc tests manually. This results in a bit more legwork than seen in SPSS.

Our case study dataset for this chapter contains two variables. The first is 'webdesign', with values 1, 2, 3 and 4. These represent Designs A, B, C and D, respectively. The second is 'seconds', which contains the number of seconds each visitor to the website lingered. Thus, the first line of the dataset (1, 55) indicates a person who was shown Design A and stayed 55 seconds before moving on.

To conduct ANOVA on these data, we must first sort the dataset so that we can copy/paste scores from each group into new columns. Using the sorting technique discussed in Chapter 9 (see p. 281), sort the dataset by webdesign.

In D1 through G1, type: Design A, Design B, Design C, Design D. These will be the column headings for our copied data. You should at this point have something like Figure 10.39.

	A	B	C	D	E	F	G
1	webdesig	seconds		Design A	Design B	Design C	Design D
2	1	55					
3	1	71					
4	1	72					
5	1	62					
6	1	67					
7	2	115					
8	2	86					
9	2	98					
10	2	120					
11	2	115					
12	2	103					
13	3	86					
14	3	108					

FIGURE 10.39   Setting up the Excel case study dataset to organize group data

Next, copy/paste each set of data into the appropriate column. Since 'webdesign 1' is 'Design A', those values should go under 'Design A'; 'webdesign 2' should go under 'Design B', and so on. When done, you should see Figure 10.40.

	A	B	C	D	E	F	G
1	webdesig	seconds		Design A	Design B	Design C	Design D
2	1	55		55	115	86	71
3	1	71		71	86	108	62
4	1	72		72	98	66	48
5	1	62		62	120	37	69
6	1	67		67	115	90	55
7	2	115			103		57
8	2	86					
9	2	98					

FIGURE 10.40   Case study dataset after reorganizing data by group in Excel

Next, open the **Data Analysis** tool and select **ANOVA: Single Factor** (Figure 10.41).

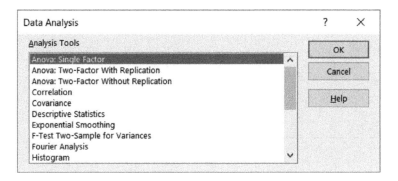

FIGURE 10.41   Excel's data analysis tool, one-way ANOVA option highlighted

In the next screen, highlight the new table you just created for **Input Range** and check the 'Labels in First Row' checkbox. Specify a new worksheet called 'ANOVA' for your output (Figure 10.42).

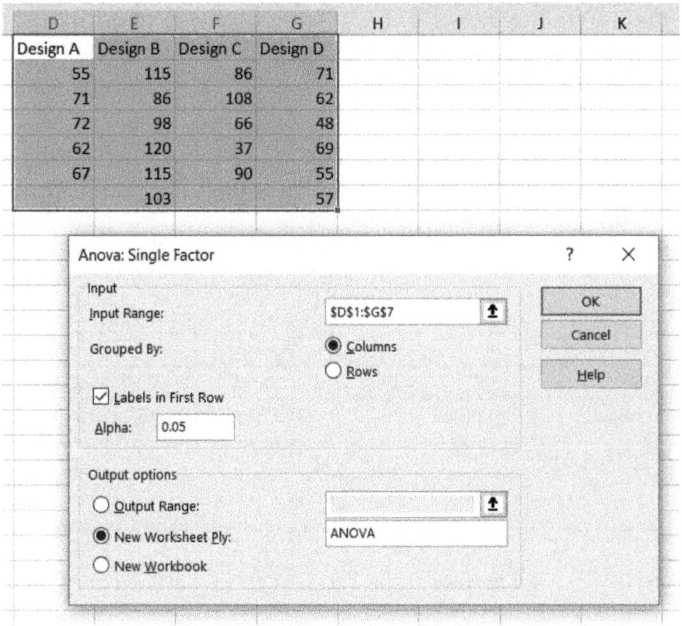

FIGURE 10.42   Within Excel's data analysis tool, group data selected for analysis

All of this tells Excel to treat each column as a group, labelled with the words in the first row. Click **OK** and you should see a now-familiar ANOVA summary table and some group descriptive statistics (Figure 10.43).

(Continued)

(Continued)

	A	B	C	D	E	F	G
1	Anova: Single Factor						
2							
3	SUMMARY						
4	*Groups*	*Count*	*Sum*	*Average*	*Variance*		
5	Design A	5	327	65.4	49.3		
6	Design B	6	637	106.1667	166.1667		
7	Design C	5	387	77.4	732.8		
8	Design D	6	362	60.33333	76.66667		
9							
10							
11	ANOVA						
12	*Source of Variation*	*SS*	*df*	*MS*	*F*	*P-value*	*F crit*
13	Between Groups	7428.024	3	2476.008	10.26309	0.000365	3.159908
14	Within Groups	4342.567	18	241.2537			
15							
16	Total	11770.59	21				
17							

FIGURE 10.43   Output from Excel's one-way ANOVA

Because Excel can compute a precise *p*-value, it displays this with a precise critical *F* in addition to the standard ANOVA table. Otherwise, these numbers are identical to those we calculated by hand.

Excel does not compute effect sizes or post-hoc tests for you. Instead, we must form each equation manually. First, in A18, type: Eta-squared. In B18, type: =B13/B16 (see Figure 10.44).

11	ANOVA						
12	*Source of Variation*	*SS*	*df*	*MS*	*F*	*P-value*	*F crit*
13	Between Groups	7428.024	3	2476.008	10.26309	0.000365	3.159908
14	Within Groups	4342.567	18	241.2537			
15							
16	Total	11770.59	21				
17							
18	Eta-squared	0.631066					

FIGURE 10.44   Excel's output panel after adding computation for eta-squared

This is all we need to do for eta-squared.

For post-hoc tests, things are a little trickier. We will need to manually compute the same information we computed earlier in this chapter. First, recreate the post-hoc comparison table in A20 through G26 (Figure 10.45).

18	Eta-squared	0.631066						
19								
20	Group 1	n1		Group 2	n2		Mean Diff	Critical M(Significant?
21	A	5		B	6			
22	A	5		C	5			
23	A	5		D	6			
24	B	6		C	5			
25	B	6		D	6			
26	C	5		D	6			

FIGURE 10.45 Excel's output panel after adding template to conduct post-hoc tests

For each mean difference, we'll create a formula to subtract the relevant means and take the absolute value (that is, drop the negative sign) of each.

- In E21, type: = ABS(D5-D6).
- In E22, type: = ABS(D5-D7).
- In E23, type: = ABS(D5-D8).
- In E24, type: = ABS(D6-D7).
- In E25, type: = ABS(D6-D8).
- In E26, type: = ABS(D7-D8).

You should end up with Figure 10.46.

20	Group 1	n1		Group 2	n2		Mean Diff	Critical M(Significant?
21	A	5		B	6		40.76667	
22	A	5		C	5		12	
23	A	5		D	6		5.066667	
24	B	6		C	5		28.76667	
25	B	6		D	6		45.83333	
26	C	5		D	6		17.06667	

FIGURE 10.46 Excel's output panel after computing mean differences for post-hoc tests

In F21, type: =SQRT((4-1)*$G$13)*SQRT($D$14*((1/B21)+(1/D21))).

This formula only involves one new function: SQRT, which returns the square root of whatever you put inside it. Otherwise, this is just the Scheffe formula – see Figure 10.47.

$$\bar{x}_{D_{crit}} \equiv \sqrt{(k-1)F_{crit}}\sqrt{MS_W\left(\frac{1}{n_1}+\frac{1}{n_2}\right)}$$

$$= SQRT\left((4-1)*\$G\$13\right)*SQRT\left(\$D\$14*\left((1/B21)+(1/D21)\right)\right)$$

FIGURE 10.47 Illustration aof the relationship between the Scheffe formula and Excel's version of it

(Continued)

(Continued)

We also added '$' to the cells referencing the critical *F* and MS$_w$. This is so that when we fill down, those cell references always stay the same. Do this now – fill from F21 to F26. You should end up with Figure 10.48.

20	Group 1	n1	Group 2	n2	Mean Diff	Critical M	Significant?
21	A	5	B	6	40.76667	28.95813	
22	A	5	C	5	12	30.24578	
23	A	5	D	6	5.066667	28.95813	
24	B	6	C	5	28.76667	28.95813	
25	B	6	D	6	45.83333	27.61049	
26	C	5	D	6	17.06667	28.95813	

FIGURE 10.48   Excel's output panel after computing critical mean differences

In F21, type: =SQRT((4-1)*$G$13)*SQR.
Finally, in G21, we'll add a formula to say 'Yes' if the result is statistically significant.

- In G21, type: =IF(E21>F21,"Yes","No").

This formula has three parts, separated by commas – see Figure 10.49.

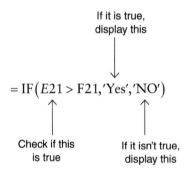

If it is true,
display this

$$= \mathrm{IF}\left(E21 > \mathrm{F}21, \text{'Yes'}, \text{'NO'}\right)$$

Check if this   If it isn't true,
is true   display this

FIGURE 10.49   Annotation of an Excel =IF() function

Fill down from G21 to G26, and you'll end up with the completed table (Figure 10.50).

20	Group 1	n1	Group 2	n2	Mean Diff	Critical M	Significant?
21	A	5	B	6	40.76667	28.95813	Yes
22	A	5	C	5	12	30.24578	No
23	A	5	D	6	5.066667	28.95813	No
24	B	6	C	5	28.76667	28.95813	No
25	B	6	D	6	45.83333	27.61049	Yes
26	C	5	D	6	17.06667	28.95813	No

FIGURE 10.50   Completed post-hoc tests in Excel

SPSS

Download the SPSS dataset for the demonstration below as **chapter10.sav**. As you read this section, try to apply the terms you've learned in this chapter to the dataset and follow along with SPSS on your own computer.

You can also get a video demonstration of the section below under **SPSS Videos: Chapter 10.**

Our case study dataset for this chapter contains two variables. The first is 'webdesign', with values 1, 2, 3 and 4. These represent Designs A, B, C and D, respectively. The second is 'seconds', which contains the number of seconds each visitor to the website lingered. Thus, the first line of the dataset (4, 71) indicates a person who was shown Design D and stayed 71 seconds before moving on.

To run the ANOVA, open the **Analyze** menu, select **Compare Means**, and then **One-Way ANOVA** – see Figure 10.51.

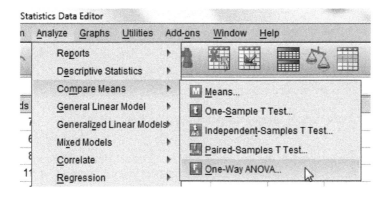

FIGURE 10.51   Finding the One-Way ANOVA analysis in SPSS

Place *seconds* in the 'dependent list' and *webdesign* as the 'factor' (Figure 10.52). You might recognize this interface from our exploration of independent-samples *t*-tests.

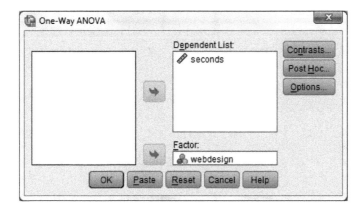

FIGURE 10.52   One-Way ANOVA dialogue in SPSS, with case study data

(Continued)

(Continued)

Next, click on **Post Hoc** to open the post-hoc panel. Here you can see a handful of the many types of post-hoc test available. For now, click the checkbox for Scheffe (Figure 10.53).

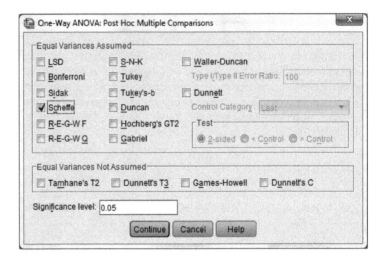

FIGURE 10.53   Post-hoc test dialogue within One-Way ANOVA dialogue in SPSS

Click **Continue,** then open the **Options** panel. Here, select **Descriptive** to get information about group means and **Means plot** to get a visualization of the data (Figure 10.54).

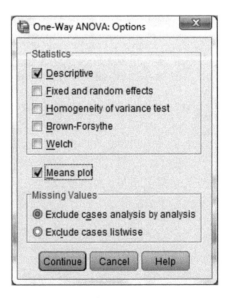

FIGURE 10.54   Options dialogue within One-Way ANOVA dialogue in SPSS

Click **Continue** and then **OK** to run the ANOVA.

First, you'll see descriptive statistics for each group, including mean and standard deviation – see Figure 10.55.

Descriptives

seconds

	N	Mean	Std. Deviation	Std. Error	95% Confidence Interval for Mean Lower Bound	Upper Bound	Minimum	Maximum
Design A	5	65.40	7.021	3.140	56.68	74.12	55	72
Design B	6	106.17	12.891	5.263	92.64	119.69	86	120
Design C	5	77.40	27.070	12.106	43.79	111.01	37	108
Design D	6	60.33	8.756	3.575	51.14	69.52	48	71
Total	22	77.86	23.675	5.048	67.37	88.36	37	120

FIGURE 10.55   First output table from ANOVA in SPSS: group and total descriptive statistics

Second, you'll see the ANOVA summary table we created earlier (Figure 10.56).

ANOVA

seconds

	Sum of Squares	df	Mean Square	F	Sig.
Between Groups	7428.024	3	2476.008	10.263	.000
Within Groups	4342.567	18	241.254		
Total	11770.591	21			

FIGURE 10.56   Second output table from ANOVA in SPSS: the ANOVA summary table

Third, you'll see the results of the post-hoc tests – see Figure 10.57. In this table, an asterisk (*) beside the mean difference indicates the result was statistically significant (although you can also simply look at the *p*-values).

Multiple Comparisons

seconds
Scheffe

(I) webdesign	(J) webdesign	Mean Difference (I-J)	Std. Error	Sig.	95% Confidence Interval Lower Bound	Upper Bound
Design A	Design B	-40.767*	9.405	.004	-69.72	-11.81
	Design C	-12.000	9.824	.689	-42.25	18.25
	Design D	5.067	9.405	.961	-23.89	34.02
Design B	Design A	40.767*	9.405	.004	11.81	69.72
	Design C	28.767	9.405	.052	-.19	57.72
	Design D	45.833*	8.968	.001	18.22	73.44
Design C	Design A	12.000	9.824	.689	-18.25	42.25
	Design B	-28.767	9.405	.052	-57.72	.19
	Design D	17.067	9.405	.376	-11.89	46.02
Design D	Design A	-5.067	9.405	.961	-34.02	23.89
	Design B	-45.833*	8.968	.001	-73.44	-18.22
	Design C	-17.067	9.405	.376	-46.02	11.89

*. The mean difference is significant at the 0.05 level.

FIGURE 10.57   Third output table from ANOVA in SPSS: post-hoc tests

(Continued)

(Continued)

Fourth, you'll see an analysis similar to the drawing exercise we did earlier in this chapter. While we drew lines earlier, SPSS displays means – see Figure 10.58.

seconds

Scheffe[a,b]

webdesign	N	Subset for alpha = 0.05	
		1	2
Design D	6	60.33	
Design A	5	65.40	
Design C	5	77.40	77.40
Design B	6		106.17
Sig.		.376	.052

Means for groups in homogeneous subsets are displayed.

a. Uses Harmonic Mean Sample Size = 5.455.
b. The group sizes are unequal. The harmonic mean of the group sizes is used. Type I error levels are not guaranteed.

FIGURE 10.58   Fourth output table from ANOVA in SPSS: tests for homogeneous subgroups

We can interpret this chart the same way, however. Designs D, A and C are one homogeneous subgroup, while Designs C and B are another.

SPSS does Scheffe tests slightly differently than we did by hand in that it computes a 'harmonic mean' instead of determining critical values for each comparison separately. However, unless your group sizes are dramatically different from one another, the results of SPSS's analysis and your own by hand should be the same.

Finally, SPSS helpfully provides a line graph of the means (Figure 10.59).

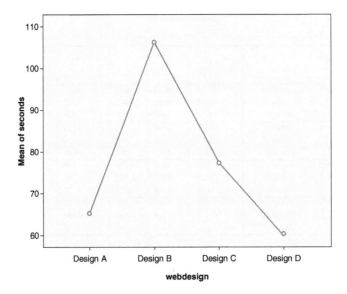

FIGURE 10.59   Line graph produced by SPSS to illustrate relationship between group means (does not imply significant differences)

You may want to update this graph to be less misleading and more appropriately formatted (see Chapter 2) – note that the *y*-axis does not go down to zero, and the chart title is missing.

The only piece of information that SPSS does not calculate is the effect size, η^2. However, you can easily do this with a calculator and the results of the ANOVA summary table in the output.

STATISTICS IN THE REAL WORLD

These web links can be accessed directly from the book's website.

A marketing analyst provides a step by step process for conducting A/B tests, a technique for comparing the effects of two or more business strategies by conducting a research study and analysing the results with a statistical test: https://neilpatel.com/blog/ab-testing-introduction/.

When would this type of testing require a *t*-test, and when would it require an ANOVA?

Writing for chron.com, Vanessa Cross describes how ANOVA can be used in business planning: http://smallbusiness.chron.com/role-variance-analysis-businesses-22641.html.

What types of questions could you address with ANOVA to help you manage or run a business?

TEST YOURSELF

After you've completed the questions below, check your answers online.

1 When is an independent-samples *t*-test appropriate versus one-way ANOVA?

2 What is the null hypothesis when comparing seven independent group means? What is the alternative?

3 For each of the following, complete this sentence: This statistic captures the total variability between the _____ and the _____.
   a SS_B.
   b SS_W.

4 Given this result from a one-way ANOVA: $F(2,15) = 4.57, p < .05$
   a How many groups were compared?
   b What was the sample size?
   c What was alpha?
   d What was the critical value?
   e Did the researcher conclude the difference was statistically significant?

5 For each of the following, find the missing value:
   a $df_T = 29$, $df_W = 27$, $df_B = ?$
   b $SS_W = 10$, $SS_B = 25$, $SS_T = ?$
   c $SS_W = 30$, $MS_W = 3$, $df_W = ?$
   d $F = 3.5$, $MS_W = 4$, $MS_B = ?$

(Continued)

(Continued)

DATA SKILL CHALLENGES

☑ **After you've completed the questions below, check your answers online.**

1 Fill in the rest of the ANOVA summary table in Figure 10.60. Given the information provided, state the critical value, and make a formal statement of the results of this ANOVA.

	SS	df	MS	F
Between-groups		3		
Within-groups			100	
Total	100	13		

FIGURE 10.60   ANOVA summary table for Data Skill Challenge 1

2 Fill in the rest of the ANOVA summary table in Figure 10.61. Given the information provided, state the critical value, and make a formal statement of the results of this ANOVA.

	SS	df	MS	F
Between-groups		4		11.25
Within-groups			.2	
Total		59		

FIGURE 10.61   ANOVA summary table for Data Skill Challenge 2

3 Colleen decides to run a second wave of tests, keeping Designs B and C, but adding Designs E, F, G and H. Her data appear in Figure 10.62. By hand, using Excel, or using SPSS, conduct the full hypothesis testing procedure for her data and draw any appropriate conclusions. Report the full ANOVA summary table.

Design B	Design C	Design E	Design F	Design G	Design H
110	94	103	81	56	140
86	84	141	79	60	115
97	116	107	70	80	130
118	65	113	57	57	146
106	35	93	93	55	109
	88	97			126

FIGURE 10.62   Colleen's group data for Data Skill Challenge 3

4 Lionel is a waiter at a local diner. He notices that he seems to earn less in tips when he works the lunch shift compared with the breakfast or dinner shift. Lionel is curious whether customers tip differently depending on the time of day, so he decides to test this by comparing the average amount tipped during each shift for one week. His data appear in Figure 10.63. By hand, using Excel, or using SPSS, conduct the full hypothesis testing procedure for his data and draw any appropriate conclusions. Report the full ANOVA summary table.

Breakfast	Lunch	Dinner
3	3	5
2	1	4
3	2	5
6	5	6
1	4	8
4	4	5
5	2	2

FIGURE 10.63 Diner group data for Data Skill Challenge 4

NEW TERMS

analysis of variance: ANOVA table: between-groups variability: F-ratio: mean square: n-way ANOVA: one-way ANOVA: sum of squares: within-groups variability:

NEW STATISTICAL NOTATION AND FORMULAS

F: the ratio of between-group variability to within-group variability used in ANOVA; compared with the F-distribution

η^2: a common measure of overall effect size for ANOVA; pronounced 'eta-squared'; calculated as SS_B/SS_T

k: the number of groups being compared in ANOVA; or the number of groups in chi-square

df_B: between-groups degrees of freedom, calculated as $k - 1$

df_W: within-groups degrees of freedom, calculated as $N - k$

SS: sum of squares

SUM OF SQUARES CONCEPTUAL FORMULAS

$$SS_B = \sum (\bar{x}_j - \bar{x})$$

$$SS_W = \sum (x_j - \bar{x}_j)$$

$$SS_B = \sum (x - \bar{x})$$

(Continued)

(Continued)

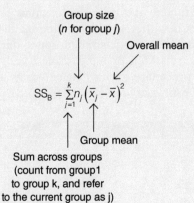

FIGURE 10.64   Annotated formula for the sum of squares between

$$SS_W = SS_T - SS_B$$

FIGURE 10.65   Formula for the sum of squares within

$$SS_T = \sum x^2 - \frac{(\sum x)^2}{n}$$

FIGURE 10.66   Formula for the sum of squares total

Visit https://study.sagepub.com/landers2e **for free additional online resources related to this chapter.**

11 CHI-SQUARED (X^2) TESTS OF FIT

WHAT YOU WILL LEARN FROM THIS CHAPTER

- How to complete the hypothesis testing procedure for chi-squared goodness-of-fit tests and tests of independence
- How to identify when chi-squared is appropriate given the data available
- How to describe the chi-squared distribution and identify critical values
- How to interpret effect sizes for chi-squared

DATA SKILLS YOU WILL MASTER FROM THIS CHAPTER

- Computing chi-squared
- Computing Cramér's V

CASE STUDY   WHICH OF THESE PRODUCTS DO CUSTOMERS PREFER?

Maria is the head of research and development at Chew With Flavour, a manufacturer of many varieties of chewing gum. Maria is principally responsible for developing new flavours of chewing gum and testing their popularity with consumers.

Initial product ideas are not a problem. Maria's team is very creative and comes up with new flavours all the time: Crunchy Blueberry and Tangy Vegetable Spread are just a couple of their recent creations. Unfortunately, all this creativity comes with a price. Sometimes, consumers just hate the flavours they come up with! That's why Maria's testing process is so critical to the success of Chew With Flavour.

Using what she learned from reading Chapters 9 and 10, Maria has to this point asked focus groups to try a random flavour of chewing gum

(Continued)

(Continued)

and make a rating of its quality on a five-point scale. She then compares each group of tasters to determine if ratings are highest for any particular flavour. But recently she's realized that's not exactly what she wants to know. What she actually wants to know is this: when each person tastes multiple flavours, which one do they prefer? That way, she can make a better guess as to which product people will buy given the option to purchase any of them. She is currently interested in customer preferences between a new mint flavour proposed by her creative team and the two dominant mint flavours from her two major competitors.

However, Maria recently read online that women are pickier about their mint flavours than men are. So when examining her new mint flavours, she is worried that women will have different preferences between her mint and her competitors' mints. Or, in other words, she believes men and women may have different preferences among these four gums.

To address these questions she sets up a focus group where each customer tastes all three flavours and marks which one they like best. She also has them record their gender.

But now what? All she has available are frequencies – how many people chose each flavour, and how many of each of those groups were men versus women. How can she answer her research questions with frequencies alone? Since customers just stated their preference, she doesn't have any means, and you definitely need means for a *t*-test. How can you compare groups without means? What should she do?

Take a look at Maria's focus group frequency data for yourself in chapter11.xls (Excel) or chapter11.sav (SPSS) online.

Maria's data differ from the data that we've looked at in Chapters 8, 9 and 10 in an important way: scale of measurement. Up to this point, we've generally had one of two designs: for one-sample tests, we had a single interval- or ratio-level variable; for independent-samples tests, we've had one nominal variable (group membership) and one interval- or ratio-level variable; for paired-sample tests, we've had two interval- or ratio-level variables. The common link between all of these tests is that they require an interval- or ratio-level variable as the 'measured' variable.

In Maria's data, she will instead have one (looking at preferences) or two (looking at the cross between preferences and gender) *nominal* variables. Because nominal variables don't have means, and because *z*-tests, *t*-tests and *F*-tests are all about comparing means, we can't use any of these tests to address her questions.

If any part of that last paragraph was confusing, do yourself a favour and review scale of measurement way back in Chapter 1 (see p. 7) before continuing here.

In this chapter, we must learn about two new tests that can be used to answer Maria's question using a new statistic called chi-squared. Although we still follow the same basic hypothesis testing process that we learned in Chapter 7, several details have changed from other tests. As you read, consider the similarities and differences between the tests you've learned and the new tests covered here.

11.1 PARAMETRIC VS NON-PARAMETRIC TESTS

FOUNDATION CONCEPTS

There are four **scales of measurement**, which determine the type of information a variable contains. First, a variable with **nominal** scale of measurement has meaningful labels. Second, a variable with **ordinal** scale of measurement is nominal, but also has a meaningful order. Third, a variable with **interval** scale of measurement is ordinal, but also has meaningful distances between values. Fourth and finally, a variable with **ratio** scale of measurement is interval, but also has a meaningful zero point (see Chapter 1, p. 7).

A **population** is a theoretical group that you want to draw conclusions about (see Chapter 1, p. 11), whereas a **parameter** is a number summarizing something about that population (see Chapter 3, p. 87).

A **sample** is a group gathered from a population (see Chapter 1, p. 11), whereas a **statistic** is a number summarizing something about that sample (see Chapter 3, p. 87). A statistic is typically calculated to be our best **point estimate** (see Chapter 6, p. 167) of a parameter.

Up to this point in the text, we've looked exclusively at parametric tests. Such tests include z-tests, t-tests and F-tests, and are named 'parametric' because they all involve making assumptions about parameters and testing sample statistics against those parameters. In such tests, we often assume that a population mean equals a certain value or that the difference between two population means is a certain value, and then compare numbers from our sample with those assumptions.

However, we cannot always safely make assumptions about the parameters underlying data. For example, for a variable to have a meaningful mean and standard deviation, it must be interval or ratio scale of measurement. Since t-tests incorporate means and standard deviations, that means we cannot compute a t-test with nominal or ordinal scales of measurement. These variables simply do not contain enough information to make any safe assumptions about the population.

But that doesn't mean such data are useless. Instead, we must use tests with more relaxed assumptions about the quality of information the data contain. In fact, we must use tests that don't require us to estimate parameters at all – these are called non-parametric tests, the most common of which is chi-squared (χ^2; pronounced 'kye', rhymes with 'pie').

Instead of estimating a parameter, chi-squared tests estimate fit. The higher the χ^2, the worse our actual data match our idea of what the data *should* look like. We call this idea about data a model. In t-tests and F-tests, we test assumptions about parameters. In chi-squared tests, we test assumptions about models.

In practice, there are two major types of chi-squared test you are likely to need: goodness-of-fit tests and tests of independence. Each has a different purpose, but most of the steps of hypothesis testing are identical between the two. We'll cover both in the sections below.

11.1.1 CHI-SQUARED TESTS: STEP 1 (STATE THE RESEARCH QUESTION)

In our case study, Maria has two questions. First, she wants to know if customers have a preference between her new mint flavour and her competitors' mint flavours. She must assume that customers have no preference and see if there is sufficient evidence to prove otherwise. This assumption – that there is no preference – is our model. Testing this model involves a chi-squared goodness-of-fit test, where we test a model about a single nominal variable and then test to see if the data are likely to have occurred if that model were true. This is why it is called goodness-of-fit: we want to know how good the fit is. We assume the model is accurate until we have evidence to indicate otherwise.

RQs for goodness-of-fit tests question the assumed model and are always non-directional. They should emphasize the number of levels of the variable being tested. In this case, gum preference is picked among two possibilities, so we state that in the RQ:

RQ$_1$: Are any of the three gums chosen more often by focus group participants?

Maria also wants to know if gum preferences are different by gender. Perhaps men prefer the competitor's gum while women prefer Chew With Flavour's gum! A chi-squared test of independence will address this question. With the test of independence, we test a model assuming that two variables are independent from one another – in this case, that gender and gum preference are not related.

RQs for tests of independence also question the assumed model and are always non-directional. They should emphasize the two variables being compared. In this case:

RQ$_2$: Does gum preference differ by gender?

11.1.2 CHI-SQUARED TESTS: STEP 2 (STATE THE HYPOTHESES)

For chi-squared tests, hypotheses are always the same. First, RQ$_1$ requires a goodness-of-fit test, so we will state the hypotheses as so:

RQ$_1$ H_0: There is no difference between observed and expected frequencies of gum preference.

RQ$_1$ H_1: There is a difference between observed and expected frequencies of gum preference.

The first part of these hypotheses (everything except 'gum preference') is always the same for all goodness-of-fit tests – just change the name of the variable at the end.

RQ$_2$ requires a test of independence, so we will state the hypotheses differently:

RQ$_2$ H_0: Gum preference is independent of gender.

RQ$_2$ H_1: Gum preference is not independent of gender.

To change these hypotheses for other problems, simply swap out the names of the two variables.

11.1.3 CHI-SQUARED TESTS: STEP 3 (SET SIGNIFICANCE LEVEL AND DECISION RULE)

As with all hypothesis testing, we must first set our acceptable Type I error rate (α). Lacking any information to the contrary, we will set $\alpha = .05$.

The chi-squared distribution (Figure 11.01) is similar to the F-distribution (see Chapter 10) in that it is one-tailed. At high degrees of freedom, some shapes of the chi-squared distribution even appear similar to F. However, at low degrees of freedom, it is dramatically different. At one degree of freedom, the chi-squared distribution swoops downward asymptotically to zero. But at three degrees of freedom, a lopsided hump appears. Above eight degrees of freedom, the chi-squared distribution appears similar to (but not precisely identical to) the normal distribution. However, in practice we rarely need the chi-squared distribution except when degrees of freedom are fairly low (as in the case of our example problem, as shown in Figure 11.02).

Both chi-squared tests involve checking the χ^2-table for a critical value. Procedurally, this is the same as we've done in previous chapters: identify degrees of freedom and find the critical value in the table.

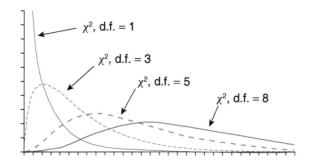

FIGURE 11.01 The sampling distribution of chi-squared at several different degrees of freedom

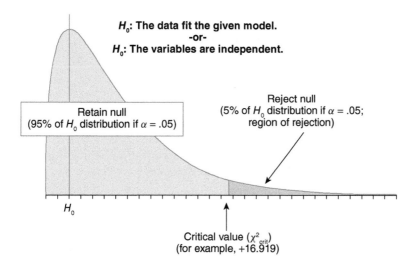

FIGURE 11.02 The sampling distribution of chi-squared for the example problem, at d.f. = 2

Degrees of freedom for the goodness-of-fit test and test of independence require slightly different calculations. For goodness-of-fit (RQ_1):

(Goodness of fit) d.f. $= k - 1$

where k = number of categories within the variable being tested.

Note that this is the same character (k) used to indicate the number of groups in ANOVA. Be careful not to mix them up.

Since the gum preference variable contains three possibilities (Chew With Flavour's flavour, Competitor #1 and Competitor #2), $k = 3$. Thus:

d.f. $= k - 1 = 3 - 1 = 2$

We can next look up the critical value in the chi-squared table, which appears in Appendix A5. As before, find the intersection of alpha (.05) and degrees of freedom (Figure 11.03).

d.f.	$\alpha = .05$	$\alpha = .01$
1	3.841	11.345
2	5.991	15.086
3	7.815	18.475
4	9.488	21.666
5	11.070	24.725

FIGURE 11.03   Looking up a critical value in the χ^2-table in Appendix A5

Because χ^2 are always positive, $RQ_1\chi^2_{crit}(2) = +5.991$.

For tests of independence, degrees of freedom incorporate information about both variables:

(Test of independence) d.f. $= (k_1 - 1)(k_2 - 1)$

where k_1 = number of categories within variable 1 and k_2 = number of categories within variable 2.

Gum preference has three categories (Chew With Flavour's flavour, Competitor #1 and Competitor #2), so $k_1 = 3$, whereas gender has two categories (female and male) so $k_2 = 2$. Thus:

d.f. $= (k_1 - 1) (k_2 - 1) = (3 - 1)(2 - 1) = (2)(1) = 2$

Looking up this value is the same process as for the goodness-of-fit test. Since they have identical degrees of freedom, the values are the same: $\chi^2_{crit}(2) = +5.991$.

11.1.4 CHI-SQUARED TESTS: STEP 4 (COLLECT A SAMPLE)

As with *t*-tests and *F*-tests, Step 4 is a good time to collect all the information we have determined so far in one place before actually collecting data. Here's the recap:

RQ$_1$: Are any of the three gums chosen more often by focus group participants?

H_0: There is no difference between observed and expected frequencies of gum preference.

H_1: There is a difference between observed and expected frequencies of gum preference.

$\alpha = .05$

$\chi^2_{crit}(2) = +5.991$

RQ$_2$: Does gum preference differ by gender?

H_0: Gum preference is independent of gender.

H_1: Gum preference is not independent of gender.

$\alpha = .05$

$\chi^2_{crit}(2) = +5.991$

For our case study, Maria runs her focus group, ultimately collecting data from 33 people: 16 women and 17 men.

11.1.5 CHI-SQUARED TESTS: STEP 5 (CONDUCT STATISTICAL TEST)

The chi-squared statistic is computed with counts, so it works a little differently from the statistics we've covered to this point. Instead of computing sample means and comparing those to population means, we will determine observed counts and compare these values with expected counts.

The formula for chi-squared is shown in Figure 11.04.

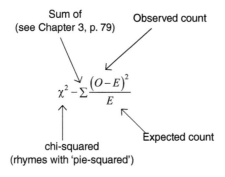

Sum of
(see Chapter 3, p. 79)

Observed count

$$\chi^2 = \Sigma \frac{(O-E)^2}{E}$$

chi-squared
(rhymes with 'pie-squared')

Expected count

FIGURE 11.04   Annotated formula for chi-squared

When computing this statistic, these formulas imply that you'll need two lists: a list of expected counts (which comes from your assumed model) and a list of observed counts (which comes from the data themselves). You'll then find the differences between each pair of counts, square those differences, and divide by each expected count within each pair. Sum these together, and you end up with chi-squared.

Conceptually, each squared-difference-divided-by-expected-value tells us what proportion of the expected value the squared difference is. For example, if we expected ten and found a difference of three, we have found a squared difference $(3)^2/10 = 90\%$ of our expected value. We square the difference for a similar reason to why we squared differences for standard deviation (in Chapter 3) and used sum of squares (in Chapter 10): we want to get rid of the negative signs. The bigger the deviation from the expected (assumed) model – in either direction, positive or negative – the more likely it is that the model described by the null hypothesis does not describe the data.

When comparing to the critical value, we then test this question: what proportion would we expect to find given a particular number of degrees of freedom, if all observed differences occurred by chance alone?

The process for deriving this chi-squared statistic differs a bit depending on which type of chi-squared you need.

11.1.5.1 GOODNESS-OF-FIT TEST

The first step in computing chi-squared for goodness-of-fit tests is creating a computation table. Figure 11.05 gives the template.

Category	Observed (O)	Expected (E)	(O − E)	(O − E)^2	$\dfrac{(O - E)^2}{E}$

FIGURE 11.05   Chi-squared computation table template

In our case study data, Maria found ten people expressed a preference for Chew With Flavour's gum, 14 expressed a preference for the gum of Competitor #1, and nine people expressed a preference for the gum of Competitor #2. We can record that in the table, as in Figure 11.06.

Category	Observed (O)	Expected (E)	(O − E)	(O − E)^2	$\dfrac{(O - E)^2}{E}$
Chew With Flavour	10				
Competitor #1	14				
Competitor #2	9				

FIGURE 11.06   Chi-squared computation table, observed counts recorded

The expected values are driven by the model assumed in the null hypothesis. So how do we get these values? For hypotheses proposing no differences among categories, we divide the number of cases by the number of possible categories. In our case study, there are three possible values for gum preference among a sample of 33, so we divide 33 by three: the expected value for each is 11 (Figure 11.07).

Category	Observed (O)	Expected (E)	(O − E)	(O − E)²	$\frac{(O-E)^2}{E}$
Chew With Flavour	10	11			
Competitor #1	14	11			
Competitor #2	9	11			

FIGURE 11.07   Chi-squared computation table, expected counts recorded

You can double-check that you have appropriate expected values by adding them together – the sum of the values in the 'Observed' column should be equal to the sum of the values in the 'Expected' column. In this case they both equal 33, so we are good to proceed to the next step.

Next, subtract each expected value from each observed value (Figure 11.08).

Category	Observed (O)	Expected (E)	(O − E)	(O − E)²	$\frac{(O-E)^2}{E}$
Chew With Flavour	10	11	10−11 = −1		
Competitor #1	14	11	14−11 = 3		
Competitor #2	9	11	9−11 = −2		

FIGURE 11.08   Chi-squared computation table, O − E calculated

Next, square the differences you just calculated (Figure 11.09).

Category	Observed (O)	Expected (E)	(O − E)	(O − E)²	$\frac{(O-E)^2}{E}$
Chew With Flavour	10	11	−1	(−1)² = 1	
Competitor #1	14	11	3	(3)² = 9	
Competitor #2	9	11	−2	(2)² = 4	

FIGURE 11.09   Chi-squared computation table, O − E squared

Finally, divide each of those squared differences by E (Figure 11.10).

Category	Observed (O)	Expected (E)	(O – E)	(O – E)²	$\frac{(O-E)^2}{E}$
Chew With Flavour	10	11	–1	1	1/11 = 0.090909
Competitor #1	14	11	3	9	9/11 = 0.818182
Competitor #2	9	11	–2	4	4/11 = 0.363636

FIGURE 11.10   Chi-squared computation table, O – E squared divided by E

To compute chi-squared, simply add those values together (round to three digits at the end, since that's the precision of the chi-squared critical values in Appendix A5):

$$RQ_1\chi^2 = .090909 + .818182 + .363636 = 1.272727 = +1.273$$

ARE EXPECTED VALUES IN GOODNESS-OF-FIT TESTS ALWAYS EQUAL?

Not necessarily! Chi-squared is extremely flexible. You can technically put any values in the expected column that you want, as long as you have a good reason for it. For example, imagine that, in the past, Maria had found that Chew With Flavour's gum was preferred two to one (2:1) to one of her competitors' flavours. She might want to run a test to see if a new gum was even better: in that case, the expected value for her flavour would be double the value of the expected value for the competitor's flavour.

Expected values are always driven by the null model. In this textbook, we'll focus on questions of the 'is there a difference?' variety. These questions assume a null hypothesis of 'no differences among categories'. If you couldn't safely assume no differences (or had a different question), you could use whatever values you wanted.

11.1.5.2 TEST OF INDEPENDENCE

Instead of looking for deviations from a hypothetical model driven by randomness (in the goodness-of-fit example above, we assumed that the 33 cases should be spread equally across the three categories), tests of independence assume that the breakdown between categories *within* each variable represents the population. The goal instead is to identify an interaction between the two variables being analysed. That means that the unique combination of one or more categories on the first variable with one or more categories on the second variable creates a joint effect that we would not expect given either one of the variables alone.

To analyse tests of independence, we create a contingency table highlighting the counts crossed between the two tables. I'll use contingency tables to highlight what interactions (statistically significant tests of independence) might look like.

First, let's look at a contingency table highlighting non-significant goodness-of-fit tests and tests of independence. For these examples, we'll consider the case study variables, but with false data, as depicted in Figure 11.11.

		Gum preference			
		Gum A	Gum B	Gum C	Total
Gender	Male	50	50	50	150
	Female	50	50	50	150
	Total	100	100	100	300

FIGURE 11.11 Contingency table demonstrating non-significant goodness-of-fit test and test of independence

In Figure 11.11, we see equal counts appearing in every cell (50 per cell, 300 in total). If we conducted a goodness-of-fit test on either variable, we would not find statistically significant results. Next, let's look at a statistically significant goodness-of-fit test for gum preference, but not for gender, as shown in Figure 11.12.

In Figure 11.12, we have a clear preference for Gum B (200 vs 50 and 50), but no effect of gender (150 vs 150). In a focus group context, where we choose research participants (often using stratified random sampling to ensure a balance of men and women; see Chapter 5, p. 148), we would not expect a difference by gender.

		Gum preference			
		Gum A	Gum B	Gum C	Total
Gender	Male	25	100	25	150
	Female	25	100	25	150
	Total	50	200	50	300

FIGURE 11.12 Contingency table demonstrating significant goodness-of-fit test but non-significant test of independence

So what does an interaction (that is, a statistically significant test of independence) look like? There are many possibilities, but the key is that there is some unique combination of the two variables that leads to an unexpected result. As an example, see Figure 11.13.

		Gum Preference			
		Gum A	Gum B	Gum C	Total
Gender	Male	100	40	10	150
	Female	10	40	100	150
	Total	125	80	125	300

FIGURE 11.13 Contingency table demonstrating significant test of independence

In Figure 11.13, a goodness-of-fit test alone would be misleading – you would conclude that Gum A and Gum C were preferred equally (125 and 125), but more than Gum B (80). However, the interaction hides a better conclusion: men overwhelmingly prefer Gum A while women overwhelmingly prefer Gum C.

The expected model for a chi-squared test of independence thus makes different assumptions than a goodness-of-fit test. Tests of independence assume that the breakdown within each variable accurately reflects the population. It then asks, 'Are there any unique combinations of categories observed that we would not have expected given that breakdown?' This is the definition of 'interaction'.

Computationally, this gets a little more complicated because we are crossing two variables (instead of considering one, as in goodness-of-fit). Separate tables are needed for each step of the process. For our case study, we'll first create a contingency table for the observed values. When determining this by hand, ensure you mark clearly that this is the 'observed' table, as we'll have several. You can also find these values for yourself by analysing the case study dataset as depicted in Figure 11.14.

Observed		Gum preference			
		Chew With/Flavour	Competitor #1	Competitor #2	Total
Gender	Male	3	11	3	17
	Female	7	3	6	16
	Total	10	14	9	33

FIGURE 11.14   Contingency table of observed values for case study dataset

Next, we need to compute the expected values. To do this, multiply the row total count by the column total count, then divide by the overall count. For example, for the top left cell, you'll multiply the top row total (17) by the left column total (10), then divide by the overall total (33). Mark this table clearly as the 'expected' table, as shown in Figure 11.15.

Expected		Gum preference			
		Chew With/Flavour	Competitor #1	Competitor #2	Total
Gender	Male	(17*10)/33=5.151515	(17*14)/33=7.212121	(17*9)/33=4.636364	17
	Female	(16*10)/33=4.848485	(16*14)/33=6.787879	(16*6)/33=4.363636	16
	Total	10	14	9	33

FIGURE 11.15   Contingency table of observed values for case study dataset

Once we have our expected values, we return to our calculation table from goodness-of-fit, with an added column to represent the second variable. Ensure you represent every combination of values – you should have as many rows in this table as there were cells in your contingency table (in this case, six). Copy the observed and expected values from your contingency table, as shown in Figure 11.16.

Variable 1	Variable 2	Observed (O)	Expected (E)	(O – E)	(O – E)²	$\dfrac{(O-E)^2}{E}$
Male	Chew With/ Flavour	3	5.151515			
Male	Competitor #1	11	7.212121			
Male	Competitor #2	3	4.636364			

Variable 1	Variable 2	Observed (O)	Expected (E)	(O – E)	(O – E)²	$\frac{(O-E)^2}{E}$
Female	Chew With/ Flavour	7	4.848485			
Female	Competitor #1	3	6.787879			
Female	Competitor #2	6	4.363636			

FIGURE 11.16   Chi-squared test of independent computation table, O and E transferred

Complete this table as you did for goodness-of-fit. You should end up with Figure 11.17.

Variable 1	Variable 2	Observed (O)	Expected (E)	(O – E)	(O – E)²	$\frac{(O-E)^2}{E}$
Male	Chew With/ Flavour	3	5.151515	–2.151515	4.629017	.898574
Male	Competitor #1	11	7.212121	3.787879	14.348027	1.989432
Male	Competitor #2	3	4.636364	–1.636364	2.677687	.577540
Female	Chew With/ Flavour	7	4.848485	2.151515	4.629017	.954735
Female	Competitor #1	3	6.787879	–3.787879	14.348027	2.113772
Female	Competitor #2	6	4.363636	1.636364	2.677687	.613637

FIGURE 11.17   Chi-squared test of independent computation table, completed

Finally, just like in goodness of fit, add all of the values in the last column to determine chi-squared. Round to three decimal places.

RQ$_2$ χ^2 = .898574 + 1.989432 + .577541 + .954735 + 2.113772 + .613637 = 7.147690 = +7.148

AVOID CELL SIZES LESS THAN FIVE

Because of the way it is calculated, chi-squared tests are very sensitive to small cell sizes. If you have fewer than five observed or expected cases in any particular cell, you risk an artificially inflated chi-squared statistic. While our examples above have fewer than five cases in some cells, it is strongly recommended that you collect a sufficient amount of data to avoid this when collecting data for your own organization.

11.1.6 CHI-SQUARED TESTS: STEP 6 (FORMALLY STATE RESULTS)

Just as for all other hypothesis tests, we next compare the observed statistic with the critical statistic and make a conclusion about statistical significance – see Figure 11.18. If the observed statistic is beyond the critical, reject the null. Otherwise, retain. Remember to report degrees of freedom.

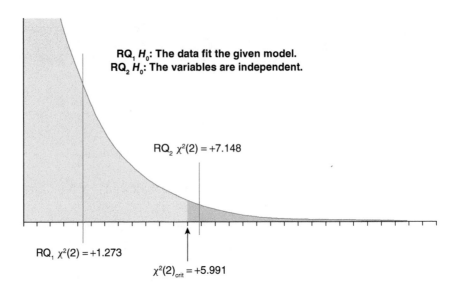

RQ$_1$ H_0: The data fit the given model.
RQ$_2$ H_0: The variables are independent.

RQ$_2$ $\chi^2(2) = +7.148$

RQ$_1$ $\chi^2(2) = +1.273$

$\chi^2(2)_{crit} = +5.991$

FIGURE 11.18   Sampling distribution of chi-squared at two degrees of freedom, with results of sample problem

$$RQ_1\chi^2(2) = +1.273, p >.05$$
$$RQ_2\chi^2(2) = +7.148, p <.05$$

11.1.7 CHI-SQUARED TESTS: STEP 7 (CONDUCT SUPPLEMENTAL ANALYSES)

When chi-squared is not statistically significant, we do not need any supplemental analyses. But when chi-squared is statistically significant, we must calculate a measure of effect size called Cramér's V, which is represented with ϕ_c ('phi-sub-c', pronounced 'fye-sub-see').

Cramér's V varies between 0 and +1, with larger numbers representing larger effects. To calculate it, you only need three pieces of information, as shown in Figure 11.19.

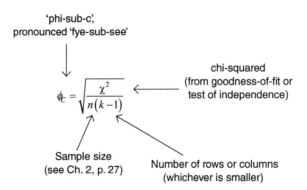

'phi-sub-c',
pronounced 'fye-sub-see'

chi-squared
(from goodness-of-fit or
test of independence)

$$\phi_c = \sqrt{\frac{\chi^2}{n(k-1)}}$$

Sample size
(see Ch. 2, p. 27)

Number of rows or columns
(whichever is smaller)

FIGURE 11.19   Annotated formula for Cramér's V

The only part of this formula that should look strange is the k: in this case, look at the contingency table and compare the number of columns (three in our case study) and rows (two in our case study). Whichever is smaller becomes the value for k (for the case study, 2).

For our case study, the calculation is shown in Figure 11.20.

$$\Phi_C = \sqrt{\frac{\chi^2}{n(k-1)}} = \sqrt{\frac{7.147690}{33(2-1)}} = \sqrt{\frac{7.147690}{33(1)}} = \sqrt{\frac{7.147690}{33}} = \sqrt{0.216597} = 0.465400 = 0.47$$

FIGURE 11.20 Step by step calculation of Cramér's V

Cramér's V is difficult to interpret. But like all effect sizes, it is most useful when comparing the effects of two different analyses. For example, we might conduct two research studies and compare the Cramér's V found in each to determine which approach produced a larger effect.

It's also worth noting that Cramér's V has another name when conducted on a 2×2 contingency table which you might read: the phi coefficient (ϕ). However, calculation and interpretation are the same as for any other Cramér's V.

11.1.8 CHI-SQUARED TESTS: STEP 8 (DRAW ALL CONCLUSIONS)

Finally, we must collect all of our results and interpretations in one place. Procedurally, it's most similar to the final set of conclusions we draw with t-tests. However, when statistical significance is found, we must also interpret the observed counts in words. To do this, look at the tables of observed values and explain what you see phrased as an answer to the research question (an example for RQ_2 appears below).

RQ_1: Are any of the three gums chosen more often by focus group participants?

H_0: There is no difference between observed and expected frequencies of gum preference.

H_1: There is a difference between observed and expected frequencies of gum preference.

$\alpha = .05$

$\chi^2_{crit}(2) = +5.991$

$\chi^2(2) = +1.273, p > .05$

Conclusion: Retain the null. The chi-squared is not statistically significant. None of the gums is chosen more often by focus group participants.

RQ_2: Does gum preference differ by gender?

H_0: Gum preference is independent of gender.

H_1: Gum preference is not independent of gender.

$\alpha = .05$

$\chi^2_{\text{crit}}(2) = +5.991$

$\chi^2(2) = +7.148, p < .05$

$\phi_c = .47$

Conclusion: Reject the null and accept the alternative. The chi-squared was statistically significant. Gum preference does differ by gender. Cramér's V was .47. From the contingency table, it appears that males prefer Competitor #1's gum, whereas women do not show strong preferences for any gum.

Given this analysis, Maria may want to develop different gums targeted at different genders.

11.2 APPLYING CHI-SQUARED TESTS OF FIT

To apply what you've learned from this chapter, consider the following case study, questions posed about that case study, and discussion of those questions.

11.2.1 APPLICATION CASE STUDY

Javier is the owner of Babelfish, a developer of translation software. His program is unique in that it is used as a tool for professional translators, marking portions of texts as 'verified correct', 'unsure' and 'unable to be translated automatically'. In the past, his program has been moderately successful, translating documents with a 80%/15%/5% success rate. That is, 80% of paragraphs were verified correct automatically, 15% of paragraphs were translated but the program could not verify them automatically, and 5% of paragraphs simply could not be translated.

Javier has just finished development of a new version of the program. He feeds it 100 sample documents and gets back the output: 2000 paragraphs verified correct, 100 paragraphs unsure, and 75 paragraphs unable to be translated.

With these data, Javier would like to test to see if his new translation program is superior to his old one.

1 What type of test does Javier need here and why?

2 What is the expected model and what is the observed model?

3 What is Javier's research question?

4 What are the hypotheses?

5 If Javier rejects the null, what can he conclude?

6 If Javier retains the null, what can he conclude?

11.2.2 APPLICATION DISCUSSION

We will again cover these questions one by one.

1 Javier needs to conduct a chi-squared goodness-of-fit test because he has already developed a model of how well the software program should perform if it is performing at the level of the old program. He wants to find evidence that his new program is improved from this previous model.

2 The observed model is provided: 2000, 100 and 75. The expected model will be based upon these numbers. Since there are a total of 2175 paragraphs, we would expect 80% * 2175 = 1740, 15% * 2175 = 326.25, 5% * 2175 = 108.75. Our expected model is therefore: 1740, 326.25, 108.75.

3 Javier's research question is: Does the performance of the new software fit the model of the old software?

4 The hypotheses are:

H_0: There is no difference between observed and expected frequencies of software performance.

H_1: There is a difference between observed and expected frequencies of software performance.

5 If Javier rejects the null, he can conclude that the new software performs *differently* from the old software. However, he cannot make specific conclusions as to how. To do this, he should examine the observed frequencies table and examine the pattern of findings, looking for the largest deviations between the observed and expected model.

6 If Javier retains the null, he can conclude only that there was insufficient evidence to reject the null model. He will need to assume that the new software performs as well as the old software until he finds evidence to the contrary.

EXPLORING CHI-SQUARED TESTS IN EXCEL AND SPSS

EXCEL

Download the Excel dataset for the demonstration below as **chapter11.xls**. As you read this section, try to apply the terms you've learned in this chapter to the dataset and follow along with Excel on your own computer.

You can also get a video demonstration of the section below under **Excel Video: Chapter 11.**

Excel does not have any built-in analytic tools for chi-squared, so we must create all calculation and contingency tables by hand. We'll start with the goodness-of-fit test for RQ_1.

(Continued)

(Continued)

GOODNESS-OF-FIT TEST

First, create the row labels and headings for the goodness-of-fit calculation table. Place these values in E1 through J8, as in Figure 11.21.

	A	B	C	D	E	F	G	H	I	J
1	gum_pref	gender			Goodness of Fit Test					
2	2	1								
3	3	1				Observed	Expected	O-E	(O-E)^2	(O-E)^2/E
4	2	2			1					
5	1	1			2					
6	3	1			3					
7	1	2							chi-sq	
8	2	2							p-value	
9	2	2								
10	2	1								

FIGURE 11.21   Setting up a goodness-of-fit calculation table in Excel

Next, we need to determine the observed counts. While you could do this by sorting and counting, Excel will do some of the legwork for you.

In F4, type: =COUNTIF(A:A,E4).

This formula looks at all the numbers in Column A (designated as A:A) and counts how many times it finds the value in E4 (in this case, the number '1'). When you fill down to F6, E4 will update to read E5 and E6, giving you observed counts of all three, as found in Column A. When done, it should look like Figure 11.22.

F6			f_x	=COUNTIF(A:A,E6)		

	A	B	C	D	E	F	G
1	gum_pref	gender			Goodness of Fit Test		
2	2	1					
3	3	1				Observed	Expected
4	2	2			1	10	
5	1	1			2	14	
6	3	1			3	9	
7	1	2					

FIGURE 11.22   Adding observed counts for goodness-of-fit test in Excel

In G4, type: =COUNT(A:A)/3

This counts all numbers in Column A (regardless of their value). It then divides this value by three (the number of categories) to determine the expected values. Fill down once again (Figure 11.23).

	A	B	C	D	E	F	G	H
1	gum_pref	gender			Goodness of Fit Test			
2	2	1						
3	3	1				Observed	Expected	O-E
4	2	2			1	10	11	
5	1	1			2	14	11	
6	3	1			3	9	11	
7	1	2						
8	2	2						

FIGURE 11.23 Adding expected counts for goodness-of-fit test in Excel

The rest of the cells across are just algebra, so try them on your own. You should come up with the following:

- In H4, type: =F4-G4.
- In I4, type: =H4^2.
- In J4, type: =I4/G4.

Fill down, and you should have the complete calculation table (Figure 11.24).

E	F	G	H	I	J
Goodness of Fit Test					
	Observed	Expected	O-E	(O-E)^2	(O-E)^2/E
1	10	11	-1	1	0.090909
2	14	11	3	9	0.818182
3	9	11	-2	4	0.363636

FIGURE 11.24 Adding final cell calculations for goodness-of-fit test in Excel

Next, we'll calculate chi-square by summing the values above. In J7, type: =SUM(J4:J6).

Finally, we need to calculate the *p*-value. The chi-squared formula requires two terms: the chi-square statistics and degrees of freedom. We'll refer to J7 for the chi-squared statistic and type the number '2' for degrees of freedom.

- In Excel 2010, in J8, type: =CHISQ.DIST.RT(J7,2).
- In Excel 2007, in J8, type: =CHIDIST(J7,2).

If your degrees of freedom are different in your own analyses, remember to change the '2' in those formulas.

That's it! You have a precise *p*-value, and should report your chi-squared accordingly:

$\chi^2(2) = +1.273$, $p = .53$

(Continued)

(Continued)

TEST OF INDEPENDENCE

Several tables are needed for the chi-squared test of independence, and this will take up a fair amount of space in Excel. Start by, in E11, typing: 'Test of Independence'. All of our analyses will be placed below this point.

First, we need to create a PivotTable. This is a function in Excel that allows us to count the number of cases falling within each combination of our two variables. We need to produce six counts (3 preferences × 2 genders), and Excel will do this automatically with a PivotTable.

For reasons that will become clear in a few moments, add a new column labelled 'counter' in C1. In C2, type the number '1' and then fill down (a full column of nothing but the number 1) – see Figure 11.25.

	A	B	C
1	gum_pref	gender	counter
2	2	1	1
3	3	1	1
4	2	2	1
5	1	1	1
6	3	1	1
7	1	2	1
8	2	2	1
9	2	2	1

FIGURE 11.25   Adding counter variable in Excel for use in a PivotTable

Next, we need to actually create our PivotTable. Click on the **Insert** ribbon and select **PivotTable** (Figure 11.26).

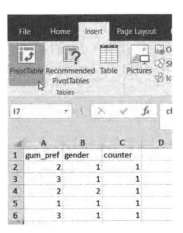

FIGURE 11.26   Selecting PivotTable from the Insert ribbon in Excel

Click on the **Cell Selection Tool** on the right (Figure 11.27).

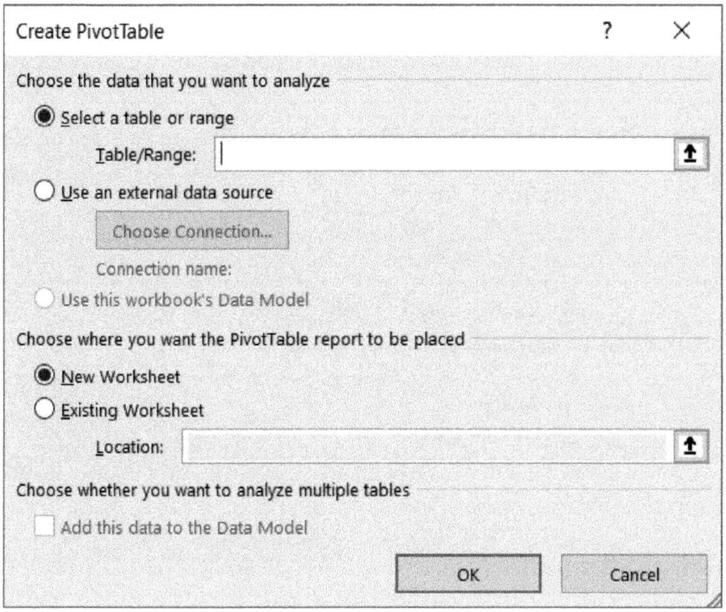

FIGURE 11.27 The PivotTable dialogue in Excel

Click-drag to highlight the first three columns of data. Then click on the **Save Selection** button to confirm – see Figure 11.28.

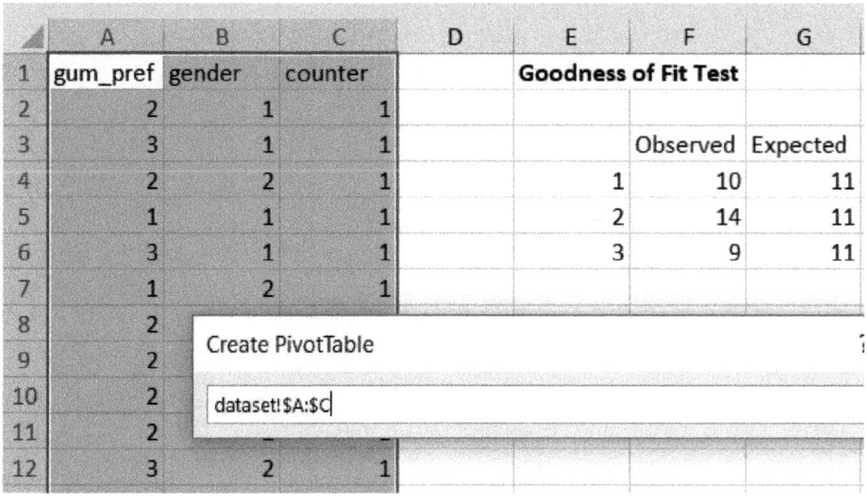

FIGURE 11.28 Selecting range of values for input into a PivotTable

(Continued)

(Continued)

   When back on the other screen, click on the second **Cell Selection Tool** and select E12 on the next screen. When you return to the Create PivotTable screen, you should see Figure 11.29.

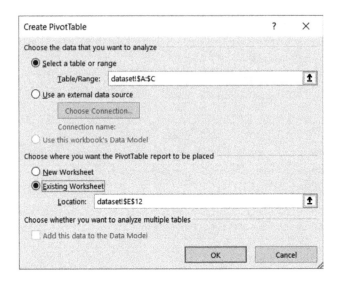

FIGURE 11.29   PivotTable dialogue after inputting information for case study dataset

   Click **OK** to open the PivotTable sidebar to the right side of your screen. Click-drag 'gum_pref' to **Row Labels**, click-drag 'gender' to **Column Labels**, and click-drag 'counter' to **Values**. It should look like Figure 11.30.

FIGURE 11.30   Specifying columns and rows for Excel PivotTable to conduct test of independence

A new table has appeared in E12:I18 – see Figure 11.31. This is your observed contingency table.

10	2	1	1						
11	2	2	1		**Test of Independence**				
12	3	2	1		Sum of counter	gender ▾			
13	1	2	1		gum_pref ▾		1	2 (blank)	Grand Total
14	2	2	1	✛		1	7	3	10
15	3	1	1			2	3	11	14
16	2	2	1			3	6	3	9
17	1	1	1		(blank)				
18	2	1	1		Grand Total		16	17	33
19	3	1	1						

FIGURE 11.31   Case study data and completed PivotTable for use as observed table in chi-squared test of independence

Next, we need the expected contingency table. Copy the row labels and headings down to E22:I26, but label the new table 'Expected' (Figure 11.32).

Test of Independence				
Count of counter	gender ▾			
gum_pref ▾		1	2 (blank)	Grand Total
	1	7	3	10
	2	3	11	14
	3	6	3	9
(blank)				
Grand Total		16	17	33
Expected	gender			
gum_pref		1	2	Total
	1			10
	2			14
	3			9
Total		16	17	33

FIGURE 11.32   Creating template for expected table in Excel chi-squared test of independence

To compute the first expected value in F22 (Figure 11.33), type: =($I22*F$26)/$I$26.

(Continued)

(Continued)

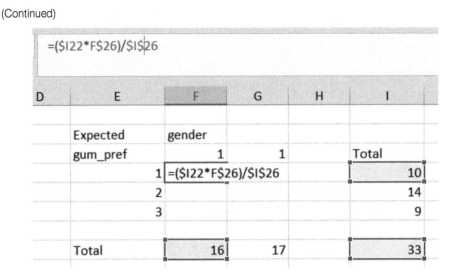

=($I22*F$26)/$I$26

D	E	F	G	H	I
	Expected	gender			
	gum_pref	1	1		Total
	1	=($I22*F$26)/$I$26			10
	2				14
	3				9
	Total	16	17		33

FIGURE 11.33   Inputting formulas to calculate expected values in Excel chi-squared test of independence

This multiplies the row total by the column total, then divides by the overall total, just as we'd do by hand. It contains dollar signs ($) so that when we fill right and down, the formula won't update the position of those cells. Fill right to G22, then down to G24. You should end up with Figure 11.34.

Expected	gender				
gum_pref	1	1		Total	
1	4.848485	5.151515			10
2	6.787879	7.212121			14
3	4.363636	4.636364			9
Total	16	17			33

FIGURE 11.34   Completed expected table in Excel

We'll compute all in one step. Once again, copy all the column headings and row labels a little lower (E28), but this time skip the totals (Figure 11.35).

Expected	gender			
gum_pref	1	2	Total	
1	4.848485	5.151515		10
2	6.787879	7.212121		14
3	4.363636	4.636364		9
Total	16	17		33
(O-E)^2/E	gender			
gum_pref	1	2		
1				
2				
3				

FIGURE 11.35   Creating template for (O-E) ^ 2/E table in Excel

In F30, type: = (F14-F22) ^ 2/F22.

You should recognize this as the Excel version of the chi-squared formula (apart from the capital sigma), all in one calculation. You should see Figure 11.36.

	=(F14-F22)^2/F22		
D	E	F	G
	(O-E)^2/E	gender	
	gum_pref	1	2
	1	0.9547348	
	2		
	3		

FIGURE 11.36   Entering the formula to calculate first (O-E) ^ 2/E

Fill across and down, as before (Figure 11.37).

(Continued)

(Continued)

	E	F	G
28	(O-E)^2/E	gender	
29	gum_pref	1	2
30	1	0.9547348	0.898574
31	2	2.1137716	1.989432
32	3	0.6136364	0.57754

FIGURE 11.37   Completed table of (O-E) ^ 2/E values in Excel

The next two steps match what we did for goodness-of-fit.

In F34, type: chi-sq.
In G34, type: =SUM(F30:G32).
In F35, type: p-value.
In Excel 2010, in G35, type: =CHISQ.DIST.RT(G34,2).
In Excel 2007, in G35, type: =CHIDIST(G34,2).

You should end up with Figure 11.38.

	E	F	G
28	(O-E)^2/E	gender	
29	gum_pref	1	2
30	1	0.9547348	0.898574
31	2	2.1137716	1.989432
32	3	0.6136364	0.57754
33			
34		chi-sq	7.147689
35		p-value	0.028048

FIGURE 11.38   Computed chi-squared and p-value in Excel

Given this, you can make a formal statement of your results:

$\chi^2(2) = +7.148, p = .03$

Since the result is statistically significant, we need to also calculate Cramér's V.

In F36, type: Cramer's V.
In G36, type: =SQRT(G34/(33*(2-1))).

You should recognize this as the Excel version of the Cramér's V formula that you calculated by hand earlier. For other problems, remember to change the values for N (33, in this case) and k (2, in this case). The final results are shown in Figure 11.39.

33			
34		chi-sq	7.147689
35		p-value	0.028048
36		Cramer's V	0.465399
37			

FIGURE 11.39   Completed chi-squared test of independence in Excel

SPSS

Download the SPSS dataset for the demonstration below as **chapter11.sav**. As you read this section, try to apply the terms you've learned in this chapter to the dataset and follow along with SPSS on your own computer.

You can also get a video demonstration of the section below under **SPSS Videos: Chapter 11**.

SPSS places goodness-of-fit tests and tests of independence in very different parts of its interface. We'll cover each in turn.

GOODNESS-OF-FIT TEST

First, open the **Analyse** menu, select **Nonparametric Tests**, then **Legacy Dialogs**, then **Chi-square** – see Figure 11.40.

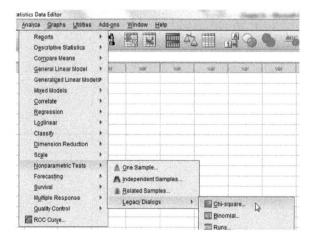

FIGURE 11.40   Menu option in SPSS for chi-squared goodness of fit

(Continued)

(Continued)

In this dialogue, drag **gum_pref** to the right. If you have specific hypothesized values for the levels of your variable, you could specify these in the **Expected Values** section of this dialogue. Since we don't, just click **OK** (Figure 11.41).

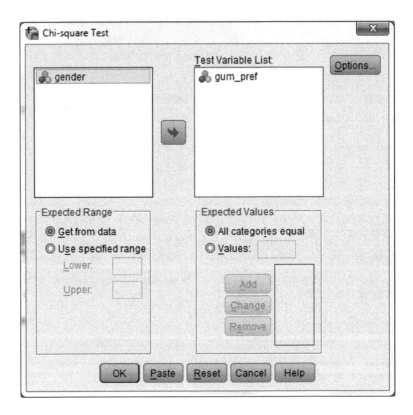

FIGURE 11.41 Dialogue for specifying chi-squared goodness of fit in SPSS

A partial calculation table will appear, with the observed and expected values for the goodness-of-fit test (Figure 11.42).

Gum Preference

	Observed N	Expected N	Residual
Taste With Flavour	10	11.0	-1.0
Competitor #1	14	11.0	3.0
Competitor #2	9	11.0	-2.0
Total	33		

FIGURE 11.42 First table of output from chi-squared goodness-of-fit test, containing observed and expected frequencies

The next table (Figure 11.43) provides all information about the chi-squared test itself.

Test Statistics

	Gum Preference
Chi-Square	1.273[a]
df	2
Asymp. Sig.	.529

a. 0 cells (.0%) have expected frequencies less than 5. The minimum expected cell frequency is 11.0.

FIGURE 11.43 Second table of output from chi-squared goodness-of-fit test, containing chi-squared statistic and p-value

From this, we can conclude:

$$\chi^2(2) = +1.273, p = .53$$

If the results are statistically significant and you need to compute Cramér's V, you must do so by hand.

TEST OF INDEPENDENCE

For the chi-squared test of independence, we navigate to the **Analyse** menu, followed by **Descriptive Statistics**, followed by **Crosstabs** (which stands for 'cross-tabulations') – see Figure 11.44.

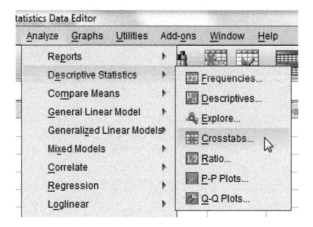

FIGURE 11.44 Menu option in SPSS for cross-tabulation, which contains chi-squared test of independence

(Continued)

(Continued)

Here, place **gum_pref** in Rows and **gender** in Columns (Figure 11.45).

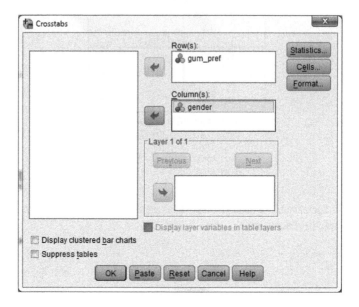

FIGURE 11.45   Dialogue for conducting cross-tabulation

Next, click the **Statistics** button. On this panel, check **Chi-square** and **Phi and Cramer's V** (Figure 11.46).

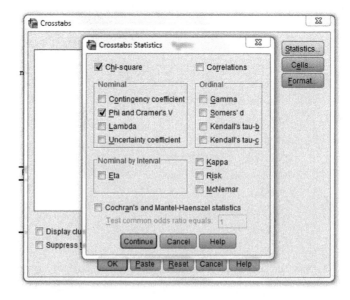

FIGURE 11.46   Statistics subdialogue for cross-tabulation, where chi-square and Cramer's V can be selected

Click **Continue** and then **OK**. The Output Pane will pop up with the results of your analysis.

The first table provides summary information about your sample. This is a good place to verify that you have entered the data correctly (that is, no missing cases).

The second table that pops up (Figure 11.47) contains your observed contingency table, which you will need for interpretation if the results are statistically significant.

Gum Preference * Gender Crosstabulation

Count

| | | Gender | | |
		Female	Male	Total
Gum PreferenceTaste With Flavour		7	3	10
	Competitor #1	3	11	14
	Competitor #2	6	3	9
Total		16	17	33

FIGURE 11.47 First outputted table from cross-tabulation, containing observed table for chi-squared test of independence

The third table that pops up contains several tests. We only need to worry about the first, which reads Pearson Chi-Square (Figure 11.48).

Chi-Square Tests

	Value	df	Asymp. Sig. (2-sided)
Pearson Chi-Square	7.148[a]	2	.028
Likelihood Ratio	7.495	2	.024
Linear-by-Linear Association	.054	1	.816
N of Valid Cases	33		

a. 3 cells (50.0%) have expected count less than 5. The minimum expected count is 4.36.

FIGURE 11.48 Second outputted table from cross-tabulation, containing chi-squared statistic and p-value From this, we can conclude:

$\chi^2(2) = +7.148, p = .03$

Since the results are statistically significant, we need to compute Cramér's V. The final table reports this (Figure 11.49).

(Continued)

(Continued)

Symmetric Measures

		Value	Approx. Sig.
Nominal by Nominal	Phi	.465	.028
	Cramer's V	.465	.028
N of Valid Cases		33	

FIGURE 11.49   Third outputted table from cross-tabulation, containing computed Cramér's V

From this, we can conclude: $\phi_c = .47$.

STATISTICS IN THE REAL WORLD

   These web links can be accessed directly from the book's website.

Bala Deshpande, Senior Managing Director at NEA India, describes how chi-squared tests of independence can be used to address common business problems: www.simafore.com/blog/bid/54594/How-to-use-Chi-Square-test-for-3-common-business-analytics-problems.

How could you use chi-squared tests in your own business?

Jonathan Weber, Data Evangelist at LunaMetrics, explains how chi-squared tests are critical in web marketing to understand the effects of advertising: www.lunametrics.com/blog/2014/07/01/statistical-significance-test.

How could you advertise your business and test effectiveness with chi-squared? Are the applications of chi-squared limited to web advertising?

TEST YOURSELF

☑   **After you've completed the questions below, check your answers online.**

1   What are degrees of freedom for each of the following situations:

   a $n = 28$, $k = 6$, goodness-of-fit.
   b $n = 200$, $k_1 = 10$, $k_2 = 2$, test of independence.
   c $n = 130$, $k_1 = 5$, $k_2 = 8$, test of independence.
   d $n = 5$, $k = 2$, goodness-of-fit.

2.   Identify the critical value for each of the following situations:

   a   d.f. = 3, $\alpha = .05$.
   b   d.f. = 1, $\alpha = .01$.
   c   d.f. = 6, $\alpha = .05$.
   d   d.f. = 24, $\alpha = .01$.

3.   Given this result from a chi-square goodness-of-fit test: $\chi^2(2) = 2.48$, $p > .05$:

   a   How many groups were compared?
   b   What was alpha?

   c What was the critical value?

   d Did the researcher conclude the difference was statistically significant?

4. A researcher selects a sample of 40 people to investigate the relationship between brand preference (Brand A or Brand B) and gender (male or female). Of the 20 males in the sample, five prefer Brand A. Of the 20 females in the sample, 12 prefer Brand A. Based on the information in this scenario:

   a What is the expected frequency for females who prefer Brand A?

   b What is the expected frequency for males who prefer Brand B?

   c What is the observed frequency for females who prefer Brand B?

   d What is the observed frequency for males who prefer Brand A?

DATA SKILL CHALLENGES

 After you've completed the questions below, check your answers online.

1 Maria decides to run a second focus group, comparing four of Chew With Flavour's gums to each other to determine which is preferred. Gum flavours A, B, C and D are picked 12, 7, 8 and 21 times, respectively. Complete the full hypothesis testing process, given these data.

2 Nandi is a manager of a paper company. He wants to update the look of his logo, so he asks a designer to create three options for a redesign. Nandi then asks his employees to vote on the logo they prefer – see Figure 11.50. Is there a clear preference among the logos or are they all chosen the same number of times? Complete the full hypothesis testing process, given these data.

Logo #	# of votes
1	14
2	16
3	25

FIGURE 11.50 Nandi's data for Data Skill Challenge 2

3 Chaitra from our Chapter 6 case study decides to track the number of accidents at the 12 manufacturing plants she manages. Right now, safety training is conducted by two separate units: one trains the day shift, while the other trains the night shift. Both are generally effective, but she is worried that the night-shift trainers aren't getting out to some of the plants further from the home office. Complete the full hypothesis testing process, given the observed numbers of accidents recorded in Figure 11.51, to see if accident counts by shift and by plant are related over the past year.

	1	2	3	4	5	6	7	8	9	10	11	12
Day	3	5	1	3	0	6	2	7	2	0	4	3
Night	4	7	0	1	1	7	0	6	9	13	6	12

FIGURE 11.51 Chaitra's data for Data Skill Challenge 3

4 Sebastian manages the food services division at an amusement park. He wants to know if there is an interaction between the type of food sold and the colour of the food cart. His carts currently sell hot dogs, ice cream and popcorn. Sebastian paints half of his food carts red and half blue. Sebastian records the number of sales for each food cart – the data are included in Figure 11.52.

(Continued)

(Continued)

Complete the full hypothesis testing process, given the observed numbers of sales recorded, to see if sale counts by food type and colour interact.

	Hot dogs	Ice cream	Popcorn
Red	10	8	15
Blue	12	22	19

FIGURE 11.52   Sebastian's data for Data Skill Challenge 4

NEW TERMS

contingency table: Cramér's V: goodness-of-fit: model: non-parametric tests: parametric tests: test of independence:

NEW STATISTICAL NOTATION AND FORMULAS

ϕ: phi coefficient, another name for Cramér's V when conducted on a 2×2 contingency table from a chi-squared test of independence

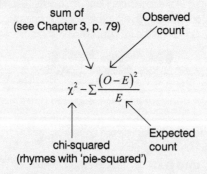

$$\chi^2 - \sum \frac{(O-E)^2}{E}$$

FIGURE 11.53   Annotated chi-square (χ^2) formula

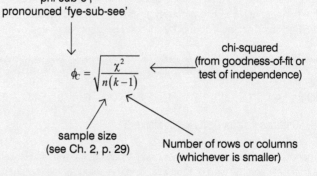

$$\phi_C = \sqrt{\frac{\chi^2}{n(k-1)}}$$

FIGURE 11.54   Annotated formula for Cramér's V

Visit https://study.sagepub.com/landers2e **for free additional online resources related to this chapter.**

12 CORRELATION AND REGRESSION

WHAT YOU WILL LEARN FROM THIS CHAPTER

- How to describe the difference between covariance and correlation
- How to identify when correlation is appropriate given the data available
- How to distinguish between magnitude and direction of correlation
- How to recognize different correlations by their scatterplot
- How to complete the hypothesis testing procedure for correlation
- How to determine when regression is appropriate
- How to compute and interpret the coefficient of determination

DATA SKILLS YOU WILL MASTER FROM THIS CHAPTER

- Computing a correlation
- Computing the coefficient of determination
- Deriving a regression line and predicting values from it

CASE STUDY   HOW MUCH VALUE ARE WE PROVIDING?

Ryan is the marketing manager for Smarter Sales, an organization that provides business intelligence to other businesses specializing in sales. Generally, their business model involves researching the client organization, conducting targeted surveys or interviews, implementing a change, and observing the effect on organizational profits.

For example, one of Smarter Sales' clients was Jill's Used Cars, who you may remember from Chapter 4. Jill hired Smarter Sales to conduct a survey of her customers. In that survey, Smarter Sales worked to identify the specific factors that were leading customers to walk off her used car lot without making a purchase. With the results of that survey, Jill

(Continued)

(Continued)

was able to change her staff's sales techniques to improve sales.

As marketing manager, Ryan's job is to find ways to bring in new clients. One of the problems that he faces is that Smarter Sales' services are often expensive. Employee time is recorded hourly, and this expense is billed directly to clients. However, Ryan wants to find a way to assure clients that this time and expense is worthwhile – that Smarter Sales only spends additional hours on a project when those hours will lead to higher profits.

To that end, Ryan collects records from all of Smarter Sales' clients over the past six months. He wants to find evidence that there is a relationship between the ultimate amount of money charged by Smarter Sales and the increase in organizational profitability.

That means he'll have two numbers for each client – the total cost to the client (in €) and the percentage increase in monthly profit as a result of changes suggested by Smarter

Sales. Each set of data will be paired; that is, he'll have two variables for each case.

In this textbook so far, he's read about two types of analyses that involve paired data. One is the paired-samples t-test he learned about in Chapter 9. But he doesn't want to know if there are differences between his cost and profits variables – he wants to know if there's a relationship! Given that, a paired-samples t-test can't be the right approach. The other test using paired data was the chi-square test of independence from Chapter 11.

That's closer to what Ryan wants – he wants to know if the two variables are related (that is, not independent). But the chi-square test of independence requires nominal data. His variables are both at a ratio scale of measurement – no categories to compare. So what should he do? How can he look for a relationship between two ratio-level variables?

Take a look at Ryan's costs and profit data for yourself in chapter12.xls (Excel) or chapter12.sav (SPSS).

Although the chi-square test of independence allows us to look for a relationship between two nominal variables, it is not very useful when we do not have specific categories within each variable for comparison. For example, although 'gender' can be split into specific categories (which can be placed in a contingency table quite easily), 'cost in €' cannot. In our case study, as in the real datasets you are likely to come across, you will have different values for *every* case when data are interval- or ratio-level scale of measurement.

To address this, we use two distinct but related analyses: correlation and regression. Each analysis produces one or more effect sizes that we can use to interpret the relationship between the variables. Additionally, we can conduct one-sample t-tests on the correlations to determine if the size of the relationship is significantly different from zero.

Although we must learn to calculate correlation and regression coefficients, the hypothesis testing process on those calculated numbers is very similar to what we've done before. As you read this chapter, consider the situations where correlation and regression would be most useful, as well as the similarities and differences between this analysis and those we covered earlier in this text.

12.1 QUANTIFYING RELATIONSHIPS WITH CORRELATION

In most of the other hypothesis tests in this book, we are concerned with differences. In *z*-tests, we examine the difference between a sample mean and a given population mean. In *t*-tests, we look at sample means, or differences between sample means, and examine the differences between those values and assumed values (usually zero). In ANOVA, we look at differences among multiple sample means, and in post-hoc tests we look at differences between each group mean. In chi-square goodness-of-fit, we examine differences between each observed count and expected counts.

In chi-square test of independence, for the first time we did not look for a difference. Instead, we assumed the two variables being analysed were independent of one another and looked for evidence to show otherwise.

In other words, we were interested in the relationship between those two variables. Did we get unique counts when Variable A was a particular value and Variable B was another particular value?

When the two variables are interval- or ratio-level scale of measurement, we are typically no longer concerned with specific levels because our data are often continuous (see Chapter 1, p. 10). With continuous data, there are too many possible values for categorical labels to be helpful. So how do we summarize the relationship between two such quantitative variables?

The most common approach is to compute a correlation coefficient. There are many types of correlation but all of them are descriptive statistics that summarize the relationship between two variables with a single number. The most common correlation is the Pearson's product-moment correlation coefficient, also called Pearson's r, which is an index of linear relationship between two variables.

There were several new terms in that sentence, so let's break it down. First of all, the name Pearson's product-moment correlation (PPMC) coefficient is very long and complicated. It is also the name of the *most common* correlation used today. As a result of its popularity, the word 'correlation' has itself become shorthand for a PPMC. In other words, if a non-professional statistician asks you, 'What's the value of the correlation?', they are almost always referring to PPMC. In this textbook, we'll generally follow this convention too: without any other context, 'correlation' will usually refer to PPMC.

'Correlation' is also a commonly misused word. To people unfamiliar with statistics, the word correlation is used as a synonym for 'relationship'. However, 'correlation' and 'relationship' are not the same. A correlation is a number used to summarize a relationship. Although one can calculate a PPMC with the hope of summarizing the relationship between two variables, the PPMC does not necessarily describe that relationship – it only describes the extent to which the variables are *linearly* related.

So what is a linear relationship? The term 'linear', on its own, refers to a straight line. So when we say 'linear relationship', we are really trying to determine how well the relationship between those two variables can be summarized with a straight line (you can see several examples of linear relationships in the scatterplots in Figure 12.01).

Each of the cells in Figure 12.01 represents a dataset with $n = 200$. You can see the shape of the correlation based upon the spread of cases, along with the value of the correlation for that cell.

When looking at this figure, you might think to yourself: 'so that correlation is .5 − .5 of what?' The answer is: nothing. We called correlation an 'index' because it does not have meaningful units. Instead, the only value of correlation by itself is to compare it with other correlations. However, in this regard, it can be very useful.

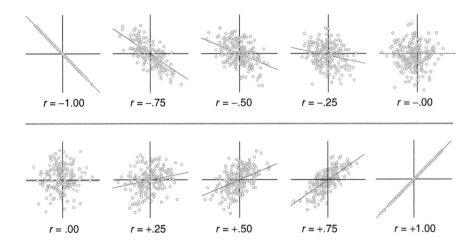

$r = .00$ $r = +.25$ $r = +.50$ $r = +.75$ $r = +1.00$

FIGURE 12.01   Illustration of positive and negative correlations ranging from −1 to +1

Given that, it's critical to recognize generally what the different values of correlation look like, so take a moment to become familiar with Figure 12.01. There are two rules that govern the actual value of a correlation:

1 Magnitude. The closer the correlation is to −1 or +1, the stronger the linear relationship. You can see the two strongest relationships in Figure 12.01 at $r = -1.00$ and $r = +1.00$. For every value of the first variable, there is one and only one possible value for the second variable. We call these perfect relationships. The absence of a relationship is depicted at $r = .00$ – the variables are completely unrelated, so the scatterplot appears to be a shapeless cloud of data.

2 Direction. There are two possible directions for linear relationships: positive (+) and negative (−). In positive relationships, both variables go in the same direction at the same time; for example, in our case study, as costs go up, profits go up (and the reverse: as costs go down, profits go down). In negative relationships, one variable goes up while the other goes down. For example, decreased employee salaries are associated with increased unexpected absences.

Each of these rules affects the value of correlation differently. Magnitude only affects the number itself (0 to 1), while direction affects the sign (+ or −). Thus, $r = -.7$ is a *stronger* relationship than $r = .5$, although the number itself is larger ($.5 > -.7$).

Next, we'll learn how to actually compute the value of correlation.

WHAT ABOUT LINES THAT AREN'T STRAIGHT?

After reading about linear relationships, you might wonder if two variables can be related in the shape of a curve. Short answer: yes, but these relationships are far less common than linear ones. Relationships that can be best summarized with a curved line are called curvilinear relationships, and the statistics you learn in this chapter won't work very well on them.

For example, if you ran a business that serves coffee early in the morning and the midday meal at noon, you might expect a curvilinear relationship between time since opening and monetary value of sales: from store opening to 8 a.m. store sales are consistent and high (for the morning rush), from 8 a.m. to 11 a.m. they are slow but stable, at 11 a.m. they begin to climb until a peak at 1 p.m. (for the midday rush), followed by a sharp drop until store closing. Although there is a relationship between time and sales, it is a curvilinear relationship. As a result, it would not be described well by a statistic summarizing *linear* relationships. We'll discuss this (and what your options would be in such a situation) more in Chapter 13.

12.2 THE LOGIC BEHIND CORRELATION

Correlation is actually derived from another statistic called the covariance – see Figure 12.02.

$$\mathrm{cov} = \frac{\sum(x - \bar{x})(y - \bar{y})}{n - 1}$$

FIGURE 12.02   Formula for covariance

In this formula, we treat the first variable as x and the second variable as y. It doesn't matter which is which – just that you keep them consistent.

If you can remember way back to Chapter 3, the covariance should look a bit familiar. Figure 12.03 shows the conceptual formula for variance.

$$s^2 = \frac{\sum(x - \bar{x})^2}{n - 1}$$

FIGURE 12.03   Formula for variance, for comparison with covariance formula

There are many similarities between covariance and variance. But what's important here is the one major difference: instead of squaring the difference between each value and its mean, we multiply the difference between each value and its own mean across *two* variables.

When calculating variance, if we have a lot of scores that are close to the mean, we end up with a small variance. If we have a lot of scores that are far away from the mean, we end up with a larger variance (review Chapter 3 if this doesn't seem familiar).

By multiplying across two variables, we make this slightly more complicated but end up describing the relationship between the variables instead of either variable alone. If *either* of the values in each pair is small, we end up with a small covariance. If *both* of the values in each pair are small, we end up with a value near zero. However, if *both* of the variables are large, the covariance gets larger. Since we divide by degrees of freedom, this calculation ultimately produces the average distance each pair of values is from forming a straight line. Consider the example in Figure 12.04.

In this scatterplot, the amounts that four scores contribute to covariance are highlighted. When the value on both x and y are large and the same, covariance increases a lot. The closer one or both variances is to zero, the less covariance increases.

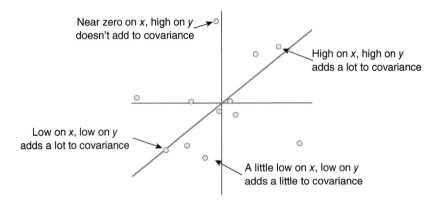

FIGURE 12.04   Annotated scatterplot demonstrating the effect of score placement on covariance

More scores close to the line (the linear relationship) produce a larger covariance. More scores far away from the line produce a smaller covariance. In this way, covariance captures how close the dataset is to a straight line (that is, a linear relationship).

However, there's one major problem with covariance – it depends entirely on the natural scale of the variances being measured. If we compute the covariance on a dataset with values ranging from 1 to 10 and another dataset with values ranging from 10000 to 20000, the covariance for the second dataset will be much, much larger. That means that a covariance of '100', without context, could mean anything – it could be a strong or weak relationship.

In Chapter 8, we learned that standardized effect sizes allow us to more easily compare the size of effects across studies. We use the same technique to make covariance more interpretable: we standardize it. A correlation is, in fact, a standardized covariance; we remove the original scales of measurement so that it always varies from -1 to $+1$, regardless of what the original data looked like. This is why correlation is an index; we get rid of the natural scales on purpose so that we can compute correlations across datasets. We always know, regardless of the original measurement, that a correlation of .6 represents a stronger relationship than a correlation of .5. We cannot make the same conclusion about covariance.

Correlation is standardized by dividing by each variable's standard deviation. It is otherwise identical to the covariance formula – see Figure 12.05.

$$r = \frac{\sum(x - \bar{x})(y - \bar{y})}{(n-1)s_x s_y}$$

FIGURE 12.05   Conceptual formula for correlation, based upon covariance formula

Correlation can also be expressed in terms of z-scores, if you happen to have z-scores available for both variables – see Figure 12.06.

$$r = \frac{\sum z_x z_y}{n-1}$$

FIGURE 12.06   Conceptual formula for correlation, using z-scores

If you compare these two formulas closely, you will see two z-score formulas embedded in the first formula – score minus mean, divided by standard deviation (once for x, once for y).

12.3 CALCULATING CORRELATION

The formulas above are conceptual formulas for correlation, and they both involve a lot of subtraction and small, potentially many-decimal-placed, calculations. As in previous chapters, we try to avoid extensive subtraction whenever possible to reduce computational errors. Thus we'll use the computational formula for correlation instead. It looks more complicated, but it is substantially easier to compute by hand – see Figure 12.07.

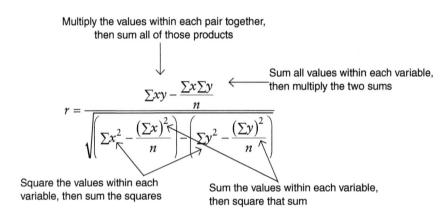

Multiply the values within each pair together, then sum all of those products

Sum all values within each variable, then multiply the two sums

$$r = \frac{\sum xy - \dfrac{\sum x \sum y}{n}}{\sqrt{\left(\sum x^2 - \dfrac{(\sum x)^2}{n}\right)\left(\sum y^2 - \dfrac{(\sum y)^2}{n}\right)}}$$

Square the values within each variable, then sum the squares

Sum the values within each variable, then square that sum

FIGURE 12.07   Annotated computational formula for correlation

While this may appear intimidating, this formula implies you'll only need five unique values for each line of your dataset, each of which is fairly easy to compute: x, y, x^2, y^2 and xy. Ryan's dataset appears in Figure 12.08.

Cost (in hundreds of euros)	Percentage increase in monthly profit
256	53
281	71
131	38
95	51
329	64
358	50
291	65
153	54
205	45
485	72
183	39
201	67

FIGURE 12.08   Chapter 12 case study dataset

With the dataset, we already have the x and y columns. Add the three remaining required columns and solve, as shown in Figure 12.09.

Cost (in hundreds of euros) (x)	Percentage increase in monthly profit (y)	x^2	y^2	xy
256	53	256 * 256 = 65536	53 * 53 = 2809	256 * 53 = 13568
281	71	281 * 281 = 78961	71 * 71 = 5041	281 * 71 = 19951
131	38	131 * 131 = 17161	38 * 38 = 1444	131 * 38 = 4978
95	51	95 * 95 = 9025	51 * 51 = 2601	95 * 51 = 4845
329	64	329 * 329 = 108241	64 * 64 = 4096	329 * 64 = 21056
358	50	358 * 358 = 128164	50 * 50 = 2500	358 * 50 = 17900
291	65	291 * 291 = 84681	65 * 65 = 4225	291 * 65 = 18915
153	54	153 * 153 = 23409	54 * 54 = 2916	153 * 54 = 8262
205	45	205 * 205 = 42025	45 * 45 = 2025	205 * 45 = 9225
485	72	485 * 485 = 235225	72 * 72 = 5184	485 * 72 = 34920
183	39	183 * 183 = 33489	39 * 39 = 1521	183 * 39 = 7137
201	67	201 * 201 = 40401	67 * 67 = 4489	201 * 67 = 13467

FIGURE 12.09   Chapter 12 case study dataset with added columns for calculation of correlation

Next, calculate each of the required sums:

Σx = 256 + 281 + 131 + 95 + 329 + 358 + 291 + 153 + 205 + 485 + 183 + 201 = 2968

Σy = 53 + 71 + 38 + 51 + 64 + 50 + 65 + 54 + 45 + 72 + 39 + 67 = 669

Σx^2 = 65536 + 78961 + 17161 + 9025 + 108241 + 128164 + 84681 + 23409 + 42025 + 235225 + 33489 + 40401 = 866318

Σy^2 = 2809 + 5041 + 1444 + 2601 + 4096 + 2500 + 4225 + 2916 + 2025 + 5184 + 1521 + 4489 = 38851

Σxy = 13568 + 19951 + 4978 + 4845 + 21056 + 17900 + 18915 + 8262 + 9225 + 34920 + 7137 + 13467 = 174224

Finally, plug these values into the formula (Figure 12.10).

From this, we can descriptively conclude that the correlation between cost and profits is .61. But is this correlation likely to have occurred by chance, if the population correlation were really zero? This is where we return to the familiar process of hypothesis testing.

12.3.1 CORRELATION: STEP 1 (STATE THE RESEARCH QUESTION)

In our case study, Ryan has one major question: are client costs (in €) and increase in profits (as a percentage) related? Research questions involving correlation always require two paired variables with interval- or ratio-level measurement.

$$r = \frac{\sum xy - \frac{\sum x \sum y}{n}}{\sqrt{\left(\sum x^2 - \frac{(\sum x)^2}{n}\right)\left(\sum y^2 - \frac{(\sum y)^2}{n}\right)}}$$

$$= \frac{174224 - \frac{2968 * 669}{12}}{\sqrt{\left(866318 - \frac{(2968)^2}{12}\right)\left(38851 - \frac{(669)^2}{12}\right)}}$$

$$= \frac{174224 - 165466}{\sqrt{(866318 - 734085)(38851 - 37296.75)}}$$

$$= \frac{8758}{\sqrt{(132233)(1554.25)}}$$

$$= \frac{8758}{14336.078273}$$

$$= .610906$$

$$= .61$$

FIGURE 12.10   Step by step formula for calculating correlation

In the stated research question, when calculating a Pearson's r, we must remember to stress that we are looking for a *linear* relationship.

RQ: Is there a linear relationship between client costs and percentage increase in profits?

12.3.2 CORRELATION: STEP 2 (STATE THE HYPOTHESES)

Although it is possible to conduct directional tests on correlation, this is rarely justified in practice. For our purposes here, we will assume all hypothesis tests of correlation are two-tailed.

All hypotheses involving parametric tests refer to parameters instead of statistics. We are interested in determining if the observed samples came from some hypothetical population of interest. In the case of z-tests, t-tests and ANOVA, our hypotheses involved testing against the values of μ, μ_D and $\mu_1 - \mu_2$. That's because we were comparing our sample means to these values.

That means, in the case of correlation, we need a parameter to represent a population correlation. The symbol for the population correlation is the Greek character ρ (rho; pronounced 'roe'). Other than the change in parameter, these hypotheses should look quite familiar:

H_0: $\rho = 0$

H_1: $\rho \neq 0$

12.3.3 CORRELATION: STEP 3 (SET SIGNIFICANCE LEVEL AND DECISION RULE)

As in all prior tests, lacking any information or rationale to the contrary, we will set $\alpha = .05$.

To determine the statistical significance of a correlation, we will actually conduct a one-sample t- test with $n - 2$ degrees of freedom. In this case, Ryan's sample has 12 cases, so $n - 12 = 10$. Using the technique you learned in Chapter 6 (see p. 178), look up the critical value for a two-tailed test with 10 degrees of freedom. You should find:

$$t_{crit}(10) = \pm 2.228$$

12.3.4 CORRELATION: STEP 4 (COLLECT A SAMPLE)

As in all other hypothesis tests, now is a good time to collect all the information we have so far in one place before actually collecting any data.

RQ: Is there a linear relationship between client costs and percentage increase in profits?

$H_0: r = 0$
$H_1: r \neq 0$
$\alpha = .05$
$t_{crit}(10) = \pm 2.228$

We've gone a little out of order this chapter (which is not typically a problem), but given our traditional set up, Ryan would now conduct his study, finding data from 12 clients.

12.3.5 CORRELATION: STEP 5 (CONDUCT STATISTICAL TEST)

To actually conduct the hypothesis test on correlation, we must now convert that correlation to a t- statistic. Fortunately, the formula is not very complicated – see Figure 12.11.

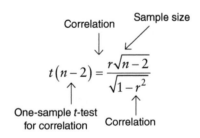

$$t(n-2) = \frac{r\sqrt{n-2}}{\sqrt{1-r^2}}$$

FIGURE 12.11   Annotated formula for conducting a t-test on a correlation

To compute it, we only need the sample size ($n = 12$) and the correlation (which we already computed: $r = +.610906$; remember to use the six-digit version) – see Figure 12.12.

$$t(10) = \frac{0.610906\sqrt{12-2}}{\sqrt{1-.610906^2}}$$

$$= \frac{0.610906\sqrt{10}}{\sqrt{1-.373206}}$$

$$= \frac{0.610906\sqrt{10}}{\sqrt{1-.373206}}$$

$$= \frac{(.610906 * 3.162278)}{\sqrt{.626794}}$$

$$= \frac{1.931855}{.791703}$$

$$= 2.440126$$

$$= +2.44$$

FIGURE 12.12   Step by step calculation of a t-test on a correlation

12.3.6 CORRELATION: STEP 6 (FORMALLY STATE RESULTS)

The procedure for formally stating results for correlation is a little different than for a one-sample t-test. First, we will look for the region of rejection just as we would have for one-sample t – see Figure 12.13.

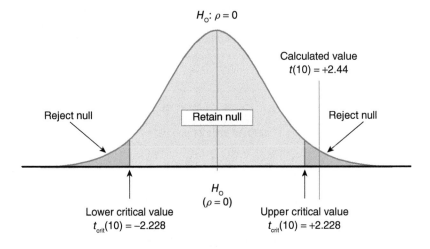

FIGURE 12.13   Sampling distribution for ρ and t in sample problem

Our observed t-statistic is in the region of rejection, so we will reject the null hypothesis and accept the alternative. However, when we report this, we will report the value of the correlation instead. The p-value is based upon the t-test, however:

$r(10) = .61, p < .05$

12.3.7 CORRELATION: STEP 7 (CONDUCT SUPPLEMENTAL ANALYSES)

As with most previous tests, if we do not find statistical significance, we do not conduct any supplemental analyses. However, if we do find statistical significance, we have one or two extra steps.

First, we always compute the coefficient of determination. This is also an effect size measure (like correlation), but it is more easily interpretable than correlation.

Second, we may also conduct a regression analysis. This is optional, and only conducted if you need the results of regression. We'll cover this in more detail below.

12.3.7.1 COEFFICIENT OF DETERMINATION

First, we must compute the coefficient of determination. The calculation for this is very easy: it's r^2. In this case, since $r = .610906$, $r^2 = .610906^2 = .373206 = .37$.

We compute the coefficient of determination because it is much easier to interpret than correlation. With correlation, the most complex conclusion we can make is 'this correlation is bigger than that correlation' or 'this correlation is significantly different from zero'. For more precise conclusions, we need r^2.

r^2 can be interpreted as the proportion of variance in one variable that can be explained by the variance in the other variable. For example, since $r^2 = .37$ in our case study, 37% of the variance in profits can be explained by the variance in costs. We can also conclude that 37% of the variance in costs can be explained by the variance in profits – both directions are correct.

So what exactly does that mean? Remember that variance captures the extent to which scores within a variable vary from the mean. The more they vary from the mean, the greater the variance. When we have two variables, each has its own variance. To some extent, those variances overlap – this is what we call covariance. We can use the variance in one variable to explain some portion of the variance in the other variable – see Figure 12.14.

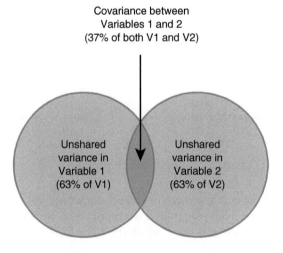

FIGURE 12.14   Venn diagram demonstrating allocation of variance in case study dataset

The goal of the coefficient of determination is to quantify this overlap. What percentage of each variable is explained by the other? In this case: 37%.

12.3.7.2 SIMPLE LINEAR REGRESSION

The term regression actually describes an entire family of analyses used to predict one variable from another. They seek to answer the question, 'Given a particular value for one variable, what would we expect the value of a particular paired variable to be?'

For example, one well-known relationship that is sometimes demonstrated in college statistics labs is the relationship between height and the distance of a standing long jump. Each student jumps as far as they can, and their height is also measured. These two characteristics are correlated strongly – typically around $r = .7$ in university classrooms. With regression, we can take the analysis a step further by making conclusions like, 'Jimmy is 5 foot 11 inches (1.8 meters) tall; how far would we expect him to jump?'

There are many types of regression. In fact, regression analysis can be used as a statistical test of interest without ever computing a correlation. However, the only form of regression we'll be covering in this textbook is simple linear regression, which is the prediction of exactly one interval- or ratio-level variable from exactly one other interval- or ratio-level variable. These are the same requirements as Pearson's r. If you want to use more than one variable on either side, you'll need a more complicated form.

At the core of all regression analysis is the creation of the regression line, also called the line of best fit. You've actually seen several regression lines in this textbook already; each of the scatterplots of correlations in Figure 12.01 contains a red regression line. Let's get a close-up of one such line to explore it a bit more – see Figure 12.15.

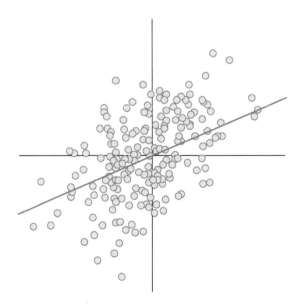

FIGURE 12.15 Scatterplot demonstrating $r = .75$ with red regression line

The red line in this scatterplot is the only possible regression line for these data because it describes ('fits') the data better than any other line can. It does this by computing the line that minimizes the sum of squared vertical deviations between each data point and the line.

Let's look at a more detailed example, with only ten cases, in Figure 12.16.

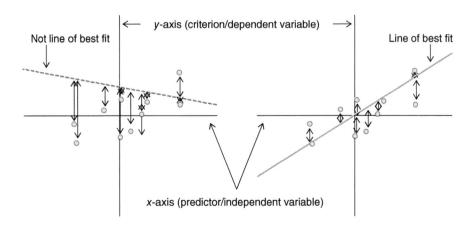

FIGURE 12.16   Side-by-side comparison of deviations from randomly drawn line versus line of best fit

In Figure 12.16, the two scatterplots (that is, the datasets themselves) are identical. The only difference between the two is where the line is drawn. In the left scatterplot, I've drawn a dotted line. You can see that the distances between my dashed red line and the actual data are quite large. These distances are called residuals. There are many points below the dashed line and not many above the line. In statistical terms, the dashed line does not fit the data well. The residuals are quite large. There are an infinite number of poorly fitting lines that I could have drawn here.

In the right scatterplot, I've drawn the line of best fit from a regression analysis as a continuous red line. You can see that the line slices cleanly between all of the data, resulting in very small deviations at all points on the line. There is only one line of best fit for any given dataset which minimizes the sum of the squared residuals (that's why it's the 'best'!). Every other possible line (like the dashed line) will result in a larger sum of squared residuals than the line of best fit. That's why regression can also be called least squares regression. The end of the analysis produces the line with the smallest sum of squared residuals possible.

The ultimate result of regression analysis is a formula to describe this line. Figure 12.17 gives the prototype for that formula in simple linear regression.

Predicted *y*-value ('*y* prime')

A given *x*-value

$$y' = bx + a \quad \leftarrow \quad \text{*y*-intercept of the regression line}$$

Slope of the regression line

FIGURE 12.17   Annotated formula prototyping the regression line from simple linear regression

Since the purpose of regression analysis is to create a useful formula, we must calculate the value of b (the slope) and the value of a (the y-intercept). An example of a solved regression formula looks like this:

$$y' = .5x + 2$$

Regression always works by using values on the x-axis to predict values on the y-axis. That means that unlike correlation, the order of variables in regression is important. If you put a variable on the wrong axis, you'll get an entirely different answer than what you want. For example, in our case study, would Ryan want to predict costs from profits or profits from costs?

Since Ryan believes increased costs lead to increased profits, 'costs' is his predictor, whereas 'profits' is his criterion. We always predict a criterion from a predictor.

Regression also uses somewhat confusing shorthand to describe the relationship between variables. We regress a criterion *on* a predictor. The order here is important – when using the word 'on', we always say the criterion first. Since Ryan is predicting profits from costs, we would say that Ryan is regressing 'profits on costs'.

The formula for the regression line involves some concepts that you might remember from geometry (slopes and intercepts). But if they seem unfamiliar, let's review them in Figure 12.18.

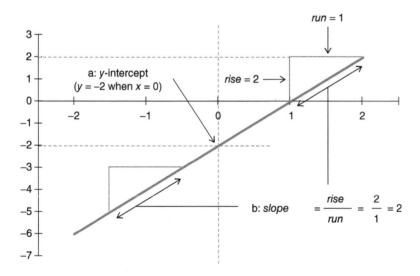

FIGURE 12.18   Annotated figure depicting $y = 2x - 2$

In this graph, the solid red line represents the regression line $y = 2x - 1$. In this regression line, '2' is the slope (the value of b). This means that for every one point increase in x, y increases two points. You can see this in Figure 12.18. Similarly, if the slope was .5 (that is, ½), a two point increase in x would be associated with a one point increase in y.

The y-intercept represents the value of y when $x = 0$. In the figure, when $x = 0$ (the vertical red dashed line), $y = -1$. Thus, -1 is the y-intercept (the value of a).

CORRELATION IS NOT CAUSATION

Although we are predicting profits from costs, that does not necessarily mean that increased costs *cause* increased profits. The only way to show that anything causes anything else is *experimental design*. We talked about experiments in Chapter 1 (see p. 13).

The case study is not an experiment. It is a correlational study (see p. 13). In a correlational study, we cannot ever show causation statistically. Instead, Ryan must make a logical argument that setting cost as the predictor and profit as the criterion is a reasonable thing to do.

This can be risky. Consider this potentially alarming fact: there is a correlation between ice cream sales and murder! Looking across the year, as ice cream sales increase, so does the murder rate. Does that mean ice cream sales cause murder? Or, perhaps even more troubling, that murder causes ice cream sales?!

Certainly not! There is a third, omitted, variable that is causing both: heat. In the summer, it becomes warm, sticky and unpleasant. Because it's warm, more people purchase ice cream. But also because of the warmth, tempers run hot and the murder rate increases. The relationship between ice cream sales and murder is in fact the result of an unmeasured third variable (heat) which causes both.

Although you are unlikely to be considering murder variables in your own work, this highlights the importance of not confusing correlation with causation. The only process that demonstrates causation is experimental design – not statistics! If you want to know how to demonstrate causality, a research methods text will help you learn how.

12.3.7.3 DETERMINING THE REGRESSION LINE

The calculation for the slope is pretty straightforward, assuming you have already calculated the correlation – see Figure 12.19.

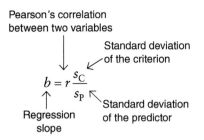

FIGURE 12.19   Annotated formula for a regression slope in simple linear regression

Since Ryan wants to predict profits from costs, profits will be our criterion while costs will be our predictor. Use the standard deviation formula from Chapter 3 (see p. 90) to determine the value for each s. If you do so correctly, you should find:

$$s_C = 11.886776$$

$$s_p = 109.641012$$

We can then plug these values plus the value of our correlation from earlier into the formula – see Figure 12.20.

$$b = r\frac{s_C}{s_P}$$
$$= .610906\frac{11.886776}{109.641012}$$
$$= .610906*.108415$$
$$= .066231 = .07$$

FIGURE 12.20   Step by step computation of a regression slope in simple linear regression

Next, we calculate the intercept with the formula shown in Figure 12.21.

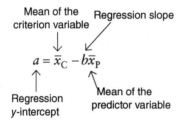

FIGURE 12.21   Annotated formula for the y-intercept in simple linear regression

Again, using the mean formulas from Chapter 3 (see p. 83) to determine the value for each:

$$\bar{x}_C = 55.75$$

$$\bar{x}_P = 247.333333$$

Finally, plug these values plus the slope we just calculated into the formula to determine the value of a:

$$a = \bar{x}_C - b\bar{x}_P$$
$$= 55.75 - 0.066231*247.333333$$
$$= 55.75 - 16.381134 = 39.368866$$
$$= 39.37$$

Thus, the final value of our regression line is:

$$y' = .07x + 39.37$$

For interpretation, the slope is most useful. In this case, for every hundred euros spent, we'd expect a .07% increase in profit.

12.3.7.4 PREDICTING VALUES FROM A REGRESSION LINE

Once we have a regression line, we can quite easily predict new values of the criterion given any value of x in which we're interested. First, write out your regression line (before rounding):

$$y' = .066231x + 39.368866$$

Remember that y' means 'predicted y' – that's what we need to solve for. Next, replace x with the value of the predictor you want to use. Once solved, this will provide you with the y-value of the regression line given that x. For example, if we wanted to predict what percentage increase in profits is most likely given 20000 euros (200 hundreds) spent, we replace x with 200, as in Figure 12.22.

$$
\begin{aligned}
y' &= .066231x + 39.368866 \\
&= .066231 * 200 + 39.368866 \\
&= 13.2462 + 39.368866 \\
&= 52.615066 \\
&= 52.62
\end{aligned}
$$

FIGURE 12.22   Step by step calculation for predicted value from a regression line

Thus, we'd expect a 52.62% increase in profits if the client spent 20000.

When predicting y-values from x-values, it's important to use x-values only within the range of the dataset's x-values. In this case study, costs ranged from 95000 to 48500, so numbers between 95 and 485 are the only ones we can use this way. We restrict ourselves this way because it's safer. Since there's no way to know if the regression line beyond the values we measured begins to curve, we simply do not look at those values without collecting more data first.

12.3.7.5 WHEN TO CONDUCT A REGRESSION

If all you want to know is 'is there a relationship?', a regression analysis is not needed. Correlation is sufficient. Regression is specifically used when you want to predict one variable from the other. If you need the formula for the regression line, for example if you wanted to predict specific values of one variable from the other, you should conduct a regression then.

Therefore, three things need to be true to justify a simple linear regression in addition to correlation:

1 The correlation is statistically significant.

2 There is some reason to assign one variable to be the predictor and the other to be the criterion.

3 You need to predict that criterion from the predictor.

While a simple linear regression can be calculated on its own (without correlation), the *p*-value associated with the slope (i.e. 'is this slope significantly different from zero?') is always equal to the *p*-value associated with the correlation (i.e. 'is this correlation significantly different from zero?'). Therefore, if you are only interested in one predictor and one criterion, correlation is easier to calculate first and allows you to compare that value with other correlations.

Regardless, remember that *correlation is not causation*. Conducting a regression analysis does not change this. Although you have chosen a *y* and an *x*, you cannot conclude that the *x* causes *y* without an appropriate experimental design. If you have not conducted an experiment – as in this case study – you can only conclude that the variables are related.

12.3.8 CORRELATION: STEP 8 (DRAW ALL CONCLUSIONS)

Correlation is a little unusual in that you may conduct regression analysis separately. Pay careful attention to the requirements of the situation (or the word problem!) to determine whether or not you need a regression line.

RQ: Is there a linear relationship between client costs and percentage increase in profits?

$H_0: r = 0$

$H_1: r \neq 0$

$\alpha = .05$

$t_{crit}(10) = \pm 2.228$

$r(10) = .61, p < .05$

$r^2 = .37$

$y' = .07x + 39.37$

Conclusion: Reject the null and accept the alternative. The correlation is statistically significant. There is a linear relationship between client costs and percentage increase in profits. 37% of the variance in percentage increase in profits was explained by the variance in client costs. For every hundred euros spent, we'd expect a .07% increase in profit.

Ryan might use this information to put together projected profits based upon project costs for clients. However, he must be careful. Since he didn't run an experiment, he can't say, 'If you spent more money, you'll make greater profits!' He can only conclude that the two are related. While that's promising (and good to know!), it doesn't demonstrate causality.

12.4 BEYOND REGRESSION

While we've discussed regression here as a supplemental analytic tool, it is also a powerful tool itself. The type of regression covered above is called simple linear regression because it is only the most simple of an entire family of regression analyses. A common, more powerful, type of regression is multiple regression. This analytic approach still produces a single regression line, but it incorporates multiple predictors. This also enables us to examine interactions, just as we do in n-way ANOVA and the chi-squared test of independence.

For example, although our case study's Ryan predicted client profits from costs, he might hypothesize that this relationship is stronger when the project team consists of more-experienced personnel. Thus, he could regress profits on both costs and the percentage of experienced personnel. This is therefore an example of multiple regression.

The difference between this and other interaction-focused analyses is again scale of measurement. The interaction between two or more grouping (nominal) variables predicting an interval- or ratio-level variable is examined by n-way ANOVA. The chi-squared test of independence examines the interaction between two nominal counts. Multiple regression examines the interaction between two interval- or ratio-level variables in predicting another interval- or ratio-level variable. And perhaps even more valuably, it can produce a single regression line incorporating all of that information.

Regression, multiple regression, and even ANOVA and t- tests are all specific cases of the general linear model, which is a general purpose statistical approach to modelling relationships between variables. If you want to proceed in learning statistics beyond this text, the general linear model is your next step. Although we won't cover the general linear model in any further detail in this text, it is important to recognise when you have a research question sufficiently complex that you will be required to take that next step.

12.5 APPLYING CORRELATION AND REGRESSION

To apply what you've learned from this chapter, consider the following case study, questions posed about that case study, and discussion of those questions.

12.5.1 APPLICATION CASE STUDY

Sofia is the owner of Recommend to Renovate, a residential housing general contractor. She is hired by homeowners, hiring and coordinating workers who renovate houses. This involves a great deal of people management, because she needs to coordinate across many different professions: plumbers, electricians, framers, demolition experts, and so on. She also needs to ensure that each renovation job is still profitable despite the many hands seeking payment for services rendered.

Sofia takes on a wide variety of renovation projects, but she believes she has begun to notice a pattern: the big jobs never pay off. The complexity of the larger projects seems to result in substantially more overhead expenses than the smaller projects, ultimately leading to less profit for the amount of time spent on the job. If Sofia earns more money working only on smaller jobs, then she wants to prioritize smaller jobs. But she is not sure if she is imagining this pattern – she needs data.

To investigate this, Sofia looks through her records and notes the number of days required to complete each job, along with the average profit per day on the job.

1 What type of test does Sofia need here and why?

2 What is Sofia's research question?

3 What are the hypotheses?

4 If Sofia rejects the null, what can she conclude? What else should she do before making any broad conclusions?

5 If Sofia retains the null, what can she conclude?

12.5.2 APPLICATION DISCUSSION

We will again cover these questions one by one.

1 Sofia needs a correlation, because she is interested in the relationship between two ratio-level variables: number of days and a ratio of profit per day.

2 Sofia's research question: Is there a relationship between length of job and profit per day?

3 $H_0: \rho = 0$

$H_1: \rho \neq 0$

4 If Sofia rejects the null, she can conclude that there is a relationship between length of job and profit per day. However, this is not the end of her analysis. Regression of profit on days will tell her the difference in profit per day attributable to each additional day of work. For example, if she found a slope of -500, she could conclude that each additional day a project dragged on resulted in a loss of -500 profit per day. A larger number of small jobs would be likely to be more profitable than a small number of large jobs.

5 If Sofia retains the null, she can conclude that there is not enough evidence to support a relationship between the two variables.

EXPLORING CORRELATION AND REGRESSION IN EXCEL AND SPSS

EXCEL

Download the Excel dataset for the demonstration below as **chapter12.xls**. As you read this section, try to apply the terms you've learned in this chapter to the dataset and follow along with Excel on your own computer.

You can also get a video demonstration of the section below under **Excel Video: Chapter 12**.

Both correlations and simple linear regression can be conducted simultaneously in Excel. In the **Data Analysis** tool, select **Regression** – see Figure 12.23.

(Continued)

(Continued)

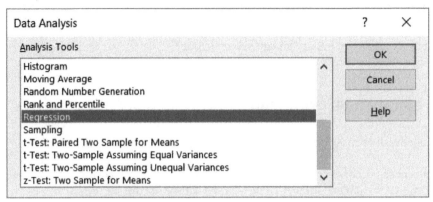

FIGURE 12.23 Excel data analysis tool, with regression analysis selected (used for both correlation and regression)

If you won't be using the results of the regression analysis, the choice of '*x*' versus '*y*' doesn't matter on the next screen. However, if you do want the regression line formula, correct specification here is very important.

In the case study, Ryan wants to predict profits from costs. That means 'cost' (in euros) is the predictor while 'perc_profit' (percentage increase in profit) is the criterion. Select the values in the profits column (including the label in Row 1) for 'Input Y Range' and the values in the costs column (including the label in Row 1) for 'Input X Range'. Also check 'Labels'. Specify a new worksheet called 'output'. When you've got everything updated, it should look like Figure 12.24.

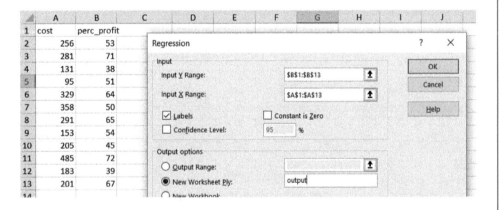

FIGURE 12.24 Excel data analysis regression dialogue, with options for case study data selected

Click **OK**.

A new worksheet will appear with several sections. The first tells us the correlation and r^2 (Figure 12.25).

	A	B
1	SUMMARY OUTPUT	
2		
3	*Regression Statistics*	
4	Multiple R	0.610907
5	R Square	0.373207
6	Adjusted R Square	0.310528
7	Standard Error	9.870119
8	Observations	12

FIGURE 12.25 Excel output for correlation data resulting from regression analysis

From this, we can conclude that $r = .61$, $r^2 = .37$ and $n = 12$ (and therefore: d.f. = 10).

The second output table contains information on ANOVA related to regression; we won't interpret this here. The third table provides details about statistical significance and the regression line – see Figure 12.26.

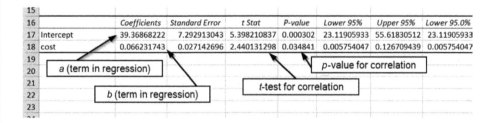

FIGURE 12.26 Annotated regression line information outputted by regression analysis in Excel

With the information from Figure 12.26, we can now conclude:

$r(10) = .61$, $p = .035$
$r^2 = .37$
$y' = .07x + 39.37$

If you need to predict a y , you can do so with a formula referencing the slope and intercept. For example, we could find the predicted value of y for $x = 200$ by typing: =B18*200+B17.

(Continued)

Both correlations and simple linear regression can be conducted simultaneously in SPSS. In the **Analyse** menu, select **Regression**, then **Linear** – see Figure 12.27.

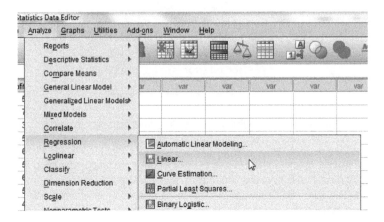

FIGURE 12.27   Menu option for linear regression in SPSS

If you only want to know the correlation between these two variables, the choice of 'independent' versus 'dependent' doesn't matter on the next screen. However, if you do want the formula for the regression line, correct specification here is very important.

In the case study, Ryan wants to predict profits from costs. That means 'cost' (in euros) is the predictor while 'perc_profit' (percentage increase in profit) is the criterion. Move the 'perc_profit' variable to 'Dependent' (another word for 'criterion') and the 'costs' variable to 'Independent' (another word for 'predictor') – see Figure 12.28.

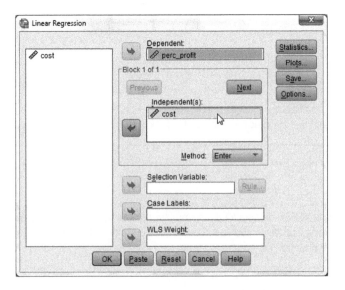

FIGURE 12.28   Linear regression dialogue box in SPSS, with case study data

Click **OK** and the Output Pane will pop up (Figure 12.29).

Model Summary

Model	R	R Square	Adjusted R Square	Std. Error of the Estimate
1	.611[a]	.373	.311	9.870

a. Predictors: (Constant), Costs to Client (in hundreds of euros)

FIGURE 12.29   First output table from SPSS regression analysis containing correlation and coefficient of determination

The Model Summary table provides you with the correlation and r^2. From this, we can conclude that $r = .61$ and $r^2 = .37$.

The second table contains information on ANOVA related to regression; we won't interpret this here.

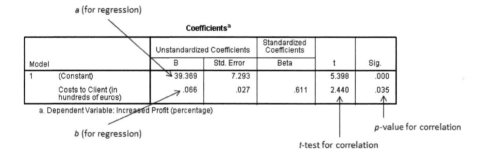

FIGURE 12.30   Annotated third output table from SPSS regression analysis containing regression line coefficients and p-value

Note that the table shown in Figure 12.30 does not report degrees of freedom. You can get this two ways. First, you could look at degrees of freedom in the ANOVA table in the 'Residual' row. Second, you could conduct descriptive statistics (for example, mean and standard deviation), and compute $n - 2$ on your own. With this information, combined with the information from the previous table, we can now conclude:

$r(10) = .61, p = .035$

$r^2 = .37$

$y' = .07x + 39.37$

(Continued)

STATISTICS IN THE REAL WORLD

These web links can be accessed directly from the book's website.

Writing for *Harvard Business Review*, Amy Gallo provides a rundown of regression analyses and their business applications: https://hbr.org/2015/11/a-refresher-on-regression-analysis.

What outcomes can you predict in your business using regression?

Writing for *PC Mag*, Rob Marvin describes what happens when regression and 'big data' collide: you end up with machine learning: www.pcmag.com/article/345858/predictive-analytics-big-data-and-how-to-make-them-work-for.

Much of what we now call 'machine learning' or 'artificial intelligence' is still regression, at its core. When might your organization benefit from machine learning, and when would regression be sufficient?

TEST YOURSELF

☑ **After you've completed the questions below, check your answers online.**

1. For each of the scatterplots shown in Figure 12.31, which of these correlations (-1, $-.7$, $-.5$, $-.3$, 0, $+.3$, $+.5$, $+.7$, $+1$) is the closest to the relationship depicted?

a)

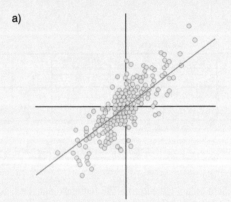

b)

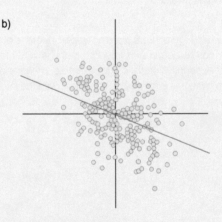

FIGURE 12.31   Scatterplots for Test Yourself Question 1

2. Which in each pair of correlations represents a stronger relationship?
   a .50 vs −.80.
   b .00 vs. 90.
   c −.90 vs −.60.
   d −.50 vs. 50

3. Can you compute Pearson's *r* in each of the following situations? Why or why not?
   a Sales to each customer (in €) vs customer satisfaction ratings (survey: 1–5).
   b Sales to each customer (in €) vs customer satisfaction ratings ('great' or 'bad').
   c Customer satisfaction ratings (survey: 1–5) vs number of purchases by each customer.
   d Customer satisfaction ratings (survey: 1–5) vs customer hair colour.

4. Given this result from a non-directional **Pearson's correlation**: $r(30) = +.02$, **$p > .05$**:
   a What was the sample size?
   b What was alpha?
   c What was the critical value?
   d Is the relationship positive or negative?
   e What was the value for *t*?
   f Did the researcher conclude the relationship was statistically significant?

DATA SKILL CHALLENGES

 After you've completed the questions below, check your answers online.

1. Sue from Tastetastic, way back in Chapter 3, discovered that her Dish 2 and Dish 7 shared several more ingredients than she thought. Do people perceive their flavour to be similar? Using the dataset from Chapter 3, answer Sue's question.
2. Jill from Jill's Used Cars in Chapter 4 wonders if she could have predicted August's sales by each employee from their July sales. If so, how many cars would she have expected someone to sell in August if they sold 14 in July? Using the dataset from Chapter 4, answer Jill's question.
3. Shane works at an ice cream store. He notices that on every warm day, his boss makes sure to stock extra supplies in anticipation of having a lot of customers. Shane decides to test whether he can predict the number of customers based on the temperature. If so, how many customers should he expect if the temperature is 38°C? He tracks the temperature and the number of customers for one week. His data are provided in Figure 12.32. By hand, using Excel, or using SPSS, conduct the full hypothesis testing procedure for his data and draw any appropriate conclusions.

Temperature (degrees C)	# of customers
22	28
25	24
29	32
28	33

(Continued)

(Continued)

Temperature (degrees C)	# of customers
35	52
32	47
30	45

FIGURE 12.32   Shane's data for Data Skill Challenge 3

4   Klaus is an office manager at a data entry company. He is interested in finding ways to improve employee productivity. Klaus wonders if the number of hours worked is related to productivity. To test this, he installs software on each of his employees' computers that measures how many cells of data they enter and how long they work. The data are provided in Figure 12.33. By hand, using Excel, or using SPSS, conduct the full hypothesis testing procedure for his data and draw any appropriate conclusions.

# of hours worked (in minutes)	# of cells entered
240	500
390	618
495	592
270	340
345	689
525	703
330	440
435	478

FIGURE 12.33   Klaus's data for Data Skill Challenge 4

NEW TERMS

coefficient of determination: correlation (coefficient): covariance: criterion: general linear model: index: line of best fit: linear relationship: Pearson's correlation: Pearson's product-moment correlation coefficient: Pearson's r: perfect relationship: predictor: regression: regression line: residual: simple linear regression:

Visit https://study.sagepub.com/landers2e **for free additional online resources related to this chapter.**

PART 3

WRAP-UP

Part 3 is a one-chapter Wrap-Up integrating everything you learned from Parts 1 and 2. Up to this point, we have covered statistical tests one at a time, but that's not how the real world works! Instead, you'll be faced with a research question and an opportunity to collect data, but not much else to go on.

In Chapter 13, we meet Clara, new director of human resources at a technology company. Clara has been tasked with improving employee job performance at her organization – not a small task. She collects many data but must now face the difficult decision of figuring out how to analyse them. By reading Chapter 13 with Clara, you'll learn how to make decisions regarding data in order to analyse them most appropriately. You'll also receive a great deal of practical advice on the various pitfalls and challenges commonly faced when doing so.

13 MATCHING STATISTICAL TESTS TO BUSINESS PROBLEMS

WHAT YOU WILL LEARN FROM THIS CHAPTER

- How to choose an approach to data analysis
- How to clean and annotate data to make analysis easier
- How to plan appropriately for later statistical analysis
- How to accurately interpret data
- How to fit the role of statistics into a larger analytic strategy

DATA SKILLS YOU WILL MASTER FROM THIS CHAPTER

- Determining which statistical test is appropriate given your data

CASE STUDY   HOW MUCH VALUE ARE WE PROVIDING?

Clara is the new Director of Human Resources at Quince Computers. Quince is a mid-sized company, specializing in the design, sales and support of a handheld music player called qPod. The company has approximately 1500 employees spread across five units: Sales, Technical Support, Administration, Research and Development, and Shipping and Receiving.

Quince has grown steadily but rapidly over the past five years. It began as a small technology start-up with only five employees (all of whom are now the executives in charge of the company!), but the qPod's explosive popularity has necessitated a rapid expansion of its workforce.

Unfortunately, this means that employee job performance has slowed. When the company was smaller and leaner, everyone pitched in to do their fair share. But now a general impression

(Continued)

(Continued)

from management is forming that some employees aren't working as hard as others.

Clara's first major responsibility is to fix this problem. Emboldened by her mastery of inferential statistics from reading this book, she decides the first step is to collect a variety of pieces of data from human resources files and see what's related to job performance. She collects gender, age, tenure, department, status as a full-time or part-time employee, and supervisory ratings of job performance

both now and from six months ago from 150 employees that have been working for Quince for at least six months.

But now that she has this large pile of data, she's not quite sure what to do with it. While she knows from Chapters 7 through 12 how to evaluate if a particular test is appropriate given the data, how do you know which test is best given a lot of data? Can she just run every possible test on these data and see what she finds? That seems haphazard, but what else can she do?

In the real world, data are usually big, unwieldy and ugly. We often have more variables than specific research questions about those variables. It is tempting to simply conduct as many tests as possible and see what comes up as 'statistically significant'.

Unfortunately, blindly conducting statistical tests like this can often do more harm than good. Statistics are inherently probabilistic, and the odds are not always in your favour. But with some careful consideration of your data and what they really have the power to tell you, you can avoid fooling yourself.

This chapter is split into two sections. In the first portion of this chapter, we'll discuss techniques for picking statistical tests given the data available. Although this has been provided in each chapter, here we'll discuss it as you'd face such a problem in a real business context: given a pile of data, what do you do with it? In the second portion of this chapter, we'll discuss specific stumbling points and challenges often faced by new statisticians trying to answer important questions for their businesses.

In that way, this chapter is a wrap-up of all the previous chapters in this book. As you read, consider how every concept, statistic and test we've covered are used in real business settings. If you have a job now, consider how data and statistical analysis would be used to answer the questions you have – and most importantly, think about how you could unwittingly mislead yourself if you forget the advice contained here.

13.1 DETERMINING THE APPROPRIATE TEST GIVEN THE DATA

FOUNDATION CONCEPTS

An **assumption** is a condition that must be true for a statistic to be meaningful. For example, data must be normally distributed for the mean to accurately represent central tendency. See Chapter 3, p. 80.

Robustness is the degree to which a statistic produces an accurate result even when its assumptions are not met. See Chapter 3, p. 84.

Way back in Chapter 3, we introduced the idea of assumptions. Every statistic has assumptions. For a statistic to be meaningful, the assumptions must be met. We also discussed the mean and standard deviation. For both to be meaningful, data must be normally distributed; thus, normality is an assumption of both these statistics. Each statistic is robust to minor deviations from perfect normality, but substantial skew will bias both.

A second assumption of mean and standard deviation is that you have independent data. For a mean calculated across cases to be meaningful, each case must come from a unique source of information. For example, consider the dataset in Figure 13.01.

Business unit	Season	Employee absences
Sales	Spring	5
Sales	Fall	4
Technical Support	All year	8

FIGURE 13.01   Example of non-independent data

In this dataset, the Sales unit absences are split into Spring and Autumn, while the Technical Support absences are all in one row. If we compute a mean on this, we'll be dividing by three. Since there are only two independent units (Sales and Technical Support), this inappropriately biases the mean towards Sales – it is counted twice. Thus, this is non-independent data, so mean and standard deviation are inappropriate.

In such cases, you have two options: (1) measure your variables again so that your data will be independent the second time, or (2) combine data. For example, because in this dataset absences have been split, we could add them together to create a new dataset, depicted in Figure 13.02.

Business unit	Season	Employee absences
Sales	All year	9
Technical Support	All year	8

FIGURE 13.02   Data from Figure 13.01 cleaned so that they are independent

Now the data are independent, so a mean would be appropriate for this revised dataset. Although addition was the solution for this dataset, it isn't always the correct approach. You must carefully think about what your data represent and how to change them so that cases are independent. Sometimes, this can be very complicated.

This concept is important now because every test we've covered in this textbook assumes independent data in some way. In the case of z-tests, one-sample t-tests, independent-samples t-tests, ANOVA and chi-square, every value being tested must be independent. In the case of paired-samples t-tests, correlation and regression, every *pair* must be independent. Every test *except* chi-square assumes normally distributed data as well.

The reason for this is that tests inherit the assumptions of all the statistics that they incorporate in their own calculations. For example, ANOVA includes in its calculations means and standard deviations; therefore, the assumptions of mean and standard deviation must be met for the results of ANOVA to be meaningful.

When choosing a test, if you can't avoid non-independent data or data that are not normally distributed, you haven't learned a test for that in this textbook. Many alternative tests exist, however. If you need one of these, you should have learned enough in this book to research it elsewhere. Figure 13.03 lists some possible alternatives to the tests we've learned here – if you need one, I suggest putting some of these terms into an online search engine. Note that these are not *necessarily* the test you need, but will point you in the right direction to discovering what the correct test is. Most of these tests are available in SPSS, and some are available in Excel.

Test we learned here	If non-normal data	If non-independent data
z-test	chi-square goodness-of-fit	N/A
One-sample *t*-test	chi-square goodness-of-fit	N/A
Paired-samples *t*-test	Wilcoxon signed-rank test	N/A
Independent-samples *t*-test	Mann-Whitney U test; rank-sum test	Paired-samples *t*-test; repeated-measures ANOVA
One-way ANOVA	Kruskal-Wallis Test	Repeated-measures ANOVA; Friedman's test
chi-square tests	N/A (χ^2 does not require normality)	McNemar's test
Correlation	Spearman's rho; Kendall's Tau	Intraclass correlation
Regression	nonparametric regression	Hierarchical linear modelling

FIGURE 13.03   Some alternatives to tests learned in this book if assumptions are not met

Procedurally, you should check assumptions immediately after collecting data. For example, before running a *t*-test, you should make a judgement regarding case independence and then check your measured variable for normality by examining histograms of all values and then of only values within each group. If you discover you can no longer run a test you planned due to any violation of any assumption, you'll need to derive new decision rules.

The rest of this section will assume that you have normally distributed, appropriately independent data. If this is true, how do you know which test to run? The first question to ask yourself: What is my research design?

13.1.1 QUESTION 1: WHAT'S MY RESEARCH DESIGN?

All of the tests we've covered in this textbook have involved one or two variables of interest. If you have more than that, you will again need a test not covered here. If you only have one variable, you can skip to Question 2. If you have two variables, you need to figure out what purpose each variable serves.

It's important to note that this purpose is driven entirely by your research question. Any particular variables could serve one purpose in one type of analysis but a second purpose in another. This is where interpreting the research question becomes critical.

In general, we first need to decide if any variables among those we are looking at should theoretically cause, or influence, other variables. The variables being caused are called dependent variables (DVs) whereas the variables doing the influencing are called independent variables (IVs). Thus, IVs cause changes in DVs. We use the word 'dependent' because the value of a DV *depends upon* the value of its IVs. Importantly, these words do not necessarily describe anything about these variables 'in the real world'. Instead, these terms are used to describe how the researcher conceptualizes the relationships in their theories (see Chapter 1, p. 13).

In our case study, we have two variables to consider: job performance six months ago and job performance right now. Both are on a seven-point scale, ranging from 1 (extremely low job performance) to 7 (extremely high job performance). The only difference between them is time. If we want to examine these two variables in one analysis, we could call them *repeated* DVs. Neither is an IV because we do not believe that job performance six months ago *causes* job performance now; instead, we believe they are both caused by outside factors. When DVs are repeated, it enables us to examine *change* – and in this textbook, we've covered only one analysis that examines change: the paired-samples *t*-test.

If your variables are not repeated, there are two different options. The first is that you are simply comparing the two variables to each other. In this case, you have two *unrepeated* dependent variables. In our case study, we might ask the following research question: are age and tenure related? In this case, we do not expect either variable to influence the other, so we have two unrepeated DVs. Our theory does not state that age affects tenure or that tenure affects age. We just want to know if they covary.

Contrast that with this research question: does age predict tenure? In this research question, we are implying that people have different tenures *because of* their age. In this case, tenure is still a DV, because it is the outcome of interest. But age is now an IV, because we expect it to exert influence over the DV. Note that data alone cannot tell you what the relationship between the variables necessarily is; a research question describing the causal beliefs of the researcher is needed.

Each of the tests we've covered so far has one DV, two DVs, or an IV and a DV, and these requirements are summarized in Figure 13.04.

Test	DVs?	IVs?
z-test	one	none
One-sample *t*-test	one	none
Paired-samples t-test	two (repeated)	none
Independent-samples *t*-test	one (outcome)	one (group membership)
One-way ANOVA	one (outcome)	one (group membership)
chi-square goodness-of-fit	one	none
chi-square test of independence	two (unrepeated)	none
Correlation	two (repeated or unrepeated)	none
	-or-	
	one (criterion)	one (predictor)
Regression	one (criterion)	one (predictor)

FIGURE 13.04   Required number of independent and dependent variables for tests in this text

Critical to interpreting this chart is the dual role of correlation: it can be used to describe the relationship between two DVs or between one IV and one DV. If it is used to describe the relationship between one IV and one DV, regression is also appropriate. In Chapter 12, we discussed the ordering in regression as 'predicting the criterion from the predictor'. A criterion in regression is always a DV; a predictor is always an IV. If you've been identifying predictors and criteria, you've already been identifying IVs and DVs.

Once you have identified the combination of IVs and DVs in your dataset, you can move on to Question 2.

13.1.2 QUESTION 2: WHAT SCALES OF MEASUREMENT ARE MY VARIABLES?

FOUNDATION CONCEPTS

There are four **scales of measurement**, which determine the type of information a variable contains. First, a variable with **nominal** scale of measurement has meaningful labels. Second, a variable with **ordinal** scale of measurement is nominal, but also has a meaningful order. Third, a variable with **interval** scale of measurement is ordinal, but also has meaningful distances between values. Fourth, and finally, a variable with **ratio** scale of measurement is interval, but also has a meaningful zero point (see Chapter 1, p. 8).

The scale of measurement of each variable determines which tests are appropriate, and there are different requirements for IVs and DVs within each test. If the requirements for scale of measurement are not met, you'll need a different test. Figure 13.05 contains a summary of the scale of measurement requirements of each test covered in this text.

Test	DV scale of measurement	IV scale of measurement
z-test	interval or ratio	N/A
One-sample t-test	interval or ratio	N/A
Paired-samples t-test	interval or ratio	N/A
Independent-samples t-test	interval or ratio	nominal or ordinal
One-way ANOVA	interval or ratio	nominal or ordinal
chi-square goodness-of-fit	nominal or ordinal (counts)	N/A
chi-square test of independence	nominal or ordinal (counts)	N/A
Correlation	interval or ratio	N/A
Regression	interval or ratio	interval or ratio

FIGURE 13.05   Required scales of measurement for variables in tests covered in this textbook

With scale of measurement requirements complete, you can move to the final question.

13.1.3 QUESTION 3: WHAT INFORMATION DO I NEED?

The third question you must ask yourself is: What kind of information do I need?

Only in one case that we've covered in this textbook does this affect which test you should choose: paired-samples *t*-test versus correlation. In both analyses, you have two repeated DVs with interval or ratio scale of measurement. So how do you know which test is appropriate?

You should use paired-samples *t*-tests if you're interested in the difference between the two repeated DVs. For example, in this case study, you might want to ask: 'Is job performance now higher than job performance six months ago?'

You should use correlation if you're interested in the relationship between the two repeated DVs. For example, using the same variables, you might want to ask: 'Is there a relationship between job performance now and job performance six months ago?'

This question is still *relevant* to all tests, however. There are typically two pieces of output in any given statistical analysis, either of which might be your intended target: a finding of statistical significance (or not) and an effect size.

If you're interested in answering a 'yes/no' question – for example, 'is there a difference?' or 'is there a relationship?' – you want the results of your analysis of statistical significance. Remember that the *p*-value from these analyses tells you how likely the observed result is given your null hypothesis. When we reject the null, we are concluding that that null is unlikely to be true given our data. When we accept the alternative, we conclude 'there is a difference' or 'there is a relationship'.

If you're interested in answering a 'how much' question – for example, 'how big is the difference?' or 'how strong is the relationship?' – you want an effect size. Remember that effect sizes quantify the strength of the difference or relationship tested. When we reject the null and compute an effect size, we are concluding 'the difference is small/large' or 'the relationship is weak/strong'.

Even if your primary question points you towards statistical significance, it is most responsible and informative to consider the effect size afterward. It is possible to find statistical significance even when the difference/relationship is not very important, practically speaking. We'll discuss this more in the second portion of this chapter.

13.1.4 QUESTION 4: ANY SPECIAL REQUIREMENTS FOR THIS TEST?

Some tests have special requirements or questions you must ask in order to determine if that test is appropriate.

In this text, we have two such sets of special requirements. First, we decide between a *z*-test and a one-sample *t*-test based upon the availability of the population standard deviation.

Second, we decide between an independent-samples *t*-test and one-way ANOVA based upon the number of levels of the IV (2 for independent-samples *t*-test; 3+ for ANOVA).

With answers to all four questions, you should be able to identify the appropriate test given your data.

13.1.5 PUTTING IT ALL TOGETHER

All of the rules discussed above can be summarized with the table in Appendix B1 and the chart in Appendix B2. For each of the questions above, you should pass from a higher level of this chart to a lower level of this chart, until you reach the name of the required test. If you come to a junction where you don't see an accurate description of your data, that means we haven't covered a test that can answer your question.

For example, imagine Clara from our case study had the following research question: Are there any differences in job performance six months ago between departments?

Question 1: To determine research design, we need to examine our variables closely and identify the relationship between them based upon this research question. One variable is job performance six months ago. The second is the department. The outcome of interest is job performance, so this must be the DV. We want to know how job performance changes as a function of department, so department must be the IV. The answer to Question 1 is 1 IV and 1 DV, which puts us on the far right side of this chart – see Figure 13.06.

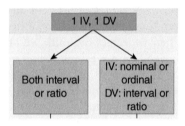

FIGURE 13.06   Question 1 answered, facing Question 2

Question 2: Now we must identify the scale of measurement for each variable. Job performance six months ago is on a scale of 1–7, based upon supervisors' ratings. These are survey data, which makes them interval-level data. Department is a number 1–5, but each number represents a different department. Thus, these data are nominal. The answer to Question 2 is nominal IV and interval DV (Figure 13.07).

Question 3: In this case, our answer to Question 3 will only affect whether we are concerned with the result of the statistical significance test or the effect size. Since Clara wants to know 'are there any differences?', there is a 'yes' or 'no' answer to her question. That means the primary target will be a statistical significance test. However, we should still compute effect size to be thorough (and for other reasons we'll discuss in the second portion of this chapter).

Question 4: Given that we have a nominal IV and interval DV, there are two possible tests: independent-samples *t*-test and one-way ANOVA. The key distinguishing factor between these two tests is the number of levels of the IV. Here, there are five possible values for the Department variable. That means we need one-way ANOVA – see Figure 13.08.

Using this procedure, you should be able to determine the appropriate statistical test for any data addressable with the tests we've covered in this textbook. If you are looking for an appropriate test for something not described in this chart, you will need a test not contained in this textbook.

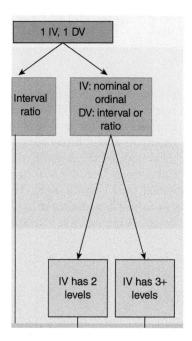

FIGURE 13.07   Question 2 answered, Question 4 faced

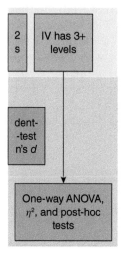

FIGURE 13.08   All questions answered, test chosen

For example, what if we wanted to know the relationship between the order that people leave the office in the evening (recorded as 1st, 2nd, 3rd, etc.) and job performance? These are two unrepeated DVs, one ordinal and one interval. Neither answer to Question 2 under 'unrepeated 2 DVs' describes this combination. Thus, we would need a test not described here (the appropriate test for these data, if you are curious, is 'Spearman's rho').

13.2 COMMON STUMBLES AND CHALLENGES WHEN ANALYSING DATA

When working to solve problems statistically in a business setting, the specific rules for choosing a test are only half the battle. The decisions that must be made to collect those data and the ultimate consequences of those decisions can have important implications for the value of your data. While a textbook on research methods will give you a more complete understanding of these issues, this portion of the chapter will introduce you to some common roadblocks and interpretive challenges faced by statisticians working with real data.

This section is further subdivided into two sections. The first, Working with Data, describes common challenges you face when staring at a dataset in SPSS or Excel. The second, The Meaning of Data, describes interpretive challenges you face after that dataset has been analysed.

13.2.1 WORKING WITH DATA

Freshly trained statisticians often come away from their first statistics course with a somewhat rosy picture of the process of analysing real data. In this view, a dataset will simply be available with precisely the two or three needed variables, and one can commence with a procedure outlined in this book. In reality, a good dataset is something for which a statistician must fight. Data are often collected from multiple sources and combined, producing difficult-to-manage massive datasets with far more information than is actually needed to answer the research question being investigated. I still have nightmares about one of my own datasets from early in my career where I had well over one thousand variables, with informative names for only a handful of them!

Unfortunately, there are no easy solutions to unwieldy datasets. The following recommendations do not solve this problem but do provide some guideposts and recommendations so that when you do face such a dataset, you won't be overwhelmed.

13.2.1.1 EXPLORATORY VS CONFIRMATORY DATA ANALYSIS

There are two broad categories of data analysis: exploratory data analysis and confirmatory data analysis.

The eight-step hypothesis testing process that we've used in this textbook is a confirmatory approach. This means that you form your research questions and then collect data to address those research questions – you are attempting to confirm (or disconfirm) your hypotheses. The first step in confirmatory approaches is always to create hypotheses based upon your theories.

Exploratory data analysis is an approach that many statisticians in the real world find attractive. In an exploratory approach, you simply explore the data, looking for relationships wherever they might exist. One type of exploratory data analysis is data mining, in which any available data are examined for all possible relationships. If Clara were to engage in data mining, she might start by looking for every correlation between every pair of variables and all possible mean differences between all of her variables on similar scales. Then, she would consider anything she found as potentially meaningful. For example, if she discovered in her data that part-time employees who were also men and had worked for less than 12 months in the company tended to have lower job performance than other groups, she might then plan to follow up with additional data analysis focusing on this group. The first step in exploratory approaches is to collect data – research questions and interpretation come later.

In summary, using a confirmatory approach, your ideas about constructs and their relationships drive your research questions. You then use data to provide evidence in support of or against your hypotheses. In an exploratory approach, you use data to drive you to whatever seems interesting.

Although exploratory approaches sound attractive, especially when facing massive datasets, they can be dangerous, because they often discount the effects of Type I error. Remember that we typically set $\alpha = .05$, such that there is a 5% chance of rejecting the null when we should not have done so in any particular test. However, if you set $\alpha = .05$, and then compute every possible correlation between (for example) ten variables looking for statistical significance, the probability that you will commit at least one Type I error among all of those analyses increases to .40. If you start slicing your variables into subsets, this can get even worse.

Such approaches are sometimes negatively referred to as fishing – implying that the statistician simply throws his statistical bait into the water to see what bites without any specific plan or rationale. From these terms, you can see that this approach is viewed by many as opportunistic and inappropriate. However, exploratory approaches can be useful as part of a carefully considered larger-scale data-analytic strategy. For example, a company interested in tracking and taking advantage of sales patterns might conduct an exploratory study first and then use a confirmatory approach with a new sample to verify what they discovered in the exploratory study.

What is clearly inappropriate is to utilize an exploratory approach but then represent it later as a confirmatory one. This is called p-hacking, which refers to the practice of fiddling with the data until you find a statistically significant *p*-value and then presenting that value to stakeholders as if you had initially set out to test that one value all along. Thus, *p*-hacked findings have dramatically inflated Type I error rates above what would be expected based upon setting $\alpha = .05$. *p*-hacked statistics are unlikely to represent the parameters they should. You should never *p*-hack.

Because data mining can be risky, it is strongly recommended that you stick to confirmatory approaches until you have training in advanced research methods. This will minimize the probability that you will conclude you have found an effect or difference when one really does not exist. The eight-step hypothesis testing process introduced in this text will serve you well in this regard.

In our case study, Clara doesn't have much direction for her data, so she is more likely to take an exploratory approach. But she should then be cautious to later confirm these with more carefully controlled data collection and analysis.

13.2.1.2 CLEAN DATA ARE HAPPY DATA

In real business settings, data rarely arrive at the statistician's computer as clean data. Clean datasets (sometimes called 'tidy') are the types of dataset that come with this textbook. You have exactly the variables you need, everything is labelled clearly (at least in the case of SPSS), and there are no missing data.

In this chapter, we've already discussed one type of cleaning that might be necessary. When data are not independent, there are relatively few statistical analyses available. So part of the cleaning process might include modifying the dataset so that the data become independent. Sometimes this isn't possible. In the example provided earlier, the Sales unit was represented twice in the dataset, whereas the Technical Support unit was represented once. By combining the two Sales rows into one, we were able to 'clean' the data, making it ready for subsequent analyses.

Another common necessity for cleaning is the combination of multiple datasets, often from multiple sources, into one. This process is sometimes called data wrangling or data munging. For example, Human Resources data, like tenure, age and gender, are typically kept separately from job performance data. The data from each employee in one dataset must be matched and combined with the data for the same employees in another dataset. Thus, the dataset for this chapter's case study was cleaned before you ever saw it.

Incorrectly entered data can also be a problem, although this was much worse in the days of paper surveys and manual data entry. For example, a person doing data entry might accidentally type a '9' when intending to type a '0', creating errors. When working on a dataset, one of the first things you should do is create frequency tables, conduct basic descriptive statistics, and create histograms and bar charts to check that the data appears as it should. For example, if you are looking at a survey item that contains only responses from 1 to 5, a '9' is clearly an error and should be deleted. Note that this approach won't catch all such errors; if a '3' was accidentally entered as a '5', there is no way to easily discover this after the data have already been recorded.

Missing data are one of the most frustrating issues in data cleaning, and you are likely to find an entire chapter devoted to this topic in an advanced research methods text. People don't always respond to every item in a survey, leaving gaps in the data they provide. Other times, human resources data are only available for employees who have given permission to share it for research purposes, creating large gaps in otherwise complete datasets. Although these limitations are certainly just to protect the privacy rights of research participants, they do create headaches for the statistician analysing their data.

Regardless of the specific problem faced, statisticians working with datasets from real businesses must clean their datasets before they start; otherwise, they risk drawing conclusions from inaccurate or incomplete data, potentially drawing invalid conclusions. Always clean your data before beginning analysis in earnest.

13.2.1.3 DATA WITHOUT CONTEXT ARE MEANINGLESS

As you might have noticed in the first portion of this chapter, the researcher's intentions and the way that data are collected have important implications for the type of test that is appropriate. A dataset without context is meaningless. There is no way to know what the numbers mean – they are only numbers and nothing more.

With context, numbers are no longer just numbers – they are representations of constructs. While the job_perf_now variable in our dataset is technically just 'numbers ranging from 1 to 7', context changes that into 'supervisors' ratings of their employees' job performance'. This context is critical to accurate interpretation.

To encourage accurate interpretation, it is always recommended to create a code sheet, or codebook, that indicates what each variable in your dataset is, what it represents, and what values are appropriate for that variable and their meanings. Figure 13.09 contains the code sheet for the case study dataset, as an example.

Variable name	Description	Valid values
gender	Self-reported gender of the employee, taken from human resources records	0 = Male 1 = Female
age	Self-reported age of the employee in years, taken from human resources records	Whole numbers above 17
tenure	Total number of months the employee has worked for Quince, in months; calculated by human resources data specialist	Whole positive numbers
department	Numeric code representing department the employee works for, taken from human resources records	1 = Sales 2 = Technical Support 3 = Administration 4 = Research and Development 5 = Shipping and Receiving
workstatus	Current weekly hours in the company; less than 35 hours per week considered part-time; more than 35 hours per week considered full-time	0 = Part-time 1 = Full-time
job_perf_6mos	Supervisor's rating of job performance six months ago; collected from semi-annual performance evaluation records six months ago	1 through 7, whole numbers only
job_perf_now	Supervisor's rating of job performance at last semi-annual performance evaluation	1 through 7, whole numbers only

FIGURE 13.09   Code sheet for the case study dataset

By keeping a code sheet with your dataset, you will always have the required contextual information for that dataset. Even if you remember all of this information now, you may not remember it when you return to the dataset a year from now. Always create code sheets.

13.2.1.4 CONSIDER YOUR STATISTICAL APPROACH BEFORE COLLECTING DATA

Although the eight-step hypothesis testing process discussed in this text includes the creation of a decision rule before collecting data, this often does not happen in practice. The risk of skipping this step is that you create a disconnection between the data you wanted and the data you have.

For example, imagine that Clara's primary research question of interest was: 'How big are the differences in job performance between departments?' Further imagine that job performance data were not available, so she needed to survey current supervisors to collect those data. She collects data asking supervisors to rate each employee as 'Above Expectations' or 'Below Expectations'.

After cleaning her data, she realizes that she cannot conduct a one-way ANOVA. She has two variables, one an IV and the other a DV, but her DV is nominal instead of interval. Thus, she is limited to the chi-square test of independence. She wanted to know 'how big are the differences?', which means she wanted a Cohen's *d*. Cohen's *d* cannot be calculated from her data as collected, so she has just wasted a great deal of effort and time.

By considering the statistical test you want to run before you collect your data, you ensure that your data will contain sufficient information to run that test. This is not always possible, but it is always worth pursuing. As renowned English statistician Ronald Fisher, creator of ANOVA, once said, 'To consult the statistician after an experiment is finished is often merely to ask him to conduct a post mortem examination. He can perhaps say what the experiment died of.'

13.2.1.5 THERE ARE MANY PATHS TO THE FINISH, AND THAT CAN BE DANGEROUS

There is an old saying popularized by American writer Mark Twain: 'There are three kinds of lies: lies, damn lies, and statistics.' This statement rather strongly implies that statistics are the worst and most extreme kind of lie. There is some truth to this, because statistics can be manipulated to convince others of a wide variety of half-truths or untruths. Data can be cleaned inappropriately, or exploratory data analysis can be used selectively to look at only the results that are favourable to a particular point of view. The concepts that you've learned from this text should help you identify such deceptions, but a more subtle form of untruth can arise in data analysis – when you fool yourself without realizing it.

The full procedure of conducting data analysis can be very complex. There are many decisions you need to make, from creation of the research question, through data cleaning, to your choice of appropriate statistical test and interpretation of the results of that test. Some of these steps are more objective (for example, choice of a critical value given a particular test), whereas others are more subjective (for example, interpretation of results).

There are multiple valid approaches to most questions. For example, the equivalent of an independent-samples *t*-test can also be conducted with regression by recording the IV as '1' and '0' in your dataset and using that variable as the predictor. In fact, ANOVA can even be considered a specific type of regression. That doesn't mean your choice of approach when analysing data where both are appropriate, between ANOVA or regression, is more or less valid. Instead, this choice more often reflects which approach your statistics instructor emphasized and what sorts of conclusions you're trying to draw. For some, post-hoc tests are more easily interpretable than a regression line; for others, the opposite is true.

Because there are so many ways to approach any given question, care must be taken that we don't mislead ourselves in data analysis. It's easy to get excited with a finding of 'statistical significance', and this can blind us to the truth of our datasets. The safest path is for two statisticians to independently ask the same research questions of the same dataset. If they both come to the same conclusion, it is more likely that their conclusion is valid. If they don't, then they should explore why that happened.

The biggest risk factor to drawing inappropriate or inaccurate conclusions is the statistician's own bias. Know your dataset well, and think carefully through every analytic decision you make, however small it seems.

13.2.1.6 PAY CAREFUL ATTENTION TO THE ASSUMPTIONS OF STATISTICAL TESTS

At the beginning of this chapter, we discussed two major assumptions behind most tests contained within this book: independence and normality.

The implications of non-independence should already be clear. If cases are not independent, your results will be biased towards whichever group (or groups) is represented more than once, unless you take steps to address this bias. Solutions include restructuring your data or using a test specifically designed for repeated or hierarchical data.

The effects of non-normality are more subtle, and they can lead to increased Type I and Type II errors. We'll look at an example of both, using correlation. Let's start with the correlation depicted in Figure 13.10 alongside histograms of each variable it includes.

The scatterplot in Figure 13.10 depicts the relationship between work experience and job performance in a hypothetical organization. This is an example of the sort of analysis you might conduct if you wanted to evaluate how well your hiring system worked. In this figure, both variables are normally distributed and the correlation between work experience and job performance is .50 – a moderate to strong relationship for this context.

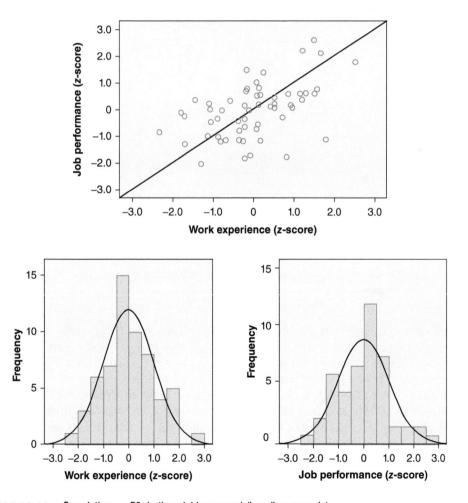

FIGURE 13.10   Correlation = .50, both variables normal (baseline example)

But what happens if we decide to only include 'high performers' and 'low performers' in our study – employees in the top 10% and bottom 10% of job performance scores? The result is depicted in Figure 13.11.

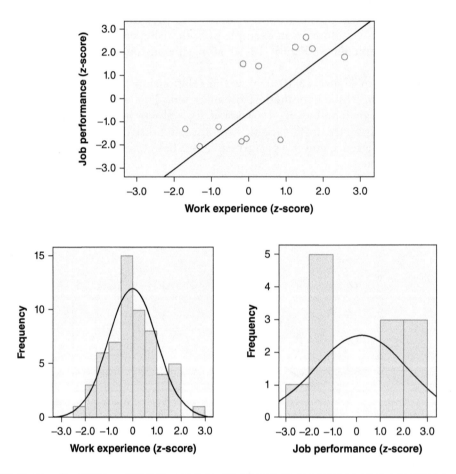

FIGURE 13.11   Correlation = .50 but appears to be .72, job performance is bimodal (example of range enhancement)

In this set, you can see that the job performance variable is no longer normal – there are now two clusters of data, one containing the bottom 10% of scores and the other containing the top 10% of scores. In the scatterplot, you can see the data in the middle of job performance are missing – only the very high and very low scores remain.

What's the effect? Although we know the correlation between work experience and job performance to be .50, it would be calculated here as .72 – a substantial increase. This effect is called range enhancement. By only including the extreme scores on job performance, the apparent difference increases, also increasing Type I error. However, a simple glance at the histogram of job performance would have told the researcher that correlation was inappropriate – the criterion variable is not normally distributed.

Another common problem with employment data is that values may be missing. Imagine, for example, that the population correlation between work experience and job performance is as depicted in Figure 13.10. Now imagine that we only employed above-average applicants (above zero, in z-score terms). Suddenly, half of our predictor variable is missing. What would happen? The result is in Figure 13.12.

FIGURE 13.12   Correlation = .50 but appears to be .37, work experience is positively skewed (example of range restriction)

In this set, you can see that the work experience variable is no longer normal – it is instead positively skewed, because all values below zero are missing. In the scatterplot, you can see the data on the left side are missing.

What's the effect this time? Although we know the correlation between work experience and job performance to be .50, it would be calculated here as .37 – a substantial decrease. This effect is called range restriction. By only including a portion of the scores on work experience, the apparent difference decreases, also increasing Type II error. However, a simple glance at the histogram of job performance would have told the researcher that correlation was inappropriate – the predictor is not normally distributed.

When you analyse data, always create and critically evaluate histograms and other visualizations of all available variables before conducting any analyses. You must ensure that your planned tests are appropriate by checking their assumptions. Otherwise, you increase your risk of drawing inaccurate conclusions. In our case study, Clara has several bar charts and histograms to check!

13.2.2 THE MEANING OF DATA

In the previous section, we discussed challenges faced when analysing data. But analysis itself is only a small portion of working with a dataset. With the results of a formal statistical test in hand, we must also extrapolate and interpret those results into a meaningful business decision. This section will discuss several specific interpretive challenges that you may face in business settings.

13.2.2.1 CORRELATIONAL RESEARCH ALONE CANNOT DEMONSTRATE CAUSATION

In Chapter 12, we discussed a cardinal rule in statistics: correlation is not causation. Discovering a relationship between two variables does not imply that one causes the other. All we can conclude is that there is covariance – variance in one explains variance in the other. It is still possible that one causes the other, but a correlational analysis does not tell us this.

What we did not discuss is that this logic extends to all statistical tests. No correlational research can by itself justify conclusions about causation. For example, if you were to conduct an independent-samples t-test and found that women had higher job performance than men, you could not conclude that gender *caused* increased job performance. It would be inappropriate, for example, to conclude that 'women work harder' or 'women are evaluated more leniently'. The statistical test alone only says 'scores for men and women are different'.

Any conclusions about causation require a research method appropriate to making such conclusions. The most common approach to do this is one we discussed in Chapter 1: an experiment. By randomly assigning people to two groups that researchers treat differently, we can conclude that the difference in the way we treated them *caused* the difference in some outcome of interest. For example, we might randomly assign a large group of taste testers to different foods and observe differences in their ratings of those foods. We can then reasonably conclude that the differences in those foods must have led to any observed differences in mean ratings.

Gender, like many variables especially interesting to researchers, is a much more complicated problem. Since we can't randomly assign people to different genders, *we can never conclude, using any statistical test, that gender causes differences in anything else*. Instead, we can only conclude that 'there is a difference' or 'there is not a difference' and provide reasons that we believe are plausible as to why that difference did or did not occur.

Be cautious in interpreting your own data. When conducting correlational research, whether that involves a t-test, ANOVA, regression, chi-squared or something else, you cannot make conclusions about causation. Only experimental research can accomplish this easily, and many research questions cannot be examined experimentally.

In our case study, Clara has collected a number of interesting variables which beg causal conclusions. However, her approach is correlational, and she cannot make such conclusions. For example, she might want to conclude that differences in organizational tenure lead to increased job performance – that more experience leads to better performance. While this is intuitively desirable, she cannot conclude causation with this research design alone.

INFERRING CAUSALITY FROM CORRELATIONAL DATA

Although causality cannot be inferred from simple correlational studies, with two variables, recent statistical research does enable the inference of causality from correlational data under certain circumstances. This body of work is sometimes called *counterfactual modelling*, because it seeks to answer a straightforward question that is contrary to the present facts: what would have happened now if things had been different in the past? With counterfactual modelling, you can make causal conclusions using correlational data under certain circumstances and by using a powerful analytic system called *structural equation modelling*. If you think being able to draw conclusions about alternative futures sounds amazing, a doctoral degree in statistics may be in your future.

13.2.2.2 DON'T UNDER-INTERPRET EFFECT SIZES

It is tempting, once you have found statistical significance, to stop there. After all, you've rejected the null and concluded that a relationship or difference is present in the data. Why do more work?

The reason is that although you may have found statistical significance, you may not have found practical significance. Practical significance describes the real-world value of a research conclusion, which we typically assess using supplemental analyses, especially effect sizes. It is possible to have statistical significance but little practical significance, and this problem is more common when sample sizes are large.

For example, consider if Clara found in an ANOVA that job performance was different between departments. With a significance F-test, she can safely conclude that there are in fact differences somewhere. But she doesn't stop there. Post-hoc analyses identify two homogeneous subsets: one containing every department except Sales, and a second containing every department except Technical Support. In other words, Technical Support differs from Sales, but no other departments differ from any other departments. Additionally, the Sales and Technical Support departments only differ by $d = .2$.

What can she do with this result? How can she follow up on this to make a positive change for her company? If several departments were different from several other departments, she might plan follow-up studies to investigate those departments or target the weaker group. But in this case, all departments are *practically* the same. Even the largest observed difference among departments is a small effect. Therefore, the differences are not large enough to be useful. Although Clara found statistical significance – the mean job performance among departments does in fact differ – these differences lack practical significance.

Without supplemental analyses, Clara might have acted on these differences, making changes with little overall benefit. With supplemental analyses, she knows that such actions would have been a waste of time.

13.2.2.3 DON'T OVER-INTERPRET EFFECT SIZES

Just as we run the risk of under-interpreting effect sizes, forgetting to consider them after finding statistical significance, we can also over-interpret effect sizes. The biggest risk of this is when group differences are found. In the context of independent-samples *t*-tests and ANOVA, a statistically significant finding indicates that two or more groups differ in their means. However, it does not imply that everyone within those groups is higher or lower than everyone in another group.

For example, imagine that Clara conducted an independent-samples *t*-test on our case study dataset, finding that men had longer tenures at the company than women. Given any random male employee and female employee, could you conclude that the man had a longer tenure than the woman?

Absolutely not! The statistical test conducted only says that the *mean* of male tenure is greater than the *mean* of female tenure. Any particular two individuals from those groups could have any relationship to one another. While *our best guess* is that the man has a longer tenure within this pair, we cannot say this conclusively.

The logical error we make when making conclusions about individuals based upon evidence about the groups to which they belong is called the ecological fallacy. Statistical tests examine differences and relationships among groups, not the members of those groups. We can never generalize our conclusions to specific members.

If you extend the logic of this to a more mundane example, it is easy to see why such generalizations are a fallacy. For example, there is a statistically significant difference in height between men and women. On average, men are taller. However, if I asked you to guess who was taller between Bill and Susan, you wouldn't have an answer! Although there is a difference between the two groups they belong to (men and women), there is no way to make specific conclusions about these two particular people.

Don't interpret effect sizes to be anything more than what they are: informative summaries of the size of the differences or relationships measured.

13.2.2.4 YOU CAN'T PROVE ANYTHING WITH STATISTICS

One of the features of statistics that students find most surprising about interpretation is this: you cannot prove *anything* with statistics. Statistics are instead a toolkit, something to be used as part of an overall analytic strategy. But we can never prove anything with statistics alone.

Many of the research questions we try to address in business can be labelled wicked problems. Wicked problems are issues which have no easy solution and often are not themselves well-defined. These are the 'big problems' that we face in making business decisions, ones with massive consequences and no way to know if the path we are taking is 'correct' or 'incorrect'.

In human resources, you might face this wicked problem: 'Should I employ this person?'

While we can demonstrate statistically that a person with the traits that this applicant has typically performs well in our organization, we cannot control for the myriad of contextual factors that might change that. Perhaps this person has family issues or a history of mental illness that we cannot know. Perhaps this person will have a personality conflict with her assigned supervisor. Perhaps this person is in the midst of a major life change and will quit in two weeks. These are factors we cannot control. While statistics can tell us 'she looks like a good employee', they cannot actually answer our question.

From a strategy standpoint, a recent example of a wicked problem can be seen in the global financial crisis of the late 2000s and early 2010s. While the origin of the crisis is complex, many claim the trigger to be the bursting of the housing bubble in the United States. The cause of that bursting can in large part be credited to unrealistic or incomplete statistical models in banking institutions. These institutions did not accurately predict the effect their policies would ultimately have. Although they used the best statistics available to them at the time, they did not know (and perhaps could not have known) what the outcome of those policies would be, in the broader context of global financial markets.

It is a major bias of our species that we want simple answers to complex problems. Sometimes this simplification is good, providing us with clear actions for the future. But other times, it can be quite harmful, leading us blindly to outcomes we cannot foresee.

Clara might face this wicked problem: Is job performance different by department? Based upon our procedure outlined in the beginning of this chapter, Clara would be likely to conduct a one-way ANOVA, concluding that job performance did in fact differ by department. But does that mean employees in some departments outperform employees in other departments? Perhaps! But it is also possible that supervisors in some departments are harsher than in other departments. It is even possible that supervisors in one department didn't make ratings as thoughtfully as those in other departments. With just this dataset, it is impossible to know. This is a wicked problem, and such problems cannot be solved with data alone.

This does not mean that statistics are useless. Far from it – statistics help us make sense out of the overwhelming, confusing information thrown at us. Instead, statistics *alone* do not provide the final answer to any meaningful question. They are only one step along the path to developing meaningful knowledge about our organizations and our world.

13.3 APPLYING FINAL LESSONS LEARNED

To apply what you've learned from this chapter, consider the case study most important to you: your own. Think of your own experiences as a manager/owner or as an employee of an organization.

- What questions did you have that could be better answered with data?

- How many times did you rely on gut feelings or the status quo to drive your decision-making?

- How can you use statistics and research methods to improve your own organization?

- How many times have you regretted making a decision based upon spotty information?

Statistics are powerful tools in the right hands. With the tools you've learned in this text, you have added specific skills to your toolkit that will help you in a wide variety of contexts, in business and everyday life. Every time you face a major decision, consider if you really have enough information to make an informed decision. If you don't have enough, see if you can conduct a research study to get what you need. Check if others have conducted such a study before you, and critique their methods before adopting them wholeheartedly.

With what you've learned from this textbook, you're now well on your way to developing the skills to tackle any business problem and solve it with a critical eye. Good luck!

EXPLORING CORRELATION AND REGRESSION IN EXCEL AND SPSS

EXCEL

 Download the Excel dataset for the demonstration below as **chapter13.xls**.

Although there are no new statistical tests to learn in this chapter, the case study dataset will be used extensively in the questions at the end of this chapter, so you should become familiar with it. There are two worksheets in this dataset: **dataset**, which contains the raw data, and **codesheet**, which contains the code sheet for this dataset (also found in Figure 13.09).

Unlike SPSS, Excel does not have built-in data labels and descriptors, so you are entirely on your own to keep up with appropriate documentation. The **codesheet** tab of this dataset is a good example of the sort of documentation you might want to keep.

SPSS

 Download the SPSS dataset for the demonstration below as **chapter13.sav**.

Although there are no new statistical tests to learn in this chapter, the case study dataset will be used extensively in the questions at the end of this chapter, so you should become familiar with it.

Unlike Excel, SPSS contains a set of built-in data labels and descriptors which you can find in the **Variable View**. When creating your own datasets, take advantage of this as a code sheet. Label your variables descriptively and mark the meaning of your values appropriately to keep track of them.

STATISTICS IN THE REAL WORLD

 These web links can be accessed directly from the book's website.

Oxford mathematician Peter Donnelly explains how humans commonly misunderstand statistics and some dire consequences: www.ted.com/talks/peter_donnelly_shows_how_stats_fool_juries.

Data scientist Kevin Novak describes how misinterpreting data can put you out of business: www.youtube.com/watch?v=FL9Y0YvNjq8.

Economist editor Kenneth Cukier describes how the incredible and growing availability of data comes with some significant downsides: www.youtube.com/watch?v=Z_HdhhzG-b0.

Data scientist Sebastian Wernicke walks us through how organizations with massive data warehouses successfully and unsuccessfully make data-based decisions: www.ted.com/talks/sebastian_wernicke_how_to_use_data_to_make_a_hit_tv_show.

TEST YOURSELF

☑ All of the following questions require the case study dataset.

☑ **After you've completed the questions below, check your answers online.**

1 For each of the following research questions, what statistical test is most appropriate?
   a Are there any differences in job performance six months ago by gender?
   b Is the split of men and women that we have data on equal to the split of men and women in our company?
   c Can we predict current job performance from employee age?
   d Is the number of part-time employees versus full-time employees different across departments?

2 Describe how Clara might take a confirmatory approach to analysing these data.

3 Describe what would need to be cleaned in the dataset shown in Figure 13.13, based upon the code sheet for the case study dataset.

job_perf_6mos	job_perf_now
6	8
3	2
2	1
	6
1	4

FIGURE 13.13   Dataset for Test Yourself Question 3

4 Are the data in the case study sufficient to address each of the following research questions? Why or why not?
   a Can job performance now be predicted from department?
   b Can tenure be predicted from age?
   c Have people changed departments between six months ago and now?
   d Are our employees younger than the national average in our industry, 31?

5 An industry report has been released describing the relationship between yearly sales in pounds (£) and stock price fluctuations. The analysis involved surveying the top ten firms and asking for reports of these two numbers. The report concluded that increased sales leads to increased stock price. Do you have reason to be suspicious of this report? Why or why not?

(Continued)

(Continued)

DATA SKILL CHALLENGES

   Ater you've completed the questions below, check your answers online.

1   Using the case study dataset, analyse and draw all appropriate conclusions for each of the following research questions. Include ANOVA summary table, if appropriate.
2   Is job performance now less than job performance six months ago?
3   The average age of employees in this industry is 31. Are our employees the same age?
4   Do the ages of employees differ by department?
5   Are there more women in relation to men in some departments?

NEW TERMS

clean data: code sheet: confirmatory data analysis: data mining: data munging: data wrangling: dependent variable (DV): ecological fallacy: exploratory data analysis: fishing: independent data: independent variable (IV): *p*-hacking: practical significance: range enhancement: range restriction: wicked problem:

Visit https://study.sagepub.com/landers2e **for free additional online resources related to this chapter.**

BIBLIOGRAPHY

Abelson, R.P. (1995) 'On suspecting fishiness', in R.P. Abelson, *Statistics as Principled Argument*. Hillsdale, NJ: L. Erlbaum Associates, pp. 78–88.

Anderson, D.R., Sweeney, D.J., Williams, T.A., Freeman, J. and Shoesmith, E. (2010) *Statistics for Business and Economics* (2nd ed.). London, UK: Cengage.

Behrens, J.T. (1997) 'Principles and procedures of exploratory data analysis', *Psychological Methods*, 2, 131–60.

Cohen, J. (1994) 'The earth is round ($p < .05$)', *American Psychologist*, 49, 997–1003.

Cook, T., Campbell, D. and Perrachio, L. (1990) 'Quasi-experimentation', in M.D. Dunnette and L. Hough (eds), *Handbook of Industrial and Organizational Psychology* (2nd ed.). Palo Alto, CA: Consulting Psychologists Press, pp. 491–576.

Cortina, J.M. and Dunlap, W.P. (1997) 'On the logic and purpose of significance testing', *Psychological Methods*, 2, 161–72.

Frobinger, M.Q. (2009) *Linking Business Problems to Statistical Procedures*. Unpublished manuscript.

Gelman, A. and Nolan, D. (2002) *Teaching Statistics: A Bag of Tricks*. Oxford, UK: Oxford University Press.

Graham, J.W., Cumsille, P.E. and Elek-Fisk, E. (2003) 'Methods for handling missing data', in J.A. Schinka and W.F. Velicer (eds), *Handbook of Psychology: Research Methods in Psychology*, vol. 2. New York, NY: John Wiley & Sons, Inc., pp. 87–114.

Grant, A.M. and Wall, T.D. (2009) 'The neglected science and art of quasi-experimentation: Why-to, when-to, and how-to advice for organizational researchers', *Organizational Research Methods*, 12, 653–86.

Hauer, E. (2004) 'The harm done by tests of significance', *Accident Analysis and Prevention*, 36, 495–500.

Hofmann, D.A. (2002) 'Issues in multilevel research: Theory development, measurement, and analysis', in S.G. Rogelberg (ed.), *Handbook of Research Methods in Industrial and Organizational Psychology*. Malden, MA: Blackwell Publishers, pp. 247–74.

Howell, D.C. (2010) *Fundamental Statistics for the Behavioral Sciences*. Belmont, CA: Wadsworth.

Krueger, J. (2001) 'Null hypothesis significance testing: On the survival of a flawed method', *American Psychologist*, 56, 16–26.

Lykken, D.T. (1968) 'Statistical significance in psychological research', *Psychological Bulletin*, 70, 151–9.

Nodine, B.F., Ernst, R.M., Broeker, C.B. and Benjamin, L.T. (1999) *Activities Handbook for Teaching Psychology*. Washington, DC: American Psychological Association.

Ree, M.L and Carretta, T.R. (2006) 'The role of measurement error in familiar statistics', *Organizational Research Methods*, 9, 99–112.

Sackett, P.R. and Larson, J. (1990) 'Research strategies and tactics in I/O psychology', in M.D. Dunnette and L. Hough (eds), *Handbook of Industrial and Organizational Psychology* (2nd ed.). Palo Alto, CA: Consulting Psychologists Press. pp. 435–66.

Salkind, N.J. (2011) *Statistics for People Who (Think They) Hate Statistics*. Thousand Oaks, CA: SAGE Publications.

Sawyer, J. (1966) 'Measurement and prediction, clinical and statistical', *Psychological Bulletin*, 66, 178–200.

Schmidt, F.L. and Hunter, J.E. (1996) 'Measurement error in psychological research: Lessons from 26 research scenarios', *Psychological Methods*, 1, 199–233.

Schmidt, F.L. and Hunter, J.E. (2002) 'Are there benefits from NHST?', *American Psychologist*, 57, 65–6.

APPENDIX A

A1 Z-TABLE

Values in the table represent the proportion of scores falling in the tail beyond the given z-score (see highlighted area in Figure A.01). Row and column headings should be added to create the complete referenced z-score; for example, to find $z = 1.12$, look at row 1.1 and column 0.02. You should see the value 0.1313, which means that: 13.13% of cases fall above $z = 1.12$ (and also that 13.13% of cases fall below $z = -1.12$).

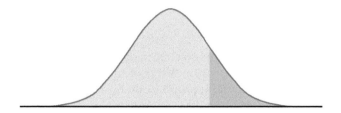

FIGURE A.01   Appendix A1: z-table

z	0	0.01	0.02	0.03	0.04	0.05	0.06	0.07	0.08	0.09
0	0.5000	0.4960	0.4920	0.4880	0.4840	0.4801	0.4761	0.4721	0.4681	0.4641
0.1	0.4602	0.4562	0.4522	0.4483	0.4443	0.4404	0.4364	0.4325	0.4286	0.4247
0.2	0.4207	0.4168	0.4129	0.4090	0.4052	0.4013	0.3974	0.3936	0.3897	0.3859
0.3	0.3821	0.3783	0.3745	0.3707	0.3669	0.3632	0.3594	0.3557	0.3520	0.3483
0.4	0.3446	0.3409	0.3372	0.3336	0.3300	0.3264	0.3228	0.3192	0.3156	0.3121
0.5	0.3085	0.3050	0.3015	0.2981	0.2946	0.2912	0.2877	0.2843	0.2810	0.2776
0.6	0.2743	0.2709	0.2676	0.2643	0.2611	0.2578	0.2546	0.2514	0.2483	0.2451
0.7	0.2420	0.2389	0.2358	0.2327	0.2296	0.2266	0.2236	0.2206	0.2177	0.2148
0.8	0.2119	0.2090	0.2061	0.2033	0.2005	0.1977	0.1949	0.1922	0.1894	0.1867
0.9	0.1841	0.1814	0.1788	0.1762	0.1736	0.1711	0.1685	0.1660	0.1635	0.1611
1	0.1587	0.1562	0.1539	0.1515	0.1492	0.1469	0.1446	0.1423	0.1401	0.1379
1.1	0.1357	0.1335	0.1314	0.1292	0.1271	0.1251	0.1230	0.1210	0.1190	0.1170
1.2	0.1151	0.1131	0.1112	0.1093	0.1075	0.1056	0.1038	0.1020	0.1003	0.0985
1.3	0.0968	0.0951	0.0934	0.0918	0.0901	0.0885	0.0869	0.0853	0.0838	0.0823
1.4	0.0808	0.0793	0.0778	0.0764	0.0749	0.0735	0.0721	0.0708	0.0694	0.0681
1.5	0.0668	0.0655	0.0643	0.0630	0.0618	0.0606	0.0594	0.0582	0.0571	0.0559
1.6	0.0548	0.0537	0.0526	0.0516	0.0505	0.0495	0.0485	0.0475	0.0465	0.0455
1.7	0.0446	0.0436	0.0427	0.0418	0.0409	0.0401	0.0392	0.0384	0.0375	0.0367
1.8	0.0359	0.0351	0.0344	0.0336	0.0329	0.0322	0.0314	0.0307	0.0301	0.0294
1.9	0.0287	0.0281	0.0274	0.0268	0.0262	0.0256	0.0250	0.0244	0.0239	0.0233
2	0.0228	0.0222	0.0217	0.0212	0.0207	0.0202	0.0197	0.0192	0.0188	0.0183
2.1	0.0179	0.0174	0.0170	0.0166	0.0162	0.0158	0.0154	0.0150	0.0146	0.0143
2.2	0.0139	0.0136	0.0132	0.0129	0.0125	0.0122	0.0119	0.0116	0.0113	0.0110
2.3	0.0107	0.0104	0.0102	0.0099	0.0096	0.0094	0.0091	0.0089	0.0087	0.0084
2.4	0.0082	0.0080	0.0078	0.0075	0.0073	0.0071	0.0069	0.0068	0.0066	0.0064
2.5	0.0062	0.0060	0.0059	0.0057	0.0055	0.0054	0.0052	0.0051	0.0049	0.0048
2.6	0.0047	0.0045	0.0044	0.0043	0.0041	0.0040	0.0039	0.0038	0.0037	0.0036
2.7	0.0035	0.0034	0.0033	0.0032	0.0031	0.0030	0.0029	0.0028	0.0027	0.0026
2.8	0.0026	0.0025	0.0024	0.0023	0.0023	0.0022	0.0021	0.0021	0.0020	0.0019
2.9	0.0019	0.0018	0.0018	0.0017	0.0016	0.0016	0.0015	0.0015	0.0014	0.0014
3	0.0013	0.0013	0.0013	0.0012	0.0012	0.0011	0.0011	0.0011	0.0010	0.0010
3.1	0.0010	0.0009	0.0009	0.0009	0.0008	0.0008	0.0008	0.0008	0.0007	0.0007
3.2	0.0007	0.0007	0.0006	0.0006	0.0006	0.0006	0.0006	0.0005	0.0005	0.0005
3.3	0.0005	0.0005	0.0005	0.0004	0.0004	0.0004	0.0004	0.0004	0.0004	0.0003
3.4	0.0003	0.0003	0.0003	0.0003	0.0003	0.0003	0.0003	0.0003	0.0003	0.0002
3.5	0.0002	0.0002	0.0002	0.0002	0.0002	0.0002	0.0002	0.0002	0.0002	0.0002

A2 *T*-TABLE

Values in this table represent the critical *t*-statistic in one or both tails given a variety of conditions (see highlighted areas Figures A.02). Users of this table should identify the appropriate degrees of freedom and also the appropriate number of tails to determine $t(\text{d.f.})_{\text{crit}}$. If α is not specified, you usually want $\alpha = .05$.

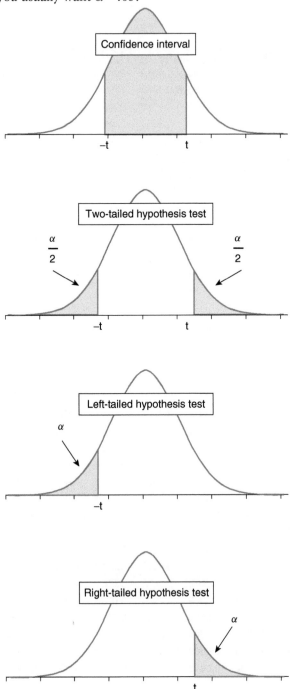

d.f. ↓	Confidence intervals			
	90%	95%	98%	99%
	Two-tailed α			
	.10	.05	.02	.01
	One-tailed α			
	.05	.025	.01	.005
1	6.314	12.706	31.821	63.657
2	2.920	4.303	6.965	9.925
3	2.353	3.182	4.541	5.841
4	2.132	2.776	3.747	4.604
5	2.015	2.571	3.365	4.032
6	1.943	2.447	3.143	3.707
7	1.895	2.365	2.998	3.499
8	1.860	2.306	2.896	3.355
9	1.833	2.262	2.821	3.250
10	1.812	2.228	2.764	3.169
11	1.796	2.201	2.718	3.106
12	1.782	2.179	2.681	3.055
13	1.771	2.160	2.650	3.012
14	1.761	2.145	2.624	2.977
15	1.753	2.131	2.602	2.947
16	1.746	2.120	2.583	2.921
17	1.740	2.110	2.567	2.898
18	1.734	2.101	2.552	2.878
19	1.729	2.093	2.539	2.861
20	1.725	2.086	2.528	2.845
21	1.721	2.080	2.518	2.831
22	1.717	2.074	2.508	2.819
23	1.714	2.069	2.500	2.807
24	1.711	2.064	2.492	2.797
25	1.708	2.060	2.485	2.787
26	1.706	2.056	2.479	2.779
27	1.703	2.052	2.473	2.771
28	1.701	2.048	2.467	2.763
29	1.699	2.045	2.462	2.756
30	1.697	2.042	2.457	2.750
40	1.684	2.021	2.423	2.704
50	1.676	2.009	2.403	2.678
100	1.660	1.984	2.364	2.626
150	1.655	1.976	2.351	2.609
200	1.653	1.972	2.345	2.601
Inf	1.645	1.960	2.326	2.576

A3 *F*-TABLE (α =.05 – FIGURE A.03)

Values in this table represent the critical *F*-statistic in the upper tail given various combinations of between-groups and within-groups degrees of freedom. Users of this table should identify the appropriate df_B and df_W to determine $F_{crit}(df_B, df_W)$. If =.01, refer to Appendix A4.

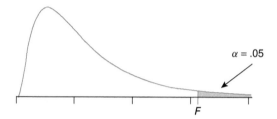

α = .05

F

FIGURE A.03 Appendix A3: *F*-table (α =.05)

	Between groups degrees of freedom (dfB)													
	1	2	3	4	5	6	7	8	9	10	15	20	25	30
1	161.5	199.5	215.7	224.6	230.2	234.0	236.8	238.9	240.5	241.9	246.0	248.0	249.3	250.10
2	18.51	19.00	19.16	19.25	19.30	19.33	19.35	19.37	19.38	19.40	19.43	19.45	19.46	19.46
3	10.13	9.55	9.28	9.12	9.01	8.94	8.89	8.85	8.81	8.79	8.70	8.66	8.63	8.62
4	7.71	6.94	6.59	6.39	6.26	6.16	6.09	6.04	6.00	5.96	5.86	5.80	5.77	5.75
5	6.61	5.79	5.41	5.19	5.05	4.95	4.88	4.82	4.77	4.74	4.62	4.56	4.52	4.50
6	5.99	5.14	4.76	4.53	4.39	4.28	4.21	4.15	4.10	4.06	3.94	3.87	3.83	3.81
7	5.59	4.74	4.35	4.12	3.97	3.87	3.79	3.73	3.68	3.64	3.51	3.44	3.40	3.38
8	5.32	4.46	4.07	3.84	3.69	3.58	3.50	3.44	3.39	3.35	3.22	3.15	3.11	3.08
9	5.12	4.26	3.86	3.63	3.48	3.37	3.29	3.23	3.18	3.14	3.01	2.94	2.89	2.86
10	4.96	4.10	3.71	3.48	3.33	3.22	3.14	3.07	3.02	2.98	2.85	2.77	2.73	2.70
11	4.84	3.98	3.59	3.36	3.20	3.09	3.01	2.95	2.90	2.85	2.72	2.65	2.60	2.57
12	4.75	3.89	3.49	3.26	3.11	3.00	2.91	2.85	2.80	2.75	2.62	2.54	2.50	2.47
13	4.67	3.81	3.41	3.18	3.03	2.92	2.83	2.77	2.71	2.67	2.53	2.46	2.41	2.38
14	4.60	3.74	3.34	3.11	2.96	2.85	2.76	2.70	2.65	2.60	2.46	2.39	2.34	2.31
15	4.54	3.68	3.29	3.06	2.90	2.79	2.71	2.64	2.59	2.54	2.40	2.33	2.28	2.25
16	4.49	3.63	3.24	3.01	2.85	2.74	2.66	2.59	2.54	2.49	2.35	2.28	2.23	2.19
17	4.45	3.59	3.20	2.96	2.81	2.70	2.61	2.55	2.49	2.45	2.31	2.23	2.18	2.15
18	4.41	3.55	3.16	2.93	2.77	2.66	2.58	2.51	2.46	2.41	2.27	2.19	2.14	2.11
19	4.38	3.52	3.13	2.90	2.74	2.63	2.54	2.48	2.42	2.38	2.23	2.16	2.11	2.07
20	4.35	3.49	3.10	2.87	2.71	2.60	2.51	2.45	2.39	2.35	2.20	2.12	2.07	2.04
21	4.32	3.47	3.07	2.84	2.68	2.57	2.49	2.42	2.37	2.32	2.18	2.10	2.05	2.01
22	4.30	3.44	3.05	2.82	2.66	2.55	2.46	2.40	2.34	2.30	2.15	2.07	2.02	1.98
23	4.28	3.42	3.03	2.80	2.64	2.53	2.44	2.37	2.32	2.27	2.13	2.05	2.00	1.96
24	4.26	3.40	3.01	2.78	2.62	2.51	2.42	2.36	2.30	2.25	2.11	2.03	1.97	1.94
25	4.24	3.39	2.99	2.76	2.60	2.49	2.40	2.34	2.28	2.24	2.09	2.01	1.96	1.92
30	4.17	3.32	2.92	2.69	2.53	2.42	2.33	2.27	2.21	2.16	2.01	1.93	1.88	1.84
40	4.08	3.23	2.84	2.61	2.45	2.34	2.25	2.18	2.12	2.08	1.92	1.84	1.78	1.74
50	4.03	3.18	2.79	2.56	2.40	2.29	2.20	2.13	2.07	2.03	1.87	1.78	1.73	1.69
75	3.97	3.12	2.73	2.49	2.34	2.22	2.13	2.06	2.01	1.96	1.80	1.71	1.65	1.61
100	3.94	3.09	2.70	2.46	2.31	2.19	2.10	2.03	1.97	1.93	1.77	1.68	1.62	1.57
150	3.90	3.06	2.66	2.43	2.27	2.16	2.07	2.00	1.94	1.89	1.73	1.64	1.58	1.54
200	3.89	3.04	2.65	2.42	2.26	2.14	2.06	1.98	1.93	1.88	1.72	1.62	1.56	1.52
∞	3.84	3.00	2.61	2.37	2.21	2.10	2.01	1.94	1.88	1.83	1.67	1.57	1.51	1.46

Within groups Degrees of Freedom (df_w)

A4 F-TABLE (=.01 – FIGURE A.04)

Values in this table represent the critical *F*-statistic in the upper tail given various combinations of between-groups and within-groups degrees of freedom. Users of this table should identify the appropriate df_B and df_W to determine $F_{crit}(df_B, df_W)$. If $\alpha = .05$, refer to Appendix A3.

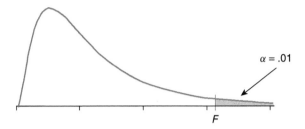

$\alpha = .01$

F

FIGURE A.04   Appendix A4: F-table ($\alpha = .01$)

	Between groups degrees of freedom (df$_B$)													
	1	2	3	4	5	6	7	8	9	10	15	20	25	30
1	4052	5000	5403	5625	5764	5859	5928	5981	6022	6056	6157	6209	6240	6261
2	98.50	99.00	99.17	99.25	99.30	99.33	99.36	99.37	99.39	99.40	99.43	99.45	99.46	99.47
3	34.12	30.82	29.46	28.71	28.24	27.91	27.67	27.49	27.35	27.23	26.87	26.69	26.58	26.50
4	21.20	18.00	16.69	15.98	15.52	15.21	14.98	14.80	14.66	14.55	14.20	14.02	13.91	13.84
5	16.26	13.27	12.06	11.39	10.97	10.67	10.46	10.29	10.16	10.05	9.72	9.55	9.45	9.38
6	13.75	10.92	9.78	9.15	8.75	8.47	8.26	8.10	7.98	7.87	7.56	7.40	7.30	7.23
7	12.25	9.55	8.45	7.85	7.46	7.19	6.99	6.84	6.72	6.62	6.31	6.16	6.06	5.99
8	11.26	8.65	7.59	7.01	6.63	6.37	6.18	6.03	5.91	5.81	5.52	5.36	5.26	5.20
9	10.56	8.02	6.99	6.42	6.06	5.80	5.61	5.47	5.35	5.26	4.96	4.81	4.71	4.65
10	10.04	7.56	6.55	5.99	5.64	5.39	5.20	5.06	4.94	4.85	4.56	4.41	4.31	4.25
11	9.65	7.21	6.22	5.67	5.32	5.07	4.89	4.74	4.63	4.54	4.25	4.10	4.01	3.94
12	9.33	6.93	5.95	5.41	5.06	4.82	4.64	4.50	4.39	4.30	4.01	3.86	3.76	3.70
13	9.07	6.70	5.74	5.21	4.86	4.62	4.44	4.30	4.19	4.10	3.82	3.66	3.57	3.51
14	8.86	6.51	5.56	5.04	4.69	4.46	4.28	4.14	4.03	3.94	3.66	3.51	3.41	3.35
15	8.68	6.36	5.42	4.89	4.56	4.32	4.14	4.00	3.89	3.80	3.52	3.37	3.28	3.21
16	8.53	6.23	5.29	4.77	4.44	4.20	4.03	3.89	3.78	3.69	3.41	3.26	3.16	3.10
17	8.40	6.11	5.18	4.67	4.34	4.10	3.93	3.79	3.68	3.59	3.31	3.16	3.07	3.00
18	8.29	6.01	5.09	4.58	4.25	4.01	3.84	3.71	3.60	3.51	3.23	3.08	2.98	2.92
19	8.18	5.93	5.01	4.50	4.17	3.94	3.77	3.63	3.52	3.43	3.15	3.00	2.91	2.84
20	8.10	5.85	4.94	4.43	4.10	3.87	3.70	3.56	3.46	3.37	3.09	2.94	2.84	2.78
21	8.02	5.78	4.87	4.37	4.04	3.81	3.64	3.51	3.40	3.31	3.03	2.88	2.79	2.72
22	7.95	5.72	4.82	4.31	3.99	3.76	3.59	3.45	3.35	3.26	2.98	2.83	2.73	2.67
23	7.88	5.66	4.76	4.26	3.94	3.71	3.54	3.41	3.30	3.21	2.93	2.78	2.69	2.62
24	7.82	5.61	4.72	4.22	3.90	3.67	3.50	3.36	3.26	3.17	2.89	2.74	2.64	2.58
25	7.77	5.57	4.68	4.18	3.85	3.63	3.46	3.32	3.22	3.13	2.85	2.70	2.60	2.54
30	7.56	5.39	4.51	4.02	3.70	3.47	3.30	3.17	3.07	2.98	2.70	2.55	2.45	2.39
40	7.31	5.18	4.31	3.83	3.51	3.29	3.12	2.99	2.89	2.80	2.52	2.37	2.27	2.20
50	7.17	5.06	4.20	3.72	3.41	3.19	3.02	2.89	2.78	2.70	2.42	2.27	2.17	2.10
75	6.99	4.90	4.05	3.58	3.27	3.05	2.89	2.76	2.65	2.57	2.29	2.13	2.03	1.96
100	6.90	4.82	3.98	3.51	3.21	2.99	2.82	2.69	2.59	2.50	2.22	2.07	1.97	1.89
150	6.81	4.75	3.91	3.45	3.14	2.92	2.76	2.63	2.53	2.44	2.16	2.00	1.90	1.83
200	6.76	4.71	3.88	3.41	3.11	2.89	2.73	2.60	2.50	2.41	2.13	1.97	1.87	1.79
∞	6.63	4.61	3.78	3.32	3.02	2.80	2.64	2.51	2.41	2.32	2.04	1.88	1.77	1.70

Within groups degrees of freedom (df$_W$)

A5 X^2-TABLE (CHI-SQUARED – FIGURE A.05)

Values in this table represent the critical χ^2-statistic in the upper tail given various degrees of freedom. Users of this table should identify the critical value $[\chi^2(d.f.)_{crit}]$ at the appropriate combination of needed d.f. and α.

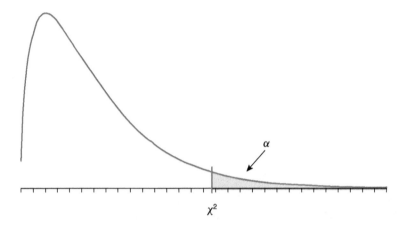

FIGURE A.05

d.f.	$\alpha = .05$	$\alpha = .01$
1	3.841	11.345
2	5.991	15.086
3	7.815	18.475
4	9.488	21.666
5	11.070	24.725
6	12.592	26.217
7	14.067	29.141
8	15.507	30.578
9	16.919	32.000
10	18.307	34.805
11	19.675	36.191
12	21.026	38.932
13	22.362	40.289
14	23.685	41.638
15	24.996	42.980
16	26.296	45.642
17	27.587	46.963
18	28.869	48.278

d.f.	$\alpha = .05$	$\alpha = .01$
19	30.144	50.892
20	31.410	52.191
21	32.671	53.486
22	33.924	54.776
23	35.172	57.342
24	36.415	58.619
25	37.652	59.893
26	38.885	61.162
27	40.113	63.691
28	41.337	64.950
29	42.557	66.206
30	43.773	67.459
40	55.758	82.292
50	67.505	96.828
100	124.342	163.546
150	179.581	225.933
200	233.994	286.139

APPENDIX B

B1 INFERENTIAL TEST REFERENCE TABLE

Test	DVs?	DV Scale of measurement	IVs?	IV scale of measurement	Test statistic	Supplemental analyses
z-test	one	interval or ratio	none	N/A	z	confidence interval and Cohen's d
One-sample t-test	one	interval or ratio	none	N/A	t	confidence interval and Cohen's d
Paired-samples t-test	two (repeated)	interval or ratio	none	N/A	t	confidence interval and Cohen's d
Independent-samples t-test	one (outcome)	interval or ratio	one (group membership)	nominal or ordinal	t	Cohen's d
One-way ANOVA	one (outcome)	interval or ratio	one (group membership)	nominal or ordinal	F	x^2 and post-hoc tests
chi-square goodness-of-fit	one	nominal or ordinal (counts)	none	N/A	x^2	Cramer's V
chi-square test of independence	two (unrepeated)	nominal or ordinal (counts)	none	N/A	x^2	Cramer's V
Correlation	two (repeated or unrepeated)	interval or ratio	none	N/A	t	r2
Correlation	one (criterion)	interval or ratio	one (predictor)	interval or ratio	t	r2 and regression

B2 INFERENTIAL TEST DECISION TREE

For more information on how to use this chart, see Chapter 13, p. 406.

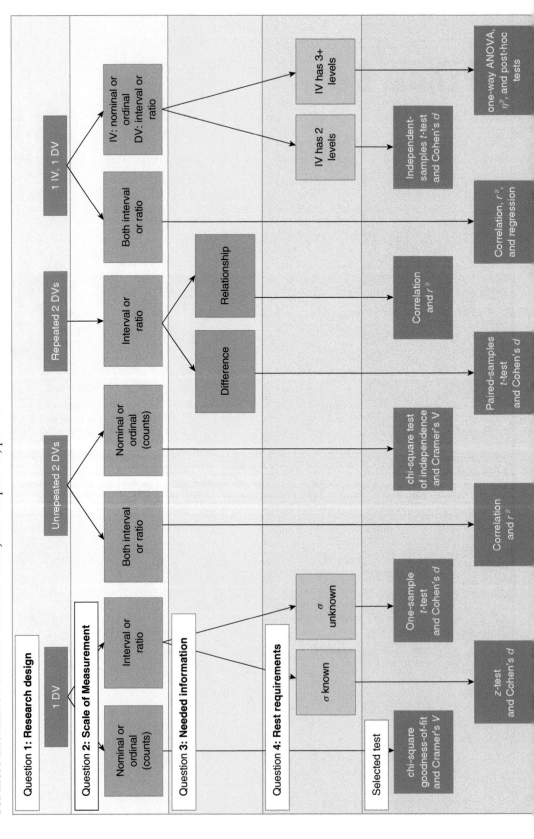

APPENDIX C

GLOSSARY

alternative hypothesis: a hypothesis implied by the null hypothesis; what we assume must be true if the null hypothesis has been rejected, although it is never tested directly.

analysis of variance: a hypothesis test where the variance of group means is compared with variance within those groups; produces an F-ratio; abbreviated ANOVA.

ANOVA: see analysis of variance.

ANOVA table: a common format for presenting the results of ANOVA; a table containing nine pieces of information produced for ANOVA: SS_B, SS_W, SS_T, df_B, df_W, df_T, MS_B, MS_W, F.

area under the curve: the visual space beneath the curvy line in a probability distribution; 100% of this space represents 100% of the data within that distribution.

assumption: a condition that must be true for a statistic to be meaningful, for example the mean assumes normally distributed data.

bar chart: an illustration of qualitative data representing a variable's categories on the x-axis as independent vertical bars and simple frequencies on the y-axis.

Bayesianism: an alternative system of assumptions to frequentism in which your degree of certainty about an event occurring is the focus of inference instead of parameters.

between-groups variability: the degree to which group means vary from one another within ANOVA; if overall variability, this is the sum of squares between; if average variability, this is the mean square between.

bias: a systematic inaccuracy in a statistic in measuring what it is intended to measure.

bin: a range of values represented as a single bar in a histogram.

case: a source of data about one or more variables, usually represented in a dataset as a row.

central limit theorem: a statistical principle stating that when sample means of a particular sample size are infinitely drawn from a particular population, the sampling distribution of those means will be approximately normally distributed.

central tendency: the 'middle' of a dataset, which can be determined by calculating a mode, median or mean.

chance: variation that occurs at random, i.e. luck.

classical method of assigning probability: a process used to determine precise values for probabilities by collecting large quantities of data and observing the probability directly; contrast with the relative frequency of occurrence method of assigning probability

clean data: real-world data that has been treated by a statistician so that it is ready to be analysed; this may involve addressing missing data, cutting out unnecessary variables, or converting variables to appropriate metrics.

code sheet: a document recording contextual information about each variable in a dataset; usually contains the variable name, a description of the variable, and a list of valid values for that variable and their meanings.

coefficient of determination: calculated as the square of a Pearson's r; interpreted as the percentage of variance in one variable explained by the variance in another.

Cohen's d: a standardized effect size measure that quantifies the difference between two means in terms of their pooled standard deviation.

computational formula: a formula defining a statistic or parameter that is simplified or restructured in comparison to its conceptual formula in order to make it easier or faster to calculate.

conceptual formula: a formula defining a statistic or parameter that clearly illustrates the underlying relationships between variables it summarizes, often at the expense of calculation difficulty; contrast with computational formula.

conditions: two or more categories into which a sample is split in order to examine differences between those categories.

confidence: a chosen level of probability that defines the width of a confidence interval (for example, with 99% confidence, we determine the range of values in which 99% of sample statistics should fall given a particular parameter).

confidence interval: a range of values within which we would expect sample statistics to fall, given a particular sample size, a particular parameter and a particular level of confidence.

confirmatory data analysis: an approach to data analysis in which a statistician states a research question and then tests that research question with data.

constant: a named value that does not change, such as pi (π), which can be contrasted with variables.

construct: a characteristic or property of interest in a population.

contingency table: a table splitting counts of two variables by the categories they contain; includes total columns and rows; used in chi-squared test of independence.

continuous: a label for data that can be divided infinitely into smaller amounts but remain meaningful (for example, 142.31241 millimetres).

control condition: a condition where the subject's treatment is not changed in order to provide a frame of reference for the effect of a treatment; contrasted with a treatment condition.

convenience sampling: sampling by drawing from a convenient source, instead of at random; substantially inferior to random sampling at worst, equal at best.

correlation (coefficient): a descriptive statistic that summarizes the relationship between two variables with a single number; often used as shorthand for the most common type of correlation: Pearson's product-moment correlation coefficient.

correlational study: a study where more than one variable is assessed at the same time without any changes made on behalf of the researcher.

covariance: an unstandardized measure of the average distance scores are from falling in a linear relationship; a standardized covariance is a Pearson's product-moment correlation coefficient.

Cramér's V: a measure of effect size for chi-squared; ranges from 0 to +1.

criterion: the y-variable in regression; the criterion is what is being predicted in regression analysis.

critical value: the threshold at which a test statistic is considered sufficiently unlikely that we believe it to have come from a different population than the one described by the null hypothesis; if a test statistic is greater than a positive critical value or less than a negative critical value, we conclude that the test statistic is statistically significant.

cumulative frequency: a count of how many times a value and all values below it (alphanumerically) appear in a variable; represented by cum. f.

cumulative percentage: cumulative frequency expressed as a percentage of sample size.

data: the plural of datum.

data mining: a type of exploratory data analysis where a dataset is examined from multiple perspectives simultaneously in order to find interesting or provocative relationships.

data munging: see data wrangling.

dataset: a collection of data linked together in a meaningful way.

Data View: a view in SPSS, selectable via the tabs at the bottom of the screen, that displays the current dataset.

data wrangling: combining multiple sources of data into one and ensure the resulting data are clean.

datum: a single value collected for research purposes.

degrees of freedom: the number of independent pieces of information that are available to estimate a value of interest; in this textbook, might be $n - 1$, $n - 2$, $n - k$ or $k - 1$, depending on the test.

dependent samples: describes data from two or more variables coming from the same conceptual source (for example, when collecting Time 1 and Time 2 customer satisfaction data, we would need to collect both pieces of information from every person; see also independent samples).

dependent variable (DV): an outcome of interest. See also criterion.

deviation: the difference between a score and the mean it is associated with.

dichotomous: a term used to refer to nominal data with only two possible values (for example, 'male' and 'female').

difference score: the difference between two numbers; typically used as an unstandardized measure of effect size.

discrete: a label for data that cannot be divided beyond a certain point (for example, 'five employees').

distribution: a common shape in which data tend to fall (for example, normal, uniform or Poisson distributions).

DV: see dependent variable.

ecological fallacy: a logical error in which findings about groups (for example, in the context of independent-samples t-tests or ANOVA) are used to make conclusions about specific individuals.

effect size: the difference between two values; may be unstandardized (for example, a difference score) or standardized (for example, see Cohen's d).

experiment: the random assignment of members of a sample to different conditions in order to provide evidence of causality.

exploratory data analysis: an approach to data analysis in which a statistician examines a dataset without any research questions or hypotheses to guide them.

fill: a technique used in Excel to copy cell contents.

fishing: a derogatory term for exploratory data analysis.

fit: the degree to which actual data match expected data.

formula: a concise definition of a statistical concept, using statistical notation.

fraction: a portion of a whole represented as one number divided by another (for example, ½).

F-ratio: the ratio of variance between group means to the variance within those groups.

frequency (or simple frequency): a count of how many times a value appears in a variable, represented with f.

frequency polygon: an illustration of quantitative data representing bins as segments on a line graph.

frequency table: a table containing all categories, simple frequencies, relative frequencies and cumulative frequencies for a given variable.

frequentism: the system of assumptions underlying all statistics and statistical tests in this book in which there are existing parameters and statistics are used to estimate those parameters; contrast with Bayesianism.

general linear model: a general purpose statistical analysis framework for examining linear relationships between variables which includes regression, multiple regression, analysis of variance, t-tests, and more.

goodness-of-fit: a non-parametric chi-squared (χ^2) test in which a set of observed frequencies on a single variable is compared with a model of expected frequencies.

histogram: an illustration of quantitative data representing the range of a variable's values on the x-axis and frequencies of those ranges on the y-axis, with no gaps between bars.

hypothesis: a testable relationship between operational definitions that reflects a theory.

hypothesis test(ing): the process of considering whether or not a sample statistic is likely to have occurred given a particular null hypothesis, and then rejecting or retaining that null.

independent data: describes a dataset where each case is completely independent of every other case; if there is an overlap, data are not independent.

independent samples: describes data coming from two or more unique sources (for example, a measure of job satisfaction can be given to a sample of women and to a sample of men; see also dependent samples).

independent-samples t-test: a two-sample hypothesis test where the difference between two sample means is compared with the difference between two population means as specified in the null hypothesis.

independent variable (IV): a variable believed to influence a dependent variable. See also predictor.

index: a type of statistic with no natural units of measurement (for example, correlation).

indicator variable: a variable that reveals to which independent sample each case in a dataset belongs (for example, a 'gender' indicator variable might contain '1's and '2's to indicate whether each case came from the male or female sample; typically a nominal or ordinal variable).

interaction: occurs when the combined effects of two variables produce a unique effect not expected from those two effects alone; interaction is needed to find statistical significance in a chi-squared test of independence.

intersection: the probability that two or more probabilities are true simultaneously; signified with the word 'and', as in 'what is the probability that both A and B are true?'.

interval: a scale of measurement for ordinal data with meaningful distances between values (for example, temperature in degrees Celsius).

interval estimate: a range of values derived from a sample as an estimate of a parameter (for example, a confidence interval surrounding is an interval estimate of μ).

least squares regression: see regression.

legend: part of a chart or figure explaining what the symbols and colours used in that chart or figure represent.

Likert-type item: a common type of survey item containing a numerical scale (often 1 to 5 or 1 to 7).

Likert-type scale: a group of Likert-type items measuring the same construct.

linear relationship: a relationship between two variables that can be summarized with a straight line.

line of best fit: see regression line.

lower bound: the smaller value in an interval estimate (usually a confidence interval).

margin of error: the width of half of a confidence interval, converted into a percentage of the value being estimated; summarizes the uncertainty of an estimate in comparison to the estimate's value.

matched-samples t-test: see paired-samples t-test.

mean: the arithmetic average of the values in a variable and a measure of central tendency, represented with $\bar{x}$ (x bar) in a sample and μ (mu) in a population.

mean square: mean sum of squares per degree of freedom in ANOVA.

median: the middlemost value in a variable and a measure of central tendency.

mode: the most common value in a variable and a measure of central tendency.

model: an expected structure of data; in chi-squared tests, observed frequencies are compared with a model of expected frequencies.

multiple regression: a regression analysis with more than one predictor variable.

negative skew: data for which the tail of the skewed data leads to the left (toward negative numbers).

nominal: a scale of measurement for data with meaningful labels.

non-parametric tests: statistical tests that do not require making assumptions about parameters (for example, chi-squared (χ^2)).

normal distribution: a common shape in which data are found, resembling a bell or hill.

null hypothesis: a statement of our assumptions about the value of a population parameter.

n-way ANOVA: an ANOVA comparing two or more independent grouping variables on one outcome variable; can detect interactions between grouping variables.

one-sample test: a hypothesis test comparing a sample mean to a given population mean.

one-sample t-test: a one-sample test where a sample mean is compared with a given population mean as stated in the null hypothesis, when the population standard deviation is not known.

one-tailed test: a hypothesis test in which the region of rejection falls in either the upper or lower tail; represented with a < or > in the alternative hypothesis and ≤ or ≥ in the null hypothesis.

one-way ANOVA: an ANOVA comparing multiple independent group means against one another; similar in purpose to an independent-samples t-test but can compare any number of groups.

operational definition: the 'real world' way of representing a construct in a dataset.

operationalization: see operational definition.

order of operations: the set of rules describing the four-step series of calculations used in solving any maths formula, summarized with the acronyms BIDMAS or PEMDAS (1, brackets/parentheses; 2, indices/exponents; 3, multiplication and division; 4, addition and subtraction).

ordinal: a scale of measurement for nominal data with order (for example, '1st', '2nd', '3rd').

outlier: an unusual case in a variable that has undue influence on statistics computed on that variable.

paired data: two variables that are linked together by some research study design characteristic (for example, two spouses, parent and child, before and after an event).

paired-samples t-test: a two-sample hypothesis test where the difference between two related sample means is compared with a population mean difference as specified in the null hypothesis; also called related-samples t-test or matched-samples t-test.

parameter: a numeric summary of a population, for example, a population mean μ (mu).

parametric tests: statistical tests that require making assumptions about parameters (for example, z-tests, t-tests and F-tests).

Pearson's correlation: see Pearson's product-moment correlation coefficient.

Pearson's product-moment correlation coefficient: a type of correlation that summarizes linear relationships; varies from -1 (representing a perfect negative relationship), through 0 (representing no relationship), up to $+1$ (representing a perfect positive relationship); also called Pearson's r, Pearson's correlation, or correlation.

Pearson's r: see Pearson's product-moment correlation coefficient.

percentage: a portion of a whole represented as its share of 100 (for example, 50%.)

percentile: the point at which a particular percentage of a dataset falls below a given point (for example, if the 75th percentile equals 5, 75% of data are less than 5 and 25% of data are greater than 5.

perfect relationship: a linear relationship where exactly one value of one variable is associated with each value of another variable; represented with a Pearson's product-moment correlation coefficient with a value of -1 (perfect negative relationship) or $+1$ (perfect positive relationship).

p-hacking: conducting an exploratory data analysis but representing it to stakeholders as if it were confirmatory, which dramatically inflates the Type I error rate.

phi coefficient: see Cramér's V.

pie chart: an illustration of qualitative data representing a variable's categories as portions of a circle (or slices of a pie).

point estimate: a single 'best guess' from a sample as an estimate of a parameter (for example, a point estimate of μ).

Poisson distribution: a distribution of data that occurs with small numbers of independent counts (for example, counts of unusual complaints at a call centre).

pooled standard deviation: a standard deviation summarized across two or more groups that is calculated by weighting itself more heavily toward the groups with larger sample sizes; equal to the square root of the pooled variance.

pooled variance: a variance summarized across two or more groups that is calculated by weighting itself more heavily towards the groups with larger sample sizes; equal to the pooled standard deviation, squared.

population: a theoretical group that you want to draw conclusions about (for example, all potential customers).

population size: the number of cases in a particular population, represented with N.

population standard error of the mean: the standard deviation of all possible sample means (i.e. the sampling distribution), often shortened to 'population standard error'.

positive skew: data for which the tail of the skewed data leads to the right (towards positive numbers).

post-hoc tests: follow-up statistical tests comparing individual pairs of group means conducted after finding a statistically significant F-test in an ANOVA.

power: the probability that we will correctly reject the null when that null should have been rejected; equals $1 - \beta$.

practical significance: the real-world value of a research finding; often assessed with an effect size.

precision: the accuracy of a statistic in measuring what it is supposed to measure.

predictor: the x-variable in regression; the value of the criterion is predicted for values of the predictor; also called the independent variable.

probability: the likelihood that a particular event will occur, expressed as a proportion, ranging from .00 (impossible to occur) to 1.00 (will definitely occur).

proportion: a portion of a whole represented as a decimal (for example, .5).

p-value: the probability that the given sample was drawn from the population described by a given null hypothesis.

qualitative: data referring to qualities, usually represented as words or letters.

quantitative: data referring to quantities, usually represented as numbers.

quasi-experiment: a correlational study resembling an experiment (subjects split into multiple categories) but using non-random assignment.

random assignment: the placement of participants into two or more conditions at random.

range: the differences between the largest and smallest scores in a variable and a measure of variability.

range enhancement: an artificial increase in correlation created by including two or more distinct segments of a previously continuous variable to be included in analysis; increases Type I error.

range restriction: an artificial decrease in correlation created by including only one segment of a continuous variable in analysis; increases Type II error.

ratio: a scale of measurement for interval data with a meaningful zero point (for example, sales in euros).

raw data: data recorded in a dataset as it was collected (for example, scores recorded as 1 through 5 resulting from a survey question asked on a five-point scale).

region of rejection: the area of the sampling distribution surrounding the null hypothesis beyond which we would reject that null.

regression: an analysis creating the formula of a regression line used in predicting quantitative variables from other quantitative variables.

regression line: the line created as the result of regression; the line that minimizes the sum of the squared residuals for a given dataset; also called the line of best fit.

reject the null: shorthand for 'reject the null hypothesis'.

reject the null hypothesis: a conclusion made when the null hypothesis is sufficiently unlikely to be true, given a particular sample and alpha level.

related-samples t-test: see paired-samples t-test.

relative frequency: a count of how many times a value appears in a variable, calculated as a proportion of the total number of cases; represented by rel. f.

relative frequency of occurrence method of assigning probability: a process used to estimate probabilities by consulting historical data and calculating a relative frequency; contrast with the classical method of assigning probability

repeated measures: a type of research design where the same variable is measured at two or more time points; if measurement occurs twice, you have collected paired data.

representative: how well the characteristics of a sample reflect the characteristics of a population.

residual: the vertical distance any particular datum is from the regression line.

retain the null: shorthand for 'retain the null hypothesis'.

retain the null hypothesis: a conclusion made when there is insufficient evidence to say that the null hypothesis is false, given a particular sample and alpha level.

robustness: the degree to which a statistic produces an accurate result even when its assumptions are not met.

sample: a group gathered at random from a population (for example, a focus group).

sample size: the number of cases in a particular sample, represented with n.

sample standard error of the mean: an estimate of the population standard error computed using the sample standard deviation and sample size, often shortened to 'sample standard error' or 'standard error'.

sampling: the process or method used to collect a sample from a population; includes random sampling, stratified random sampling and convenience sampling.

sampling distribution: a distribution of all possible sample means given a particular population mean and sample size.

sampling error: the difference between a sample mean and the mean of the population that sample was drawn from.

scale of measurement: a way to categorize a variable based upon the quality of the information it contains.

scatterplot: an illustration of two qualitative or quantitative variables where one variable is represented on the x-axis, the other variable is represented on the y-axis, and each case is represented with a mark at the intersection of its scores on those two variables.

significance/significant: see either statistical significance or practical significance.

significance level: the probability set as acceptable by the researcher that the null hypothesis is rejected when it is in fact true.

simple linear regression: a regression of exactly one variable predicting exactly one variable.

simple random sampling: sampling by drawing from a population where each member of that population has an equal chance at being drawn.

skew: a property of data resembling a normal distribution but not perfectly symmetrical (see also: negative skew, positive skew).

standard deviation: the average distance between all scores in a variable and their mean, represented in a population as σ (sigma) and in a sample as s, and is also the square root of the variance.

standardization (or standardized): the process of converting data into a format that can be compared across datasets regardless of the type of raw data used (for example, using z-scores instead of raw data or correlation instead of covariance).

standard normal distribution: a normal distribution with a mean of 0 and standard deviation of 1.

statistic: a numeric summary of a sample, for example, a sample mean $\bar{x}$ (x bar).

statistical significance: see reject the null hypothesis.

strata: groups of interest identified in stratified random sampling; plural of stratum.

stratified random sampling: sampling by identifying important groups of interest (i.e. strata) and using simple random sampling within those strata.

stratum: a group of interest identified in stratified random sampling; plural is strata.

student's t-distribution: a sampling distribution used as an improvement upon the z-distribution when sample sizes are too small; see Appendix A2.

subject: a member of a sample.

subscript: smaller letters used beneath terms in formulas to denote where a variable came from (for example, 'Experiment' in $N_{Experiment}$).

sum of squares: shorthand for 'sum of the squared deviations'; found on top of the variance formulas and throughout ANOVA calculations.

t-distribution: see student's t-distribution.

test of independence: a non-parametric chi-squared (χ^2) test in which two nominal variables are compared to determine if they are independent from one another.

theory: a relationship between constructs.

treatment condition: a condition where the subject is treated in a particular way in order to determine the effects of that treatment; contrasted with a control condition.

t-statistic: the test statistic produced by a *t*-test.

two-tailed test: a hypothesis test in which the region of rejection falls in both tails; represented with a ≠ in the alternative hypothesis and = in the null hypothesis.

Type I error: rejecting a null hypothesis when the null should have been retained; represented with alpha (α).

Type II error: retaining a null hypothesis when the null should have been rejected; represented with beta (β).

uniform distribution: a distribution of data that occurs when all possibilities are equally probable (for example, the rolling of a die or tossing of a fair coin).

union: the probability that any of two or more probabilities are true; signified with the word 'or', as in 'what is the probability that either A or B is true?'

upper bound: the larger value in an interval estimate (usually a confidence interval).

variability: the degree to which scores within a single variable are different from one another.

variable: data with different values based upon their source, usually represented in a dataset as a column, which can be contrasted constants.

Variable View: a view in SPSS, selectable via the tabs at the bottom of the screen, that displays the properties of the variables in your dataset.

variance: the squared average distance between all scores in a variable and their mean, represented in a population as σ^2 (sigma squared) and in a sample as s^2, and is also the squared standard deviation.

wicked problem: a problem without a simple solution that cannot be solved by approaching the problem from a single perspective (for example, with statistics alone); that is, most problems in business.

within-groups variability: the degree to which members of a group vary from one another within ANOVA; if overall variability, this is the sum of squares within; if average variability, this is the mean square within.

z-distribution: see standard normal distribution.

z-score: a raw score converted to standard deviation units; negative values represent scores below the mean, while positive values represent scores above the mean (for example, $z = -1$ indicates a score one standard deviation below the mean).

z-statistic: the test statistic produced by a *z*-test.

z-test: a one-sample test where a sample mean is compared with a given population mean as stated in the null hypothesis, when the population standard deviation is known.

APPENDIX D

STATISTICAL NOTATION AND FORMULAS

cum.f: cumulative frequency

df_B: between-groups degrees of freedom in ANOVA, calculated as $k - 1$

df_W: within-groups degrees of freedom in ANOVA, calculated as $N - k$

f: frequency

F: the ratio of between-group variability to within-group variability used in ANOVA; compared with the F-distribution

H_0: the null hypothesis (can also be pronounced 'H-sub-zero')

H_1: the alternative hypothesis (can also be pronounced 'H-sub-one')

k: the number of groups being compared in ANOVA; or the number of groups in chi-square

N: population size

n: sample size

rel.f: relative frequency

SS: sum of squares

$s_{\bar{x}}$: sample standard error (or standard error statistic), pronounced 's-sub-x-bar'

t_{crit}: the critical value(s) of a t-test

z_{crit}: the critical value(s) of a z-test

α: the significance level chosen for any particular statistical test, and the probability of committing a Type I error

β: the probability of committing a Type II error (power = $1 - \beta$)

η^2: a common measure of overall effect size for ANOVA; pronounced 'eta-squared'; calculated as SS_B/SS_T

μ_d: population mean difference (for use in paired-samples t-tests)

ϕ: phi coefficient, another name for Cramér's V when conducted on a 2×2 contingency table from a chi-squared test of independence

$\sigma_{\bar{x}}$: population standard error (or standard error parameter), pronounced 'sigma-sub-x-bar'

Σ: capital Greek letter sigma, pronounced 'sum of' in formulas

$$\text{ref.}f = \frac{f}{N}$$

FIGURE D.01 Formula for relative frequency

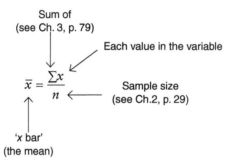

FIGURE D.02 Annotated formula for sample mean

$$\text{range} = x_{\text{largest}} - x_{\text{smallest}}$$

FIGURE D.03 Formula for range

$$\text{deviation} = x - \mu$$

FIGURE D.04 Formula for deviation

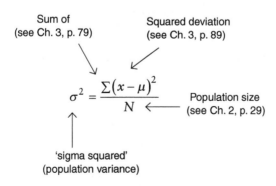

FIGURE D.05 Annotated conceptual formula for population variance

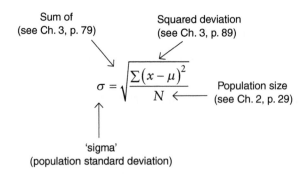

Sum of
(see Ch. 3, p. 79)

Squared deviation
(see Ch. 3, p. 89)

$$\sigma = \sqrt{\frac{\sum(x-\mu)^2}{N}}$$

Population size
(see Ch. 2, p. 29)

'sigma'
(population standard deviation)

FIGURE D.06   Annotated conceptual formula for population standard deviation

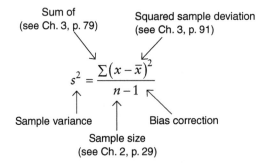

Sum of
(see Ch. 3, p. 79)

Squared sample deviation
(see Ch. 3, p. 91)

$$s^2 = \frac{\sum(x-\bar{x})^2}{n-1}$$

Sample variance

Bias correction

Sample size
(see Ch. 2, p. 29)

FIGURE D.07   Annotated conceptual formula for sample variance

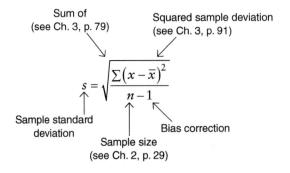

Sum of
(see Ch. 3, p. 79)

Squared sample deviation
(see Ch. 3, p. 91)

$$s = \sqrt{\frac{\sum(x-\bar{x})^2}{n-1}}$$

Sample standard
deviation

Bias correction

Sample size
(see Ch. 2, p. 29)

FIGURE D.08   Annotated conceptual formula for sample standard deviation

$$s^2 = \frac{\sum x^2 - \frac{(\sum x)^2}{n}}{n-1}$$

Sample size
(see Ch. 2, p. 29)

Bias correction

FIGURE D.09   Annotated computational formula for sample variance

$$s = \sqrt{\frac{\sum x^2 - \frac{(\sum x)^2}{n}}{n-1}}$$

Sample size
(see Ch. 2, p. 29)

Bias correction

FIGURE D.10   Annotated computational formula for sample standard deviation

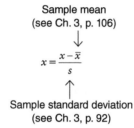

Sample mean
(see Ch. 3, p. 106)

$$x = \frac{x - \bar{x}}{s}$$

Sample standard deviation
(see Ch. 3, p. 92)

FIGURE D.11   Annotated formula for sample z-score

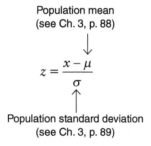

Population mean
(see Ch. 3, p. 88)

$$z = \frac{x - \mu}{\sigma}$$

Population standard deviation
(see Ch. 3, p. 89)

FIGURE D.12   Annotated formula for population z-score

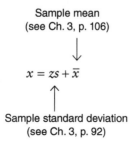

Sample mean
(see Ch. 3, p. 106)

$$x = zs + \bar{x}$$

Sample standard deviation
(see Ch. 3, p. 92)

FIGURE D.13   Annotated formula for calculating a raw score from a sample z-score

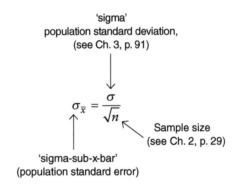

Population mean
(see Ch. 3, p. 88)

$$x = z\sigma + \mu$$

Population standard deviation
(see Ch. 3, p. 92)

FIGURE D.14   Annotated formula for calculating a raw score from a population z-score

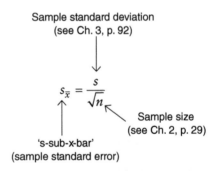

'sigma'
population standard deviation,
(see Ch. 3, p. 91)

$$\sigma_{\bar{x}} = \frac{\sigma}{\sqrt{n}}$$

Sample size
(see Ch. 2, p. 29)

'sigma-sub-x-bar'
(population standard error)

FIGURE D.15   Annotated formula for the population standard error

Sample standard deviation
(see Ch. 3, p. 92)

$$s_{\bar{x}} = \frac{s}{\sqrt{n}}$$

Sample size
(see Ch. 2, p. 29)

's-sub-x-bar'
(sample standard error)

FIGURE D.16   Annotated formula for a sample estimate of the standard error

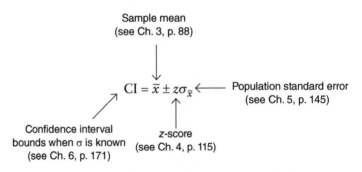

Sample mean
(see Ch. 3, p. 88)

$$CI = \bar{x} \pm z\sigma_{\bar{x}}$$

Population standard error
(see Ch. 5, p. 145)

Confidence interval
bounds when σ is known
(see Ch. 6, p. 171)

z-score
(see Ch. 4, p. 115)

FIGURE D.17   Confidence interval formula when population standard deviation/error is known

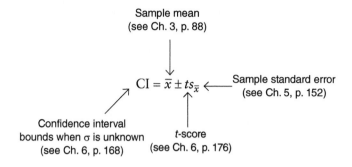

FIGURE D.18   Confidence interval formula when population standard deviation/error is unknown

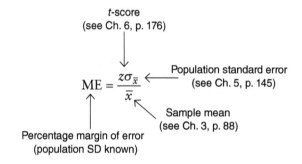

FIGURE D.19   Margin of error formula when population standard deviation/error is known

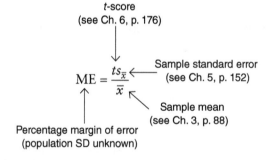

FIGURE D.20   Margin of error formula when population standard deviation/error is unknown

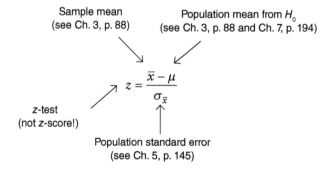

FIGURE D.21   Annotated formula to conduct a z-test

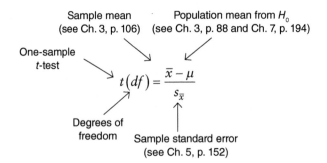

FIGURE D.22 Annotated formula to conduct a one-sample *t*-test

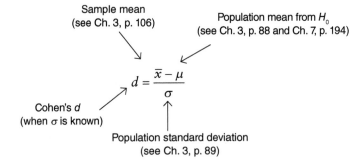

FIGURE D.23 Annotated formula for Cohen's *d* for a one-sample *t*-test when σ is known

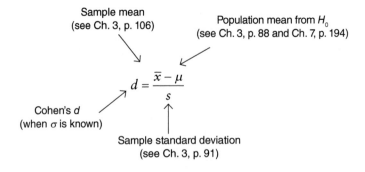

FIGURE D.24 Annotated formula for Cohen's *d* for a one-sample *t*-test when σ is unknown

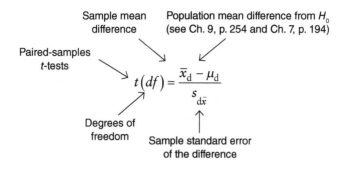

FIGURE D.25   Annotated formula for a paired-sample *t*-test

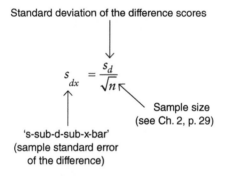

FIGURE D.26   Annotated formula for a sample estimate of the standard error of the difference

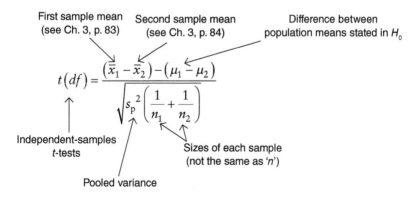

FIGURE D.27   Annotated formula for an independent-samples *t*-test

Variance of first sample
(see Chapter 3, p. 84)
Second sample size
First sample size
Variance of second sample
(see Chapter 3, p. 84)

$$s_p^2 = \frac{(n_1 - 1)s_1^2 + (n_2 - 1)s_2^2}{(n_1 - 1) + (n_2 - 1)}$$

Pooled variance
First sample size
Second sample size

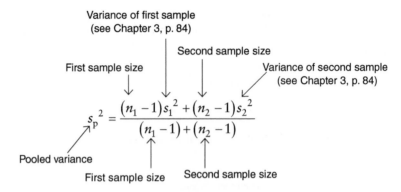

FIGURE D.28 Annotated formula for the pooled variance

$$SS_B = \Sigma\left(\bar{x}_j - \bar{x}\right)$$

$$SS_W = \Sigma\left(x_j - \bar{x}_j\right)$$

$$SS_T = \Sigma\left(x - \bar{x}\right)$$

FIGURE D.29 Conceptual formulas for sum of squares in ANOVA

Group size
(n for group j)
Overall mean

$$SS_B = \sum_{j=1}^{k} n_j \left(\bar{x}_j - \bar{x}\right)^2$$

Group mean
Sum across groups
(count from group 1
to group k, and refer
to the current group as j)

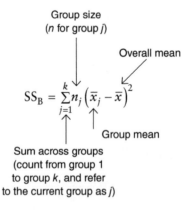

FIGURE D.30 Annotated computational formula for sum of squares between in ANOVA

$$SS_W = SS_T - SS_B$$

FIGURE D.31 Computational formula for sum of squares within in ANOVA

$$SS_T = \Sigma x^2 - \frac{(\Sigma x)^2}{n}$$

FIGURE D.32   Computational formula for sum of squares total in ANOVA

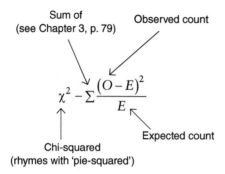

FIGURE D.33   Annotated formula for chi-squared tests

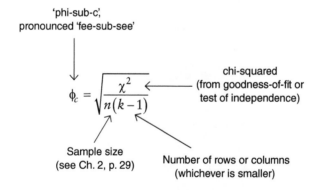

FIGURE D.34   Annotated formula for Cramér's V

APPENDIX E

ENABLING EXCEL'S DATA ANALYSIS ADD-IN

For those learning statistics with Excel, Chapters 9–13 of this text require Excel's Analysis ToolPak, which itself contains the Data Analysis tool. This is a free add-in which extends the functionality of Excel. However, it is not enabled by default.

To enable the Data Analysis tool in Excel, open the File tab and select Options – see Figure E.01.

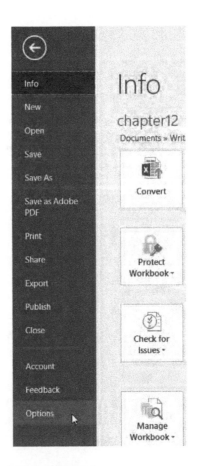

FIGURE E.01   Enabling the Data Analysis tool, step 1

Next, select the Add-Ins set of options (Figure E.02).

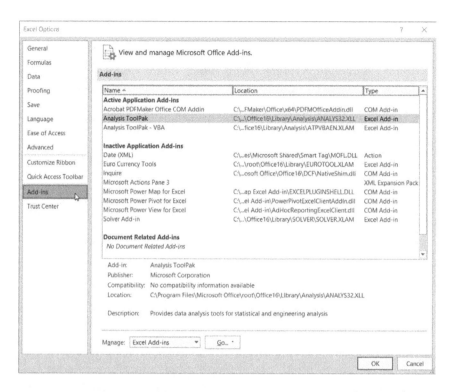

FIGURE E.02 Enabling the Data Analysis tool, step 2

Next, at the bottom of the Add-Ins panel, ensure 'Manage' is set to 'Excel Add-ins' and click Go… (Figure E.03).

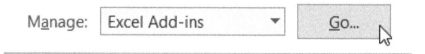

FIGURE E.03 Enabling the Data Analysis tool, step 3

Next, check the 'Analysis ToolPak' option, then click OK (Figure E.04).

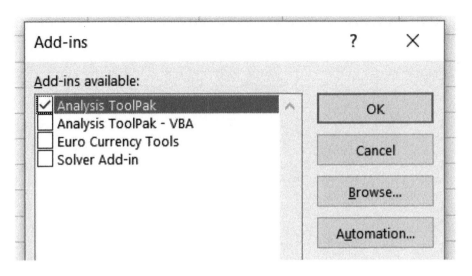

FIGURE E.04   Enabling the Data Analysis tool, step 4

You're done! To access the Data Analysis tool, click on the Data tab and select Data Analysis. If you can see the button highlighted in Figure E.05, the Data Analysis tool has been successfully enabled.

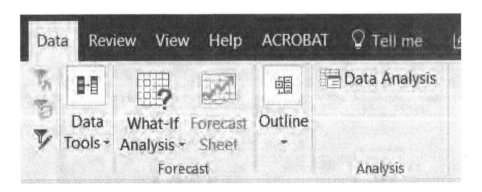

FIGURE E.05   Selecting the newly installed Data Analysis tool in Excel

INDEX